THE MACMILLAN
Bible Atlas

YOHANAN AHARONI
Professor of Archaeology
Chairman of Department of Archaeology, and Institute of Archaeology
Tel Aviv University

and

MICHAEL AVI-YONAH
Professor of Archaeology and History of Art
The Hebrew University of Jerusalem

COMPLETELY REVISED THIRD EDITION

ANSON F. RAINEY
Professor of Ancient Near Eastern Cultures
and Semitic Linguistics
Tel Aviv University

ZE'EV SAFRAI
Professor of Land of Israel Studies
Bar Ilan University

Designed and Prepared by
CARTA, JERUSALEM

MACMILLAN • USA

Macmillan General Reference
A Simon & Schuster Macmillan Company
1633 Broadway
New York, NY 10019

Library of Congress Cataloging-in-Publication Data

Aharoni, Yohanan, 1919-1976.
    The Macmillan Bible atlas/Yohanan Aharoni and Michael Avi-Yonah.
    —Completely rev., 3d ed./Anson F. Rainey, Ze'ev Safrai.
        p.   cm.
    Includes index.
    ISBN 0-02-500605-3
    1. Bible—Geography—Maps. I. Avi-Yonah, Michael, 1904-1974.
    II. Rainey Anson F., 1930-   .   III. Safrai, Ze'ev.   IV. Carta
    (Firm).   V. Title.   VI. Title: Bible atlas.
    G2230.A2 1993 <G&M>
    220.9'1'0223—dc20   92-27895
                                                                          CIP
                                                                         MAP

Portions of this volume have been previously published as follows:
Carta's Atlas of the Bible by Yohanan Aharoni, Ph.D., The Hebrew University of Jerusalem.
Copyright © 1964, 1974, by Carta, Jerusalem. All rights reserved. *Carta's Atlas of the Period
of the Second Temple, The Mishnah and the Talmud* by Michael Avi-Yonah, Professor of
Archaeology and History of Art, The Hebrew University of Jerusalem. Assisted by Shmuel
Safrai, Senior Lecturer in Jewish History, The Hebrew University of Jerusalem. Copyright
© 1966, 1974 by Carta, Jerusalem. All rights reserved.

The scripture quotations in this publication are from the Revised Standard Version of the
Bible, copyrighted in 1946 and 1952 by the Division of Christian Education, National Council of
Churches, and used by permission.

10   9   8   7   6
Printed in the United States of America

PREFACE

This Atlas is the product of cooperation between two Hebrew University scholars and Carta, Jerusalem, cartographers. Professor Y. Aharoni edited the Old Testament section (maps 1—171), while Professor M. Avi-Yonah edited the section dealing with the later periods (maps 172—271); the cartographic and technical preparation was directed by Emanuel Hausman. The two sections were originally prepared, drawn, and published in slightly different form in separate Hebrew volumes by Carta, Jerusalem.

The purpose of the Atlas is to show, as far as possible through maps of each event, the changes and historical processes in the lands of the Bible. In the first part of the Atlas, the Jewish people were located mainly in the small area of the Holy Land; by the time of the Bar Kokhba Revolt, however, a large part of the people was scattered among the nations. We were guided by the most recent knowledge in Bible, historical, and archaeological research, and new concepts in educational instruction. In the light of these, we have attempted to provide a balanced viewpoint. In many instances, of course, we have had to choose between conflicting views in matters where only additional discoveries and further research may be decisive.

The focal point of the Atlas is the Holy Land, and one of our aims was to place it within its proper relation to the surrounding lands, most of which played an important part in its history. There are, therefore, many maps showing the Holy Land as a part of the Ancient East or the Greco-Roman world as a whole. We have tried to include within these maps every place and event in neighboring lands touching upon the Bible and the history of the Land of the Bible, even if not specifically mentioned in the Scriptures. It should be noted, however, that this is not an atlas of the Ancient East or of the Hellenistic and Roman Empires, nor have we attempted to be conclusive in regard to surrounding lands.

In general, if there is any doubt as to the identification of a site, this has been indicated in the index of place names, not in the maps. As for borders we often possess only information of a general nature. We often have details on border settlements, but data as to exact bordercourses is mostly lacking. In writing texts this raises little difficulty, for it normally suffices to state that "the border runs from A in the east to B on the coast," and so forth. On maps, however, one must be definitive, for a line once drawn lends itself to only one interpretation. Many of the routes of campaigns and journeys, especially those of the New Testament, are also conjectural. Indeed, in the light of modern scholarship it is extremely difficult to accept the geographical details of the Evangelists and of the first part of Acts at face value. In many cases the starting point of a route is known, as well as the destination and often also a number of stations along the way. Details of each particular route or border were arrived at on the basis of topical and topographical logic, for in an historical atlas, conjecture must complement fact.

The impetus for this Atlas came from the late Amnon Soferman, C.E., co-founder of Carta, Jerusalem, who conceived it in its basic form and devoted to it the last months of his life.

Mr. Israel Eph'al, Instructor at the Tel Aviv University, and Dr. Shmuel Safrai, Senior Lecturer at the Hebrew University, Jerusalem, assisted in the preparation of the Old Testament and later sections, respectively. Thanks and appreciation are due to Professor William D. Davies, George Washington Ivey Professor of Advanced Studies and Research in Christian Origins, Duke University, for his valuable advice and assistance throughout the preparation of this Atlas. Clement Alexandre and Peter Nevraumont, both of the Macmillan Company, New York, read the manuscript and offered many valuable suggestions.

The physical preparation of the Atlas was devotedly carried out by the staff of Carta, Jerusalem especially M. Sofer and A. Nur, cartographers, Mrs S. Zioni and N. Karp, graphic artists, and R. Grafman, who adapted the text and maps for the English edition.

PREFACE TO THE THIRD REVISED EDITION

It has been nearly two decades since the original authors of this Atlas made their final drafts for the second edition. Meanwhile, much has been achieved in the study of ancient sources and the understanding of the ecological environment of the Land of the Bible. Archaeological surveys, under the inspiration of Yohanan Aharoni, but of which he never lived to see the fruits, have covered most of the country's terrain. Excavations in sites from all areas of the land have produced an abundance of new materials. The Graeco-Roman cities of Palestine, from Galilee to the southern steppes, including Beth-shean and Caesarea, have been extensively uncovered and their material culture illuminated.

The analysis and interpretation of all this new data make it imperative that an Atlas such as this undergo a thorough revision. In the Old Testament section the text for nearly every map has been completely rewritten. The Second Temple section has been revised to incorporate many new discoveries, especially as pertains to Jerusalem of Herodian times. The revisors have freely expressed their own judgment in every case. This has been done with the feeling that in most instances Aharoni and Avi Yonah would have appreciated the new evidence and would have probably accepted the new arguments. In any case, we have tried to work in the spirit of those two great mentors of Historical Geography.

The basic method of the original edition remains unchanged. The maps are based on the ancient written sources, the physical environment with which each document deals, and the data retrieved from archaeological research. Students of Historical Geography would do well to read each source cited for any given map if they wish to gain the full appreciation of the interpretation which the map represents. The vast array of secondary, scholarly literature could not possibly be cited in a teaching handbook such as this. An update in that area would require an entirely different format.

The land of Canaan/Israel/Palaestina is still a focal point for millions of Bible lovers, Jewish and Christian. The history of that geographical entity cannot be divorced from the wider context of the Ancient Near East and the Graeco-Roman world. Historical Geography, putting the Bible on the Map, is an attempt to understand the biblical events in their ecological and socio-cultural context. It is an essential component of biblical studies if we truly desire to empathize with the ancient people whose religious experience we claim to share. It is our hope that this third edition will enrich the Bible study of all students, teachers and scholars who sincerely desire to bring the Bible down to earth.

ANSON RAINEY   ZE'EV SAFRAI

LIST OF SYMBOLS

★	City mentioned in sources to map
•	City not mentioned in sources to map
⊛	Capital mentioned in sources to map
◉	Capital not mentioned in sources to map
⊛	District capital mentioned in sources to map
⊙	District capital not mentioned in sources to map
⊡	Fortress mentioned in sources to map
☐	Fortress not mentioned in sources to map
⊠	Camp
ⵏ	Revolt
⚔	Battlefield
⊶★	Attack, siege of city
⊷★	Conquest of city
←	Campaign, attack, or journey
⟩⟩⟩	Flight
——	Road
••••••••	Border of kingdom, state, or tribe
··············	District border
○	Spring

Other symbols appear in the legends to the individual maps.

LEGEND OF GEOGRAPHICAL NAMES

	Biblical	Contemporary Non-Biblical	Noncontemporary
Major City	**Jerusalem**	**Akhetaton**	
City or Village	Antiochus	Sennabris	(Tell el-Far'ah)
Country, Kingdom, State, or Tribe	J U D A H		
Mountain, River, or Region	*Jordan Valley*		

Names in parentheses are non-contemporary or modern; where appended to another name, however, they may be contemporary variants.

A NOTE ON SOURCES

Geographical names and quotations from the Bible are from the Revised Standard Version. Those from the Apocrypha are from the American Bible Society edition. If the spellings in the Versions are not consistent, preference has been given to that spelling closest to the Hebrew form. Geographical names and quotations from external sources are based, in the main, on *Ancient Near Eastern Texts Relating to the Old Testament*, edited by J. Pritchard, Princeton University Press, and the Loeb edition of Josephus' works, but certain modifications have been made. In the spelling of classical placenames, Latinized forms have generally been used; the "A" in "ae," however, has been eliminated in most cases, except in such names as Caesar and Aegina, where accepted usage dictates otherwise. The variant spelling "tel" and "tell" represent the Hebrew and the Arabic, respectively.

A NOTE ON THE CHRONOLOGY

Ancient Near Eastern chronology is based on the coordination of historical events, especially the years of a king's reign with known astronomical phenomena the age of which can be calculated. The chronology of the kingdoms of Assyria, Neo-Babylonia, and Persia is accurate within two years or less. There is still wide room for variation in the older historical periods. The chronology of Egypt adopted here is that generally followed by scholars at the Oriental Institute of the University of Chicago. Obviously, the Old and Middle Kingdoms are subject to revision as new data come to light; the New Kingdom is fairly well established though there are still two options, a higher and a lower. That based on the 1504 accession date for Thutmose II has been incorporated here. The wealth of data from the Third Intermediate Period, which parallels the biblical monarchies of Israel and Judah, makes the chronology more accurate though there is apparently still room for modification. By the Saite period (664 B.C.) the dates are coordinated with those of Mesopotamia.

For the Hebrew kings, the chronology as worked out by E. R. Thiele is adopted throughout. It enjoys numerous links with firm Assyrian and Babylonian dates. The pre-monarchial period, including the Age of the Patriarchs and the Age of the Judges, has no certified contacts with ancient Near Eastern history; their relative chronologies can only be surmised on the basis of comparison with the general archaeological framework.

The chronology of the Hellenistic and Roman periods is fairly well established and presents no special problems. The dates of events mentioned in the New Testament have been fitted, as far as possible, within the general chronology framework.

Names within ▢frames▢ are of places as yet unidentified, though their general location is known from the sources.

TABLE OF CONTENTS

THE FOUR WINDS OF THE HEAVENS AND THEIR NAMES

The Lord said to Abram ... Lift up your eyes, and look from the place where you are, northward and southward and eastward and westward; for all the land which you see I will give to you and to your descendants for ever.

(Genesis 13:14-15)

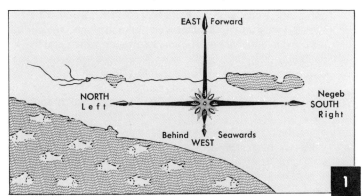

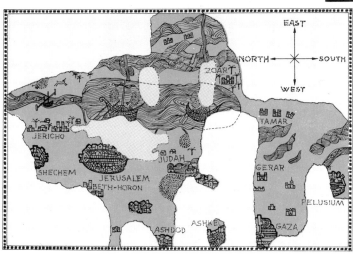

Section of the Medeba Map (Place names translated from the Greek)

To the north the winterbound, snow-covered mountains of the Lebanon; to the south the semiarid Negeb; to the east the wide desert; to the west the Great Sea — these are the natural borders of Palestine. Within their confines was enacted the history of Israel from the days of the Patriarchs on. A look at the landscape, its roads and ancient settlements, and the countries surrounding it are a prerequisite for a proper understanding of this history.

We possess no ancient map depicting the Holy Land in the biblical period. If such did exist, we can assume that it would face eastward, for in ancient Hebrew the word "forward" also indicates east, "behind" and "seaward" mean west, "right" means south, and "left" means north. Benjamin ("the son of the right hand") is the southernmost of the Rachelite tribes; the Dead Sea is also referred to in Hebrew as the "forward (eastern) sea;" the Great Sea, the Mediterranean of today, is also called the "latter (western) sea."

One of the oldest maps extant is the Medeba map. This is a mosaic floor dating from the sixth century A.D. in a church at Medeba, to the east of the Dead Sea. This map was intended to show the Holy Land of the Bible and faces eastward. At the center appears the Dead Sea, on which sail two boats. It was prepared more than one thousand years after the Destruction of the First Temple, and thus is of limited value for the identification of ancient sites.

THE WAY TO SHILOH

I will send them out that they may set out and go up and down the land, writing a description of it with a view to their inheritances...

(Joshua 18:4)

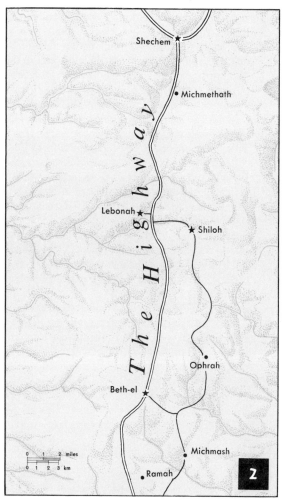

JUDG. 21:19

The Bible does not, as a rule, give many descriptions of settlements, their location and character — these matters were taken for granted then. Only a few verses diverge from this rule, the outstanding case being the description of the site of Shiloh in the story of the abduction of wives for the Benjaminites: "So they said, 'Behold, there is the yearly feast of the Lord at Shiloh, which is north of Bethel, on the east of the highway that goes up from Bethel to Shechem, and south of Lebonah'" (Judg. 21:19). Nothing could be more accurate. Why did the biblical writer give such detail to the location of a site as famous in ancient times as Shiloh? Probably because Shiloh had been destroyed by the Philistines, and early in the period of the Monarchy, when the story was written down, it lay in ruins.

Unlike Shiloh, most locations are merely described in vague terms in the Bible. Thus, in reconstructing the ancient map of the Holy Land in the various periods, we must lean heavily on four factors:

1. analysis of the history, character, and general topography of the individual site in the light of available sources;

2. identifications in later sources;

3. the preservation of the ancient name, with possible modifications during transfer from Hebrew to Aramaic and Arabic; and

4. archaeological examination of the site under consideration in the light of the above data.

From the wilderness and this Lebanon as far as the great river, the river Euphrates, all the land of the Hittites to the Great Sea toward the going down of the sun shall be your territory.

(Joshua 1:4)

Archaeological research has made great strides in our times, and many details of the map of the ancient Holy Land are now agreed upon.

The decisive geographical factor in the history of Palestine is its outermost position at the southwest end of the settled, fertile lands of the Near East. These lands stretch crescent-like from the Persian Gulf to the Sinai Peninsula: the so-called Fertile Crescent. On the west, this crescent touches the Mediterranean Sea. On the north and the east it is surrounded by high, nearly impassable mountains, the Amanus, Taurus, Ararat, and Zagros ranges. Within the hollow of the Fertile Crescent lies the extensive Syrian-Arabian Desert, extending on the west into the wilderness of Paran (the Sinai Peninsula). This latter separates the Holy Land from Egypt.

Today the Fertile Crescent is divided between Iraq, Syria, Lebanon, Jordan, and Israel; its fertility stems from two factors — flat lands and an abundance of water. This is especially true of the area known by the Greek name Mesopotamia — "between the two rivers." This is the richest part of the Fertile Crescent, whose broad plains are watered and fertilized by the flow of the two large rivers, the Tigris and the Euphrates. "THE river" of the Bible is the Euphrates. Syria and Palestine are less fortunate, for they represent the narrow and lean parts of the Fertile Crescent and of the two Palestine is the smaller and the poorer; rivers are small and do not allow passage of boats; the riverbeds are deep and in ancient times there was little possibility of utilizing their waters for irrigation. Land is uneven and ridges leave only limited plains. Rains fall mostly in one season and their amount diminishes progressively as one goes farther south.

In spite of its being the smallest and the poorest section, at the edge of the Fertile Crescent, Palestine held an important geopolitical position as a bridge between the lands of the Fertile Crescent and Egypt, the land of the Nile. Mesopotamia on the one side, and Egypt on the other, were lands of large rivers, and in both of them the foundations of civilization were laid toward the end of the fourth millennium. Similar geographical and economic features assisted in the development of both these lands; there are extensive alluvial plains, whose fertility is dependent upon large, long rivers passing through them. A river is the primary integrating factor within each of the two countries. It provides convenient arteries of communication and irrigates the land. This, of course, was dependent upon there being a governmental apparatus capable of instilling order, peace, and security, and of mobilizing manpower for the construction of dams and canals on a wide scale. Under such conditions rose the first mighty kingdoms with the power to impose organization and unity on their individual settlements, and even rule over areas beyond their own borders. In the Fertile Crescent this was the historical stage on which appeared in succession Sumer and Accad, Mitanni and the Hittites, and later the Arameans, the latter having given their name to the northern part of Mesopotamia — Aram Naharaim. In contrast, Egypt was closely confined and homogeneous in development, only the various dynasties succeeding one another over the years, from the time of the Early Kingdom down through the Middle and into the Late Kingdoms. Communications between Egypt and the kingdoms of the Fertile Crescent passed of necessity through Palestine, thus establishing its destiny as a land-bridge. Military campaigns swept in succession through Palestine, which in many periods was held by one or the other of the great powers; yet no major cultural development came about in either civilization without Palestine having some part in it.

THE ANCIENT NEAR EAST — PHYSICAL

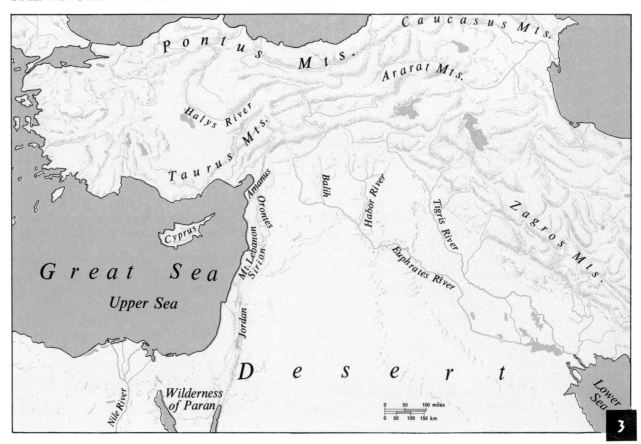

THE FERTILE CRESCENT — ANCIENT KINGDOMS

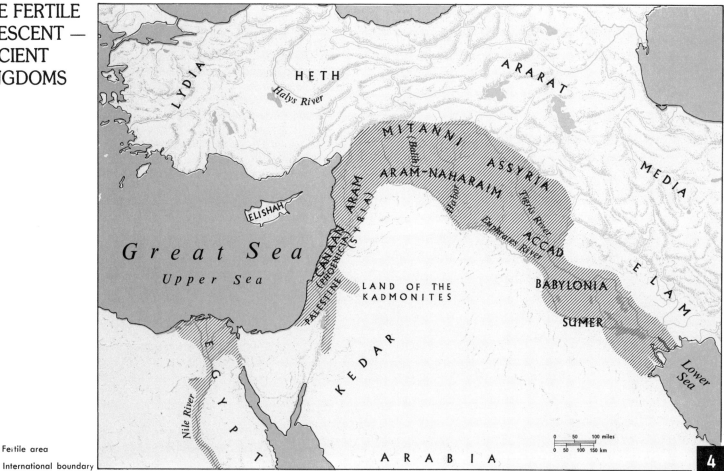

HETH

LYDIA

ARARAT

Halys River

MITANNI

MEDIA

ASSYRIA

ARAM-NAHARAIM

(Balih)

ELISHAH

Tigris River

ACCAD

Habor

Euphrates River

Great Sea

Upper Sea

ELAM

BABYLONIA

SUMER

LAND OF THE KADMONITES

Lower Sea

KEDAR

Nile River

EGYPT

ARABIA

Feitile area

International boundary

| 0 | 50 | 100 miles |
| 0 | 50 | 100 | 150 km |

4

THE FERTILE CRESCENT — MODERN STATES

Black Sea

30°   40°

U.S.S.R.

40°

Caspian Sea

TURKEY

Anatolian Plateau

KURDISTAN

IRAN (PERSIA)

CYPRUS

Mediterranean Sea

SYRIA

Mesopotamia

LEBANON

Syrian Desert

Tigris River

IRAQ

ISRAEL

JORDAN

Euphrates River

30°

EGYPT

30°

Western Desert

Sinai

Nafud Desert

KUWAIT

Persian Gulf

Nile River

NEUTRAL TERRITORY

SAUDI ARABIA

Red Sea

40°

| 0 | 50 | 100 miles |
| 0 | 50 | 100 | 150 km |

5

Raising water from river to canal (Relief from palace of Sennacherib at Nineveh)

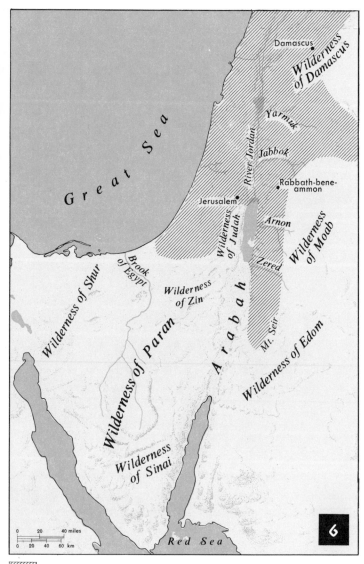

Damascus

Wilderness of Damascus

Great Sea

Yarmuk

River Jordan

Jabbok

Rabbath-bene-ammon

Jerusalem

Wilderness of Judah

Arnon

Zered

Wilderness of Moab

Brook of Egypt

Wilderness of Shur

Wilderness of Zin

Arabah

Mt. Seir

Wilderness of Edom

Wilderness of Paran

Wilderness of Sinai

| 0 | 20 | 40 miles |
| 0 | 20 | 40 | 60 km |

6

Red Sea

Area of settlement

THE GEOGRAPHICAL REGIONS OF PALESTINE

The terrain of the Holy Land is quite varied, mainly because of sharp climatic differences from region to region. The major feature of the relief of the Holy Land and Syria is the deep rift stretching from northern Syria through the Valley of Lebanon, the Jordan Valley, the Arabah and the Gulf of Elath, down to the southeastern coast of Africa. This cleft divides Palestine into its western part "Cisjordan" and the eastern "Transjordan"; there are great differences in altitude within short distances. The distance between Hebron and the mountains of Moab as the crow flies is no more than 36 miles, though in traversing this, a descent from +3000 feet down to -1,300 feet below sea-level (the lowest spot on the face of the earth) is made, followed again by an ascent to more than +3000 feet. These contrasts form the dry Arabah at the edge of the Judean Desert, with its rugged scarps, and opposite are the fertile and watered plateaus of Transjordan. These variations of land and climate brought about extremely different patterns of settlement within Palestine, which resulted in corresponding political divisions in most periods.

In several instances, the major distinct regions of the Holy Land are clearly defined and listed in the Bible according to topography and climate (Deut. 1:7; Josh. 10:40; 11:16; Judg. 1:9; and so forth).

Even such a list as the geographical administrative classification of cities of Judah is divided into four major regions: the Negeb (south), the Shephelah (lowlands), the hill-country, and the steppe, or wilderness (Josh. 15:21, 33, 48, 61).

And behold, a great wind came across the wilderness...
(Job 1:19)

THE DESERTS SURROUNDING PALESTINE

The Holy Land lies between the sea and the desert, and both influence its nature. The westerly wind brings life-giving rains, whereas the easterly brings only the dryness of the desert. The higher a place, or the closer to the sea, the more wet the climate.

The southern part of Palestine lies within an arid zone that runs around the globe; the extensive desert regions enclose the Holy Land on the south and east, with lofty Mount Seir jutting like a finger toward the heart of the wilderness.

There is no definitive natural border separating the settled area from the desert regions, and the hungry pastoralists of the steppe have beaten on the doors of the Holy Land since time immemorial. The influence of the steppe and the desert in the history of the Holy Land is profound and an awareness of this wilderness is echoed throughout the pages of the Bible.

In the hill country, in the lowland, in the Arabah, in the slopes, in the wilderness...
(Joshua 12:8)

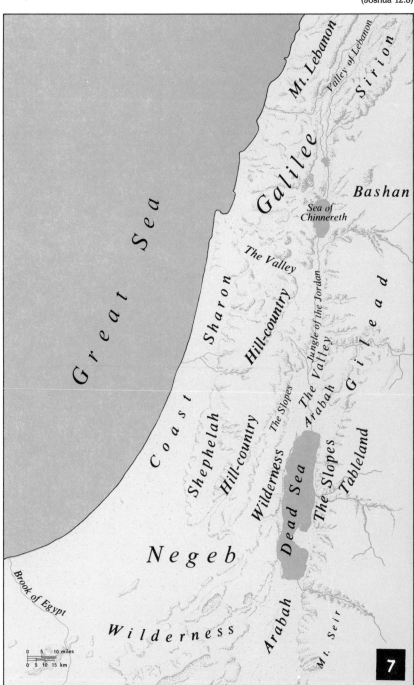

Mt. Lebanon

Valley of Lebanon

Sirion

Galilee

Bashan

Sea of Chinnereth

Great Sea

The Valley

Sharon

Hill-country

The Valley of Jordan

Jungle of the Jordan

Gilead

Coast

Shephelah

Hill-country

The Slopes

Wilderness

Arabah

The Slopes

Tableland

Dead Sea

Negeb

Brook of Egypt

Wilderness

Arabah

Mt. Seir

| 0 | 5 | 10 miles |
| 0 | 5 | 10 | 15 km |

7

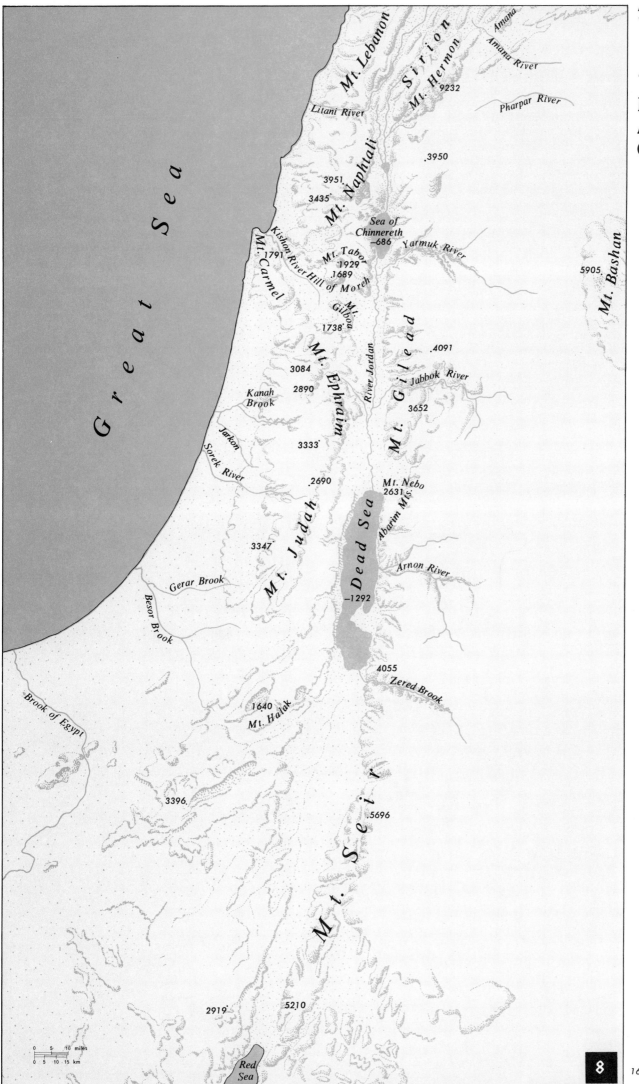

A Land of hills and valleys, which drinks water by the rain from heaven ...

(Deuteronomy 11:11)

THE MOUNTAINS AND STREAMS OF PALESTINE

Great Sea

Mt. Lebanon

Sirion

Amana

Mt. Hermon
.9232

Amana River

Pharpar River

Litani River

Mt. Naphtali

.3950

3951.

3435.

Sea of Chinnereth
−686

Yarmuk River

Mt. Bashan

5905.

Kishon River

Mt. Carmel
.1791

Mt. Tabor
.1929

Hill of Moreh
.1689

Mt. Gilboa
1738.

River Jordan

Mt. Gilead

.4091

Jabbok River

3652.

Mt. Ephraim

3084.

Kanah Brook

2890.

Jarkon

3333.

Sorek River

.2690

Mt. Nebo
2631.

Abarim Mts.

Dead Sea

Mt. Judah

3347.

Gerar Brook

−1292

Arnon River

Besor Brook

4055

Zered Brook

Brook of Egypt

1640
Mt. Halak

3396.

.5696

Mt. Seir

2919.

5210.

Red Sea

8

1640 = Altitude in feet

THE INTERNATIONAL ROUTES IN THE ANCIENT EAST

The main highways played a most important part in the history of the Holy Land. The settlements of Palestine are located at the crossroads of the Ancient East. The most important route was the highway from Mesopotamia to Egypt, and on it were founded the important political centers. From earliest times commercial caravans plied the major highways, carrying their products, precious objects, and luxuries; and providing for the needs of the caravans and their security, became a constant source of income. These ways, however, were not open for trade and commerce alone: military campaigns and conquests also trod them throughout history, leaving in their wake destruction and desolation. In most periods the Holy Land was dominated by major foreign powers, northern or southern, who mainly strove to secure a hold on these routes.

The mountainous nature of the Palestinian terrain dictates the courses of the roads. The principal international route connecting Egypt with North Syria and Mesopotamia transverses Palestine from south to north, following the line of the seacoast in the south until reaching the barrier of Nahal Kanah (Nahr el-'Auja) where it had to swerve eastward to go around Aphek.

It then skirted the eastern edge of the northern Sharon Plain and passed to the Jezreel Valley either via the valley of Aruna to Megiddo or via the valley of Dothan. From there it most probably went past Beth-shean, either north to Hazor and the Lebanese Beqa' or across the Jordan to Damascus. The segment from Egypt across Sinai was called "the Way of the god Horus" by the Egyptians and once it was called "way of the land of the Philistines" (Exod. 13:17). Apart from that, this great international trunk route has no name either in the Bible or in extra-biblical sources, Roman or otherwise.

The second international route was the King's Highway (Num. 21:22), which passes through the hill-country of Transjordan, close to the desert. This is the secondary route from Damascus to Egypt, its importance lying in the fact that the roads to Arabia branch off from it. There existed various other secondary, local roads, which were used largely by local traffic, and in time of need they also served as alternatives for international trade caravans. The maps show only the more important routes, especially those mentioned by name in the Bible.

> We will go up by the highway; and if we drink of your water, I and my cattle, then I will pay for it...
>
> (Numbers 20:19)

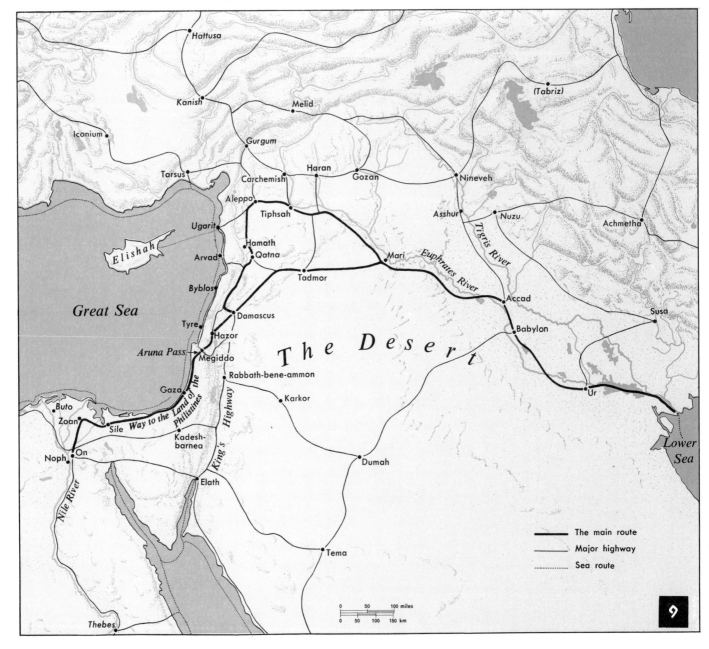

9

Build up, build up the highway,
clear it of stones...
(Isaiah 62:10)

THE ROUTES
IN PALESTINE

Sidon

To Ugarit

To Qatna

To Qatna

To Tadmor

Damascus

Ijon

Tyre   *Way of the Sea*

Kanah

Kedesh

Achzib

Hazor

Acco

Hannathon   Ashtaroth   Karnaim   Kenath

Yanoam   Edrei

Jokneam

Dor   Beth-   Beth-arbel   Bezer

Megiddo   shean   Ramoth-gilead   Salecah

Zephath   Taanach   *Way to Beth-haggan*   Jabesh-gilead

Aruna   Beth-haggan

Hepher   *Gath*   Dothan   *Road to Bashan*

Yaham

Samaria   Tirzah   Mahanaim

Shechem

1   Adam

Joppa   Aphek   *Way to the Jordan*   *Way of the Plain*

Lebonah   Rabbath-bene-ammon

Upper   Ophrah   2   *Way to Beth-jeshimoth*   *Caravan Route*   To Dumah

Beth-   3

horon   4

Jabneh   Gittaim   *Way to Beth-horon*   Michmash   Jericho   Beth-   Heshbon

Ashdod   Timnah   *Way to Beth-shemesh*   Jerusalem   jeshimoth

Ekron   *Way to Beth-*

Gath   *Way to Timnah*   shemesh   Beth-lehem

Ashkelon

Way to Ephrath   Aroer

Gaza   Lachish   En-gedi

Hebron   Ziph

Gerar   *Way to Moab*

Yurza   Arad

Raphia   *Way of the Land of the Philistines*   *King's Highway*   *Way of the Wilderness of Moab*

To Zoan   Sharuhen   Beer-sheba   Hormah   *Road to Edom*   *Road to Horonaim*   Kir-moab

Way of the Spies

Way to Moab

Bozrah

Way to the Arabah   *Way of the Wilderness of Edom*

Way to Shur

Kadesh-barnea   Punon

Way to the Reed Sea

Way to the hill-country of the Amorites

Rekem

1 *Way of the Diviners' Oak*

2 *Way to Ophrah*

3 *Way of the Wilderness*   ▬▬▬ Major highway

4 *Way to the Arabah*   ───── Local road

To On

Paran

0   5   10 miles

0 5 10 15 km

Way to Mt. Seir

Elath   To Tema

10

NOTE: Hebrew "the way of (place
name)" means "the way (leading) to..."

THE ECONOMY OF THE ANCIENT EAST

He who tills his land will have plenty of bread ...
(Proverbs 12:1'

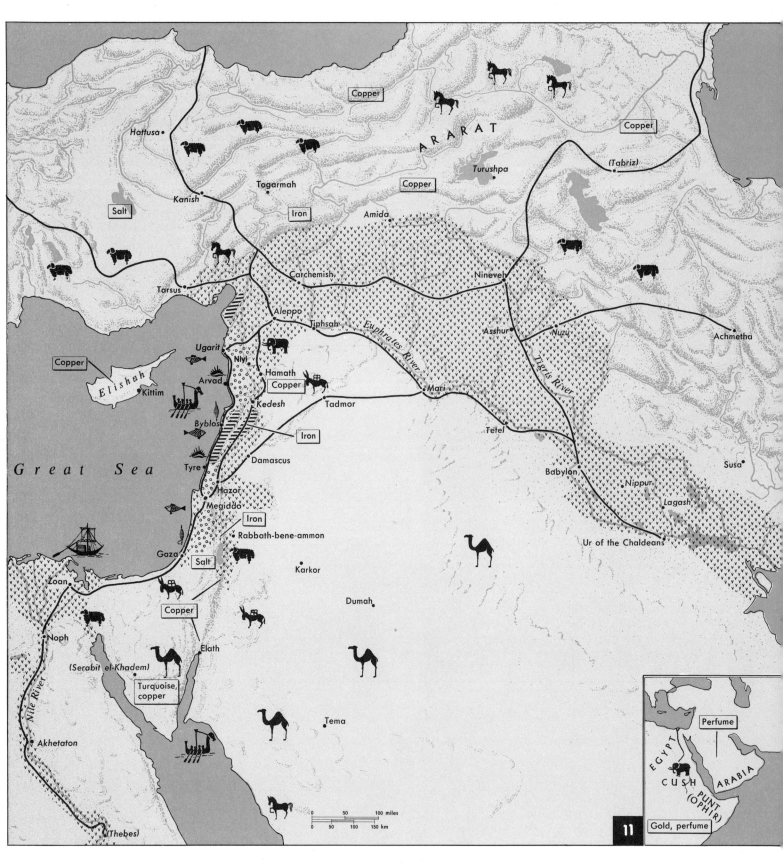

Hattusa

Copper

A R A R A T

Copper

Togarmah

Turushpa

(Tabriz)

Kanish

Salt

Iron

Amida

Copper

Tarsus

Carchemish

Nineveh

Aleppo

Tiphsah

Euphrates River

Asshur

Nuzu

Achmetha

Ugarit

Niyi

Copper

Hamath

Elishah

Arvad

Copper

Mari

Tigris River

Kittim

Kedesh

Tadmor

Byblos

Iron

Tetel

Susa

Tyre

Damascus

Babylon

G r e a t   S e a

Hazor

Nippur

Megiddo

Iron

Lagash

Rabbath-bene-ammon

Ur of the Chaldeans

Gaza

Salt

Karkor

Zoan

Copper

Dumah

Noph

(Serabit el-Khadem)

Elath

Nile River

Turquoise,
copper

Tema

Akhetaton

0   50   100 miles
0   50   100   150 km

11

Perfume

EGYPT

CUSH

ARABIA

PUNT
(OPHIR)

Gold, perfume

(Thebes)

Field produce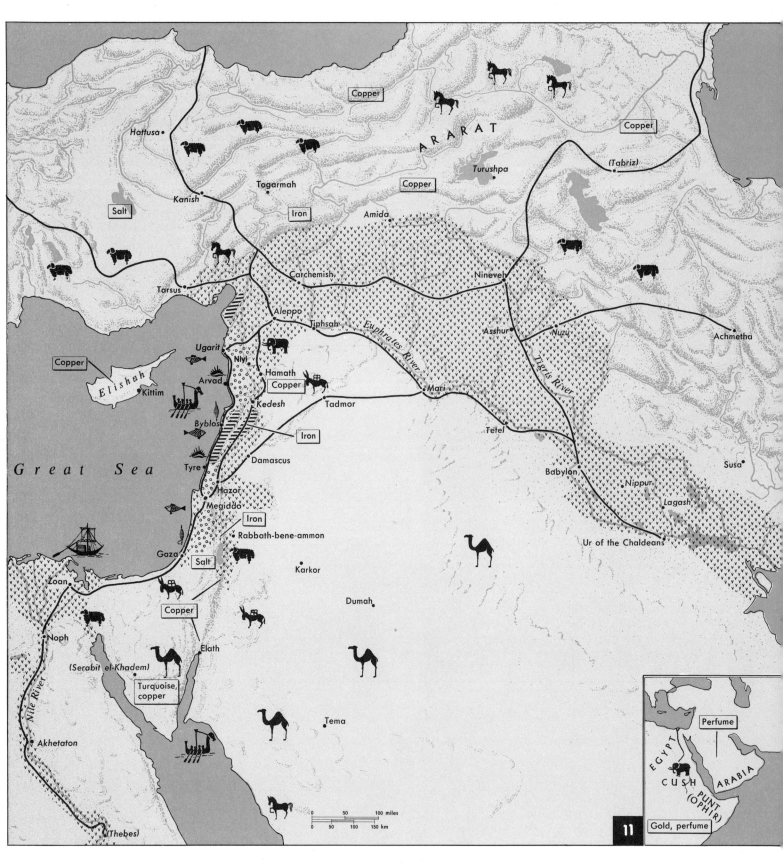
Construction timber
Fruit trees
Forests

 Dates
 Sycamores
 Cedars
 Wheat
 Barley
 Sheep
 Cattle
 Camels
Horses
Fishing
Perfume
Tyrian
purple
Textiles
Ivory
Caravans
 Phoenician
 Egyptia

C o m m e r c e

Food production was the basis of ancient economy. Diet was monotonous and much simpler than that of today; each area relied mainly upon its local produce. Although there were places where grain and other foodstuffs were marketed, the scope of such commerce was limited.

In the Ancient East grain production took place on the riverine plains. In the outlying, marginal regions, in the steppes and northern plains, sheep-raising was common, as was cattle and horse-breeding in certain areas. Camel-breeding on a large scale, mainly in the Arabian Desert, did not start until the end of the second millennium. The donkey was the chief beast of burden. In Palestine, too, grain was produced, though animal husbandry and horticulture were more important.

Another major branch of economy in the Ancient East was the smelting and working of metals. An important source of gold lay in the Land of Punt, to the south of Egypt; this may have been the biblical Ophir to which Solomon's ships sailed (1 Kings 10:11, and so forth). The two most common metals, used in weapons and tools, were copper and iron, which were mainly produced in Asia Minor and the Caucasus, as well as in Cyprus. According to the Bible, iron and copper were mined in the mountains of the Holy Land (Deut. 8:9); evidently reference is made here to the few mines in the marginal areas: the Valley of Lebanon, southern Gilead, and especially the copper mines on either side of the Arabah.

In the mountains of Lebanon and in the Anti-Lebanon (Sirion) stood forests of cedar and other woods, an important source of construction timber not only for Palestine and Syria, but also for Egypt and Mesopotamia. The forests of the Hauran and Mount Seir (Edom) probably served only local needs.

The coastal cities became centers of the textile industry, partly because they were close to the source of the Murex shells used in making "Tyrian purple," a dye reserved for precious textiles. The Hellenistic name for Canaan, Phoenicia, is connected with the Greek word for reddish-purple — *phoenix*. In documents of the fourteenth century B.C. found at Ugarit — the port city on the north Syrian coast — mention is made of textiles imported from Acco, Ashdod, and Ashkelon. In both Ugaritic documents and later Accadian sources, Ashdod and possibly also Ashkelon are mentioned as centers of fish exports. Thus, we may assume that a fish-preserving industry existed in the southern coastal cities. It seems that in various periods salt was obtained from the Dead Sea and from Mount Sodom, as witnessed by the name "Ir-hammelah" — the city of salt — at the northwestern end of the Dead Sea. The cultivation of various types of aromatic gums for perfumes in the Dead Sea region was also of some importance, the region having the proper climate for such. The main centers of perfume production, however, lay in southern Arabia.

The various crafts remained the trade secrets of family and tribal associations within particular areas. A speciality in the Jordan Valley, near Succoth, was the casting of metal utensils (1 Kings 7:46), as confirmed by archaeological excavations at Succoth proper.

A well-developed art in Canaan was ivory carving, the luxury product being used by the wealthy and royalty in architectural and furniture ornamentation. Tusks were imported from Kush (Nubia) and the land of Ni'i in northern Syria. The centers of this industry in the Canaanite period were located along the coast and, in the Israelite period, primarily at Damascus, Hamath, and perhaps Samaria.

Commerce thus generally occupied an important position in the economy of Palesine, especially in those areas along the main trade routes.

A land of wheat and barley, of vines and fig trees and pomegranates, a land of olive trees and honey ... a land whose stones are iron, and out of whose hills you can dig copper.

(Deuteronomy 8:8-9)

THE ECONOMY OF PALESTINE

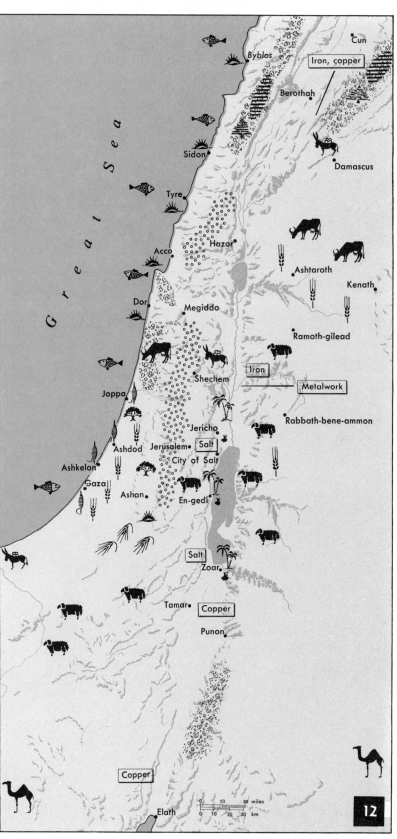

COMPARATIVE CHRONOLOGY OF EARLY CIVILIZATIONS

Period	Date	Mesopotamia	Syria-Palestine	Egypt
Neolithic (Late Stone Age)	5000	Jarmo Hassuna, Nineveh I	Jericho IX Byblos A	
			Ras Shamra V (Ugarit)	El-Fayum A
		Samarra, Nineveh II	Amuq	
	4000		Megiddo XX, Hamath L Yarmuk (Shaar Ha-Golan) Jericho VIII	Deir Tasa
Chalcolithic (Stone-Copper Age)		Tell Halaf		
	3500			El-Badari
		Tell el-Ubeid	Teleilat Ghassul, Beer-sheba	El-Amrah, Nagada I
	3150	Erech		
Early Bronze Age I		Jemdet Nasr	Early Canaanite Period I	El-Gerzeh, Nagada II
	2850			

Where you sowed your seed and watered it with your feet, like a garden of vegetables ...
(Deuteronomy 11:10)

THE EARLY CULTURES IN THE MIDDLE EAST

The first blossoms of human civilization are recognized in the development of food production (agriculture) and in the founding of towns and organized settlements. Traces of such are found already in the Middle Stone age (Mesolithic), some 10,000 years ago. According to our present knowledge, Jericho is the oldest city in the world, for in the seventh millennium it was already surrounded by a massive stone wall. Jarmo, in northern Mesopotamia, is more or less contemporary, though it appears to have been no more than a village. Only future research will prove whether Jericho was truly the first city and unique at that time, and whether to the Jordan Valley, the smallest of the river valleys of the Fertile Crescent, belongs the designation "the cradle of civilization."

During the fifth millennium (the Late Stone age — Neolithic), and the fourth millennium (the Chalcolithic), the progress of man is in evidence throughout the Fertile Crescent. In this period, Mesopotamia takes to the fore, but in Egypt, too, parallel developments are taking place, as also in the countries between — Palestine and Syria. These early cultures are today named after the sites where they were first discovered; in the comparative table the major cultures are listed chronologically.

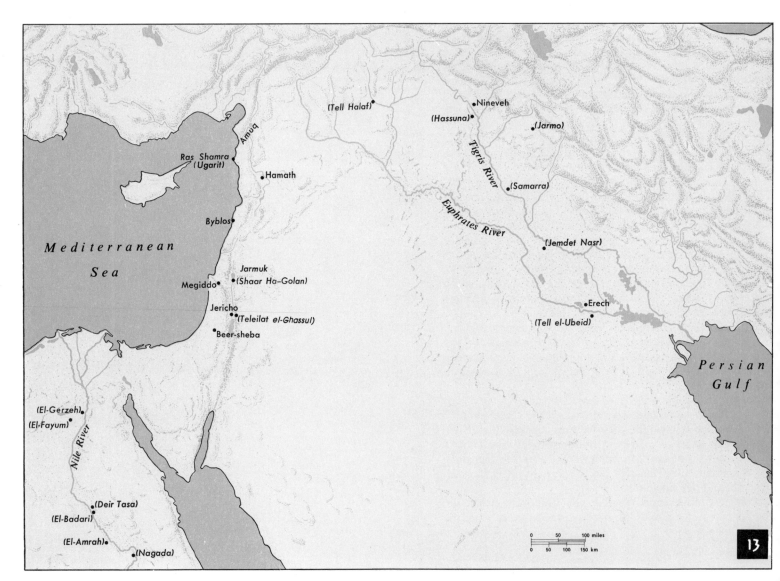

13

A river flowed out of Eden to water the garden, and there it divided and became four rivers.

(Genesis 2:10)

THE RIVERS OF THE GARDEN OF EDEN

Where are the ancient centers of civilization according to the Bible? The answer to this is hinted at in the description of the four rivers emerging from the Garden of Eden. It is natural that the ancients should believe the rivers of Eden to be those flowing through the lands most abundant in water, the foremost being the Tigris and the Euphrates in Mesopotamia. The Pishon and the Gihon have not been identified and may have merely been symbolic. But since Havilah is one of the regions of Cush (Gen. 10:7), it would seem that the two major branches of the Nile (the Blue and the White) are intended.

From these the coastland peoples spread ... in their lands, each with his own language, by their families, in their nations.

(Genesis 10:5)

THE FAMILIES OF THE NATIONS IN THEIR LANDS (TABLE OF NATIONS)

In the Bible there has been preserved a unique list of the nations of the world, within the scope of the people of Israel, the list of the family of man ("the generations of the sons of Noah"). The lands of the world and the peoples are divided into three main lines: the sons of Shem in Mesopotamia and Arabia, the sons of Ham in Egypt and within its sphere of influence, and the sons of Japheth in the northern and western lands. Included in the list are also royal cities and important centers within the Fertile Crescent: in the land of Shinar (southern Mesopotamia) and the land of Canaan. Even if not all the identifications are certain — and some of the names have not been identified at all — the general division is quite clear: three spheres of peoples and lands, which meet in the region of the Holy Land.

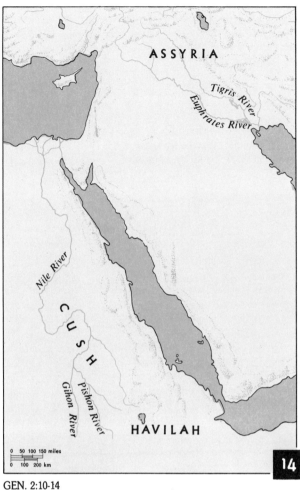

GEN. 2:10-14

Japheth — (Cretan wall painting of Cnossus)

...m — Ti, Queen of Egypt (Beginning of ...urteenth century B.C.)

...hem — Assyrian (Relief from palace of ...argon at Khorsabad)

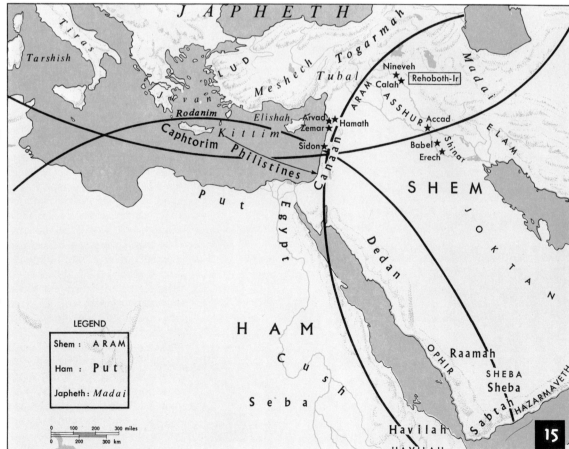

LEGEND

Shem : A R A M

Ham : Put

Japheth : Madai

GEN. 10. 1 CHRON. 1:4-23

ARCHAEOLOGICAL EXCAVATIONS IN PALESTINE

Biblical geography in a serious sense began about one hundred and fifty years ago with the survey trip of Edward Robinson in 1838. He recorded many biblical place-names still preserved in Arabic dress. However, he and many who came after him did not recognize that the village bearing a biblical name might not be on the original spot of the Old Testament site. In 1890, Flinders Petrie proved what others had been claiming for some time, namely that the prominent, flat-topped mounds located at strategic points around the country were actually the accumulation of debris from city upon city, built up during the ages. Such a mound is usually called a tell, a Semitic term signifying "mound" or "hillock," which gradually acquired the specific usage as a designation of a mound made up of ancient debris. Archaeological surveys since Robinson not only recorded Arabic place names, they also mapped the country and indicated the ecological and sociological details of the terrain and of the population. Flinders Petrie's excavation at Tell el-Hesi inaugurated the activity of excavation in Palestine

THE CHALCOLITHIC PERIOD
FOURTH MILLENNIUM B.C.

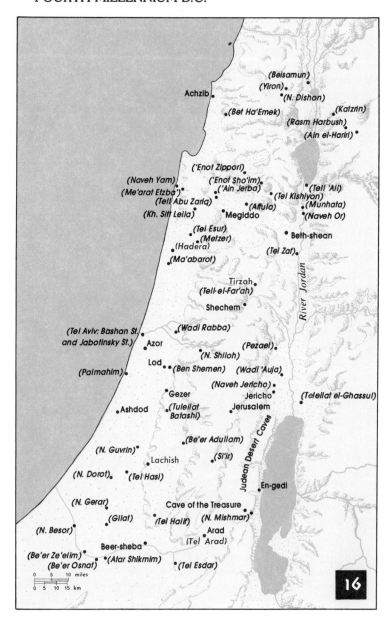

THE CANAANITE PERIOD (THE BRONZE AGE)
3150 TO 1200 B.C.

following the example of giants like Layard in Assyria and Schlieman at Troy. It became clear that these tells were built up from the successive construction and destruction of settlements on the same site. As a city was destroyed, buildings disintegrated, adding yet another layer of rubble to the height of the tell. During the Canaanite and Israelite periods, these sites tended to remain at locations with favorable conditions for sustaining human habitation, namely good water, arable land, defensible position and routes of communication.

The Arabic form of *tell* is spelled "tell" in English, whence the English loan word; the modern Hebrew form is spelled "tel." The past sixty years have seen numerous large-scale excavations at such major sites in Palestine. Techniques of recording and analyzing the finds are continually becoming more refined. The layers of debris are the main focus of the excavation; occupation layers are called *strata* (hence: stratigraphy). All the architectural features and other artifacts are ascribed to their respective layers. The meticulous differentiation of strata is based on the physical relationship of the features to one another; the relative dating is based on the nature of the artifacts found in each stratum, especially stone tools and pottery vessels (usually in fragments). Pottery is ideally suited to this task for two reasons: when a vessel is broken it becomes worthless and is discarded; but the ceramic fragments, especially of vessels fired in a kiln, are as hard as stone and thus survive the ravages of time (unlike organic materials

THE ISRAELITE PERIOD (THE IRON AGE)
1200 TO 587 B.C.

THE PERSIAN, HELLENISTIC, AND ROMAN PERIODS

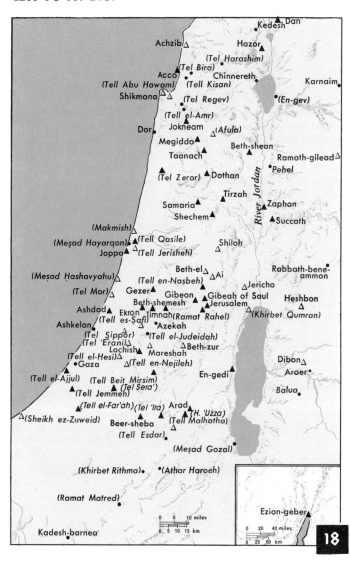

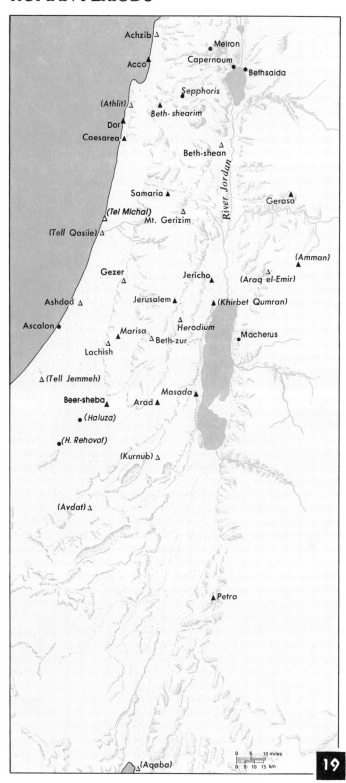

• Trial excavation or minor remains   △ Excavation   ▲ Major excavation

which soon disintegrate in the moist soil). The abundance of potsherds in each layer are classified according to their style and type (thus: typology). The progressive development of local pottery styles and the appearance of imported styles from neighboring cultures are becoming more and more recognizable as the volume of excavated (and published) material increases. Comparison of the finds in the various strata of different excavations is gradually building up an acknowledged scale of ceramic typology for archaeological dating. The discovery of inscriptions or imported objects of datable artistic styles also helps to refine the dating.

For the historical periods dealt with in this atlas, it may also be possible to compare the successive strata and occasional destruction layers with the recorded historical events pertaining to a particular site, or more often to the general region in which a site is located. However, such comparisons are a tricky business and great caution must be exercised; too often, scholars have jumped to premature conclusions about the supposed "historical" dating of this or that excavated stratum.

As a proper background for excavations, the archaeological survey seeks to gather all the relevant data available for reconstructing the means of subsistence, the pattern of site

locations and so forth. The goal is to achieve a picture of human habitation in all its facets in a particular physical setting.

The earliest cultures in the history of the Holy Land are known to us only from archaeological research. Most recent discoveries in the Jordan Valley prove that man appeared in Palestine in the Lower Pleistocene Age, estimated to be at least half a million years ago. This early man lived in Palestine before the final depression of the Jordan Valley to its present depth. In several caves in Mount Carmel and in Galilee, skeletons of Paleolithic man have been uncovered. These are of the more advanced type of Neanderthal man discovered in Europe. The scientific name of this type is *Palaeanthropus Palaestinensis* — "Early Palestinian Man." The last phase of the cave dwellers, in the Mesolithic Age (about 10,000 to 8000 B.C.), parallels the end of the last Ice Age in Europe. At this time began the first true settlement in Palestine; no major climatic changes have taken place since then. The earliest culture has been termed Natufian, after caves in Wadi en-Natuf on the western slopes of the central hill-country. This was a transitional phase of man, from hunting and gathering of food to crude agriculture and animal husbandry.

The revolutionary transition of man in Palestine, from cave dweller to founder of villages and towns, is best seen at Jericho, the one city of this period known to show such extensive accomplishments in construction and technology. This is in contrast to the usual open sites scattered here and there near readily arable land.

The progress of early civilizations was not always smooth and peaceful. Declines and retrogressions followed peaks of achievement. New conquering people dislodged inhabitants from their settlements, or settled in their midst. In the Chalcolithic period (the fourth millennium B.C.) many settlements were founded, mainly in the fertile valleys and on the edge of the desert. It was at this time that copper first came into use alongside stone implements. The later phase of this age is called the Ghassulian culture, after a group of small mounds in the southeastern part of the Jordan Valley, where the culture was first discovered (Teleilat Ghassul); it later became well known from several sites near Beer-sheba. These settlements spread over wide areas and were not fortified; the inhabitants were engaged in agriculture, herding, and household industries, including copper working. Their technical and artistic achievements are quite remarkable. A cache of copper utensils found in the "Cave of the Treasure" in the Judean Desert surpasses in both quality and beauty all other such objects known from the East from the same period. Among the lands of the early civilizations, Palestine held a respectable position till the end of the fourth millennium B.C.

SCHEMATIC SECTION OF A TELL

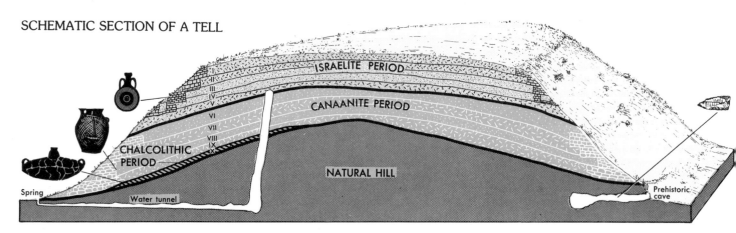

THE ANCIENT EAST IN THE THIRD MILLENNIUM

The first large empires of the Ancient East arose early in the third millennium B.C. In southern Mesopotamia, powerful city-kingdoms were centered at Kish, Larak, Lagash, Umma, Erech and Ur. This land, later referred to in the Bible as the land of Shinar, was then called Sumer. Sumerian culture laid the foundations of civilization in the Middle East, its influence extended over the "land of the west" (Syria and Palestine) as far as Egypt.

Egypt at about this time was united by its earliest kings, those of the "zero" dynasty preceding the first dynasty. From that time on, Egypt represented one of the mightiest powers, and even in the earlier periods its influence reached countries far to the north: Na'armer, thought to be the first king to unite all Egypt, saw some penetration into southern Palestine, whether for conquest or only for trade is still debated. A cosmetic palette with its cartouche, found in Egypt, is thought by some scholars to bear a graphic depiction of the conquest of a Canaanite city. The name of Na'armer has been found incised on sherds found in the excavations at Arad, Tel Erani and elsewhere. The gigantic pyramids built under the kings of the second to fifth dynasties are imposing monuments to the organizational ability and political power of Egypt in that age, the Old Kingdom period.

The political center of Mesopotamia in the twenty-fourth century B.C. moved from Sumer in the south to Semitic Accad in the north, the exact location of which has not yet been ascertained. Sargon I of Accad founded this empire and not only enforced his authority over Sumer and Dilmun (Bahrein) in the south, but also conquered the area of Subartu, north of Asshur, reaching even the Amanus mountains and the "Upper Sea," the Mediterranean.

The excavations at Tell Mardikh, south of Aleppo, have revealed the ancient city of Ebla. The archive from the end of the Early Bronze Age contains thousands of cuneiform tablets, mostly in Sumerian, with some in the local Semitic dialect. Much is now being learned about the political and social life of North Syria and its relations with Accad. No contacts with biblical history or geography have been found in the Ebla documents.

Mesopotamia, Syria and Egypt in the third millennium are known to us from many written documents, while Palestine in the same period was still in its "proto-history," since as yet no documents from this time have been discovered here. Someday inscriptions may come to light, for excavations have revealed that during this same third millennium — the Early Bronze Age — there were rich and powerful city-kingdoms with well-advanced cultures in Palestine. There were cities which covered an area of 25 to 50 acres, enclosed within strong fortifications up to 25 to 30 feet thick, like those at Megiddo and Beth-yerah (map 21 shows only the major centers). Although the history of this period is still obscure, there can be little doubt that both Palestine and Syria took an active part in its cultural development.

The beginning of his kingdom was Babel, Erech, and Accad, all of them in the land of Shinar.

(Genesis 10:10)

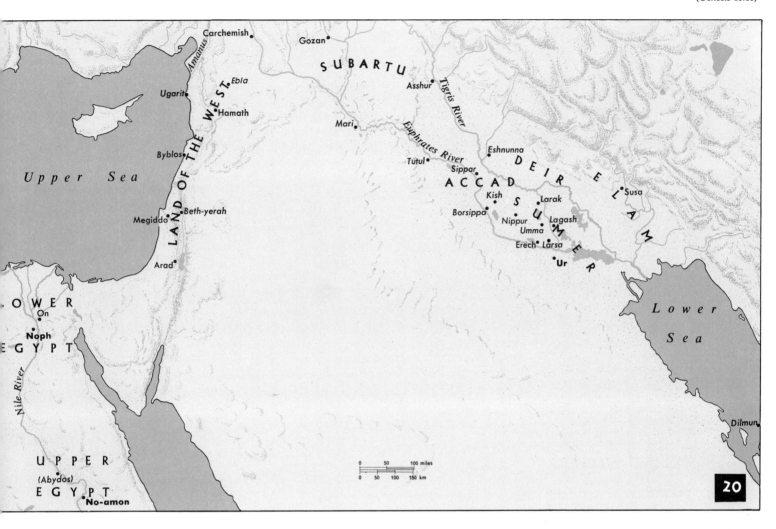

THE CAMPAIGN OF PEPI I

CA. 2350 B.C.

The sole historical information on Palestine from the Early Bronze Age is an Egyptian inscription telling of five military campaigns in the time of Pepi I (2390-2361 B.C.) to the "land of the Sand-Dwellers," the ancient Egyptian name for the lands to the east of Egypt. One campaign is described in detail — the Egyptian army set out in two columns, one by land and one by sea; the sea group arrived earlier and landed behind a prominent ridge, the "Nose of the Antelope's Head," possibly the Carmel headland. The conquered land was evidently the plain of Acco and a part of the Jezreel Valley, where the Egyptians destroyed fortresses, sacked settlements, uprooted fig trees and vines, and took booty. A picture of the settlements flourishing at the time, especially in the coastal plains, is conjured up by this vivid description.

Obviously, the "Sand Dwellers" in this ancient Egyptian text were not nomads but settled agriculturalists. Evaluation of Canaanite society must be based on the ecological (agricultural) facts and not on Egyptian pejorative terms for foreign peoples.

INSCRIPTION, TOMB OF UNI, COMMANDER, ARMY OF PEPI I — ABYDOS, EGYPT

I landed behind the high mountain in the north of the Land of the Sand-Dwellers.

(Inscription of Uni)

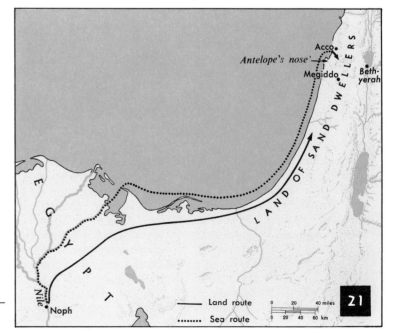

The map shows locations including Tyre, Laish, Kedesh, Hazor, Acco, Rakkath, Ashtaroth, Shimron, Beth-yerah, Edrei, Megiddo, (Tell Asawir), Taanach, Beth-shean, (Tell el-Husn), Dothan, Rehob, River Jordan, Tirzah, Zarethan, Aphek, (Azor), Lod, Ai, Jericho, Gezer, Jerusalem, (Tell es-Safi), Jarmuth, (Tel 'Erani), Eglon, Lachish, (Tell en-Nejileh), ('En HaBesor), Arad, (Bab Edh-Dhra)

0 5 10 miles
0 5 10 15 km

22

Prostrated enemies and plan of fortress
(On cosmetic palette of Na'armer)

Execration Text on clay figurine
from Şakkara

PALESTINE DURING THE TIME OF THE EGYPTIAN MIDDLE KINGDOM
20TH TO 19TH CENTURIES B.C.

In the closing centuries of the third millennium, a wave of pastoralists speaking a West Semitic tongue occupied all the main centers of culture in North Syria and penetrated southward into Mesopotamia. In Accadian documents they are called the "People of Amurru" (= Sumerian Martu, "the west"). Their population grew in the rural areas until they were strong enough to take over the great cities and to found new dynasties. This had become possible because of the decline and fall of the commercial empire under the leadership of the city of Ur (Ur III period). Of these Amurrite rulers, the most famous is 'Ammurapi (Hammurabi), whose forefathers had founded a dynasty at Babylon. His reign falls in the mid-eighteenth century B.C.

Farther south, in Palestine, every city state of the Early Canaanite era was destroyed, though not all at the same time. This cultural vacuum left the land open to the pastoralists from the steppe land of Syria and Transjordan. They roamed over the countryside, bringing with them new traditions of pottery and copper working. This intermediate period is reckoned by scholars as the last phase of the Early Bronze Age or as the first phase of the Middle Bronze Age; it is in fact an interlude between them. Scanty remains of the poor village settlements and extensive cemeteries left behind by these pastoralists have been found at most major sites but the clearest testimonies are

open air settlements in the highlands south of the biblical
[Neg]eb or in Transjordan. Throughout Canaan (Cisjordan)
[the]re were no city states and no contacts with Egypt, which
[it]self was in the throes of an intermediate period lacking any
[cen]tral government.

[T]he pastoralists of the intermediate period seem to have
[dis]appeared by about 2000 B.C. By this time, more civilized
[Am]urrites were beginning to repopulate Canaan from the
[nor]th. As commerce by sea and by land was being renewed
[bet]ween the Canaanites/Amurrites on the Phoenician coast,
[main]ly Byblos, the need for strong, fortified towns along the
[Pal]estinian coast and on the main trunk route gave rise to a
[new] urban culture, the true Middle Bronze Age, which enjoyed
[con]tinuity for the next eight centuries, that is, through the Late
[Ca]naanite period until the Israelite conquest.

[E]gypt was ruled by the twelfth dynasty (1991-1784 B.C.); under
[the] leadership of those Pharaohs, Egyptian culture reached its
[gre]atest heights of material and cultural prosperity. Its political
[influ]ence extended over Palestine and the Phoenician coast
[and] Canaanite/Amurrite merchants were encouraged to set
[up] a colony in the delta. The first written documentation
[of s]ociety in Palestine stems from this period. The principal
[sou]rce, the "Execration Texts," consists of inscribed bowls or
[of] figurines in the form of captives, bearing portions of a
[text] recording the list of Pharaoh's potential enemies in Cush
[(Su]dan), Libya, Retenu (Palestine-Syria) and Egypt itself. The
[doc]ument included imprecations and curses to be inflicted on
[the] offenders. Mention is made of cities and ethnic groups within
[the] Egyptian sphere of influence, with the respective leaders
[bein]g called "Rulers of foreign countries" (= the Hellenistic
[ter]m: Hyksos). Three groups of these texts have been found,
[the] earlier ones on saucers from the mid-twentieth century,
[and] the later group on figurines from the end of the nineteenth
[cen]tury B.C. The section on Retenu in the earlier group has only
[a fe]w, mostly unidentified names; in Palestine only Jerusalem,
[Ash]kelon and Rehob can be identified. Frequently, there are
[two] or even three or four rulers per city. In the later group
[of t]exts the Retenu chapter has sixty-four towns, many more
[of t]hem recognizable from later sources. Now there is usually
[onl]y one ruler for each town or group though a few have
[two]. The change may reflect developments in the political and
[soci]al regime, perhaps a consolidation of feudal oligarchies into
[mo]re centralized local monarchies. It is unlikely that the earlier
[soc]iety was pastoral while the later was urban.

[T]he names of the rulers are West Semitic in character,
[com]pounded of the same components such as 'ammu, 'ab,
[il] and hadad. These are identical to the Amurrite personal
[nam]es from Mesopotamia in this period.

[A]nother glimpse of life in Retenu during the twelfth dynasty
[is th]e story of Sinuhe, possibly a copy of a real tomb inscription.
[Sinu]he was a court official during the reign of Amenemhat I
[(199]1-1962) and with the death of that monarch, Sinuhe fled
[Egy]pt. He nearly died in the western Sinai desert until rescued
[by] a nomadic chieftain who helped him continue northward.
[He] moved from one city state to another until he reached
[Byb]los. There he feared the Egyptian enclave and turned back
[to] the land of Kedem in Retenu (perhaps in the Lebanese
[Beq]a' or in the region of Golan-Bashan) where a local ruler
[with] an Amurrite name appointed him as a feudal vassal and
[mad]e him his son-in-law. He prospered in his feudal fief where
[all b]ranches of agriculture were practiced: orchards, vineyards
[and] field crops. As an experienced military leader, he organized
[the] defense against nomadic intruders from the steppe and led
[raid]s against neighboring states. Finally, he was repatriated
[to E]gypt by Sen-useret I (1971-1928).

[L]ittle is known about Egyptian military activity in this period.
[A c]ertain Khu-sebek, who served as an officer under Sen-useret
[III (]1878-1842) tells in his tomb inscription about a campaign
[aga]inst the state of Shechem.

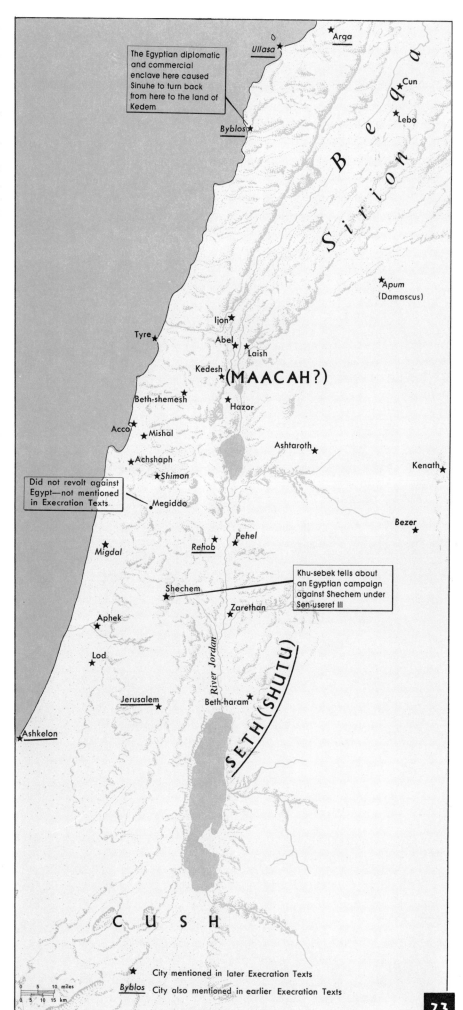

The Egyptian diplomatic and commercial enclave here caused Sinuhe to turn back from here to the land of Kedem

Did not revolt against Egypt—not mentioned in Execration Texts

Khu-sebek tells about an Egyptian campaign against Shechem under Sen-useret III

★ City mentioned in later Execration Texts

Byblos City also mentioned in earlier Execration Texts

EXECRATION TEXTS · THEBES, MERGISSA, SAKKARA, EGYPT

LIST OF LATER EXECRATION TEXTS

The Earlier Texts — Published by Sethe	The Later Texts — Published by Posener	Number S	Number P	Rulers S	Rulers P	'3mw nbw + "all the Asiatics"	Identification
	Abilum		E 47		1		Abel-(beth-maacha)
	Aksapa		E 11		1		Achshaph
Anharu		e 16-19		4			
Anharu		f 10				'3mw nbw	!***
	Apum mhty		E 34		1		Apum =
	Apum rsyt		E 33		1		Upi
	Apqum		E 9		1		Aphek
	Ari		E 21				*
Arhanu		e 30		1			
Arhanu		f 20				'3mw nbw	!***
Arhabu		e 11-12		2			Rehob
Arhabu		f 8					
	Arhabum		E 14		1	'3mw nbw	
Asannu		e 13-15		3			**
Asannu		f 14					
	Asannu		E 3		1	'3mw nbw	
	Asannus(?)		E 48		1		*
	Asapa, cf. Yasapa						
Asqalanu		e 23-25		3			Ashkelon
Asqalanu		f 14				'3mw nbw	
	Asqala		E 2		1		
Ullasa		f 3				'3mw nbw	Ullasa
Ullasa		f 3				'3mw nbw	
	Ullasa		F 2				
	Baqatum		E 20		1		
	Busranu		E 27		1		Bozrah
	Beta-samsu		E 60		1		Beth-shemesh (Naphtali)
	Haramu		E 4		1		
	Harimu		E 1		1		
	Hasora		E 15		1		Hazor
	Hasasum		F 6			'3mw nbw	*
	Yabilya		E 43		1		*
Yamuaru		e 7		1			
Yamuaru		f 6				'3mw nbw	!***
Yamuaru		e' 5		1			
Yamuaru		f' 6				'3mw nbw	
Yanuqa		e 1-3		3			
Yanuqa(!)		e 31		hq3w+nbw			
Yanuqa		f 4				'3mw nbw	
Yanuqa		e' 1-3		3			
Yanuqa		e' 6		hq3w+nbw			
	[Yanuqa]		E 36		1		
	Yanuqa		E 64		hq3w+nbw		
Yarimuta		f 9				'3mw nbw	
Yarimuta		f 13				'3mw nbw	
	Rimuta[...]		F 3			'3mw nbw	
Yasapa		f 21				'3mw nbw	**
	Asapa		E 12		1		
	Kina		E 7		1		Gina
Kupni		f 2				'3mw nbw	Byblos
Kubni		f' 2				'3mw nbw	
	Kubni		E 63			'3mw nbw whyt nt...☆	
Kusu			E 50			wr n whyt ☆☆	Tribe of Cush
Kusu			E 51			wr n whyt ☆☆	
	Lesi		E 59		1		Laish
	Luba(?)		E 31		1		Lebo-(Hamath)
	Maktulya		E 5		1		Migdal
	Makaya		E 37		1		
	Makaya		E 62				(Beth-)Maacha?
	Marsih-ki mhyt		E 24		1		
	Marsih-ki rsyt		E 23		1		*
	Masa		E 29		1		*
	Masala		E 13		1		Mishal
Mutara		e 26		1			
	Sapum		E 17		1		*
	Surudanu(??)		E 41		1		*
	'-f-r-?-a		E 42		1		
Ahumuta		e 29		1			**
Ahamuta		f 17				'3mw nbw	
	Ahumuta		E 26		1		
	Ayyanu		E 18		1		Ijon
	Akaya		E 49		1		Acco
	Enya		E 10		1		
	Aqlaya		E 58		1		Eglon? Ekron?
Irqatum		e 22		1			
Irqatum		f 12				'3mw nbw	Arkath
	Irqatum		E 54		1		
	Irqata		E 61			whyt nt...	
	'As[ta]rtum		E 25		1		Ashtaroth
	Pihilum		E 8		1		Pella
Qahlamu		e 8-10		3			**
Qahlamu		f 7				'3mw nbw	
	Qahlamu mhyt		E 40		1		
	Qahlamu rsyt		E 39		1		
	Qanaya		E 32		1		Kenath
	Qarqarum		E 56		1		*
	Sirum		E 19		1		Siri-basani
	Suruya		E 35		1		Tyre
	Rayata		E 44		1		*
Raqaha		e 20,21		2			**
Raqaha		f 11				'3mw nbw	
	Raqaha		F 4			'3mw nbw	
(U)Rusalimum		e 27, 28		2			Jerusalem
(U)Rusalimum		f 18				'3mw nbw	
	(U)Rusalimum		E 45		1		
	Sakmemi		E 6		1		Shechem
	Samuanu		E 55		1		Shimon (Shimron)
	Sariyanu(?)		E 30		1		Sirion
	Saramil(?)		E 22		1		*
	Sosu		E 57		1		Pastoralists
Sutu		e 4-6		3			
Sutu		f 5				'3mw nbw	
Sutu		e' 4		1			
Sutu		f' 5				'3mw nbw	Tribe of Seth (Upper and Lower)
	Sutu hrt		E 52		1		
	Sutu hrt		E 53		1		
	[...]raya		E 46		1		*
	[...]rayanu		E 38		1		
	[...]sa		E 16		1		

hq3w+nbw = all the rulers   ☆☆ = leaders of the clans

whyt nt... ☆ = the clans of ...

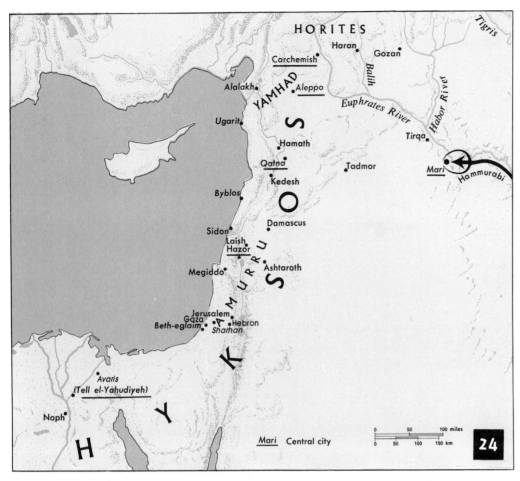

And there came, after a surprising manner, men of ignoble birth out of the eastern parts, and had boldness enough to make an expedition into our country, and with ease subdued it by force...

(Manetho, quoted by Josephus, Against Apion I, 14)

HYKSOS RULE — THE FIFTEENTH DYNASTY OF EGYPT

1668-1560 B.C.

INSCRIPTION, TOMB OF AHMOSE, SON OF EBEN, COMMANDER, ARMY OF AHMOSE - EL-KAB, UPPER EGYPT

The West Semites who had established a commercial colony at Avaris on the eastern arm of the Nile continued to thrive during the rule of the thirteenth dynasty (1784-1668) and the parallel fourteenth dynasty in the western delta (1720-1665) but the chaos at the end of the former line of rulers gave the West Semites, possibly reinforced by forces from Palestine-Syria, the opportunity to set up their own kingdom with Avaris as the new capital. This was the beginning of the fifteenth dynasty (1668-1560 B.C.) whose Egyptian vassals in Middle and Lower Egypt are reckoned as the sixteenth dynasty (1665-1565). A rival dynasty, the seventeenth (1668-1570), gained control of No-Ammon (Thebes) in Upper Egypt.

Some of the rulers of the fifteenth dynasty continued to use their Semitic names. The Egyptians continued to refer to them as "foreign rulers" in recognition of their origin in the West Semitic Levant. The influence of these "Hyksos" rulers reached at least as far as the Carmel ridge since scarabs of their kings and numerous officials are found in Middle Canaanite cities throughout southern Palestine. Objects bearing the names of Hyksos kings have been found far and wide in the ancient Near East.

The largest and apparently the most prosperous city in Canaan at that time was Hazor. It is the only city mentioned in the vast archives of the Amurrite city of Mari on the middle Euphrates (destroyed finally by king 'Ammurapi [Hammurabi] of Babylon).

The Hyksos rulers were expelled from the delta of Egypt by Ahmose I (1570-1546), founder of the eighteenth dynasty (1570-1293) in Thebes. The only testimony to the capture of Avaris, the Hyksos capital, and the subsequent siege of Sharhan/Sharhon (possibly to be equated with the corrupted biblical place name written Sharuhen) in the land of Retenu (Canaan) is the tomb inscription of Ahmose the son of Eben. He relates that the war against Sharhan/Sharhon lasted for three years. This Hyksos outpost town must have been somewhere near or just beyond Gaza (see below regarding Map 27). It is not known how many other campaigns were conducted by Ahmose I and his successor, Amenhotep I (1551-1524), but the same soldier, Ahmose son of Eben, recounts how he accompanied Thutmose I (1524-1518) on a campaign clear up to Naharina (biblical Naharaim), the upper Euphrates area. There he attacked the principal ruler before the latter had gotten his own forces together. Thutmose III later found a stele set up by Thutmose I on the eastern side of the Euphrates. From these testimonies it is obvious that the Egyptians had already achieved control of the southern Levant, otherwise, they could not have moved northward so easily.

While the Hyksos were being expelled, the Hurrians were establishing an empire of their own in north Syria and north Mesopotamia. They were taking advantage of a lightning campaign conducted by a Hittite ruler, Mursilis I, who destroyed Aleppo and penetrated to Babylon where he brought to an end the dynasty of 'Ammurapi and his successors. Now the Hurrians could expand their own kingdom, called Mitanni, from their capital of Washukanni (possibly Tell el-Fakheriyeh). These Hurrians were a non-Semitic people from the central Caucasus area. They had had some contact with Indo-Aryans from whom they had adopted some religious and other cultural features such as the breeding of horses for use with war chariots. The war chariot became the standard mobile firing platform for raining arrows on the flanks of the enemy infantry and for pursuing a routed foe. It was too light and defenseless to be used in frontal attack.

Throughout the remainder of the sixteenth and most of the fifteenth centuries B.C. the history of the Levant is primarily a tale of violent struggle between Mitanni and Egypt for control of Syria and Palestine.

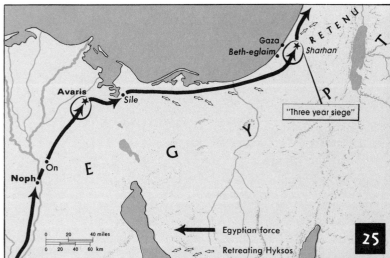

Avaris was destroyed ... Sharuhen was put to siege for
three years...
(Inscription in tomb of Ahmose, son of Eben)

THE EXPULSION OF THE HYKSOS

1560 B.C.

"Three year siege"

→ Egyptian force

⇨ Retreating Hyksos

25

THE MIDDLE EAST IN THE MID-SECOND MILLENNIUM B.C.

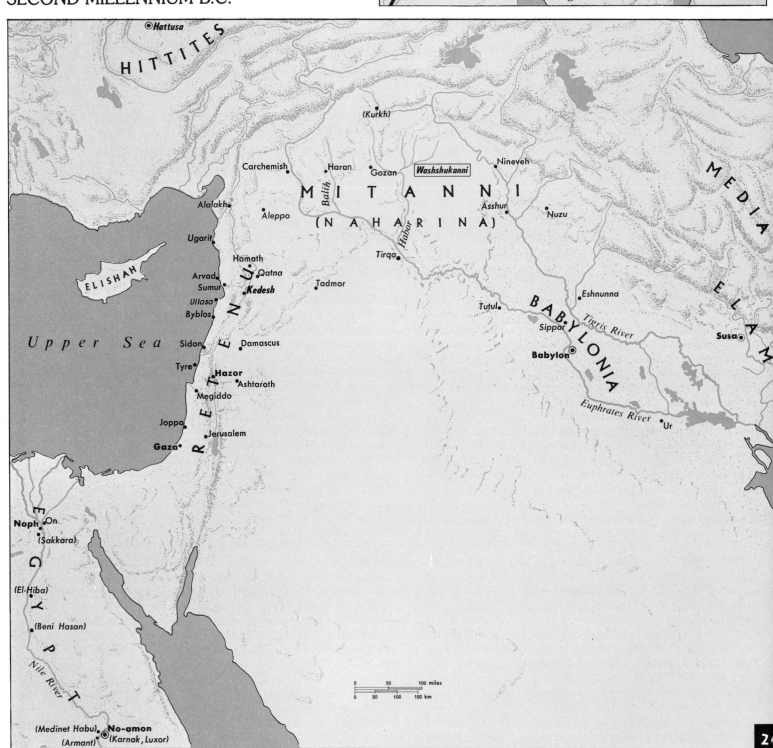

⊙ *Hattusa*

HITTITES

(Kurkh)

Carchemish•

•Haran   Gozan•   *Washshukanni*   Nineveh•

M I T A N N I

Alalakh•   Aleppo•   Balih   (N A H A R I N A)   Asshur•   •Nuzu

Ugarit•

Hamath•   Tirqa•   Habor

Arvad•   •Qatna

Sumur•   **Kedesh**   Tadmor•   Eshnunna•

ELISHAH   Ullasa•   Tutul•   BABYLONIA   Tigris River

Byblos•   Sippar•   **Susa**⊙

U p p e r   S e a   Sidon•   •Damascus   **Babylon**⊙   ELAM

Tyre•   Euphrates River

Hazor•   •Ur

Megiddo•   •Ashtaroth

Joppa•   R E T E N U

Gaza•   •Jerusalem   MEDIA

Noph•   •On

(Sakkara)

G   (El-Hiba)

E   (Beni Hasan)•

Y

P   Nile River

T   (Medinet Habu)•   **No-amon**⊙

(Armant)   (Karnak, Luxor)

0   50   100 miles
0   50   100   150 km

2

And the troops there were in Sharuhen, when from Yurza to the ends of the earth they rebelled against the king...

(Inscription of Thutmose III, Karnak)

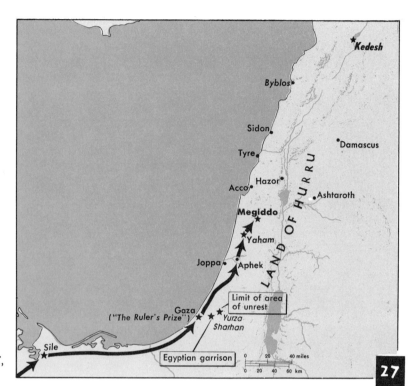

Canaanite chariot (On gold bowl from Ugarit)

INSCRIPTIONS, THUTMOSE III - KARNAK, GEBEL BARKAL, ARMANT, EGYPT

THE CAMPAIGN OF THUTMOSE III
1482 B.C.

Thutmose III (1504-1450), grandson of Thutmose I, was the most energetic of the eighteenth dynasty kings. Even during the co-regency with his mother-in-law, Hatshepsut (1503-1483), he had conducted at least one campaign to Nubia and probably at least one to Retenu where he may have had to reconquer Gaza. When his mother-in-law died, it may have been the signal for a Mitanni-inspired revolt in Retenu. The scribes began to number Thutmose III's campaigns from the time he became sole ruler. His first campaign was aimed at restoring Egyptian control over the southern Levant.

At the head of the Canaanite league stood the ruler of Kedesh on the Orontes and the king of Megiddo. The Egyptian army started out from Sile (Sillu), the fortress on the eastern border of the delta, and marched two hundred and forty kilometers (about 144 miles) in ten days to reach their main base in Retenu at Gaza, known by its title, "the Ruler's Prize." This means that the units had encamped every evening at one of the many supply points along the northern Sinai coast.

Thutmose III mentioned that his northernmost garrison was at Sharhan, evidently just beyond or near Gaza. From the next Canaanite city northward, Yurza, all the cities were in revolt against Egyptian rule. It took eleven days to reach the next major station at Yaham on the Sharon Plain, only half the distance covered in the first ten-day leg of the journey. The Egyptian army must have had to devote some time to fighting and consolidation of Pharaoh's rule over the cities in southern Palestine, such as Joppa and probably Gezer and a few others.

At Yaham, Thutmose called a council of war to discuss the next move. It was known that the Canaanites and their allies were mustering in the Jezreel Valley somewhere beside Megiddo. The alternative routes lay before them: a southern road that brought them through the Valley of Dothan to near Taanach, a northern road that passed by a prominent town called Zephath and probably reaching the plain beside Jokneam. The central route went from Aruna through the narrow defile of the brook Qina (or Gina) just south of Megiddo. The officers advised taking the southern or the northern route but Thutmose III chose the center, supposedly through valor and courage. Actually, his scouts may have informed him that the enemy was still encamped south of Megiddo, close to Taanach. Such was the case when Thutmose, at the head of his personal guards, came out first onto the narrow plain behind Megiddo. He had caught the Canaanites by surprise! After taking up positions on either side of the pass to protect his debauching troops, he encamped in a strategic spot beside the brook and his army assumed positions facing Megiddo on the southwestern side. The battle proper took place on the following day. Thutmose had forced his enemies to accept his venue for the encounter, a narrow valley behind Megiddo where the Canaanite chariots could not maneuver around his flanks. His infantry mounted a victorious charge and the Canaanites fled for safety within Megiddo.

The leaders of the enemy coalition had evidently set up their own private pavilions on the hill beside Megiddo. When the Egyptians in hot pursuit of the fleeing Canaanites passed through the enemy camp, they turned aside from the chase to seize booty for themselves. Thus, they lost the chance to end the war in one day. It took Thutmose III seven months of siege before Megiddo finally surrendered and the enemy leaders offered their submission. Their sons were taken as hostages to Egypt and they were sent home ignominiously.

Thutmose III had the account of his campaign, his first as sole ruler, inscribed on an inner wall of the Karnak temple. The list of the conquered towns was inscribed on another. Each town is represented by the figure of a captive with arms bound behind an oval body; the oval contains the name of the town in hieroglyphs. The original roster contained nearly one hundred and twenty names about half of which are identifiable. They represent a geographical spread from Gaza to Kedesh, with two notable omissions: the towns of the Lebanese coast and Shechem and Jerusalem in the hills of Palestine. It was probably because those cities did not take part in the revolt. The list probably comprised smaller geographic documents, some or all being itineraries used by official couriers. Within small groups, the towns seem to be contiguous, but the groups are not arranged in a logical order. Some geographical features such as "the mountain," or "the valley," appear in addition to town names. It is impossible to deduce any methodical arrangement of the groups of towns in accordance with some administrative pattern. Nevertheless, the list is a testimony to the many Canaanite towns of the mid-fifteenth century, most of them ranged alongside the principal valleys and plains. The settlement pattern for Canaan in the Late Canaanite period can be deduced by supplementing Thutmose's list with other sources such as the Amarna tablets and the rosters of later pharaohs.

All subsequent campaigns were directed at northern Syria. The sixth campaign was against Kedesh on the Orontes. A total of seventeen campaigns is recorded. On one of them, Thutmose crossed the Euphrates and set up a victory stele beside that of his grandfather, Thutmose I. The topographical lists from these later campaigns were added to the original list on two new copies adorning the pylon built by Thutmose on the south side of the temple. The additional text provides over two hundred names, many of them identifiable in north Syria.

THE DEPLOYMENT OF FORCES FOR THE BATTLE OF MEGIDDO

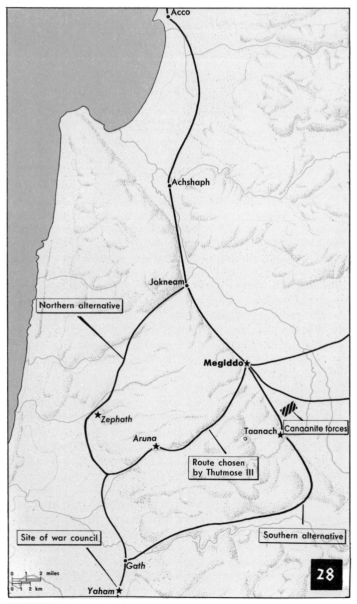

INSCRIPTION, THUTMOSE III — KARNAK, EGYPT

How is it to go through the pass which becomes narrow? When it is known that the enemy is there, waiting on the other side, more and more of them gathering. Will not the horses have to go single file ... But there are two other roads — one (to the east), emerging near Taanach, the other to the north of Zephath, emerging north of Megiddo...

(Inscription of Thutmose III, Karnak)

THE BATTLE OF MEGIDDO

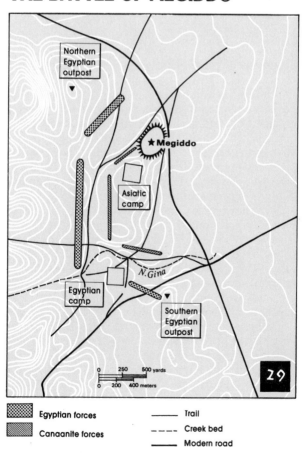

INSCRIPTION, THUTMOSE III —
KARNAK, GEBEL, BARKAL, EGYPT

st of the lands of Upper Retenu which were besieged
Pharaoh in the wretched city Megiddo
(Heading of City-list)

THE CITY-LISTS
OF THUTMOSE III

Part of list of cities conquered by
Thutmose III (Relief in Temple of
Ammon at Karnak)

CITY-LISTS, THUTMOSE III —
KARNAK, EGYPT

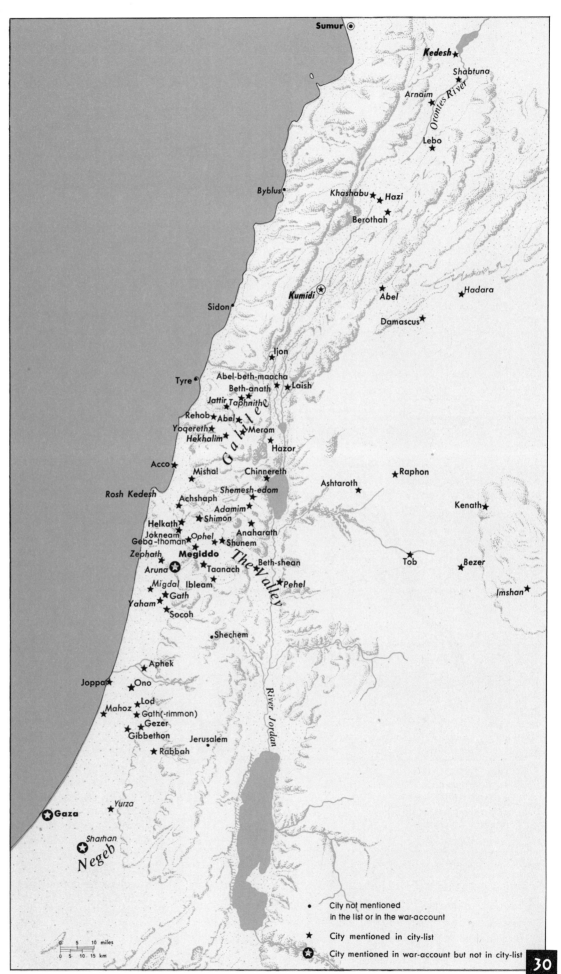

Sumur ◎

Kedesh ★

Shabtuna

Arnaim ★

Orontes River

Lebo ★

Byblus ●

Khashabu ★ Hazi

Berothah ★

Kumidi ✪

Abel ★

Hadara ★

Sidon ●

Damascus ★

Ijon ★

Tyre ●

Abel-beth-maacha ★

Beth-anath ★ ★ Laish

Jattir ★ Taphnith ★

Rehob ★ Abel ★

Yoqereth ★ Merom ★

Hekhalim ★

Galilee

Hazor ★

Acco ★

Mishal ★

Chinnereth ★

Ashtaroth ★

Raphon ★

Rosh Kedesh

Shemesh-edom ★

Achshaph ★

Adamim ★

Kenath ★

Helkath ★ Shimon ★

Jokneam ★

Anaharath ★

Geba-thoman ★ Ophel ★ ★ Shunem

Zephath ★ Megiddo ✪

The Valley

Beth-shean ★

Tob ★

Bezer ★

Aruna ✪ Taanach ★

Pehel ★

Migdal ★ Ibleam ★

Imshan ★

Yaham ★ Gath ★

Socoh ★

Shechem ●

Aphek ★

River Jordan

Joppa ★ Ono ★

Mahoz ★ Lod ★

Gath(-rimmon) ★

Gezer ★

Gibbethon ★

Jerusalem ●

Rabbah ★

Yurza ★

Gaza ✪

Sharhan ✪

Negeb

● City not mentioned
in the list or in the war-account

★ City mentioned in city-list

✪ City mentioned in war-account but not in city-list

0 5 10 miles
0 5 10 15 km

30

List of plunder: Living Maryannu, 550; their wives, 240;
Canaanites, 640; sons of rulers, 232; daughters of rulers,
323; concubines of rulers ..., 270...
(Inscription of Amenhotep II, Memphis)

THE EARLY CAMPAIGNS OF AMENHOTEP II

1450 AND 1445 B.C.

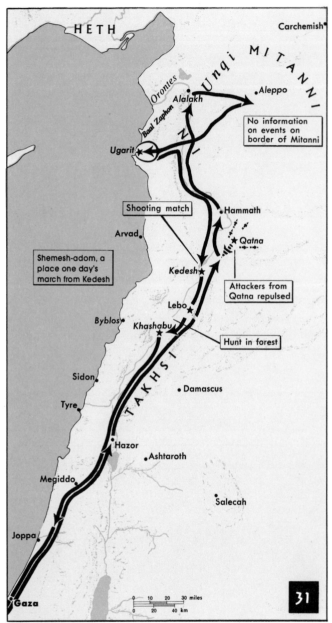

MONUMENTS,
AMENHOTEP II —
KARNAK, MEMPHIS,
AMADA, ELEPHANTINE,
EGYPT

Throughout the fifteenth, fourteenth and thirteenth centuries, Egyptian rule over Canaan was relatively stable, especially since the decisive victory by Thutmose III in his first campaign. Nevertheless, there were occasional problems. The main centers of Egyptian administration seem to have been Gaza in the south, Sumur on the northern coast and Kumidi (Komidi) in the Lebanese Beqaʻ Valley. In addition, other key towns like the seaports of Joppa in the south and Ullasa in the north and strong points on major crossroads such as Bethshean were also Egyptian bases. Just as the Canaanites had found the terrain beside Megiddo suitable for mustering their forces, so the Egyptians also favored that area as a place to maintain a strong military presence. The Egyptians permitted considerable freedom to the rulers of the local city states; these latter were generally free to manage their own affairs. Each township consisted of a class of senior ranking citizens, the "elders of the city." They held estates and often had residences within the city as well. It was to their advantage to have one of their number serving as hereditary king, a first among equals, so long as the latter protected the interests of the upper class. The craftsmen usually lived in the towns or in special villages. Their main service was to the ruler. The farms were maintained by a landless peasant class and sometimes by slaves. The Egyptians demanded loyalty as expressed by annual payment of taxes in kind from the agricultural produce. Vassal rulers were also responsible for policing the trade routes, expediting the caravans and providing particular commodities to pharaoh such as raw glass, special slave girls, etc. Above all, the function of Canaan as a land and sea bridge for commerce with the Aegean, Syria and Mesopotamia, was uppermost in Egyptian priorities. Under a strong line of pharaohs, the Canaanites could be kept under control, but when rival powers, first the Hurrians of Mitanni and then the Hittites of Hatti, exerted pressure on the Canaanite cities to defect from Egypt, it was necessary for the Egyptian king to take stern measures.

The first signs of renewed unrest came towards the end of Thutmose III's reign and his son, Amenhotep II, was appointed co-regent to meet the crisis. The young prince went into the field to put down an insurrection on the part of seven rulers in the land of Takhsi. His victorious campaign was called his "first" by the scribes who composed two stelae commemorating favors to the temples at Amada and Elephantine. By the time Amenhotep II had returned home to Egypt with the seven captured rebels, whose heads he severed, his father had died leaving him as sole ruler. On his next campaign, now reckoned as his first as sole ruler, he met no resistance until he reached the northern Beqaʻ Valley one day south of Kedesh; then he went on into North Syria, well beyond Qatna. The reason for this action may be an attempted coup d'etat by anti-Egyptian forces in Ugarit (though the spelling of the name is unusual). After a lightning police action in Ugarit, Amenhotep demonstrated his bowmanship before the residents of Kedesh, and hunted in the forest of Lebo. Military action was taken against Khashabu in the northern Lebanese Beqaʻ. On the return journey to Egypt Amenhotep captured a diplomatic courier bearing a (cuneiform) letter in a pouch around his neck. He was on a mission for the "ruler of Naharina (Mitanni)," probably to stir up rebellion behind pharaoh's back.

List of plunder which Pharaoh took: rulers of Retenu, 127; ruler's brothers, 179; Apiru, 3,600; living Shasu, 15,000; Horites, 36,300 ...
(Inscription of Amenhotep II, Memphis)

THE LAST RECORDED CAMPAIGN OF AMENHOTEP II
1443 B.C.

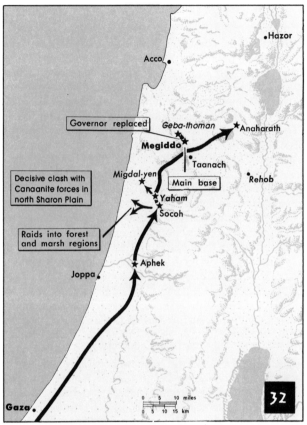

MONUMENTS, AMENHOTEP II — KARNAK, MEMPHIS, EGYPT

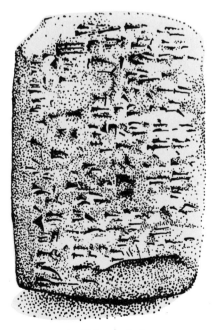

An El-Amarna Letter

In spite of the earlier show of force in North Syria, Amenhotep II did not succeed in convincing the local Canaanite rulers that loyalty to Egypt was imperative. The ruler of Naharina (Mitanni) probably stepped up his efforts to stir up trouble. This time the resistance centered on the northern Sharon Plain. On this, his second campaign as sole ruler, Amenhotep arrived at Aphek where he was well received by the local ruler. He encamped at Yaham as his father had done and the troops made forays into the scrub forest areas of the Sharon to take prisoners and cattle. The god Amon appeared to him that night and promised victory; the ensuing text is broken but shows that a decisive encounter with the Canaanite forces, perhaps at Gath-padalla, took place. Pharaoh claimed to have personally guarded the captives all night within a ring of fire. Next, the Egyptian army laid siege to Anaharath in eastern Lower Galilee in the valley leading from Mt. Tabor to the Jordan. Afterward, they returned to "the vicinity of Me(!)giddo" (corrupt spelling) for rest and regrouping. From there, troops were sent to nearby Geba-thoman where the local ruler was arrested and his son installed in his place.

Four cuneiform epistles found at Taanach date to this period. In two of them a certain Amenhotep, without royal titles, chides the local ruler for not appearing with his troops at Gaza. In a second letter he orders the ruler to come on the morrow to Megiddo with his troops and his tribute. That Amenhotep may have been an official named after the pharaoh. It has been speculated that he was pharaoh himself passing through Canaan on his early campaign as crown prince or even on one of his later campaigns against North Syria or against Anaharath. Another of the Taanach letters comes from a superior local official located at Rehob.

Amenhotep II's two stelae from Karnak and Memphis include lists of the prisoners taken; the passages disagree in their numbers but they reflect the social structure of the time: city rulers and their families, the warrior class (landed nobles called *maryannu*), Canaanites, Hurrians and North Syrians (Nughassians). There were also outcasts (*'apîrû*) and pastoralists (*shasu*) serving as mercenaries.

EGYPT IN THE AMARNA AGE

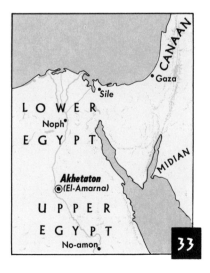

THE KINGS OF CANAAN IN THE AMARNA AGE
FOURTEENTH CENTURY B.C.

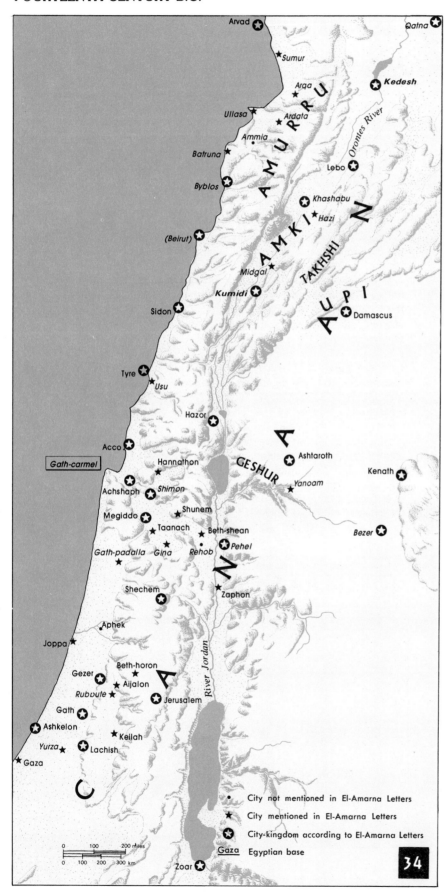

The next pharaoh, Thutmose IV, has left a few fragment[s of] monuments in Canaan that seem to testify to his presen[ce] there. A list of sacrifices from Karnak attests to prison[ers] from Gezer. Mitanni finally made peace with Egypt becau[se] she feared the reviving Hittite state in Anatolia. Through[out] most of the long reign of the Amenhotep III (1386-1349) the[re] was no need to campaign in the Levant. His son, Amenho[tep] IV (1350-1334), built a new capital called Akhetaton, "Horiz[on] of the Sun," at Amarna. A cuneiform archive discovered the[re] contained international correspondence between Amenho[tep] III and IV and the other "great powers" of the day. The lette[rs] from Mitanni had been sent to the older pharaoh while t[he] capital was at No-Amon, as were some of the epistles fr[om] Canaan. The bulk of the letters come from city rulers [in] Canaan and central Syria addressed to Amenhotep IV.

The local correspondence sheds much light on the social a[nd] political relations between the various city states in Canaan a[nd] vis à vis their Egyptian overlords. The letters from foreign cou[n]tries, including Babylon, Assyria, Alashia and Hatti, docume[nt] the collapse of Mitanni at the hands of the vigorous Hitt[ite] monarch, Suppiluliuma. The new Hittite presence in No[rth] Syria led to considerable unrest among the Canaanite rule[rs.] The three main administrative centers were Gaza, Sumur a[nd] Kumidi. Cushites from Nubia and Sherdanu from the Aege[an] region served as garrison troops alongside renegade ('ap[îrû) and nomadic (Sutû and shasu) mercenaries.

The outcasts and outlaws ('apîrû), people who had had [to] flee from the city state societies, found refuge in the mounta[in]ous areas of the Levant. They were available to any leader w[ho] might hire them, usually on condition that they be reward[ed] by citizenship and lands. One such refuge was the mount[ain] plateau behind the North Lebanese coast, around Ammia. [In] the reign of Amenhotep III, an upstart named Abdi-Ashi[rta] rallied these outlaws around himself and began subverti[ng] the local city rulers loyal to Egypt. Rib-Haddi, the ruler [of] Byblos, wrote alarming letters to pharaoh and to his responsi[ble] officials. They heeded the warnings and dispatched Egypt[ian] troops by sea. The upstart was put to death and the rebell[ion] ended. Under the next pharaoh, Amenhotep IV, some Egypti[an] officers may have favored the establishment of a small buf[fer] state to protect their northern frontier from the Hittite thre[at.] They encouraged the sons of Abdi-Ashirta, Pu-Baalu a[nd] Aziru, to use their 'apîrû troops to found just such a state, [in] the territory now called Amurru, as their father had envisag[ed.] This time, pharaoh was persuaded to ignore the protests [of] the hapless Rib-Haddi and to support Aziru, the head of t[he] new state. Aziru was called to Egypt to give accounts a[nd] convinced the Egyptians to confirm him as ruler of Amur[ru.] He also saw the growing internal weakness of the Egypti[an] social order and decided, upon his return to Amurru, to s[hift] his allegiance to Suppiluliuma! Thus was founded a dynas[tic] state with 'apîrû mercenaries that maintained its existence [for] the next century or more. It was part of the Hittite emp[ire] but during certain interludes it was forced to submit und[er] pressure from Egypt. This fatal mistake in foreign policy w[as] not because Amenhotep IV (Akhenaton) neglected his empi[re;] it was the result of faulty intelligence and poor advice on t[he] part of senior officials. Late in his reign or perhaps und[er] the next principal successor, Tutankhamen (1334-1325), [a] major campaign to Canaan was planned; orders were se[nt] out to city rulers along the proposed route for the preparati[on] of supplies and auxiliary troops.

EL-AMARNA LETTERS

Legend on map:

- • City not mentioned in El-Amarna Letters
- ★ City mentioned in El-Amarna Letters
- ✪ City-kingdom according to El-Amarna Letters
- Gaza Egyptian base

34

y the king be apprised concerning his servant and
city. I am cultivating the (fields of Shunem)... I alone
g corvée workers...
ler of Megiddo to Pharaoh, El-Amarna Letter 365).

THE CITY STATE OF SHECHEM AND ITS NEIGHBORS IN THE AMARNA LETTERS

CA. 1350 TO 1334 B.C.

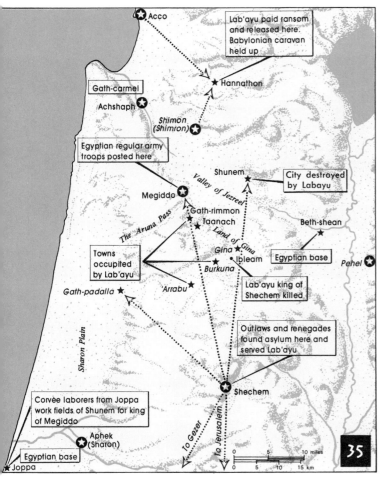

Acco

Lab'ayu paid ransom and released here. Babylonian caravan held up

★ Hannathon

Gath-carmel

Achshaph

Shimon (Shimron)

Egyptian regular army troops posted here

Shunem

City destroyed by Labayu

Megiddo

Valley of Jezreel

Gath-rimmon

The Aruna Pass

Taanach

Beth-shean

Land of Gina

Gina ★Gina

Ibleam

Egyptian base

Pehel

Towns occupied by Lab'ayu

Burkuna

Lab'ayu king of Shechem killed

Gath-padalla ★

'Arrabu ★

Sharon Plain

Outlaws and renegades found asylum here and served Lab'ayu

Shechem

To Gezer

To Jerusalem

Corvée laborers from Joppa work fields of Shunem for king of Megiddo

Aphek (Sharon)

35

Egyptian base

Joppa

0   5   10 miles
0   5   10   15 km

⊛ City-kingdom according to El-Amarna Letters

········· Intercity connection according to El-Amarna Letters

-AMARNA LETTERS

The ruler of Shechem, Lab'ayu, controlled an area contiguous with the city state of Jerusalem in the south, Gezer in the southwest, Gath-padalla to the west and Megiddo to the northwest. Lab'ayu was not a native of Shechem; his own home city and his family estate (including the family cult statue) were seized by force; the name of that town and the attacking enemy are not given. Lab'ayu had close political ties with Milkilu, ruler of Gezer, and complained that the latter went unpunished while he, Lab'ayu, had suffered the loss of property. The father-in-law of Milkilu was Tagu, ruler of Gath-carmel; Tagu furnished the soldiers for the Egyptian garrison at Beth-shean. The hills around Shechem were less densely occupied than the coastal plain and valleys. So political refugees and renegades ('apîrû) sought refuge there. Lab'ayu's son was accused of consorting with those outlaws and Lab'ayu had to turn the lad over to an Egyptian official for interrogation.

When the unit of the Egyptian standing army posted at Megiddo was called home and not replaced right away (probably due to important political events in Egypt), Lab'ayu launched a program of territorial expansion. He forced the ruler of Gath-padalla to join him; then he attacked 'Arrabu, and Burkuna, towns in the Dothan Valley, and Gath-rimmon beside Taanach. He also destroyed Shunem. His troops comprised 'apîrû renegades and he drove out the inhabitants of the conquered towns so his outlaw soldiers could take over their farm lands. The next step was an attempted conquest of Megiddo, whose ruler, Biridia, complained bitterly to pharaoh. The alliance with Gezer, Gath-padalla and Gath-carmel, plus influence over the mercenaries at Beth-shean and the family link with Lab'ayu's son at Pehel would give Lab'ayu virtual control over a major portion of the international trunk route from Egypt to Damascus and beyond.

The king of Egypt issued an order to the local rulers to arrest Lab'ayu and send him alive to Egypt for questioning. The ruler of Acco, Surata, took the prisoner from Megiddo, ostensibly to send him via ship to Egypt. Instead, he accepted ransom money from Lab'ayu at Hannathon and released Lab'ayu and also Baalu-meher of Gath-padalla to go to their homes. An ambush was laid for Lab'ayu at Gina (Jenin?) and he was slain. Afterwards, Biridia of Megiddo was charged with bringing corvée workers, including some from Joppa, to work the abandoned fields of Shunem so that the Egyptians would not lose any income.

Soon the sons of Lab'ayu renewed the league with Gezer and began pressuring the ruler of Gath-padalla to renew their father's insurrectionist policies, presumably without success. Satatna, son of Suratu, from Acco took part in the plundering of a Babylonian caravan at Hannathon; he was abetted by the ruler of Shim'on.

And now even a town in the territory of Jerusalem, called Beth-NINIB (Horon?), belonging to the king, has gone over to the people of Keilah . . . if there are no regular troops (this year) then all the king's lands will be taken over by the renegades ('apîrû)!"
(Ruler of Jerusalem to pharaoh, El-Amarna Letter No. 290).

JERUSALEM AND THE CITIES OF THE SHEPHELAH IN THE AMARNA LETTERS

CA. 1350 TO 1334 B.C.

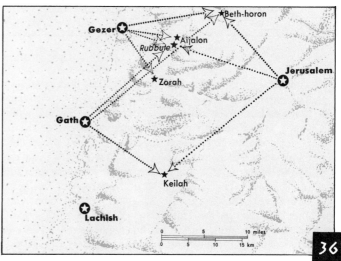

★Beth-horon

Gezer

Rubbute ★

★Aijalon

Jerusalem

★ Zorah

Gath

Keilah

Lachish

0   5   10 miles
0   5   10   15 km

36

EL-AMARNA LETTERS

The southern hill country was dominated by Jerusalem, whose ruler, 'Abdi-Kheba, was supported by a garrison of Nubian mercenaries. The Amarna letters tell of conflict between 'Abdi-Kheba and his neighbors on the coastal plain. The bone of contention was control of the approach routes from the Shephelah to the central hill country. 'Abdi-Kheba had bribed the leaders of Keilah to abandon their allegiance to Shuwardata, apparently the ruler of Gath. He wanted control over the Vale of Elah and the road leading from Keilah to Beth-zur and Bethlehem. Shuwardata complained and got permission from pharaoh to reclaim his lost town by force. Then Shuwardata

and Milkilu of Gezer, supported by Tagu of Gath-carmel, occupied Rubbute (the biblical Rabbah) and another town, Beth-NINIB, probably Beth-horon, both of which controlled other routes to the hill country. 'Abdi-Kheba and his enemies refer to each other as 'apîrû, "outlaws." Zimredda, ruler of Lachish, resisted the blandishments of his own brother, Shipti-Baalu, to be disloyal to pharaoh and was slain by "servants who have become renegades," in the words of 'Abdi-Kheba. Nevertheless, Shipti-Baalu did become ruler of Lachish. The ongoing conflict in the Shephelah involved other towns such as Aijalon and Zorah.

THE WARS OF SETI I IN THE LAND OF CANAAN AND AGAINST THE HITTITES IN SYRIA
1291-1271 B.C.

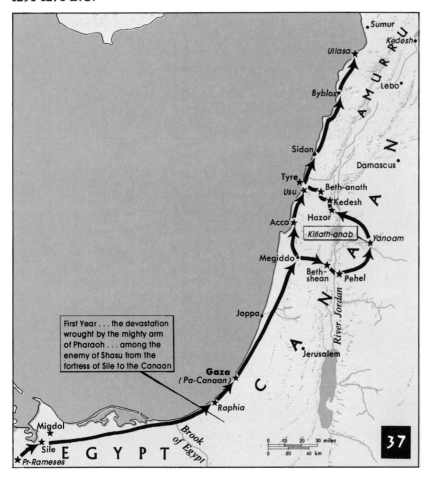

First year ... The destruction made by the mighty arm of Pharaoh — life, health, prosperity — among the enemy of the Shasu, from the fortress of Sile to Pa-Canaan.
(Inscription Karnak)

First Year ... the devastation wrought by the mighty arm of Pharaoh ... among the enemy of Shasu from the fortress of Sile to the Canaan

MONUMENT, SETI I — BETH SHEAN;
RELIEFS — KARNAK;
VARIOUS CITY LISTS — EGYPT

The last third of the fourteenth century B.C., during the reign of Tutankhamon, Ay and Horemheb, saw Egypt hard pressed to maintain her hold on Canaan. The political unrest in Egypt itself was resolved by the time Horemheb's successor, Rameses I, had founded the nineteenth dynasty (1293 B.C.). The old Hyksos town of Avaris was revived as the new dynastic capital in the eastern delta under the name Pr-Rameses, "House of Rameses." The energetic second pharaoh of this dynasty, Seti I, set out to reaffirm Egyptian control over Canaan and to challenge the Hittites for control of the Levant. For his first campaign, during his first year of reign (1291 B.C.), relatively good documentation has survived, especially his reliefs on the north wall of the hypostyle hall at Karnak and

a stele found at Beth-shean, plus several topographical lists at various temples. His relief of crossing the northern Sinai (see page 46) shows him returning victoriously after defeating the Shasu pastoralists in northeastern Sinai. The series of outposts and supply depots, used by the Egyptians during the entire New Kingdom period, are depicted on this relief. Word had come that "the foe belonging to the Shasu are plotting rebellion; their chiefs are gathered together, waiting on the mountain ridges of Khurru; they have begun clamoring and quarreling, one of them killing his fellow; they have no regard for the laws of the (Egyptian) palace." Seti I had to pacify these troublesome nomads and also to make a show of force along the main military routes of Canaan.

On this day Pharaoh was told: The wretched enemy in the city of Hamath ... holds the city of Beth-shean by treaty with Elah of Pehel. He does not allow the ruler of Rehob to leave his city.

(Beth-shean stele of Seti I)

SETI I QUELLS A REBELLION IN THE BETH-SHEAN VALLEY
1291 B.C.

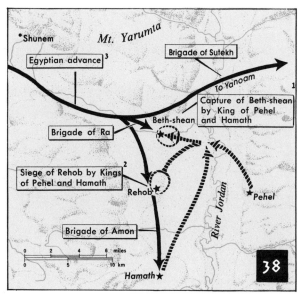

Egyptian force ◀— · Canaanite force ·◀▥▥▥▥

Though the mountainous regions were now being infiltrated by the pastoralists, the city states continued to thrive on the plain as illustrated by one phase in Seti I's first campaign, documented in a stele discovered at Beth-shean: "The wretched enemy in the town of Hamath is assembling a great host of people to himself; he has seized the (Egyptian garrison) town of Beth-shean; then, in league with the men of Pehel, he has blockaded the ruler of Rehob." Seti dispatched three brigades to reoccupy Beth-shean, to lift the siege of his loyal vassal at Rehob, and to secure the eastern town of Yanoam.

A second stele bears the fragmentary account of 'apîrû renegades in Mt. Yarumta (probably the Jarmuth/Remeth of Issachar, Josh. 19:21; 21:29, in the high plateau north of Beth-shean).

Stele of Seti I from Beth-shean

THE EXPEDITIONS OF RAMESES II TO NORTHERN CANAAN
1275 AND 1274 B.C.

The aggressive policy of Seti I was continued by his son Rameses II. An inscription on the cliff above the Dog River (Nahr el-Kelb) dates to the latter's fourth year (1275 B.C.). Rameses evidently marched up the coast and forced Amurru to return to Egyptian vassalage, thus preparing for his next campaign into central Syria. The campaign of the following year (1274 B.C.) has been immortalized in several temple reliefs and inscriptions as a deed of personal heroism on the part of Rameses. He and his troops had marched through southern Canaan "as safely as in Egypt." From a regional base at a "City of Rameses" in the land of Amki, he crossed the watershed between the Litani and the Orontes. False information from Shasu bedouin loyal to the Hittites led Rameses to believe that Muwatalli, the Hittite emperor, had withdrawn to Aleppo so the Egyptian brigades marched up the valley in column, Rameses and his headquarters unit leading the way. But the Hittite foe was hiding behind the high mound of the city of Kedesh. While

Rameses' personal guards and the Brigade of Amon were setting up the command center and the Brigade of Ra was on the road, the enemy chariots launched a surprise flank attack (No. 1 below). Rameses claims that he personally defended the demoralized troops of his entourage (No. 2 below), but some texts reveal that a unit of crack Egyptian troops arrived just in the nick of time from Amurru (No. 3 below); they had come via the coastal route and evidently been scheduled to join up with Rameses. Their arrival saved Rameses from the Hittite surprise attack. On the following day, the two armies joined battle and though Rameses claimed victory, it was he who withdrew from the field, not the Hittites. After the Egyptian retreat southwards, the Hittite general Hattusilis (brother of Muwatalli and later emperor himself) marched as far as the Damascus area and devastated the countryside. Amurru could now return to its former position as a Hittite vassal state.

And now the wretched enemy from Heth, together with many foreign lands, lay concealed and prepared for battle northeast of Kedesh.

(Kedesh Victory Poem)

THE EXPEDITIONS OF RAMESES II TO NORTHERN CANAAN

RELIEFS — THEBES, LUXOR, ABU SIMBEL;
INSCRIPTIONS — THEBES

ARZAWA

HITTITE EMPIRE

KIZZUWATNA

MITANNI NAHARINA

MUGISH

Alalakh

Aleppo

Ugarit

Orontes River

NUGHASSE

Hamath

Qatna

Sumur

AMURRU

Kedesh

Arnama

Lebo

Byblos

Year 5, confrontation at Kedesh

Year 4, campaign to northern coast

ELISHAH

(Beirut)

Sidon

CANAAN

AMKI

UPI

Damascus

Tyre

City of Rameses

Megiddo

Beth-shean

Jaffa

Gaza

Hittite forces

Egyptian force

Reinforcement from Amurru

Rameses

Sile

0 20 40 miles
0 20 40 60 km

THE BATTLE OF KEDESH
1286 B.C.

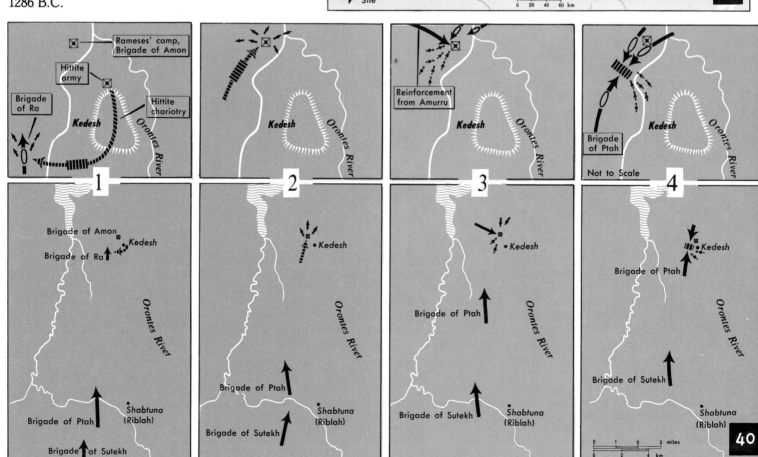

1
Rameses' camp, Brigade of Amon
Hittite army
Brigade of Ra
Hittite chariotry
Kedesh
Orontes River

Brigade of Amon
Kedesh
Brigade of Ra
Orontes River
Brigade of Ptah
Shabtuna (Riblah)
Brigade of Sutekh

2
Kedesh
Orontes River

Kedesh
Orontes River
Brigade of Ptah
Shabtuna (Riblah)
Brigade of Sutekh

3
Reinforcement from Amurru
Kedesh
Orontes River

Kedesh
Brigade of Ptah
Orontes River
Brigade of Sutekh
Shabtuna (Riblah)

4
Brigade of Ptah
Kedesh
Orontes River
Not to Scale

Kedesh
Brigade of Ptah
Orontes River
Brigade of Sutekh
Shabtuna (Riblah)

0 1 2 3 miles
0 2 4 km

40

Let me describe for you the nature of a chariot warrior
. . . Let me relate to you the territories to the border
of the land of Canaan. . .

Papyrus Anastasi I

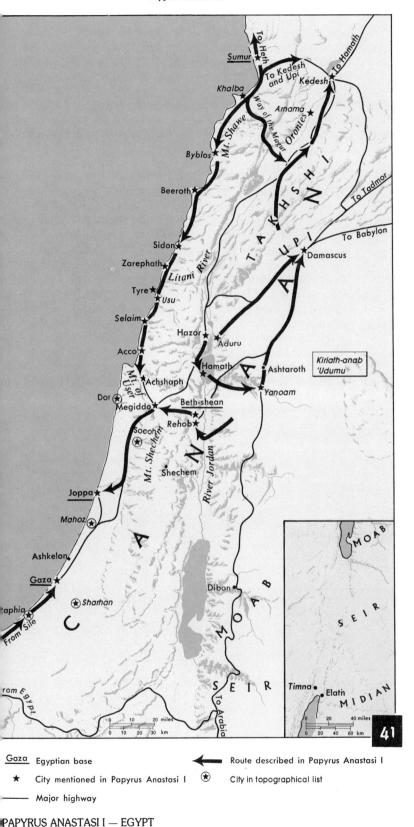

Gaza — Egyptian base

★ — City mentioned in Papyrus Anastasi I

⊛ — City in topographical list

—— — Major highway

← — Route described in Papyrus Anastasi I

PAPYRUS ANASTASI I — EGYPT

THE LAND OF CANAAN DURING THE REIGN OF RAMESES II
BEFORE 1270 B.C.

After the near defeat at Kedesh, Rameses was forced to deal with unrest in Canaan. A Luxor relief dated to his eighth year (1271 B.C.) depicts his action against several towns in Galilee and Amurru. Another victory stele at Nahr el-Kelb dates to year ten (1269 B.C.). One topographical list follows an itinerary along the coast and an undated relief shows a siege of Acco. There are also recorded activities in the south and east, as far as the land of Moab and the mountain of Seir. Rameses often boasts of his victories over the Shasu, some of which he lists by tribal or geographical names. Beginning with Seti I, there was a (seasonal?) Egyptian mining project in the copper rich wadi at Timna that continued to flourish into the days of the twentieth dynasty. Some of the labor force was local as attested by the presence of the so-called "Midianite" pottery from southern Transjordan.

The rise of an independent Assyria gave the Hittites new worries on their eastern front. Thus they were led to seek accommodation with Egypt and a peace treaty was negotiated and ratified by Rameses II's twenty-first year (1258). Amurru remained a Hittite vassal as did Kedesh. Such is the geopolitical situation reflected in the northern border of Canaan (Num. 34:1-12; see Map 50).

A school text in the form of a satirical letter depicts the life of an Egyptian scribe. Among his other duties was that of diplomatic courier for which training as a chariot warrior was also required. The geographic chapter preserves some of the main itineraries in Canaan with which an Egyptian emissary had to be familiar. Routes along the Phoenician coast, in the Lebanese Beqa', the Damascene and Lower Galilee are described. Of special interest is the route from the fords of the Jordan past Beth-shean to Megiddo and south through the Aruna pass. There the charioteer would face dangers from the difficult path and the tribesmen hiding in the forest. Even greater risks awaited in the seaport at Joppa among deceitful maidens and horse thieves. There was, however, an Egyptian ordinance base there where chariots could be repaired and weapons replenished. The final chapter lists the North Sinai coastal forts just as depicted on Seti I's Karnak relief (see Map 48).

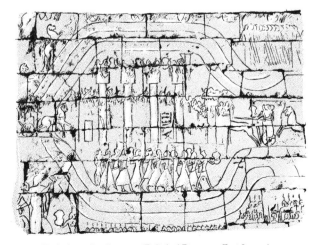

Kedesh-on-the-Orontes (Relief of Rameses II at Luxor)

Canaan is plagued by every evil, Ashkelon is carried off,
Gezer taken, Yanoam is like that which is not, Israel is
desolate, its seed is nought.

(Merneptah Stele)

THE CAMPAIGN OF MERNEPTAH
1207 B.C.

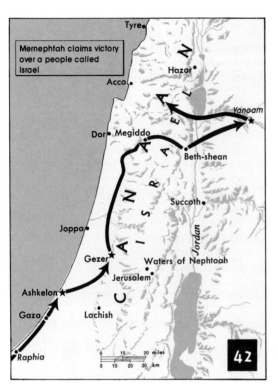

The rest of Rameses II's long reign of 67 years seems to have been relatively peaceful, giving ample time to develop Egypt's economy; but the expeditions against Moab and the Shasu of Mt. Seir may represent punitive measures in the face of new disturbances. Rameses' son, Merneptah, had to ward off an attempted invasion of the delta from the west by a coalition of Libyans and peoples from the Cretan/Aegean area. In his seventh year, Merneptah was forced to quell rebellions in Canaan. The victory poem in his victory inscription says: "Plundered is Canaan with every evil; carried off is Ashkelon; seized upon is Gezer; Yanoam has been made as that which does not exist; Israel is laid waste, his seed is not." The three towns are defined by the standard symbols for city states but Israel is clearly defined by the symbols for a non-urban ethnic group. Pharaoh Merneptah recorded his military activities on the sides of a wall perpendicular to the south side of the Karnak temple; his Libyan war on the east and his Canaanite war on the west. The latter relief had been ascribed to Rameses II because his famous treaty with the Hittites is also displayed there, but it has been shown that the war reliefs are from Merneptah. Three conquered cities are shown but only the inscription for Ashkelon is preserved: "The wretched town which his majesty seized when it was rebellious, Ashkelon." Above Ashkelon one sees the Canaanite forces being defeated by pharaoh; other panels of the relief show prisoners dressed as typical Shasu, the pastoral nomads so frequent in Egyptian texts of this time; these nomadic warriors evidently represent the Israel of the victory hymn.

VICTORY STELE OF MERNEPTAH — THEBES, EGYPT

Go from your country and your kindred and your
father's house to the land that I will show you.

(Genesis 12:1)

THE TRADITION OF ABRAHAM'S MIGRATION

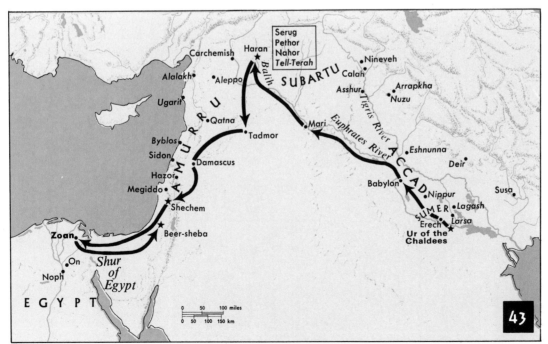

GEN. 11:31-13:1

The narrative about the migration of the patriarchal ancestor of the Israelite nation emphasizes their origin in Mesopotamia and their subsequent association with Egypt, the two great riverine cultures of the ancient Near East. Ur of the Chaldees was the venerable city of the moon god Sin in southern Mesopotamia, Sumer. It had once controlled a vast commercial empire in the late third millennium B.C. The Chaldees, however, are the former nomadic people who settled there in the early Iron Age and achieved supremacy with their capital at Babylon, during the seventh century B.C. Haran was at the principal crossroads of commerce in Upper Mesopotamia. Several of the patriarchal relatives are actually the patronyms of known cities in that vicinity; Haran and Nahor appear in the Mari letters of the eighteenth century B.C. while Tell Terah and Serug are known from later Assyrian sources.

"The Canaanite was then in the land" but Amorites lived at Hebron, said to have been founded seven years before Zoan in Egypt. Zoan was the new capital of the delta, founded after the channels near Pr-Rameses were no longer usable, probably during the eleventh century B.C. Other ethnic groups encountered in Canaan were the Midianites (Ishmaelites) and the Philistines. The latter first appear in the eastern Mediterranean as leaders of the invasion by Aegean peoples in the eighth year in the reign of Rameses III (1174 B.C.). The Ishmaelites were present in the steppe lands up to the tenth century B.C.

The Patriarchs came into the country from Transjordan and confined their migratory movements in Cisjordan to the watershed route through the hill country, from Shechem via Bethel to Hebron. They also sojourned in the Negeb, that is, Beer-sheba and vicinity. Their livelihood was based on the herding of small cattle and their movements were primarily for the seasonal utilization of local pasturage. They sought to live in symbiosis with certain urban centers, namely Shechem and Gerar, and probably also Bethel and Hebron. From Beer-sheba they made journeys into the Sinai steppe "between Kadesh and Shur," reminiscent of the Shasu from Edom in Mt. Seir who sought pasturage in the eastern Delta of Egypt. Narratives about a sojourn in the land of Gerar feature both Abraham and Isaac. The latter obtained urban living accommodations and invested in grain production but was forced back to Beer-sheba by the jealousy of the local residents. Beer-sheba seems to be on the periphery of the territory ruled by Abimelech, king of Gerar. The Patriarchs could live there without clashing with the people of Gerar, but the king preferred to legalize the relationship by means of treaties (covenants). During times of drought and famine, the Patriarchs sought respite by going to Egypt.

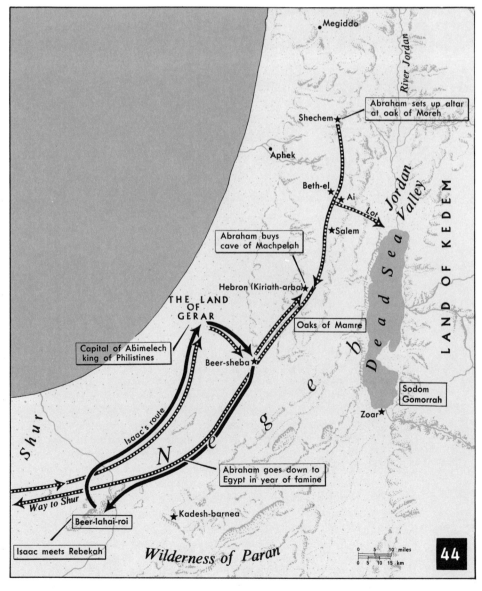

From there (Hebron), Abraham journeyed toward the territory of the Negeb; and dwelt between Kadesh and Shur; and he sojourned in Gerar.

(Genesis 20:1).

ABRAHAM AND ISAAC IN THE LAND OF CANAAN

GEN. 12:6-35:29

In the days of Amraphel king of Shinar, Arioch king of Ellasar, Chedorlaomer king of Elam, and Tidal king of Goiim, these kings made war with Bera king of Sodom, Birsha king of Gomorrah, Shinab king of Admah, Shemeber king of Zeboiim, and the king of Bela (that is, Zoar).

(Genesis 14:1-2)

THE KINGS OF THE NORTH

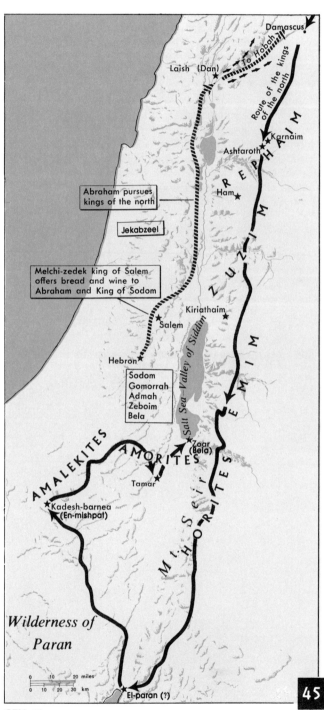

Wilderness of Paran

GEN. 14

45

The narrative in Genesis 14 about the four kings who came to attack the five kings of the "cities on the plain" is the oldest military tradition preserved in the Bible. It contained pre-Israelite geographical data exemplified by the double names of most of the towns, e.g. "Bela, that is Zoar." Besides a reverence for that ancient tradition, there is a concern that the reader be able to orient himself geographically; thus the venerable names are updated by contemporary Israelite names. None of the characters mentioned have been identified with known historical figures nor have the Sodom, Gomorrah or the other towns appeared in ancient near eastern documents.

The same night he arose and took his two wives, two maids, and his eleven children, and crossed the ford of the Jabbok.

(Genesis 32:2)

JACOB AND HIS SONS

GEN. 31-35

46

Also in the later phase of the patriarchal narratives, that pertaining to Jacob and his sons, the action is restricted almost entirely to the central hill country. Esau is now living in Mt. Seir. Peaceful symbiosis with sheep-raising Canaanites is reflected in the story of Judah and Tamar which takes place in the northern Shephelah near the junction of the Vale of Elah with the geographical "trough" separating the Shephelah from the hill country of Judah. Unlike the Abrahamic account, Jacob's entrance into Canaan via Transjordan is clearly defined. While Jacob's entourage derives from the Haran region, their contacts with the outside world after settling in Canaan are with Egypt. Joseph is sold to a caravan passing through the Valley of Dothan (on the southern route from the Jezreel Valley to the Sharon Plain as defined by Thutmose III). Jacob's sons make trips to Egypt and finally the patriarch himself migrates to the Land of Goshen in the eastern delta.

EGYPT OF THE EXODUS

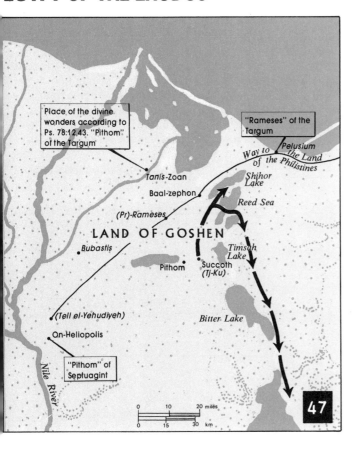

Place of the divine wonders according to Ps. 78:12,43. "Pithom" of the Targum

"Rameses" of the Targum

Way to the Land of the Philistines

Tanis-Zoan

Baal-zephon

Pelusium

Shihor Lake

Reed Sea

(Pr)-Rameses

LAND OF GOSHEN

Bubastis

Pithom

Succoth (Tj-Ku)

Timsah Lake

(Tell el-Yehudiyeh)

On-Heliopolis

Bitter Lake

"Pithom" of Septuagint

Nile River

0   10   20 miles
0   15   30   km

47

Jacob and his sons were allowed to settle in a choice portion of "the land of Rameses" (Gen. 47:11) called "the land of Goshen." The city of Rameses (Egyptian "the House of Rameses") was built on the former site of the Hyksos capital, Avaris. It served as the northern capital for the pharaohs of the nineteenth and twentieth dynasties. By the end of the twelfth century B.C. the branch of Nile beside Rameses had silted up, forcing the pharaohs of the twenty-first dynasty to build a new capital at Zoan (Tanis). They plundered the ruins of Rameses and brought many statues, stelae and other ornamented architectural pieces to their new city. The pharaohs of the twenty-second dynasty established a second delta capital at Bubastis and also brought in statues and other pieces from the ruins of Rameses. During the fourth century B.C., the worship of a deified Rameses was practiced at both Zoan and Bubastis, while the gateway city to Egypt had become Pelusium. This led late Jewish writers to identify Zoan with Rameses (Ps. 78:12, 43) or with Pithom (the Targum) and Pelusium with Rameses (Targum; Josephus). The translators of the Greek Septuagint equated Pithom with Heliopolis (biblical On) and the Goshen/Land of Rameses area as the Wadi Tumeilat.

Egyptian inscriptions point to Pithom (Egyptian Pr-Atum) as the site at the western end of an ancient overflow lake in the Wadi Tumeilat. Biblical Succoth is the name associated with watering pools farther west of Pithom, towards the modern Timsah lake. The land of Goshen was the plain between Rameses and Pithom. The Shihor was evidently an elongated lake or pond lying alongside the course of the ancient eastern branch of the Nile between Baal-zephon (Daphne) and Pelusium. The "Reed Sea" was the large marshy area that once existed to the southeast of Baal-zephon. Between these two bodies of water passed the "Way of Horus," the route taken by New Kingdom pharaohs (incarnates of Horus) on their military campaigns to Canaan and Syria. The Bible calls it "the way of the land of the Philistines (Exod. 13:17)."

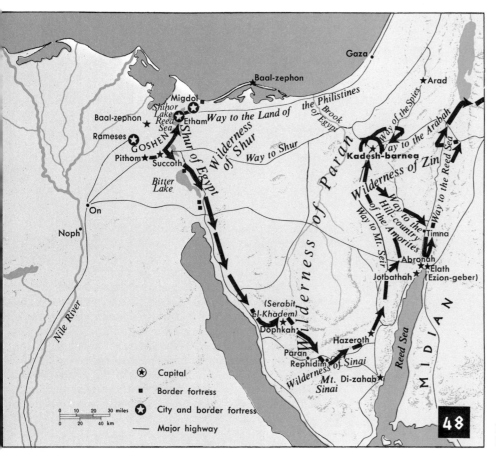

Gaza

Baal-zephon

Arad

Migdol

Shihor Lake

Baal-zephon

Reed Sea

Etham

Way to the Land of the Philistines

Brook of Egypt

Way of the Spies

Rameses

GOSHEN

Shur of Egypt

Wilderness of Shur

Way to Shur

Wilderness of Paran

Kadesh-barnea

Way to the Arabah

Way to the Reed Sea

Pithom

Succoth

Bitter Lake

Wilderness of Zin

On

Way to Mt. Seir

Way to the Hill-country of the Amorites

Timna

Noph

Abronah

Elath (Ezion-geber)

Jotbathah

(Serabit el-Khadem)

Dophkah

Hazeroth

Reed Sea

MIDIAN

Paran

Rephidim

Wilderness of Sinai

Mt. Sinai

Di-zahab

Sinai

⊛ Capital
■ Border fortress
◎ City and border fortress
— Major highway

0 10 20 30 miles
0   20   40 km

48

God did not lead them by way of the land of the Philistines, although that was near; for God said, "Lest the people repent when they see war, and return to Egypt."

(Exodus 13:17)

THE EXODUS AND WANDERING IN THE WILDERNESS

EX. 12:37-19:1;
NUM. 10:11-12; 33:1-36

The pharaonic campaigns to Canaan required logistic bases at intervals of about fifteen miles across the northern Sinai coastal route. Seti I included a depiction of the forts and water sources along this route in his reliefs on the north wall of the hypostyle hall at Karnak. This "Way of Horus," the "way of the land of the Philistines" (Ex. 13:7) was too heavily fortified to serve as an escape route for the people of Israel. Instead, they are depicted as beginning their trek from Succoth (Egyptian Tj-ku), a known pasturage area for the Shosu bedouin during the nineteenth dynasty, to Etham, on the fringe of the wilderness (of Shur). From there they turned back to a position in front (east) of Pi-hahiroth (possibly a site near Sile) "between Migdol

and Baal-zephon" (Ex. 14:2, 9). Their withdrawal in the face of the pursuing Egyptian was through the marshes east of Baal-zephon, the "sea of Reeds" (Egyptian P-Tjufy). Thence, they entered the wilderness of Shur (Ex. 15:22) and evidently headed south. Firm identifications for the remaining stations on their march are difficult since the ancient names have not survived in the Sinai peninsula. The present state of our knowledge favors a route commensurate with the Byzantine traditions for the location of Mt. Sinai at Jebel Musa. The location of Kadesh-barnea is well established and provides a focal point for the wanderings during the forty wilderness years.

Campaigns of Seti I (On the north wall of the great hall at Karnak)

So you remained in Kadesh many days ...
(Deuteronomy 1:46)

KADESH-BARNEA

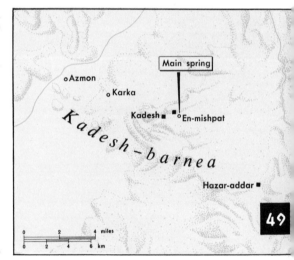

NUM. 20:13; DEUT. 1:19-46

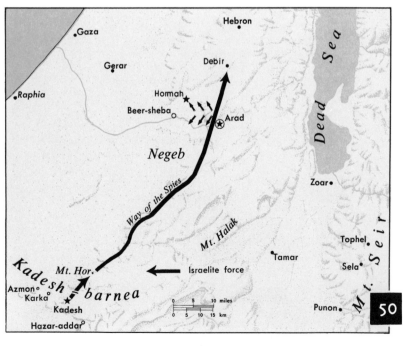

When the Canaanite, the king of Arad, who dwelt in the Negeb, heard that Israel was coming by the way of Atharim, he fought against Israel...

(Numbers 21:1)

ILL-FATED INVASION FROM THE SOUTH

The Israelites first attempted to penetrate from the south; th[e] effort failed because of stout resistance on the part of t[he] Amalekites in the Negeb and the Canaanites in the hill count[ry.] Their retreat from the hills is associated with Hormah, with [a] play on its name (Hebrew *herem* can mean "destruction" [or] "devoted," i.e. "sacred"). Two passages mention a Canaan[ite] king of Arad (Num. 21:1; 33:40) dwelling in the Negeb wh[ile] the two others ascribe the Negeb to the Amalekite and t[he] hill country to the Canaanite (Num. 14:44-45) or the Amor[ite] (Deut. 1:41-44). The defeat at Hormah was finally aveng[ed] when Judah and Simeon conquered it (Judges 1:17).

NUM. 14:44-45; 21:3; 33:40; DEUT. 1:41-44

So they went up and spied out the land from the wilderness of Zin to Rehob, near the entrance of Hamath.

(Numbers 13:21)

THE TRAVELS
OF THE SPIES
AND THE LIMITS
OF THE LAND
OF CANAAN

NUM. 13; 34:1-12; JOSH. 13:4; EZEK. 47:19

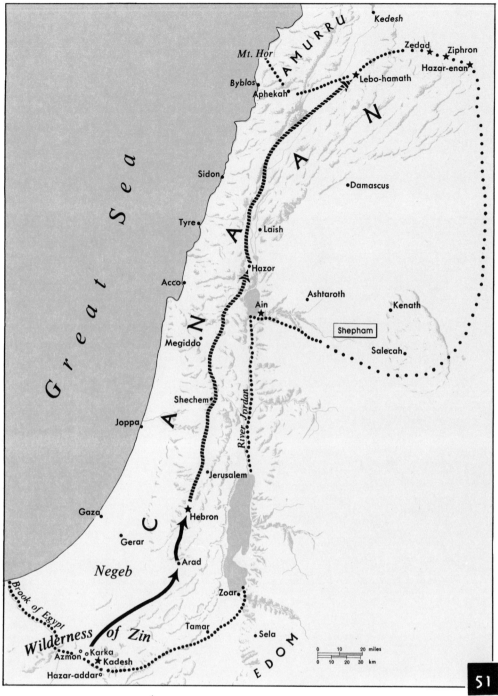

•••••••••• Border   ⬅— Spies' route

•••••• Conjectured border   ◀▐▐▐▐▐ Continuation of route to border of Land of Canaan

According to an early tradition, there was an unsuccessful attempt to invade the land of Canaan from Kadesh-barnea in the south. Although the final objective in the north was indicated as Lebo-hamath on the northern border of Canaan, the account of the twelve spies sent from Kadesh-barnea focuses on the Hebron area, precisely where Caleb, the leading spy, eventually settled with his clan. Amalek was in the Negeb, namely the valleys east and west of Beer-sheba; Kadesh-barnea was in the Wilderness of Zin. The borders of the geographical entity known as Canaan are defined in detail in Num. 34:1-12. The southern boundary, from the Dead Sea past Kadesh-barnea to the Brook of Egypt, coincides with that of the inheritance of Judah (Josh. 15:2-4). The northern boundary, also described by the prophet Ezekiel (Ezek. 47:15-18), reflects the extent of Egyptian control during the late thirteenth century B.C., probably in accordance with the peace agreement between Rameses II and the Hittites. The small kingdom of Amurru, founded during the fourteenth century B.C., was excluded. Transjordan south of the Yarmuk was never reckoned as part of Canaan (see also Josh. 22:9-10, 32).

Come to Heshbon, let it be built, let the city of Sihon
be established.

(Numbers 21:27)

THE PENETRATION INTO TRANSJORDAN

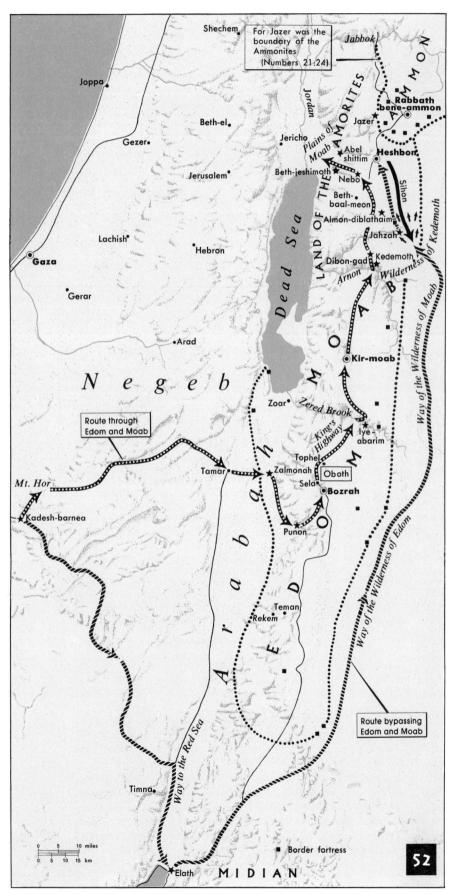

For Jazer was the boundary of the Ammonites (Numbers 21:24)

Route through Edom and Moab

Route bypassing Edom and Moab

Border fortress

The Israelite conquest began in eastern Transjordan, beyo[nd]
the borders of the Land of Canaan. In this sparsely settl[ed]
region, there were extensive lands for pasturage (Num. 32[:1-]
4). Peoples related to the Israelites had already settled [in]
the southern parts of Transjordan, soon forming organiz[ed]
kingdoms — Edom, Moab, and Ammon. The Amorite kingd[om]
of Heshbon was located between Moab and Ammon; its rul[er,]
Sihon, warred against Moab's first king and conquered t[he]
entire plateau of Moab to the Arnon River (Num. 21:2[6]).
Moses exploited this political situation by asking the Kings [of]
Moab and Edom to grant the Israelites passage through th[eir]
lands on the King's Highway, to reach the territory of Sih[on]
(Num. 20:14-21; Judg. 11:17); when refused this permissi[on]
Moses turned southward to Elath, avoiding Edom and Mo[ab]
and then penetrated Sihon's kingdom from the eastern des[ert]
(the wilderness of Kedemoth). Since that time, the Arnon h[as]
been considered the traditional border between the Israel[ite]
tribes and Moab, even though Moab never accepted the fa[ct]
and took every opportunity to regain control over "the plai[ns]"
north of the Arnon.

In contrast, the picture revealed by the list of desert statio[ns]
shows a direct route, passing through the heart of Edom a[nd]
Moab to "the plains of Moab" opposite Jericho (Num. 33:[37-]
49). Many scholars are of the opinion that this list reflects [a]
tradition of an older wave of immigration by several trib[es]
prior to the setting up of the Transjordanian kingdoms. T[he]
biblical traditions concerning the camp at Abel-shittim a[nd]
the fierce war against the Midianites are connected with t[his]
movement.

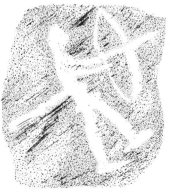

Archer (Graffito in Negeb)

NUM. 20:14-21:30; 33:37-49

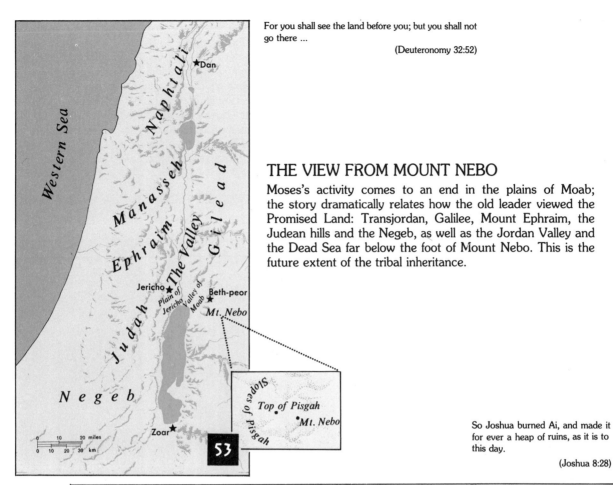

For you shall see the land before you; but you shall not go there ...

(Deuteronomy 32:52)

THE VIEW FROM MOUNT NEBO

Moses's activity comes to an end in the plains of Moab; the story dramatically relates how the old leader viewed the Promised Land: Transjordan, Galilee, Mount Ephraim, the Judean hills and the Negeb, as well as the Jordan Valley and the Dead Sea far below the foot of Mount Nebo. This is the future extent of the tribal inheritance.

So Joshua burned Ai, and made it for ever a heap of ruins, as it is to this day.

(Joshua 8:28)

THE NARRATIVE OF THE CONQUEST OF THE LAND OF CANAAN

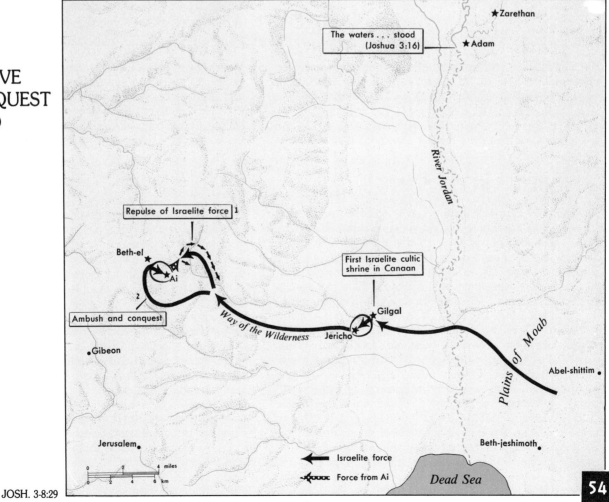

The waters . . . stood
(Joshua 3:16)

Repulse of Israelite force 1

First Israelite cultic shrine in Canaan

Ambush and conquest

→ Israelite force
⤛⚬⚬⚬⚬ Force from Ai

The conquest of the Land of Canaan begins with the crossing of the river Jordan; the first spot reached by the tribes was Gilgal, east of Jericho (Josh. 4:19). Gilgal was evidently the first place sanctified in the Land of Canaan, serving for a time as the center of the Israelite tribes; it was not by chance that Saul, the first Israelite king, was crowned there (1 Sam. 11:15).

Related to Gilgal are the stories of the conquests of Jericho and Ai. These stories contain many legendary shadings and historically they are enveloped in obscurity. The conquest of Jericho and Ai in this period has received no archaeological confirmation. At Ai this question is especially difficult, for the city seems to have been utterly destroyed a thousand years before the time of Joshua. Some scholars are of the opinion that, in the biblical narrative, Ai was substituted for nearby Beth-el; others assume that the source of the story of the conquest of Ai is a popular legend, surrounding the sanctuary at Gilgal, and was intended to explain the ruined cities dotting the landscape in this area. On the other hand, the conquest of Beth-el, described in Judges 1:22-26, has been substantiated by archaeological excavations.

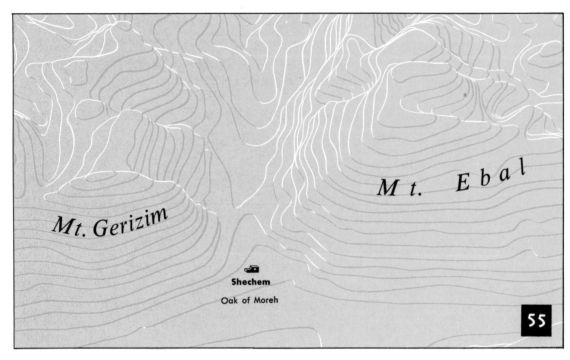

You shall set the blessing on Mount Gerizim and the curse on Mount Ebal.

(Deuteronomy 11:29)

THE REGION OF SHECHEM

Mt. Ebal

Mt. Gerizim

Shechem

Oak of Moreh

55

DEUT. 11:26-32; 27; JOSH. 8:30-35

The continuation of the story of the conquest relates the building of an altar at Mt. Ebal where there is a covenant renewal ceremony. The altar was so located that the two halves of the congregation could see it; half of them were opposite Gerizim and the other half opposite Ebal. This tradition seems to derive from the ancient sanctuary at the oaks of Moreh, near Shechem. This latter city had always been the leading urban center in the hill country of Ephraim. It is not listed among the conquered cities in Josh. 12. In fact, it would appear that Israelite penetration into this central hill region had been relatively peaceful. A modus vivendi with the Canaanites at Shechem seems to have been achieved.

CONQUESTS IN THE SOUTH

In reconstructing the Israelite occupation of the land, it must be remembered that only selected events are described in the Bible. There were probably many other conflicts between the Israelites and the indigenous population which have been lost or at best survive only as vague allusions in the record. Furthermore, there were some areas where the tribes managed to settle down without conquering the adjacent Canaanite cities. On the other hand, the Book of Joshua ascribes the entire process to a lightning campaign conducted by all the tribes together under the leadership of one man, Joshua son of Nun. Even the Transjordanian tribes are said to have crossed over to Cisjordan to help their brothers in the conquest. This tendency is most obvious with regard to the conquest of Hebron and Debir, which was first ascribed to Caleb and Kenaz (Josh. 15:13-19; Judg. 1:12-15), then to Judah (Judg. 1:10-11), and finally to Joshua and the entire people of Israel (Josh. 10:36-39). Joshua himself belonged to the clan of Beriah which lived in the hills of Beth-el between Naaran and Beth-horon (1 Chron 7:23-28). Joshua's principal activities were probably originally restricted to that central hill country, especially the victory at Gibeon. While the Book of Joshua presents this unified picture of the conquest, the victories gained by individual tribes, or local groups of tribes, is stressed in the Book of Judges. Activities in the central and southern regions are portrayed in the Book of Joshua under three stages:

1. *The battle of Gibeon.* Here the Israelites rallied around Joshua to come to the aid of the Gibeonites, a Hivite enclave living in four towns on the plateau northwest of Jerusalem. The king of Jerusalem called up his allies to punish the Gibeonites for making a covenant with Israel. He saw this as a threat to his control over the main approach route from the coastal plain to the hill country, via Beth-horon. The Canaanite forces were routed as they sought to retreat down the Beth-horon road. Their flight southward "as far as Azekah and as far as Makkedah" (Josh. 10:11) serves as a link with the subsequent campaign in the southern Shephelah.

2. *The invasion by the southern tribes.* Judah is credited with a victory over the Canaanite king Adoni-bezek at a place called Bezek. Although the identification is not certain, Map 57 portrays the campaign as if this Bezek is identical with

the Bezek of 1 Sam 11:8. The subsequent reference to the conquest of Jerusalem by Judah (Judg. 1:8) is probably an editorial retrospect concerning David's conquest of the city. While Judah and Simeon may have entered the Judean hill country from the north, the subsidiary tribes of the Calebites and the Kenazzites probably did penetrate from the south, conquering Hebron and Debir. The Kenites settled around Arad in the Negeb, having come via "the city of Palms," perhaps Tamar in the Arabah rather than Jericho (Judg. 1:16). The Simeonites originally managed to settle in five Shephelah and Negeb sites, Etam, En-rimmon, Tochen, Ether and Ashan (1 Chron. 4:31-32) and shared with Judah in the conquest of Hormah (Judg. 1:17).

3. *The conquest of the southern Shephelah.* This was probably the latest stage in the occupation of the greater Judean territory. It is noteworthy that of the three known districts in the Shephelah, the northern one, from the Valley of Sorek to the Vale of Elah (Josh. 15:33-36), was evidently occupied peacefully, without any serious conflicts (cf. Gen. 38). The conquest of the cities in the central and southern districts seems to follow a circuit based on the connection with the previous narrative (the Canaanite retreat after the battle of Gibeon) and the ensuing narrative (the conquest of Hebron and Debir in the hill country). Thus, the sequence starts with Makkedah and the capture of the fugitive Canaanite kings and leads to the ascent to Hebron and Debir. Map 57 follows the tradition of Josh. 15:13-19 (cf. Judg. 1:10-15); Map 58 follows the tradition of Josh. 10:36-39.

A metal object bearing the cartouche of pharaoh Rameses III found near the gate at Lachish indicates that that Canaanite city was under Egyptian control until at least the mid-twelfth century B.C. The votive bowl with a hieratic inscription found there previously must refer to the reign of Rameses III. Therefore, the Israelite conquest of that area could have taken place in the latter half of the twelfth century B.C.

THE BATTLE OF GIBEON

Sun, stand thou still at Gibeon, and thou Moon in the valley of Aijalon.

(Joshua 10:12)

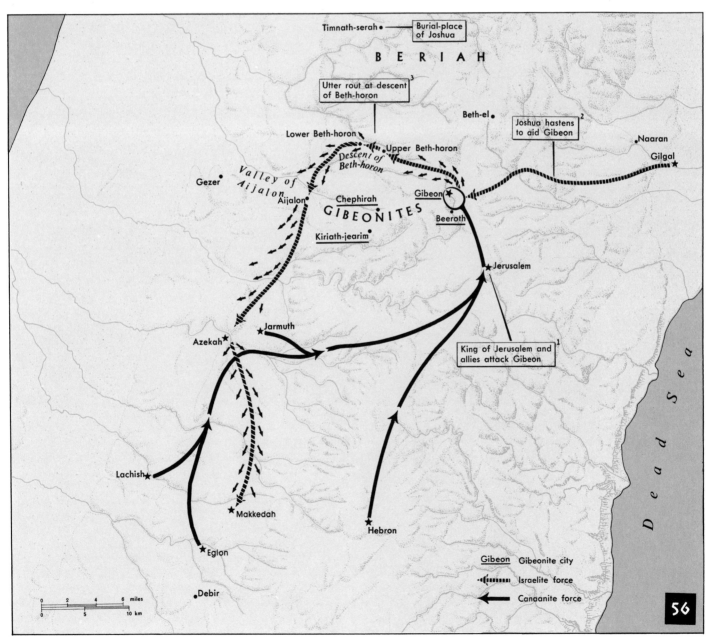

JOSH. 10:1-15

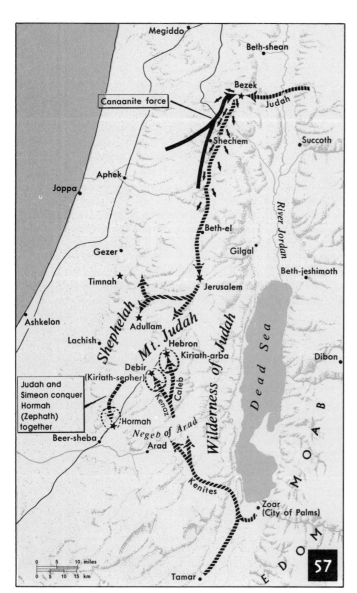

Then Judah went up and the Lord gave the Canaanites and the Perizzites into their hand; and they defeated ... them at Bezek.

(Judges 1:4)

THE RISE OF JUDAH AND THE SOUTHERN TRIBES

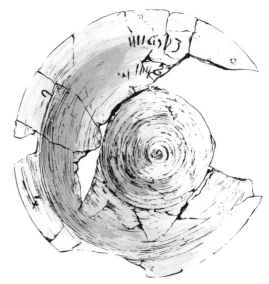

List of taxes in Egyptian hieratic script from Lachish (End of Canaanite period)

JOSH. 10:36-39; JOSH. 15:13-19; JUDG. 1:1-20; GEN. 38; 1 CHRON. 2; 4

So Joshua defeated the whole land, the hill country and the Negeb and the lowland and the slopes...

(Joshua 10:40)

CONQUEST OF SOUTHERN SHEPHELAH DISTRICTS (AND CENTRAL HILL COUNTRY)

LATTER HALF OF 12TH CENTURY B.C.

JOSH. 10:28-35

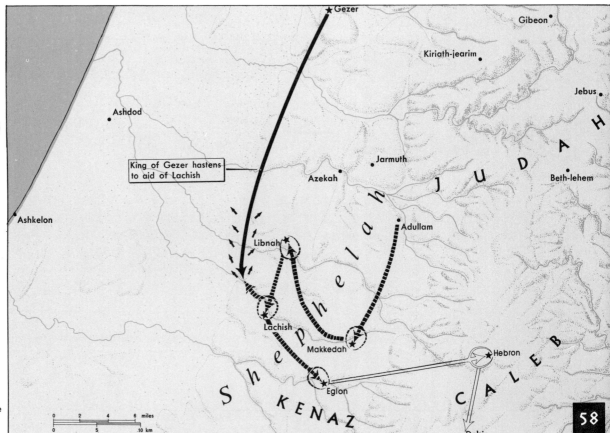

◀┤▥▥▥▥ Israelite force

◀━━━ Canaanite force

⇐━━━ Route to Hebron and Debir

Then fought the king of Canaan; at Taanach by the
waters of Megiddo they got no spoils of silver.
(Judg. 5:19)

THE WAR OF DEBORAH — THE DEPLOYMENT OF FORCES
12TH CENTURY B.C.

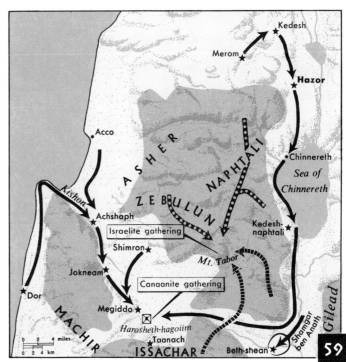

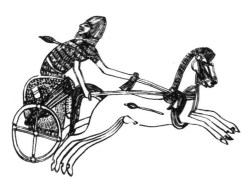

Canaanite charioteer wounded by arrow
(Decoration on chariot of Thutmose IV)

So Barak went down from Mount Tabor...
(Judges 4:14)

Israelite force
Canaanite force
Israelite volunteers
Canaanite chariot camp
Area of continuous Israelite settlement

JOSH. 12:19-23: JUDG. 4-5

THE WAR OF DEBORAH — THE BATTLE

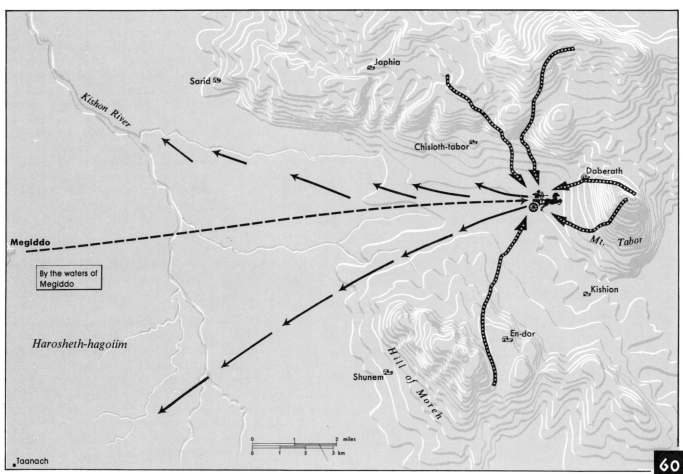

By the waters of
Megiddo

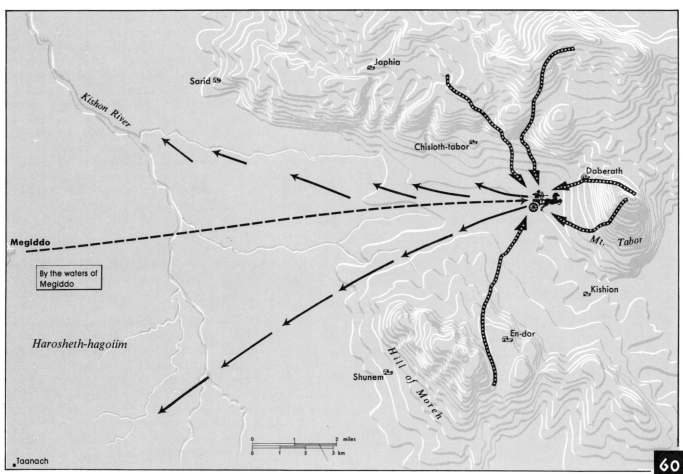

JOSH. 12:19-23; JUDG. 4-5

THE DEATH OF SISERA

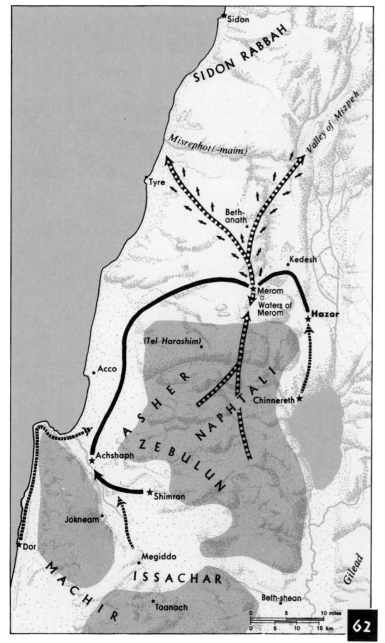

But none of the cities that stood on mounds did Israel
burn, except Hazor only that Joshua burned.

(Joshua 11:13)

THE BATTLE OF THE WATERS OF MEROM

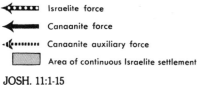

◀▭▭▭▭ Israelite force

◀━━━ Canaanite force

◀▭┉┉┉┉ Canaanite auxiliary force

▭ Area of continuous Israelite settlement

JOSH. 11:1-15

JUDG. 4:17-22; 5:24-30

The Bible records two major conflicts between the Israelite
tribes and the Canaanites of the cities in Galilee: the battle of
the waters of Merom (Josh. 11:1-15) and the battle of Deborah
(Judg. 4 & 5). In both accounts, the leader of the Canaanite
league is Jabin, king of Hazor. Thus, they are both related
to the same chronological period. Deborah's victory is said to
have brought about the decline of Jabin (Judg. 4:24) while
the battle of the waters of Merom culminates in the utter
destruction of Hazor (Josh. 11:10-11). Using that as a criterion,
scholars have suggested that Deborah's victory preceded that
of the Merom battle; it would follow that the order of the
two events became reversed when the Merom victory was
assigned to Joshua by the later author of the book of Joshua.
Others hold that the reference to Jabin in the narrative of
Deborah's victory is a later addition and that the original leader
of the Canaanite coalition in Judg. 4 & 5 was Sisera. However,
Sisera is never called a king, nor does he have a specific
city of his own. There is no city by the name of Harosheth-
hagoiim in any extra-biblical sources and attempts to find
its name in the Arabic toponymy of the Jezreel Valley have
been futile. In fact, Harosheth-hagoiim is apparently identical
with Galil-hagoiim (Isa. 9:1 [Heb. 8:23]) and is to be derived
from the root meaning "to plow." Harosheth means "cultivated
land" and refers to the rich farm area on the southern side
of the Jezreel Valley; since the time of Thutmose III it had
been known as royal domain, cultivated for the benefit of
an overlord. It was Sisera's job to protect the interests of
his master, the king of Hazor, in this highly profitable center
for agriculture. Harosheth-hagoiim of the prose account (Judg.
4:2, 13, 16) is synonymous with "at Taanach by the waters of
Megiddo" of the poetic version (Judg. 5:19).

The battle of Deborah is one of the few such narratives
which can be reconstructed geographically in considerable
detail; the prose and poetic versions complement one another.
The conflict is said to have been preceded by the deeds of
Shamgar the son of Anath who, inspired by Jael, the wife of
Heber the Kenite, smote the Philistines (Judg. 3:31). Perhaps
this echoes a clash with the Philistine garrison at Beth-shean
(1 Sam. 31:10, 12). The situation had reached an impasse
in which security along the roads was severely threatened
(compare the danger of traveling through the 'Aruna Pass for
fear of the wild tribesmen as depicted in Papyrus Anastasi I).
The tensions between the Israelite tribes living in the hills and
the Canaanite city states, who controlled most of the good
farm land and water sources, erupted into open conflict; the
tribesmen were assembled by Barak and brought to Mt. Tabor
by night. This holy mountain marked the juncture of the tribal

territories of Zebulun, Naphtali and Issachar (Deut. 33:18-19). The largest contingent came from Zebulun and Naphtali with volunteers from Issachar and the three tribes in Mt. Ephraim. Issachar was evidently living mainly along the southern edge of the Jezreel Valley in subservience to the Canaanites who imposed corvée labor on them (Gen. 49:14-15). They had not yet been settled on the plateau east of the Hill of Moreh. Machir was still dwelling in the northern part of Mt. Ephraim, just south of the Jezreel Valley; later Machir moved to Transjordan where it came to be reckoned as a branch of the Manasseh tribe (see Map 65). Kedesh in Naphtali, the birthplace of Barak, the son of Abinoam, is not the Canaanite Kedesh in Upper Galilee (Josh. 20:7; 21:32; 1 Chron. 6:61) but rather Khirbet Kedish, an extensive Israelite site overlooking the Sea of Chinnereth, only a few hours' walk from Mt. Tabor.

The names of the individual Canaanite kings involved are not enumerated in Judges but they may have been preserved in the list of conquered Canaanite cities in Josh. 12. Sisera gathered the Canaanite chariotry at Harosheth-hagoiim, and after crossing the upper reaches of the Kishon stream, proceeded towards Mt. Tabor. The Canaanites were confident that with the mobility of their chariots they could intimidate the foot troops from the Israelite tribes and soon have them scattered before a rain of arrows. On the day chosen for the confrontation, it began to rain and the chariots bogged down in the mud of the valley floor. This gave the advantage to the Israelite warriors who charged down the mountainside on foot, gaining momentum and courage as they ran. The Kishon, becoming swollen by the rains, hindered the escape of the Canaanite warriors who had abandoned their chariots and were fleeing on foot. They had gone to the battle expecting to receive great rewards upon their victorious return to "Taanach by the waters of Megiddo" but they got no "spoil of silver" there; instead, they were swept away by the torrent of the Kishon.

Sisera had also abandoned his chariot, but instead of fleeing towards his own headquarters in Harosheth-hagoiim (probably Megiddo itself though that town is never mentioned in the narrative), he struck for the Jordan Valley via the hills of Lower Galilee. Thus, he came to the settlement of Heber the Kenite. Heber's family were descendants of Hobab, the father-in-law of Moses, and ancestor of the Kenites who had settled in the wilderness of Arad (Judg. 1:16). The encampment located at Allon (Oak of) Zaanannim, on the southern border of Naphtali's territory (Josh. 19:33), was probably a cult center (compare Allon [= Oak of] Moreh, near Shechem Gen. 12:6). Jael, the wife of Heber, was probably a renowned prophetess, familiar to both Canaanites and Israelites. Sisera was evidently seeking refuge in her sanctuary. Instead, he met his death at her hands.

Only four Canaanite cities are mentioned in the narrative about the conflict at the waters of Merom. The Madon and Shimron of the Hebrew version are ghost words; the Greek Septuagint translation, based on a superior Hebrew text, proves that the originals were Maron (= Merom) and Simeon (known as Shim'on in the Egyptian sources; and compare 2 Chron. 16:9; 34:6). The Canaanites had gathered at the waters of Meron/Merom (the name is preserved in Marun er-Ras), a central point in Upper Galilee. The non-biblical references (Egyptian and Assyrian) to Meron/Merom also suggest a location in this area. The line of the Canaanite retreat, "as far as Great Sidon and Misrephoth-maim and east as far as the valley of Mizpeh" (Josh. 10:8) confirms that the battle took place in Upper Galilee. The original clans involved were probably those of Naphtali and perhaps of Asher, whose initial of settlements were in the high mountainous area of southern

Upper Galilee as demonstrated by archaeological surveys.

The leadership in this campaign is ascribed by the Book of Joshua to Joshua himself, who is also credited with the destruction of Canaanite Hazor. Archaeological excavations have revealed the wholesale destruction of the Canaanite city, but the exact date of this event cannot be determined by material remains alone. Nor is there any archaeological proof for the identity of the attackers.

And these are the kings of the land whom Joshua and the people of Israel defeated on the west side of the Jordan ...

(Joshua 12:7)

THE LIST OF KINGS OF CANAAN
12TH CENTURY B.C.

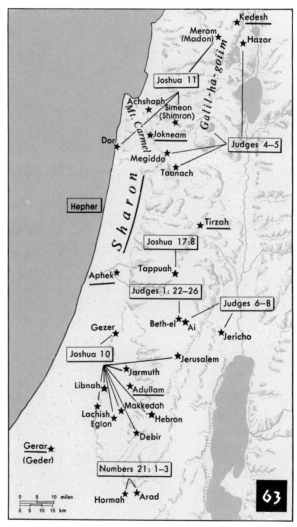

JOSH. 12:7-24

Kedesh — City or district not mentioned in account of conquest

The list of vanquished Canaanite kings is a summary of the stories of the conquest contained in the Books of Joshua and Judges. Its major importance lies in recording city names not mentioned in the actual accounts, and thus fills in some gaps in the picture of the wars of the conquest. Besides the kings of the north, the list contains several cities in Mount Ephraim and in the Sharon, Adullam in the Shephelah, and "the king of Goiim in Gilgal," or according to the Septuagint, "the king of Goiim in Galilee," that is, probably, Galil-hagoiim.

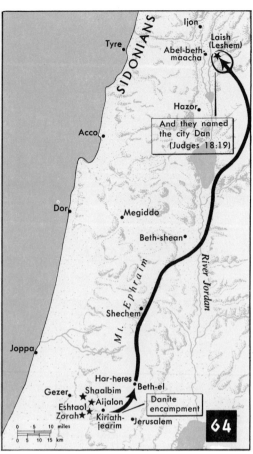

And six hundred men of the tribe of Dan, armed with weapons of war, set forth from Zorah and Eshtaol ...

(Judges 18:11)

THE MIGRATION OF THE TRIBE OF DAN
12TH CENTURY B.C.

Some of the tribes are said to have failed in taking their prospective inheritances or parts thereof. The most striking example is the migration of the tribe of Dan from the northern Shephelah (Judg. 1:34-35) to the Canaanite city of Laish at the foot of Mt. Hermon. Laish was occupied by Sidonians (the biblical term for Phoenicians) whose function was doubtless cultivation of the agricultural hinterland for the Phoenician cities whose local manpower was employed in maritime activities. When the Danites seized their city and its territory, they evidently took over the function of providing produce for the Sidonian markets; some of their young men seem to have become enamored with the seafaring way of life as well. Thus, the Danites were reluctant to join any action against the other Canaanite city states, "Dan, why did he abide in ships?" (Judg. 5:17)

To Machir the first-born of Manasseh, the father of Gilead, were allotted Gilead and Bashan, because he was a man of war.

(Joshua 17:1)

JUDG. 17-18; JOSH. 19:47

MACHIR THE SON OF MANASSEH
12TH CENTURY B.C.

NUM. 32:39-40
JOSH. 17:1-6; CHRON. 7:14-19

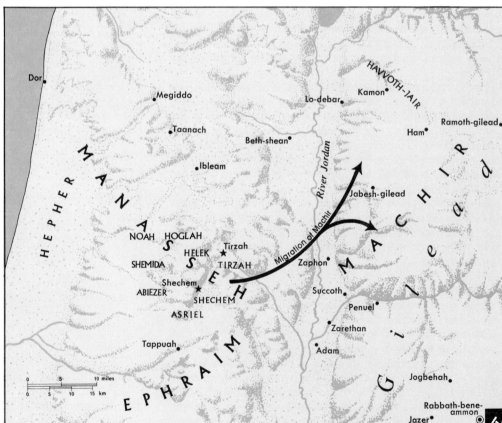

(See genealogical table on page 104)

Other movements of tribes and clans from one region to another are hinted at in passing, identical clan and place names occurring in different tribal contexts. Thus, the migration of Machir to northern Gilead is clearly reflected in the genealogical list of Manasseh. In the days of Deborah, Machir still dwelt in northern Mount Ephraim (Judg. 5:14), later becoming the "father" of Gilead, that is, the inhabitant of Gilead, while Manasseh inherited his place west of the Jordan. This explains the strange phenomenon that clans settled in northern Mount Ephraim, and still found there in the period of the Israelite Monarchy (see map 137), were included in the genealogical list as sons of Transjordanian Machir and Gilead.

d I not bring up Israel from the land of Egypt, and
e Philistines from Caphtor and the Syrians from Kir?

(Amos 9:7)

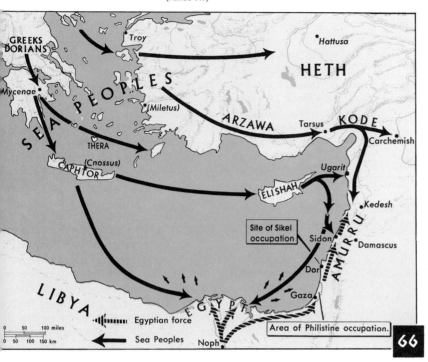

THE MIGRATION OF THE SEA PEOPLES
1174 B.C.

Peoples from the Aegean region, Greeks and other Indo-Europeans, had been in contact by maritime trade with Egypt and the Levant from at least the Middle Bronze Age. Ships from Keftiu (=Caphtor) had brought goods to Egypt during the eighteenth dynasty and during the Amarna period; Lukku (Lycians) had threatened the kingdom of Alashia (on Cyprus). Sherdanu mercenaries (from the Sardis region) had served in Egyptian garrisons in Canaan and fought under Rameses II at the battle of Kedesh, while Lukku, Dardanians and other western Asiatics of similar origin fought for the Hittites. Pharaoh Merneptah repelled an invasion of Libyans supported by several Aegean peoples, including the Akawasha (Achaeans?), the Shekelesh and the Tursha (Tyrsenoi, ancestors of the Etruscans?).

The great explosion of "sea peoples" came in the eighth year of Rameses III, 1174 B.C. Driven by famine and hunger, they erupted from their homelands in the northwest. Coming by land and by sea they destroyed the great centers like Hattusas, Kode, Arzawa, Alashia, Carchemish, and Ugarit. They set up a camp in the land of Amurru, on the border of Canaan. Rameses III was able to repulse their attempted invasion of Egypt; his victory is commemorated in text and reliefs in his mortuary temple. The five ethnic groups mentioned were the Philistines, the Sikels, the Shekelesh, the Dananu and the Washashu. Papyrus Harris I claims that the captives from this battle were settled in Egyptian garrisons. As for the coast of "Philistia," excavations at several major sites, such as Ashdod and Ekron, show that the Canaanite cities were destroyed by fire and the subsequent occupation was characterized by an Aegean style of pottery. The Philistines and others had apparently captured those coastal centers; Rameses III must have acquiesced in their occupation of southern Canaan. He and his successors, at least down to Rameses VI (1141-1134 B.C.), continued to exercise some form of control over Canaan in spite of the sea peoples' presence.

Under the first ruler of the twenty-first dynasty, Smendes at Tanis (1070-1044 B.C.), an official named Wenamon was reputedly sent to Lebanon to buy lumber for repairing the sacred bark of Amon in Thebes. The account of his adventures reveals that another of the "sea peoples," the Sikels, was settled at Dor. They have a city-state regime, operate a fleet of ships, and enjoy maritime relations with Tyre, Byblos and Alashia. Wenamon is received as a commercial customer but not as the representative of an overlord. Obviously, the Egyptian hegemony in Canaan has passed into history.

HE TRAVELS OF WEN-AMON EARLY 11TH CENTURY B.C.

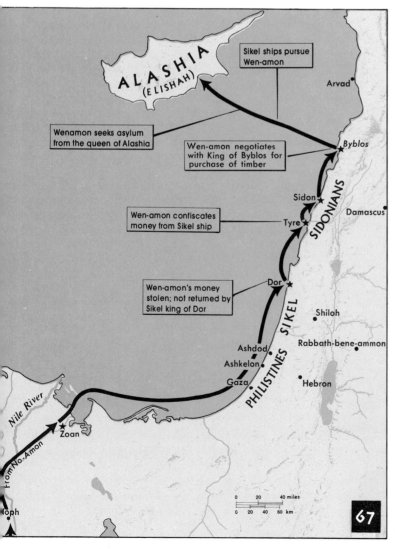

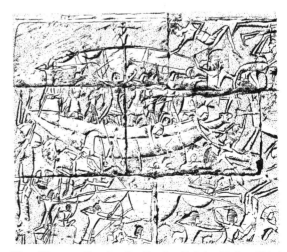

War of Rameses III against Sea Peoples (Relief at Medinet Habu)

JOURNEY OF WEN-AMON; PAPYRUS — EL-HIBA, EGYPT

And he took possession of the hill country, but he could not drive out the inhabitants of the plain, because they had chariots of iron.

(Judges 1:19)

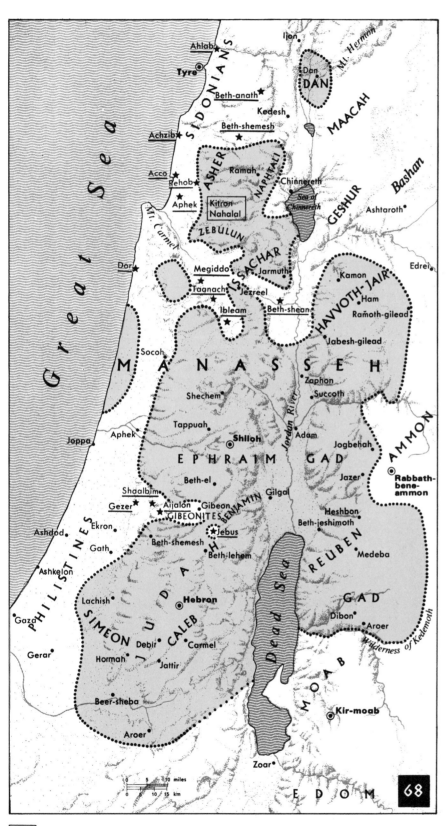

Area of Israelite control

Gezer Canaanite city not conquered (according to Judg. 1)

JOSH. 15:63; 16:10; 17: 11-18; JUDG. 1:21-35

THE LIMITS OF ISRAELITE CONTROL
12TH-11TH CENTURIES B.C.

By the twelfth century B.C. the principal rival peoples [of] Palestine were becoming well established in their respecti[ve] areas: the Canaanites continued to dwell in the northe[rn] valleys and plains, the Philistines (with other "sea peoples") in the southern coastal plain, and the tribes of Israel in t[he] hill country. The biblical tradition confirms that Israelites we[re] unable to dislodge the Canaanites and Amorites in the lowla[nd] areas, for they had "chariots of iron" (Josh. 17:18). A list [of] the areas where the non-Israelites continued to dwell is giv[en] in Judg. ch. 1 and similar allusions appear here and the[re] in the book of Joshua (Josh. 15:63; 17:11-13). Judg. 1:1[8-] 19 (LXX) confirms that Judah did not subdue the Philistine[s.] Judg. 1:27-35 lists the unconquered areas according to trib[e.] The main surviving Canaanite enclaves were in the Valley [of] Jezreel, and along the Phoenician coast. The Asherites gain[ed] acceptance among the Phoenicians (Sidonians), apparent[ly] as client farmers for a society whose manpower was heav[ily] committed to maritime activities (Judg. 1:31-32). No traditi[on] exists about the conquest of Shechem, whose situation ma[y] have been like Gezer (Judg. 1:19), a Canaanite populati[on] living in symbiosis with the Israelites. Jebus-Jerusalem, Gez[er] and the Amorite towns that resisted the Danites were [in] the center of the country. Very early traditions reveal th[at] the Ephraimites came into early contact with the indigeno[us] population of the area where the Danites were driven out [(1] Chron. 7:20-24; Judg. 1:35). Some clans from Benjamin al[so] migrated to the same area (1 Chron. 8:12-13; 2 Sam. 4:3-4).

Recent archaeological surveys in the hill country areas co[n-] firm the arrival of pastoralists who began their settlement alo[ng] the fringes of the steppe land, east of the watershed. Gradual[ly] they expanded and established settlements in the areas [of] mixed agriculture and eventually moved into the western h[ill] zones where it became necessary to develop terraces a[nd] plant orchards and vineyards. Thus, originally pastoral group[s] became transformed into a thoroughly sedentary society wi[th] varied subsistence strategies. The tribal groups that settled [in] Upper Galilee went through a similar process; their materi[al] culture reflects a certain cultural symbiosis with the Phoenicia[ns] on the coast below.

All of this data confirms the new population revolutio[n] brought about in the twelfth and eleventh centuries. In t[he] Late Bronze Age the main concentrations of population we[re] in the plains (see Maps 30 and 34); the hill country areas we[re] largely uninhabited, providing refuge for 'apiru outlaws a[nd] for the Shosu pastoralists. The latter became more and mo[re] numerous and adopted sedentary ways of life, perhaps becau[se] of a decline in the overall Canaanite agricultural productivity.

The dichotomy between Canaanites on the plains and I[s-] raelites in the hills characterizes the narratives throughout t[he] books of Judges and Samuel.

Beth-anath (Relief of Rameses II at Thebes)

This is the land that yet remains ...
(Joshua 13:2)

THE LAND THAT YET REMAINS

Ṣumur

AMURRU

Mt. Hor

Zedad Ziphron

Byblos★ Lebo-hamath Hazar-enan

Aphekah

Valley of Lebanon

Sidon

Baal-gad Damascus ◉

Misrephoth Mt. Hermon

Tyre ◉ (-maim) Dan

Beth-anath Kedesh

Achzib Beth-shemesh

Acco GESHUR Ashtaroth

Aphek Ain Kenath

Dor

Megiddo Beth-shean

Ibleam Ramoth-gilead Salecah

Shechem

Joppa River Jordan AMMON

Shiloh ◉

Gezer Rabbath-bene-ammon ◉

Jebus

Ashdod ★ ★Ekron

Ashkelon ★ ★Gath Dibon

Gaza ★ Hebron ◉

PHILISTINES MOAB

AVVITES Kir-moab ◉

Beer-sheba

Brook of Egypt

Mt. Halak Tamar

Kadesh-barnea Bozrah ●

EDOM

Great Sea

0   10   20 miles
0   10   20   30 km

JOSH. 13:1-6; JUDG. 3:1-3

69

☐ "The land that yet remains"

<u>Aphek</u> Canaanite city not conquered (according to Judg. 1)

•••••• Border of Land of Canaan

Besides the Canaanite enclaves that were later incorporated into Israel, we also find in the Bible the term "the land that remains" (Josh. 13:1-6; Judg. 3:1-3). This term included Philistia in the south, and the Phoenician-Sidonian coast up to Byblos, the Lebanon to Aphek on the Amorite border, and the Valley of Lebanon from Baal-gad beneath Mount Hermon to Lebo-

hamath, in the north. It included parts of the land of Canaan (compare Ex. 34:1-12; map 50), into which the Israelite tribes had never penetrated. These regions were beyond the area of Israelite settlement even in later periods, though in the expansionist periods of the kingdom of Israel some of them came under Israelite rule. The "boundary of the Amorites" in this connection was the border of the Amorite-Amurru kingdom in the Lebanon, well-known to us from Egyptian New Kingdom sources.

The Israelite areas of settlement were thus limited in the main to the hill. The hostility of the Philistines and the older indigenous population spurred on large-scale Israelite settlement activity, including the gradual deforestation of previously unused areas and the founding of settlements and long-term agricultural projects (orchards and vineyards). Traces of this activity in the hill region have been discovered in archaeological surveys in Transjordan, Judah, Mount Ephraim, and Galilee. This trend brought about the most important changes in the settlement pattern of Palestine in any historical period. Uninhabited areas were for the first time populated, the number of inhabitants doubled and new centers were established in the interior. The Israelite settlement radically changed the face of the map, and continuity of settlement, one of the prerequisites for the internal unification of the Holy Land into a single kingdom, was first achieved during the Israelite Monarchy.

Siege of city in Land of Amurru (Relief of Rameses III at Medinet Habu)

THE TWELVE TRIBES

The description of the tribal territories in Josh. 13-19 comprised some detailed border descriptions and lists of towns for the respective tribes. The town lists are assumed by most scholars to date to a period of centralized administration during the monarchy. This is especially relevant for the extensive lists of Judah which are organized into regions and districts (see Map 130). The border descriptions are only partial. Map 71 shows that detailed descriptions are given for only a few of the tribes. Those accounts that do exist consist of recognizable boundary points given in geographical order. The course of the border can be traced by means of the descriptive verbs used in the delineations. Comparison of parallel passages giving the same border, such as the mutual boundaries of Benjamin with Judah and Ephraim, show that the original text must have been much more detailed than the abridged versions preserved in the book of Joshua. One finds careful recording of small details only in crucial areas, such as the boundary passing around Jerusalem. The zones where definite borders are not given correspond roughly to those areas where the Israelites had not actually penetrated during the initial stages of the settlement process (as depicted in Judg. 1).

The tribes of Issachar, Dan, Simeon and the Transjordanian tribes have only town lists coupled with some general topographical designations. The Judean border is not really that of the tribe; the northern segment corresponds to that of Benjamin while the southern is evidently the political border of the Judean monarchy (also applied to the description of Canaan,

see Map 50). The northwestern extension of the border of Judah (beyond Beth-shemesh) was actually the border between Philistia and the kingdom of Israel. The Asherite border is also related to the national Israelite boundary during the monarchy (compare 2 Sam. 24:5-7; Map 106).

The only tribes with border descriptions are Benjamin, Manasseh, Ephraim, Zebulun, Asher and Naphtali, the same tribes mentioned as those who failed to conquer the Canaanite enclaves (Judg. 1:22-38). There is also an intriguing correlation with the Solomonic districts described in 1 Kings 4. For the districts defined by tribal names in the Solomonic list, we have borders in Josh. 13-19; for those Solomonic districts defined by town lists (corresponding to the lists of unconquered towns in Judg. 1) there is a lack of border descriptions in Joshua. The most prominent cult center for the northern tribes seems to have been Shiloh. During the period of the judges, the bond between these northern tribes and those of the south was rather tenuous. Judah, Simeon and the neighboring groups (Calebites, Kennizites, Kenites, Jerachmeelites) did not take part in any common war venture (such as the battles of Deborah and Gideon). It is possible that at least the non-Judean tribes in the south looked to Hebron as an important cult center. However, it is not at all certain that there were any official "leagues" of tribes, either in the north or in the south, prior to the years of conflict between David and Eshbaal (Eshbosheth).

And Joshua charged those who went to write the description of the land, saying, "Go up and down and write a description of the land, and come again to me; and I will cast lots for you here before the Lord in Shiloh."

(Joshua 18:8)

THE BORDER OF THE TRIBAL TERRITORIES
12TH-11TH CENTURIES B.C.

Mesopotamian border marker
(ca. twelfth century B.C.)

...these are the inheritances which the people of [Isra]el received in the land of Canaan ...

(Joshua 14:1)

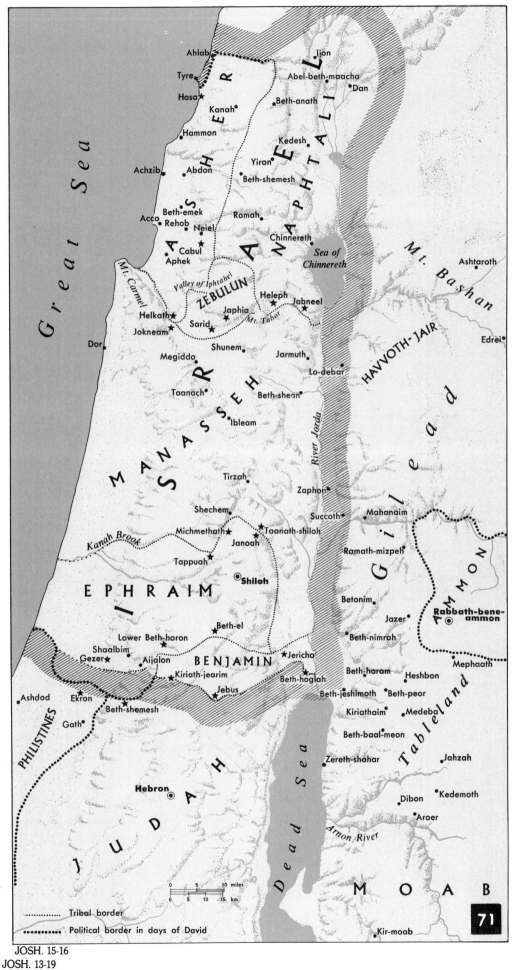

Tribal border

Political border in days of David

JOSH. 15-16
JOSH. 13-19

70

71

Then on the north the boundary turns about to Hannathon, and it ends at the valley of Iphtahel;..

(Joshua 19:14)

THE BORDERS OF THE TRIBES IN GALILEE

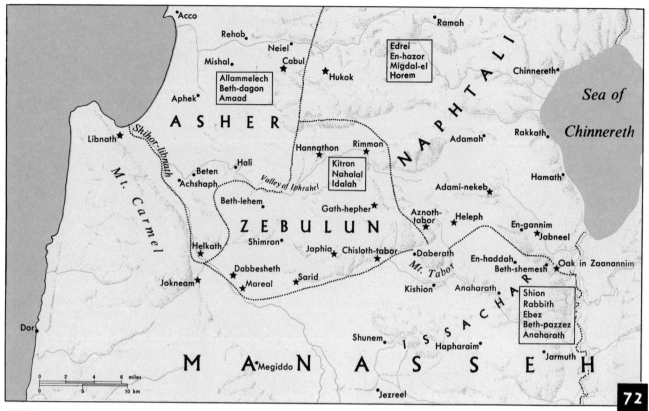

JOSH. 19:10-39

Then the boundary goes up by the valley of the son
of Hinnom at the southern shoulder of the Jebusite
(that is, Jerusalem); and the boundary goes up to the
top of the mountain that lies over against the valley
of Hinnom, on the west, at the northern end of the
valley of Rephaim ...

(Joshua 15:8)

THE BORDERS OF THE TRIBE OF BENJAMIN AND ITS NEIGHBORS

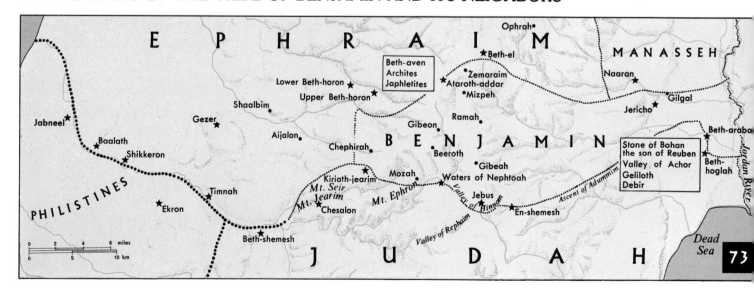

JOSH. 15-18

And the people of Israel served Eglon
the king of Moab eighteen years.
(Judges 3:14)

THE WAR OF EHUD
2TH TO 11TH
CENTURIES B.C.

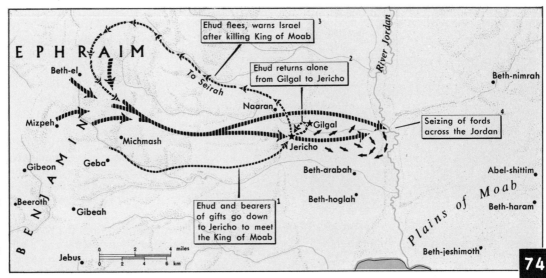

JUDG. 3:12-30

Ehud flees, warns Israel
after killing King of Moab

Ehud returns alone
from Gilgal to Jericho

Seizing of fords
across the Jordan

Ehud and bearers
of gifts go down
to Jericho to meet
the King of Moab

EPHRAIM

Beth-el

To Seirah

Naaran

Mizpeh

Michmash

Gilgal

Jericho

Beth-nimrah

River Jordan

Beth-arabah

Gibeon   Geba

Abel-shittim

Beeroth   Gibeah

Beth-hoglah

Plains of Moab

Beth-haram

Jebus

Beth-jeshimoth

74

0   2   4 miles
0   2   4   6 km

◄▐▐▐▐▐▐ Israelite force
◄— ◄— ◄— Moabites

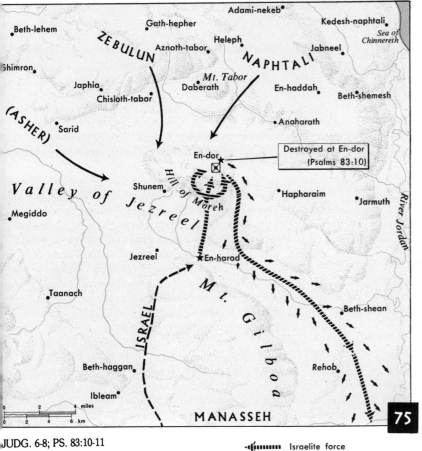

Adami-nekeb

Beth-lehem   Gath-hepher   Kedesh-naphtali

ZEBULUN   Heleph   Jabneel   Sea of Chinnereth

Shimron   Aznoth-tabor   NAPHTALI

Japhia   Mt. Tabor   En-haddah
Chisloth-tabor   Daberath   Beth-shemesh

(ASHER)   Anaharath

Sarid   En-dor   Destroyed at En-dor
(Psalms 83:10)

Valley of   Shunem   Hapharaim
Jezreel   Hill of Moreh   Jarmuth

Megiddo   River Jordan

Jezreel   En-harod

Taanach   Mt. Gilboa   Beth-shean

ISRAEL

Beth-haggan   Rehob

Ibleam   MANASSEH   **75**

0   2   4 miles
0   2   4   6 km

JUDG. 6-8; PS. 83:10-11

◄▐▐▐▐▐▐ Israelite force
☒ Midianite camp
◄— — Gathering of Israelite warriors
◄— ◄— ◄— Flight of Midianites

The Lord is with you, you mighty man of valor.
(Judges 6:12)

THE PURSUIT AFTER THE MIDIANITES
12TH TO 11TH CENTURIES B.C.

For whenever the Israelites put in seed the Midianites
and the Amalekites and the people of the East would
come up ...
(Judges 6:3)

THE WAR OF GIDEON
12TH TO 11TH CENTURIES B.C.

Arabian warriors mounted on camels
(Relief from palace of Asshurbanipal at
Nineveh)

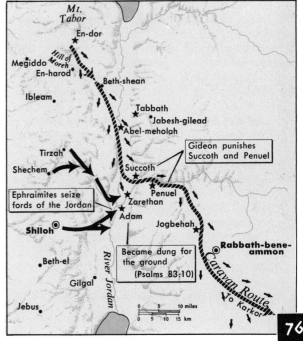

Mt. Tabor

En-dor

Megiddo   Hill of Moreh

En-harod   Beth-shean

Ibleam

Tabbath
Jabesh-gilead

Abel-meholah

Tirzah   Gideon punishes
Succoth and Penuel

Shechem   Succoth

Ephraimites seize   Penuel
fords of the Jordan   Zarethan

Adam   Jogbehah

Shiloh   Rabbath-bene-
ammon

Became dung for
the ground
(Psalms 83:10)   Caravan Route
To Karkor

Beth-el

River Jordan

Gilgal

Jebus

0   5   10 miles
0   5   10   15 km

JUDG. 7-8   **76**

Let fire come out from Abimelech, and devour the
citizens of Shechem, and Beth-millo ...

(Judges 9:20)

THE KINGDOM OF ABIMELECH
12TH TO 11TH CENTURIES B.C.

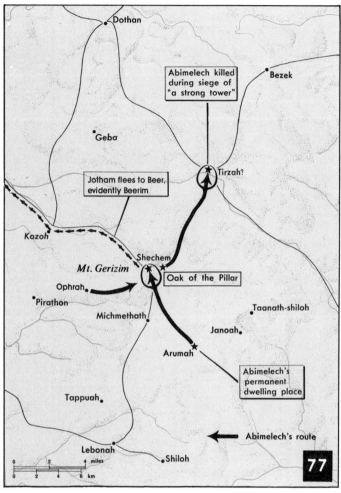

Dothan

Abimelech killed
during siege of
"a strong tower"

Bezek

Geba

Tirzah?

Jotham flees to Beer,
evidently Beerim

Kozoh

Shechem

Mt. Gerizim

Oak of the Pillar

Ophrah

Pirathon

Taanath-shiloh

Michmethath

Janoah

Arumah

Abimelech's
permanent
dwelling place

Tappuah

Abimelech's route

Lebonah

Shiloh

0   2   4 miles
0   2   4   6 km

77

JUDG. 8:30-9:57

The establishment of the tribes in their various territories
continued during the twelfth century. The bonds between the
tribes loosened under the relatively calm conditions. No strong
enemies threatened the security and holdings of the Israelite
peasants. Here lies the disadvantage of a historical atlas: it
is easier to sketch a map of a short military episode than to
show generations of peaceful toil which built the foundations
for a healthy life of a nation in its land.

The wars described in the Bible are mostly against neighbors
and invaders coming from the desert, taking every opportunity
to loot and destroy. In times of danger, leaders rose to the call
of the tribes — the divinely inspired Judges. They generally held
leadership even after their wars of deliverance. The number
of warriors mustered around them was small and they were
summoned only from among their own and neighboring tribes.
Groups of a few hundred men under audacious leadership
could by surprise overcome their enemies, who were also
small, unorganized bands.

Only one of the judges, Othniel the son of Kenaz, came from
a southern tribe. The historical and geographical circumstances
of his war are unknown. Ehud was of the tribe of Benjamin and
acted with the assistance of the people of southern Mount
Ephraim. His daring personal deed is described; the circum-

stances under which the king of Moab was able to penetrate
to Jericho, the "city of palms," with the aid of the Ammonites
and the Amalekites, are, however, unknown. Gideon was of
the tribe of Manasseh, and his family, that of Abiezer, dwelt
at Ophrah. The location of Ophrah is uncertain. Because the
death of Gideon's brothers is associated with Mount Tabor,
scholars have sought Ophrah in the Jezreel Valley. However,
the clan of Abiezer was in the hills southwest of Shechem.
There we find Kh. 'Awfar from which Jotham could easily
have walked to Mount Gerizim. The Beer to which Jotham
fled is probably to be equated with the Beerim of the Samaria
ostraca. It should be noted that Issachar is not mentioned
in the story of Gideon's war, even though the battle took
place within its territory. The enemy whom Gideon fought
were highly mobile Bedouin marauders mounted on camels;
they infiltrated from the desert and filled the valleys with their
flocks and tents, harassing the Israelite populace scattered in
open settlements. Gideon was not content with a mere attack
on the enemy camp, but chased the raiders far into the desert.
Jephtah was a Gileadite. He freed the Israelite settlements in
Transjordan from Ammonite pressure. His outstanding ability
as a leader is related in the account of his campaign. Also
noticeable is the extreme contrast between the tribes which
dwelt on either side of the Jordan. This latter found expression
even in the different dialects of Hebrew used by each group
(Judg. 12:6).

The reign of Abimelech, the son of Gideon, which lasted for
three years, represents a peculiar episode in the period of the
Judges — an attempt to pass leadership on through inheritance,
to establish a kingship. In his venture, Abimelech was aided by
the older Canaanite population of Shechem, which considered
him one of their own because of his maternal lineage. They
provided him with "silver out of the house of Baal-berith"
(Judg. 9:4). The remains of this Canaanite temple, also called
Beth-millo, were uncovered during excavations at Shechem.
Abimelech refused, however, to commit himself to the rulers
of Shechem and made Arumah, between Shechem and Shiloh,
his capital. Soon after, relations deteriorated completely, since
the Canaanites of Shechem were not prepared to accept him
as an Israelite king (Judg. 9:28). Abimelech razed Shechem to
its foundations and, moreover, tried to extend his domination
over the other Canaanite cities which remained in the midst
of Manasseh in Mount Ephraim. He met his death at the siege
of the fortress (tower) of Thebez, and thus ended his short
"reign." The location of Thebez is unknown. The identification
with Tubas is highly doubtful. Thebez may be a corruption of
the name Tirzah, an important Canaanite city near Shechem
(Josh. 12:24).

Decorated Philistine bowl

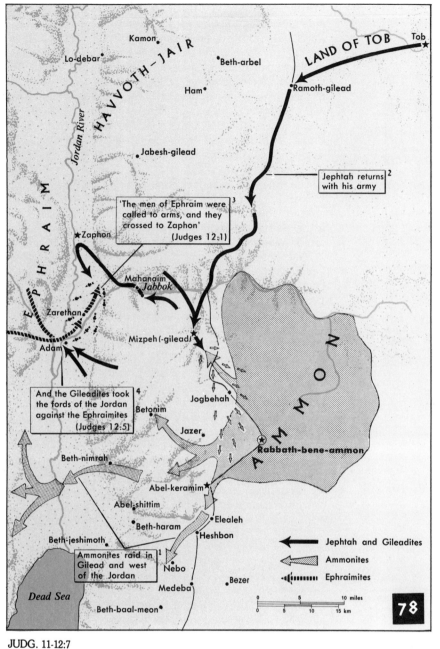

"Come and be our leader, that we may fight with the Ammonites."

(Judges 11:6)

THE WAR OF JEPHTAH
END OF 12TH TO 11TH CENTURIES B.C.

Jephtah returns with his army [2]

'The men of Ephraim were called to arms, and they crossed to Zaphon' (Judges 12:1) [3]

And the Gileadites took the fords of the Jordan against the Ephraimites (Judges 12:5) [4]

Ammonites raid in Gilead and west of the Jordan [1]

Kamon
Lo-debar
Beth-arbel
Ham
Ramoth-gilead
LAND OF TOB
Tob
HAVVOTH-JAIR
Jordan River
Jabesh-gilead
EPHRAIM
Zaphon
Mahanaim
Jabbok
Zarethan
Adam
Mizpeh (-gilead)
AMMON
Betonim
Jogbehah
Jazer
Rabbath-bene-ammon
Beth-nimrah
Abel-keramim
Abel-shittim
Elealeh
Beth-haram
Heshbon
Beth-jeshimoth
Nebo
Bezer
Medeba
Dead Sea
Beth-baal-meon

Jephtah and Gileadites
Ammonites
Ephraimites

0   5   10 miles
0   5   10   15 km

78

JUDG. 11-12:7

Decorated Philistine jug

Samson went down to Timnah ...

(Judges 14:1)

THE DEEDS OF SAMSON EARLY 11TH CENTURY B.C.

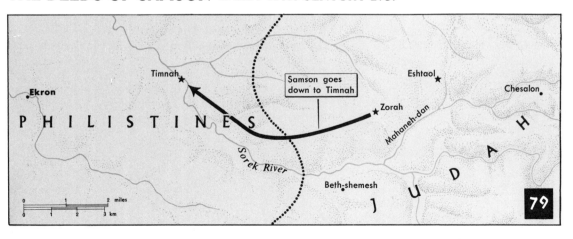

Samson goes down to Timnah

Ekron
Timnah
Eshtaol
Chesalon
PHILISTINES
Zorah
Mahaneh-dan
Sorek River
Beth-shemesh
JUDAH

0   1   2 miles
0   1   2   3 km

79

At that time the Philistines had dominion over Israel.

(Judges 14:4)

JUDAH AND PHILISTIA IN THE DAYS OF SAMSON

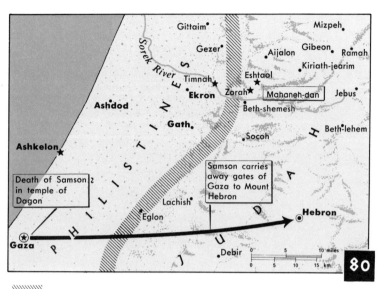

Border area between Judah and Philistia

JUDG. 13-16

From Dan to Beer-sheba, including the land of Gilead, and the congregation assembled as one man to the Lord at Mizpah.

(Judges 20:1)

THE STORY OF THE CONCUBINE IN GIBEAH
12TH TO 11TH CENTURIES B.C.

JUDG. 19-20

The struggle with the Philistines, the strongest of Israel's enemies, finds expression in the heroic tales of Samson. The Philistines had occupied the southern coastal area by force in c. 1174 B.C. and later they may have had Egyptian acquiescence in developing their confederation of five city states. Their main settlement zone was initially up to the Sorek Valley and included the coastal towns of Gaza, Ashkelon and Ashdod with two inland towns at Gath and Ekron. All of these places had seen occupation during the Late Bronze Age. The Philistines brought with them their Aegean pottery tradition of monochrome Mycenaean III C ware. After they had been in the country for a generation or two, their potters developed a bi-chrome style of pottery reminicent of their Aegean heritage but also reflecting their adaptation to the local Canaanite culture. This latter style is called "Philistine Ware." They had highly skilled metalsmiths and their soldiers wore sophisticated armor (as with Goliath the Gittite, Map 91).

Most stories of the conflict between Israel and the Philistines center on the tribal areas of Benjamin and Ephraim, i.e. the central hill country. However, the Danite Samson and his family are associated with Judah. The border between Judah and Philistia ran along the margin of the Judean Shephelah. In the Samson narratives, we have a glimpse of life in the Sorek Valley. The main events took place between Israelite Zorah and Philistine Timnah, evidently a daughter city of Ekron. Zorah is on a high ridge; Timnah is in the Sorek Valley, thus Samson "went down . . . (Judg. 14:1)." Samson and his Danite family were a remnant that had not gone north with the rest of the tribe. The Philistines were already dominating certain areas of Judah (Judg. 15:11). The heroic tales of this champion were undoubtedly quite popular among the villages of Judah especially along the border facing Philistia. Culturally, there was considerable symbiosis between Judah and the Philistines for example, a thoroughly Judean town like Beth-shemesh had large quantities of "Philistine" pottery, even though it was across the border from Philistine territory (1 Sam. 6:12).

The book of Judges ends with the story of the fraternal war between Benjamin and the other Israelite tribes, following the ravishing of the concubine of a Levite at the hands of the people of Gibeah in Benjamin. This story reflects the general situation during the period of the Judges: "In those days there was no king in Israel; every man did what was right in his own eyes" (Judg. 21:25, etc.). Although there was no central political rule in Israel in this period, there was evidently a confederation of tribes formed around a central sanctuary. If one tribe violated the laws of the league, the council would meet to confer punishment. The historical circumstances, however, of the Israelite war against Benjamin remain obscure. It must have occurred at an earlier period, for at the end of the period of the Judges, Benjamin was a strong, well-established tribe, and Gibeah in Benjamin became the first capital of Israel, under Saul. This narrative dates to an earlier stage of the Israelite settlement as indicated by the mention of the Ark being at Beth-el under the charge of Phinehas, son of Eleazar (Judg. 20:26-28).

Then the Lord raised up judges, who saved them out of the power of those who plundered them.

(Judges 2:16)

THE JUDGES ACCORDING TO THEIR TRIBES
12TH TO 11TH CENTURIES B.C.

Tyre

Dan

Kedesh

A S H E R

N A P H T A L I

Acco

Shamgar son of Anath³

Ashtaroth

ZEBULUN

Kedesh-naphtali★

Barak son of Abinoam⁴

Great Sea

Elon 10

Dor

Kamon★

Megiddo

I S S A C H A R

Jair the Gileadite⁷   Ramoth-gilead

Beth-shean

M A N A S S E H

Tola son of Puah of Issachar⁶

Shamir★   Gideon son of Joash⁵   Zaphon★

Ophrah★   Jephtah the Gileadite⁸

Pirathon★   Shechem   Succoth

Abdon son of Hillel¹¹

River Jordan

Adam

Joppa

Shiloh◎

E P H R A I M

Jazer

G A D

Beth-el   Rabbath-bene-ammon◎

Ehud son of Gera²   Gilgal

B E N J A M I N   Heshbon

D A N

Ashdod   Zorah★   Jebus

Samson 12

Beth-lehem★

Ashkelon   Ibzan 9

R E U B E N

J U D A H

Othniel son of Kenaz 1

Dead Sea

Hebron

Dibon

Gaza

Debir★

Arad

Beer-sheba

S I M E O N

Aroer   Kir-moab◎

0   5   10 miles
0   5 10 15 km

Zoar

The Book of Judges was intended to give due credit to the various tribal heroes of the pre-monarchial age. On the other hand, the book stressed the shortcomings of even the most renowned of the judges, or deliverers. Subtle stress is placed on the fact that life is much better under the monarchy. At the beginning of the book, in chapter 1, the list of unconquered cities is annotated by the references to forced labor which was later imposed on the Canaanite population. The administration of such an institution as forced labor was only possible during the reigns of David and Solomon. The two accounts at the end of the Book of Judges are more explicit. Social anarchy and moral depravity, especially at the ancestral home of Saul, were rampant in the age when "There was no king in Israel;

every man did what was right in his own eyes."

Besides the great Judges of deliverance, the Book of Judges also mentions several "minor Judges" (Judg. 10:1-5; 12:8-15), who judged the people from their native cities. Their wealth is usually emphasized in the Scriptures, and no tradition concerning wars under their leadership has come down to us. In times of peace, their authority was quite limited. Five "minor Judges" are given and it may be more than incidental that the total number of judges mentioned in the Book of Judges is twelve, a Judge for each tribe. It is doubtful whether these were the only "minor Judges;" their names may have been chosen on the basis of their tribal affiliations, in order to provide each tribe with a judge, even if not a deliverer.

Israel was defeated by the Philistines . . .

(1 Samuel 4:2)

THE BATTLE OF EBEN-EZER MID-ELEVENTH CENTURY B.C.

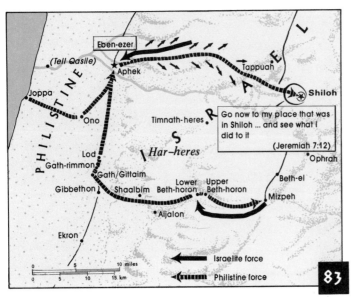

1 Sam. 4

In the mid-eleventh century events were leading toward a decisive battle between Israel and the Philistines for supremacy in the Land of Canaan. This conflict gave birth to the "Philistine empire," which lasted for a short time only, and later to the Israelite kingdom, which was founded in reaction to Philistine pressure.

Our information on the dramatic struggle is fragmentary, and only a shadow of the events is revealed by the folk stories preserved. The major battle occurred between Aphek and Eben-ezer. Ancient Aphek, located at the source of the Yarkon River, became a border city at the northern edge of Philistia. The exact location of Eben-ezer is unknown, but it may have been near 'Izbet Sarta on the best road leading from Shiloh to Aphek. The battle resulted in the absolute defeat of the Israelite tribal league, and Shiloh itself was destroyed, as indicated by excavations there. This explains the fact that Shiloh is never again mentioned as an Israelite center, that the descendants of the priests of Shiloh were settled at Nob near Jerusalem at the time of Saul (1 Sam. 21:2 ff.), and the later hints as to the fate of the city (Jer. 7:12, 14; 26:6, 9; Ps. 78:60).

The ark of the Lord was in the country of the Philistines seven months.

(1 Samuel 6:1)

THE WANDERINGS OF THE ARK OF THE COVENANT MID-ELEVENTH CENTURY B.C.

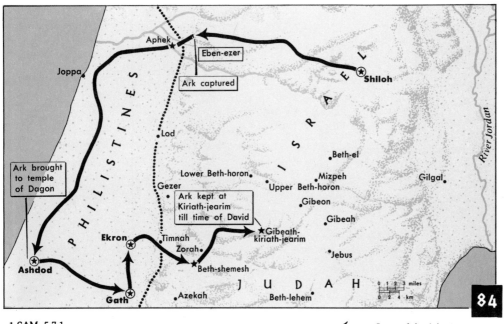

1 SAM. 5-7:1

← Route of the Ark

The Ark of the Covenant, which had been brought from Shiloh to the battlefield, fell into Philistine hands. The wonderful story of its wanderings and return gives us a glimpse into the life of the central cities of northern Philistia and their border areas. From Philistine Ekron, the Ark was removed to Beth-shemesh in Judah, where the people were harvesting wheat in the valley; this was the vale of Sorek, near Timnah, in whose fields Samson had loosed his foxes (1 Sam. 15:1-5). The people of Beth-shemesh passed the Ark on to the "hill of" Kiriath-jearim (1 Sam. 7:1; 2 Sam. 6:3-4: and see Josh. 18:28), the early Hivite-Gibeonite city on the southern border of Benjamin, which is also the southernmost border of the northern Israelite tribes there. The Ark remained there until David recovered and transferred it to Jerusalem, for lack of a ritual center to take the place of Shiloh. Consequently Samuel, the spiritual leader of Israel in those days of extreme crisis, each year made a circuit of the tribal and ritual centers on the borders of Benjamin and Ephraim.

The Bible contains the tradition about another war, this time under the leadership of Samuel (1 Sam. 7:7-14). The Israelite tribes had assembled at Mizpeh where Samuel called them to repentance. The approaching Philistine forces were routed and pursued as far as "Beth-car" which may be corrected (with the help of the Greek version) to "Beth-horon." As a result of this clash, the towns between Ekron and Gath (= Gittaim) were restored to Israelite control. This may have opened the way for the Beriah clan to settle in this area (cf. 1 Chron. 7:20-24; 8:12-13). Good relations were also established between the Israelites in this area and the Amorites who had formerly resisted the tribe of Dan (Judg. 1:34-35).

From the continuation of the account in the Book of Samuel, it would appear that Philistine harassment of Israel did not cease, but rather became more intense. The Philistines re-asserted their claim to hegemony in the hill country by posting a governor at Geba, a city of Benjamin near the border of Ephraim (1 Sam. 10:5; cf. 13:3).

Thus it appears that Israelite-Philistine relations were a continuous chain of hostile actions and reactions. The surprising Israelite victory in the days of Samuel may have brought about, in turn, more intensified efforts on the part of the Philistines. They now penetrated to the heart of the Israelite settlement in the hill country and secured their rule in the conquered regions by installing permanent occupation forces.

The time was ripe in Israel for rule by kingship. Saul, the first of the Israelite kings, arose in the midst of the Philistine oppression. He came from Gibeah of Benjamin. This city became Saul's stronghold and the first capital of the kingdom of Israel; henceforth it was known as Gibeah of Saul. The biblical account of the route taken by Saul as he found a kingdom while searching for his lost asses in the central Mount Ephraim is a fine example of the instructive topographical data included in this type of folk tale.

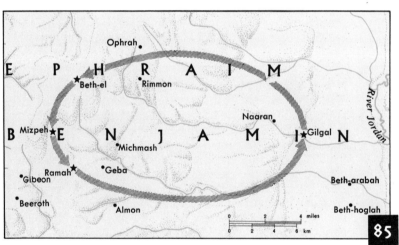

And he went on a circuit year by year to Bethel, Gilgal, and Mizpah ... Then he would come back to Ramah ...
(1 Samuel 7:16-17)

THE CITIES OF SAMUEL
CA. 1040 B.C.

1 SAM. 7:16-17

Now the asses of Kish, Saul's father, were lost.
(1 Samuel 9:3)

SAUL SEARCHES FOR HIS ASSES
CA. 1035 B.C.

Carts of Sea People drawn by oxen (Relief of Rameses III at Medinet Habu)

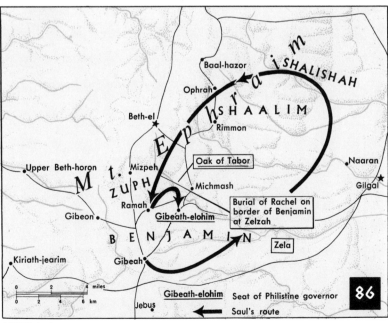

Gibeath-elohim   Seat of Philistine governor

◄──   Saul's route

1 SAM. 9-10:16

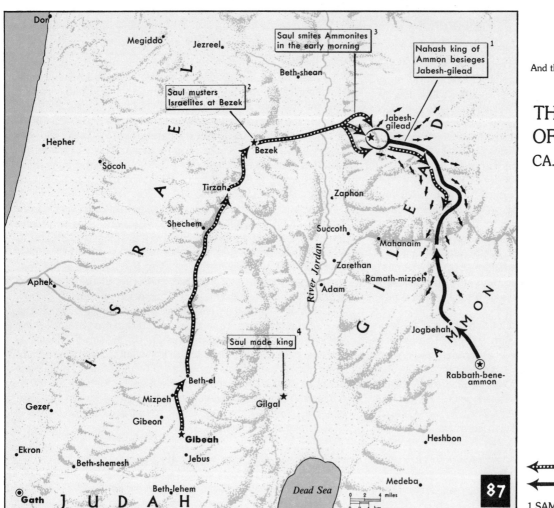

And the spirit of God came mightily upon Sa...
(1 Samuel 1...

THE SALVATION
OF JABESH-GILEAD
CA. 1035 B.C.

Saul smites Ammonites in the early morning [3]

Nahash king of Ammon besieges Jabesh-gilead [1]

Saul musters Israelites at Bezek [2]

Saul made king [4]

Israel ◀▪▪▪▪▪▪

Ammon ◀━━━

87

1 SAM. 11

Saul's ascent to kingship resembles the rise of the deliverer Judges. Jabesh-gilead had been oppressed by Nahash king of Ammon; Saul sallied forth from Bezek and by a surprise attack on the Ammonites relieved the Israelite city. After this victory Saul did not disperse the forces gathered around him; he was anointed king before God by Samuel at Gilgal. It is hardly by chance that the kingdom was founded on the very spot of the first Israelite center in the Land of Canaan.

The establishment of the kingdom meant open rebellion against Philistine rule. Saul, with 2000 men, went up to Michmash and the southern part of Mount Ephraim. His son, Jonathan, rallied 1000 men at Gibeah in Benjamin and proceeded to seize Geba and slay the Philistine governor there. The

Philistines reacted immediately, sending considerable forces. Saul retreated to Gilgal; later he and the remnants of his army joined forces with Jonathan at Geba opposite Michmash, the deep Wadi Suweinit separating the two hostile camps. Israelite victory was achieved through the overconfidence of the Philistines who were sure of easy victory, having sent punitive troops to the several Israelite regions instead of concentrating their might for a decisive battle. The courage displayed by Jonathan when surprising the Philistine forces, passing through the narrow wadi, also played an important part. Sudden confusion turned into crushing defeat as Saul's forces pursued the Philistines to the region of the vale of Aijalon.

Jonathan defeated the garrison of the Philistines...
(1 Samuel 13:3)

THE REBELLION OF SAUL AGAINST
THE PHILISTINES

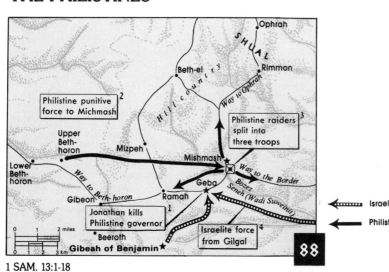

Philistine punitive force to Michmash [2]

Philistine raiders split into three troops [3]

Jonathan kills Philistine governor [1]

Israelite force from Gilgal [4]

Israel ◀▪▪▪▪▪▪

Philistines ◀━━━

88

1 SAM. 13:1-18

So the Lord delivered Israel that day...
(1 Samuel 14:23)

THE BATTLE OF MICHMASH

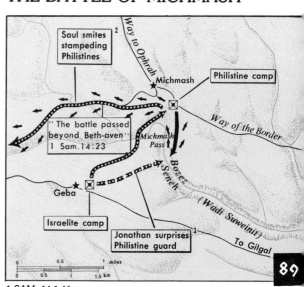

Saul smites stampeding Philistines [2]

Philistine camp

"The battle passed beyond Beth-aven"
1 Sam. 14:23

Jonathan surprises Philistine guard [1]

Israelite camp

89

1 SAM. 14:1-46

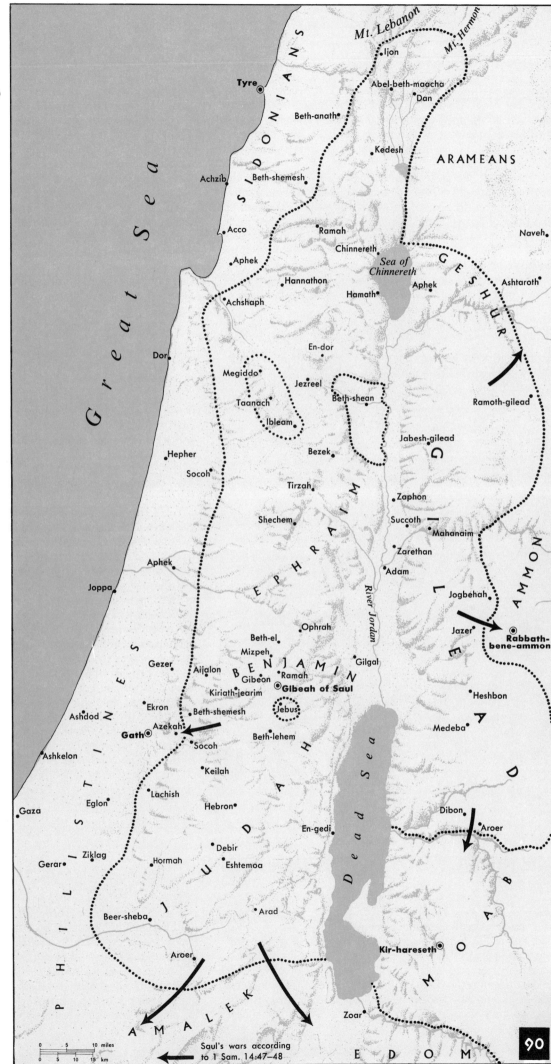

And he made him king over Gilead and the Geshurites(!) and Jezreel and Ephraim and Benjamin and all Israel.
(2 Samuel 2:9)

THE KINGDOM OF SAUL
CA. 1035 TO 1017 B.C.

Great Sea

SIDONIANS

Mt. Lebanon

Mt. Hermon

Ijon

Tyre

Abel-beth-maacha

Dan

Beth-anath

Kedesh

ARAMEANS

Achzib

Beth-shemesh

Acco

Ramah

Naveh

Chinnereth

Aphek

Sea of Chinnereth

Hannathon

Hamath

Aphek

Ashtaroth

Achshaph

G E S H U R

Dor

En-dor

Megiddo

Jezreel

Ramoth-gilead

Taanach

Beth-shean

Ibleam

Bezek

Jabesh-gilead

Hepher

G

Socoh

Tirzah

Zaphon

Shechem

Succoth

Mahanaim

Zarethan

Adam

River Jordan

L

Aphek

E

Jogbehah

A M M O N

Joppa

Ophrah

Jazer

Rabbath-bene-ammon

Beth-el

Mizpeh

Gilgal

Gezer

B E N J A M I N

Heshbon

Aijalon

Gibeon

Ramah

Kiriath-jearim

Gibeah of Saul

Medeba

Ekron

Beth-shemesh

Jebus

Ashdod

Azekah

A

Gath

Socoh

Beth-lehem

D

Ashkelon

Keilah

J

Dead Sea

Dibon

Aroer

Eglon

Lachish

U

Gaza

Hebron

D

En-gedi

Gerar

Ziklag

Hormah

Debir

A

Eshtemoa

Arad

H

Kir-hareseth

O

Beer-sheba

M

Aroer

Zoar

A M A L E K

B

E D O M

Philistine sword

0   5   10 miles
0   5   10 15 km

Saul's wars according to 1 Sam. 14:47–48

P H I L I S T I N E S

90

2 SAM. 2:9

THE KINGDOM OF SAUL

Saul was the last of the judges and the first of Israel's kings. Saul not only delivered Israel from the Philistine yoke, but also warred upon all the other surrounding enemies, and he "delivered Israel out of the hands of those who plundered them" (1 Sam. 14:48). In the account of the reign of Saul's son Eshbaal (Ishbosheth — 2 Sam. 2:9), the regions of his kingdom are listed as the five areas of "all Israel." These are the regions of dense Israelite settlement: Gilead in Transjordan; the Geshurites (incorrectly transmitted as Ashurites) in Galilee; the plain of Jezreel (named after the major city of Issachar); Ephraim in the central hill country, and Benjamin. To these must be added Judah, over which Saul had also extended his rule, but which fell to David "in the days of Eshbaal."

The mention of Jezreel in this passage probably reflects the status of the tribe of Issachar, who had settled in the town of Jezreel and who had been serving the Canaanites as corvée laborers (Gen. 49:14-15). The major towns along the sides of the great Valley were probably still maintaining their Canaanite character under nominal Philistine hegemony (like Beth-shean). Saul had died trying to dislodge the Philistines from this area. There must have been some degree of symbiosis between the Canaanites in these towns and the Israelites in the surrounding villages throughout the late twelfth and eleventh centuries B.C.

The borders of the kingdom of Israel in the days of Saul were those of the Israelite settlement (1 Sam. 13:19). He made no attempt to impose his rule over the various Canaanite enclaves; even pagan Jebus, very close to his capital, was never conquered by him. The task of uniting the entire Holy Land under a single Israelite king was left to his successor, David.

THE BATTLE OF ELAH — DAVID'S DUEL WITH GOLIATH
CA. 1020 B.C.

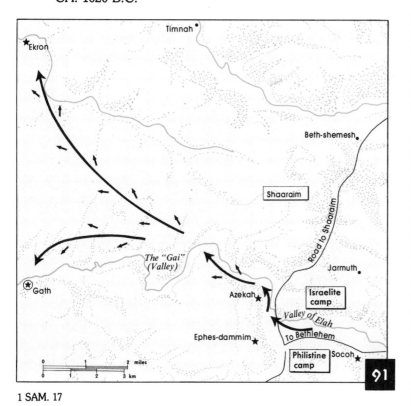

1 SAM. 17

David's home was Bethlehem, the key town in the true heartland of the tribe of Judah. His prowess as a warrior and as a musician enabled him to rise rapidly in the ranks of the young kingdom (1 Sam. 18:13). His marriage to the king's daughter (1 Sam. 18:17- 30) may reflect a tendency to draw the tribe of Judah, and its most influential clan, closer to the fledgling monarchy.

Saul's efforts to win the allegiance of Judah is reflected in the clash between his forces and the Philistines in the Vale of Elah (1 Sam. 17). The "duel of champions" so typical of Homeric tradition (but also of the ancient Near East) is perhaps the most widely known tale from all of biblical military lore; in fact there is a rival tradition that Elhanan son of Jaareoregim of Bethlehem was the actual champion on the Israelite side (cf. 2 Sam. 21:19; 1 Chron. 20:5). The geographical details of the narrative (especially in the Greek version) reflect a first-hand knowledge of the terrain. The two armies were facing one another across the valley, the Philistines on the south, Israel on the northern ridge. When the Philistines were routed, they sought to retreat westward along the winding course of the valley and as they turned northward (to go around Azekah) they were on the "road to Shaaraim." The Israelites were waiting there and inflicted many casualties on the Philistines. The pursuit followed the course of the valley westward beyond Azekah toward the gates of Gath and Ekron. The passage is one of the key texts supporting the location of Philistine Gath in northern Philistia.

THE NARRATIVE OF DAVID'S WANDERINGS
CA. 1018 B.C.

Within a short time relations between Saul and David became strained, and the two strong personalities often clashed. David fled, first to the Judean Desert, where he took refuge in caves and strong-points among its precipices. Here he gathered a band of malcontents, and tried to survive in spite of the hostility of the Judean settlements on the desert's edge. Saul pursued him even into this desolate region. The intense patriotism of the two great rivals is quite evident in the tales of this chase:

Saul, in spite of his deep hatred for David, sped to battle against the Philistines the moment he heard of an attack, thus giving David the opportunity to escape (1 Sam. 23:27-28); David, on his part, did not take advantage of various opportunities to harm Saul, out of respect to the Lord's anointed (1 Sam. 24:26). In the end Saul prevailed and David saw no recourse but to seek protection under Achish, king of Gath, a leader of his people's enemies.

And every one who was in distress, and every one
who was in debt, and every one who was discontented,
gathered to him; and he became captain over them.

(1 Samuel 22:2)

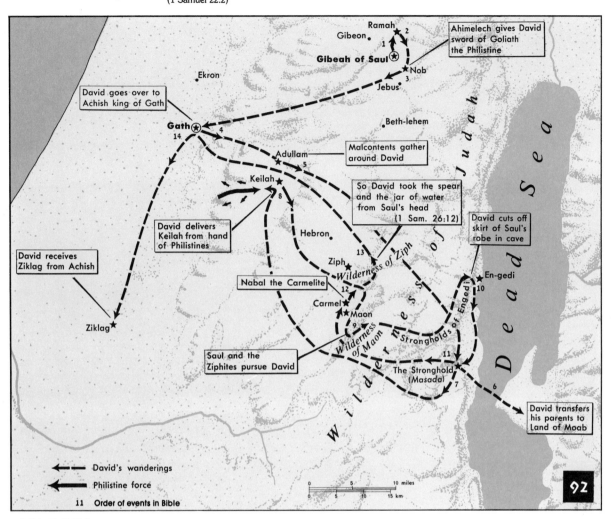

Ramah
Gibeon
Gibeah of Saul ⊛
1
2
Ahimelech gives David
sword of Goliath
the Philistine

Ekron
Nob
3
Jebus

David goes over to
Achish king of Gath

Beth-lehem

Gath ⊛
4
14

Adullam
5

Malcontents gather
around David

Keilah
8

So David took the spear
and the jar of water
from Saul's head
(1 Sam. 26:12)

David delivers
Keilah from hand
of Philistines

Hebron

David cuts off
skirt of Saul's
robe in cave

David receives
Ziklag from Achish

Ziph
13

Wilderness of Ziph

En-gedi
10

Nabal the Carmelite

12
Carmel
Maon
9

Wilderness of Maon

Strongholds of Engedi

W i l d e r n e s s   o f   J u d a h

D e a d   S e a

Ziklag ★

Saul and the
Ziphites pursue David

11
The Stronghold
(Masada)
7
6

David transfers
his parents to
Land of Moab

→ - - → David's wanderings
━━━→ Philistine force
11 Order of events in Bible

0   5   10 miles
0   5   10   15 km

92

1 SAM. 19:18-27:6

Philistine noble (Faience
plaque of time of
Rameses III, Medinet
Habu)

When Achish asked, "Against whom have you made a
raid today?" David would say, "Against the Negeb of
Judah," or "Against the Negeb of the Jerahmeelites,"
or, "Against the Negeb of the Kenites."

(1 Samuel 27:10)

DAVID AT ZIKLAG

CA 1017 B.C.

Achish not only welcomed David, but put him in charge of
Ziklag, one of the towns on the fringe of his territory. It would
appear that Achish may have been "first among equals" in
the circle of five Philistine "lords" ("tyrants"?), which entitled
him to be called "king." He intended to use David and his
troops to protect the southeastern flank of Philistia facing
the tribal elements occupying the Negeb. David would report
attacking those very tribes when in reality he was attacking
their archenemies, the Amalekites, and the other nomadic
groups that usually harassed the Negeb settlements. The local
regions were named after their inhabitants (1 Sam. 27:10;
30:14), namely, the "Negeb of the Cherethites" on the west,
the "Negeb of Judah" in the center, the "Negeb of Caleb"
in the northeast (probably including mainly the hill country
south of Hebron, Judg. 1:15), the "Negeb of the Kenite" on
the east (around Arad, Judg. 1:16) and the "Negeb of the
Jerahmeelite," probably to the southeast. Simeon is noticeably
absent; according to the proper verse division in 1 Chron.
4:31b- 32, Simeon was not introduced into the Negeb towns
until David became king.

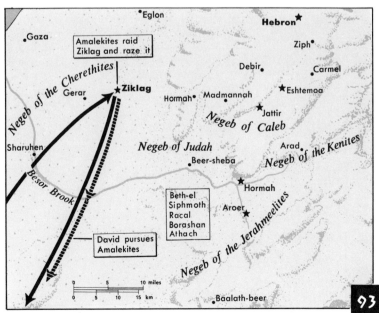

Eglon
Hebron ★
Gaza
Ziph

Amalekites raid
Ziklag and raze it

Debir
Carmel

Negeb of the Cherethites
Gerar
★ Ziklag
Hormah
Madmannah
Eshtemoa

Negeb of Caleb
Jattir

Sharuhen

Negeb of Judah
Arad
Negeb of the Kenites

Besor Brook
Beer-sheba

Hormah

Beth-el
Siphmoth
Racal
Borashan
Athach
Aroer

David pursues
Amalekites

Negeb of the Jerahmeelites

0   5   10 miles
0   5   10   15 km

Baalath-beer

93

1 SAM. 27:6-12; 30

THE ORIGINS OF DAVID'S MEN OF VALOR

CA. 1018 TO 1017 B.C.

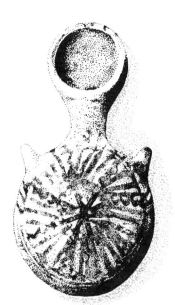

Water flask (Eleventh century B.C.)

2 SAM. 23:8-39; 1 CHRON. 11:10-12:22

David's men of valor gathered around him, some still while he was in the desert stronghold (1 Chron. 12:8) and others at Ziklag. They served as the nucleus of his army and were unquestioningly loyal and always ready for daring exploits. Most were from Judah and Benjamin, though some came from more distant tribes, from Mount Ephraim and beyond the Jordan.

The unit of "thirty chief men" became a permanent military institution during the reign of David, later their number swelling and including also foreigners, such as Zelek the Ammonite, Naharai of Beeroth, and Uriah the Hittite (2 Sam. 23:37-39; 1 Chron. 11:39, 41).

Now the Philistines gathered all their forces at Aphek; and the Israelites were encamped by the fountain which is in Jezreel.

(1 Samuel 29:1)

THE DEPLOYMENT FOR THE BATTLE OF GILBOA

CA. 1016 B.C.

The wars of the Israelites against the Philistines culminated in Saul's death on Mount Gilboa. Saul fought his last battle on the crossroads of Jezreel. The Philistines attempted to dominate the valley and threatened to cut the tribes of Galilee off from Mount Ephraim.

In order to properly understand the preparations for the battle, and the battle itself, it must be noted that the biblical narrative is not in exact chronological order, but skips from event to event in keeping an account of the activities of Saul and David. In chapter 28 (1 Sam.) there appears the story of

1 SAM. 29

Saul's meeting with the medium of En-dor the night before the battle; and in chapter 29 there is an account of the talks between the lords of the Philistines and Achish concerning David, at the start of their campaign. The proper order of events is: the Philistines rallied at Aphek in the Sharon plain, as was their custom when venturing upon campaigns to the north (1 Sam. 29:1); from there the Philistines advanced to Shunem at the foot of the hill of Moreh, while Saul deployed his army opposite them on Mount Gilboa, favoring the mountainous area as more convenient for his lightly armed Israelite warriors. He encamped at a spring at the foot of Jezreel; it was from here that Saul went to the medium of En-dor in the darkness of night. The next day he died a hero's death on the Gilboa, together with three of his sons. The Philistine victory was absolute and the important cities of Jezreel remained under their control. As a warning, the Philistines fastened the corpses of Saul and his sons to the walls of Beth-shean, and placed their weapons in the temple of Ashtaroth, possibly one of two temples there in this period, the remains of which have been unearthed in archaeological excavations. The men of Jabesh-gilead, remembering Saul's having saved their city from the Ammonites, made a daring move under cover of darkness, and recovered the corpses of Saul and his sons from the walls of Beth-shean, bringing them to Jabesh for decent burial.

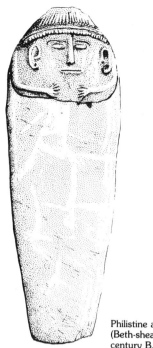

Philistine anthropoid coffin (Beth-shean, ca. end 12th century B.C.)

The men of Israel ... fell slain on Mount Gilboa
(1 Samuel 31:1)

The valiant men arose, and went all night ...
(1 Samuel 31:12)

THE DEATH OF SAUL

THE BURIAL OF SAUL

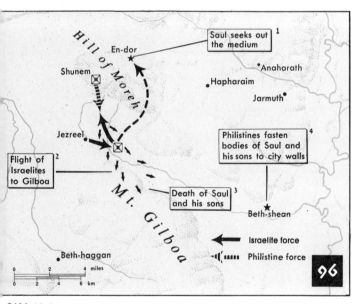

SAM. 28; 31

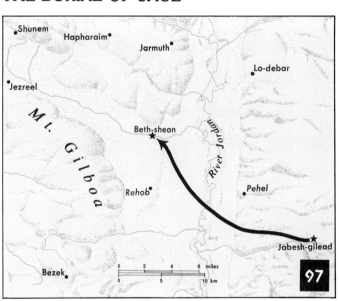

1 SAM. 31:11-13

THE KINGDOMS OF DAVID AND ESHBAAL CA. 1018 TO 1010 B.C.

Abner the son of Ner, captain of Saul's army, escaped from the battle of Gilboa with his life. He transferred the capital of Israel to Mahanaim, across the Jordan, and there crowned Eshbaal, one of Saul's surviving sons, as king (2 Sam. 2:8; 1 Chron, 8:33). It is Eshbaal who is also referred to in the Bible, in a derogatory manner, as Ish-bosheth ("man of disgrace"). Although David, as a vassal of the king of Gath, had come to the rallying point of the Philistines at Aphek, he was saved from fighting against his own people, because the lords of the Philistines were suspicious of him (1 Sam. 29). After Saul's death, David persuaded the elders of Judah to anoint him in Hebron as king over Judah, along with the affiliated tribes of the Calebites, Kenizzites, Kenites, Jerahmeelites and Simeonites. Hebron was chosen as the capital because of its central location and because it was Calebite rather than Judahite. While David reigned in Judah, Eshbaal reigned in the five remaining Israelite tribal regions of Saul's kingdom (2 Sam. 2:9-10). It seems that the Philistines welcomed this split and that Achish continued to regard David as a loyal vassal, still at his bid.

At first the Philistines seemed to be correct in their assumptions. The clash at Gibeon was only one of many hostilities which weakened the forces of the two rival kingdoms. It was as if Israel and Judah had returned to their former status of local tribal groupings, lacking strength even to venture beyond their own territories.

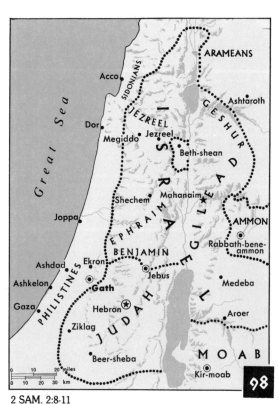

2 SAM. 2:8-11

Ish-bosheth, Saul's son, was forty years old when he began to reign over Israel, and he reigned two years. But the house of Judah followed David.

(2 Samuel 2:10)

THE KINGDOMS OF DAVID AND ESHBAAL

... And met them at the pool of Gibeon; and they sat down, the one on the one side of the pool, and the other on the other side of the pool.

(2 Samuel 2:13)

THE BATTLE BY THE POOL AT GIBEON
CA. 1015 B.C.

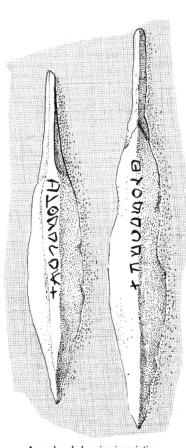

Arrowheads bearing inscription "Arrow of the servant of Lebaoth"

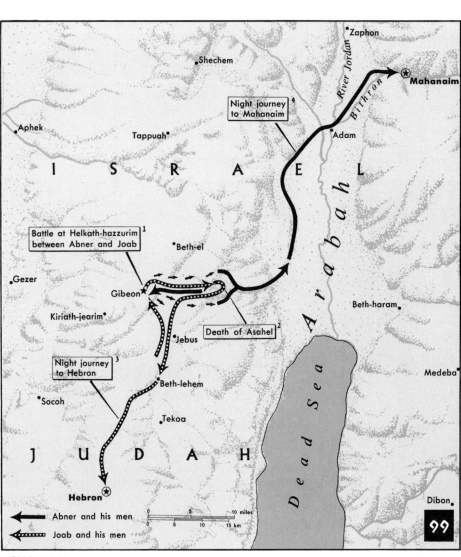

2 SAM. 2:12-32

David took the stronghold of Zion, that is, the city of Davia.

(2 Samuel 5:7)

2 SAM. 5; 1 CHRON. 11:4-9; 14:8-17

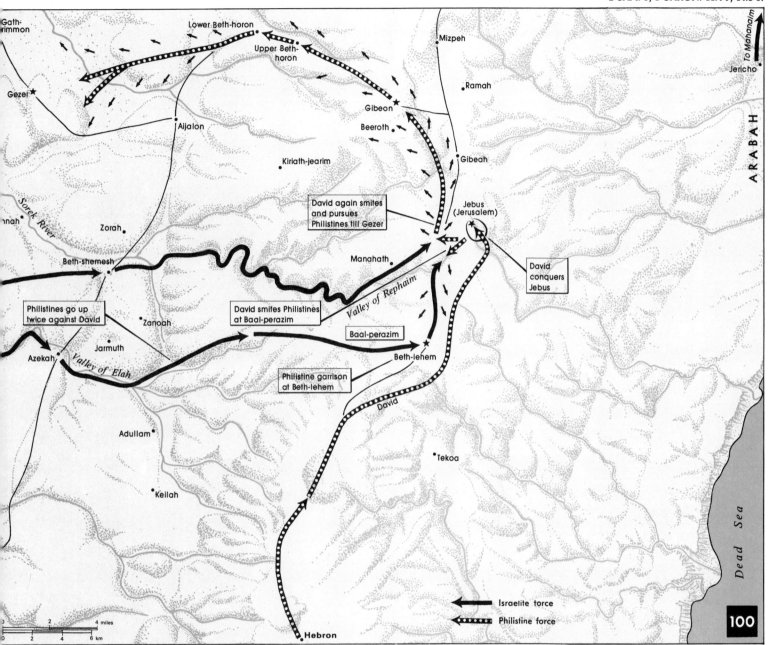

The tragic deaths of Abner and Eshbaal led to David's kingship over Israel and Judah. Abner was slain by Joab at Hebron. Eshbaal was assassinated by two of his officers from the Rimmon clan of Beeroth. The latter had fled to Gittaim, probably to escape persecution by Saul (2 Sam. 4:1-3). Hence, Gittaim is also known as Gath-rimmon.

Just as David had chosen Hebron as a capital to unite Judah and the client tribes in the south, he now chose to conquer the Jebusite enclave at Jerusalem and make that city his dynastic possession ("the city of David"). By now the Philistines realized that the unification of all the tribes under David posed a threat to their hegemony in the hill country. Twice they came up against him via the Valley of Rephaim (cf. Josh. 15:8). The first time, they had a garrison positioned at Bethlehem (2 Sam. 23:14) to prevent David from getting help from the south. David smote them and called the place of his victory Baal-perazim (2 Sam. 5:20). The second time,

David ambushed the Philistines by blocking their retreat at the western end of the Valley of Rephaim. The Philistines were forced to retreat via the watershed road, past Geba, to the Beth-horon road. David pursued them as far as Gezer (2 Sam. 5:24).

Having expelled the Philistines from the central hill country, David was free to bring the Ark of the Covenant from Kiriath-jearim to his new capital in Jerusalem. Then he took the initiative against the Philistines on the coastal plain and "took Gath and its daughter settlements from Philistine control" (1 Chron. 18:1; cf. 2 Sam. 8:1). The reference is probably not to "Gath of the Philistines" (Amos 6:2), of the pentapolis, but rather the Gath-Gittaim/Gath-rimmon northwest of Gezer. This victory secured David's control over the corridor from Gezer, where David left the indigenous Canaanites unmolested, to the seaport at Joppa (see Map 107).

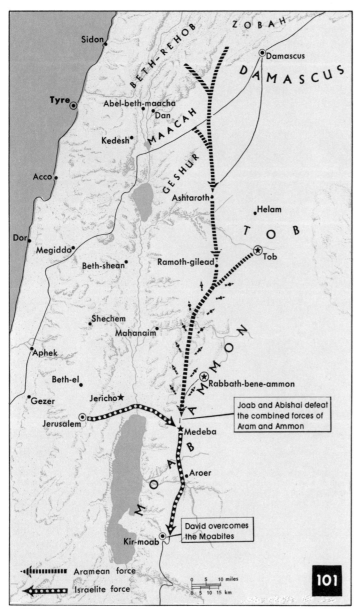

2 SAM. 8:2; 10:1-14; 1 CHRON. 18:2; 19:1-19

DEFEAT OF THE ARAMEAN COALITION AND THE CONQUEST OF RABBATH-BENE-AMMON

CA. 1000-990 B.C.

David's Transjordanian conquests may be traced chronologically by correlating the information in 2 Sam. 8:2-11 (= 1 Chron. 18:2-11) with that of 2 Sam. 10:1-19, 11:1, 26-31 (= 1 Chron. 19:1-19, 20:1-3). The course of events was apparently as follows: 1. Moab was conquered and reduced to vassal status, thus giving David firm control over the tableland north of the Arnon (2 Sam. 8:2; 1 Chron. 18:2). 2. The new Ammonite ruler, Hanun, showed his displeasure at Israel's military presence so close to his borders by insulting David's ambassadors (2 Sam. 10:1-5 = 1 Chron. 19:1-5). Then he sent for help from the Aramean kingdoms that had developed in northern Transjordan and in the Lebanese Beqa' Valley, namely Aram Beth-rehob and Aram-zobah, Maacah, and the men of Tob (2 Sam. 10:6; 1 Chron. 19:6-7a). These combined forces assembled east of Medeba, obviously intent on challenging David's hegemony over the Moabite tableland (1 Chron. 19:7a). David sent forth

When the Ammonites saw ... and hired the Syrians of Beth-rehob, and the Syrians of Zobah ... and the king of Maacah with a thousand men, and the men of Tob ...

(2 Samuel 10:6)

DAVID'S INITIAL CAMPAIGNS IN TRANSJORDAN

CA. 1000 B.C.

And when the Arameans of Damascus came to help Hadadezer king of Zobah, David slew twenty-two thousand men of the Syrians.

(2 Samuel 8:5)

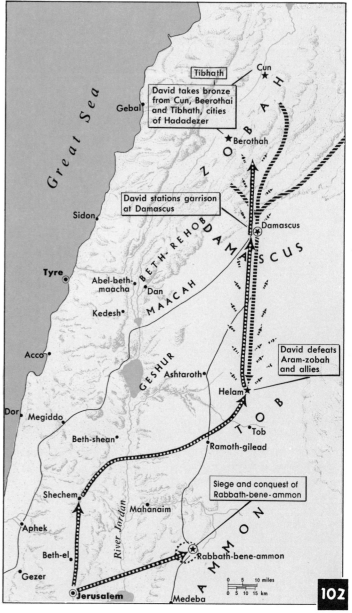

2 SAM. 8:3-10; 10:15-19; 11:1; 12:26-31; 1 CHRON. 18:3-10; 19: 16-19; 20:1-3

his army under the command of Joab; seeing the opposing forces on two sides, Joab divided the command with his brother, Abishai; the Arameans were routed by Joab and then the Ammonites retreated to their fortified city.   3. Stung by his defeat, Hadadezer, king of Aram-zobah, sent for all his vassals and associates among the Aramean kingdoms and tribes as far as the Euphrates. They assembled at Helam where David confronted them with the army of Israel. David's victory caused Hadadezer's vassals to defect and to offer allegiance to David (2 Sam. 10:15-19; 1 Chron. 19:16-19).   4. The way was now clear to settle accounts with Rabbath-bene-ammon. After the next harvest, David sent the army under Joab to attack the city and following a protracted siege, Joab was able to send for David to receive the enemy's surrender (2 Sam. 11:1, 12:26-11; 1 Chron. 20:1-3).   5. While Hadadezer was

trying to restore his authority over his former vassals along the Euphrates, David invaded his home territory and captured most of his military forces. This made David the nominal leader of the Aramean league over which he appointed governors at Damascus.   6. As a result, Toi, king of Hamath on the Orontes, the archenemy of Hadadezer, sought an alliance with David (2 Sam. 8:9-11; 1 Chron. 18:9-11).   7. Finally, the way was now open to extend Israel's control over the southern expanses of Edom. The military victory was accomplished by Abishai (probably under Joab; cf. the superscription to Psalm 60); and commissioners were appointed to administer the Edomite domains (1 Chron. 18:12-13; cf. 2 Sam. 8:13b-15). At this time, Hadad, a child from the Edomite royal house, was smuggled to Egypt where he received political asylum (1 Kings 11:15-20).

HE CONQUEST OF EDOM AND THE FLIGHT OF HADAD TO EGYPT

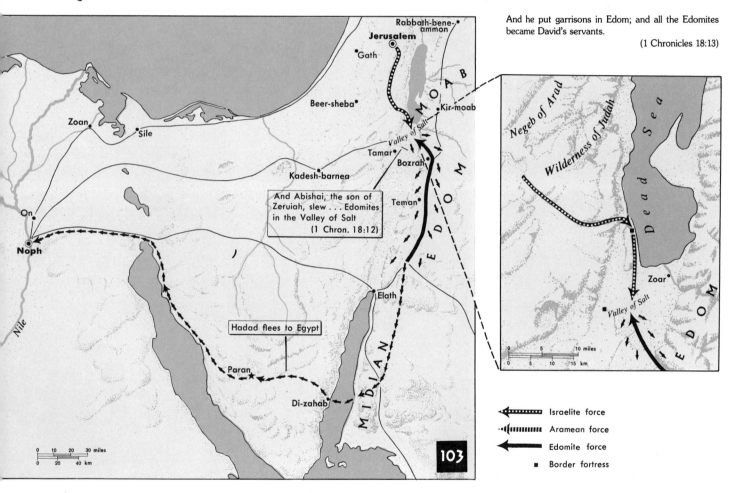

And he put garrisons in Edom; and all the Edomites became David's servants.

(1 Chronicles 18:13)

And Abishai, the son of Zeruiah, slew . . . Edomites in the Valley of Salt
(1 Chron. 18:12)

Hadad flees to Egypt

◄▭▭▭▭▭   Israelite force

-◄(|▥▥▥▥▥   Aramean force

◄━━━━━   Edomite force

■   Border fortress

THE KINGDOM OF DAVID

CA. 1000 to 970 B.C.

The kingdom of Israel reached the height of its military and political power under David. The larger kingdoms in the Ancient East were at their nadir, leaving a vacuum in the western part of the "Fertile Crescent." In David, Israel found a brilliant and far-sighted military and political leader, able to exploit the prevailing situation. Following the encounter with Aram-zobah, Israel became the major power in Syria and Palestine. The extent of the Israelite empire under David and Solomon is revealed by the passage concerning Solomon: "For he had dominion over all the region west of the Euphrates from Tiphsah to Gaza, over all the kings west of the Euphrates"

(1 Kings 4:24). In the Hebrew, "west of the Euphrates" is "the other side of the river," the name used by the peoples of Mesopotamia for this area. Thus the influence of David and Solomon spread from Tiphsah on the Great Bend of the Euphrates to Philistine Gaza on the southern border of the Land of Canaan.

This was an administratively complex empire, three main elements being discernible within it: the Israelite population; conquered kingdoms; and vassal kings. At the center of the empire stood the tribes of Israel and Judah, to which were appended the Canaanite-Amorite regions brought under

David's control. Around these lay the conquered and tributary kingdoms: Edom, Moab, Ammon, Aram-damascus, and Aram-zobah. Israelite governors were appointed over some of these territories, as in Edom and Damascus (2 Sam. 8:6, 14), while in others members of the local royal house ruled, under the tutelage of the king of Israel. These latter were actually governors, as in Ammon. One of the notables of Transjordan, who had come to David's aid during the rebellion of Absalom — Shobi the son of Nahash of Rabbath-bene-ammon (2 Sam.

17:27) — was probably the son of the king of Ammon who died before his kingdom was conquered by David (1 Chron. 19:1). The third element, the vassal kings, had been forced, in one way or another, to accept David's hegemony; they included Philistia and various kingdoms in northern Transjordan, such as Geshur, whose king was the grandfather of Absalom (2 Sam. 3:3; 13:37). The relationship with Toi king of Hamath (2 Sam. 8:10) and Hiram king of Tyre was probably of a similar nature (2 Sam. 5:11).

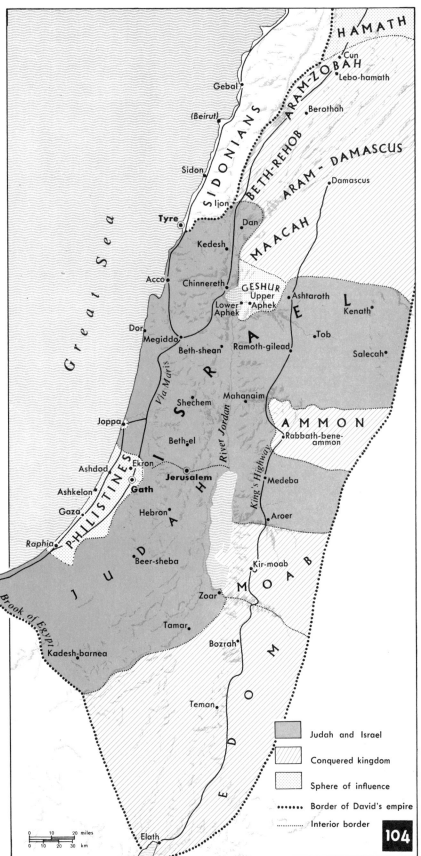

And when all the kings who were servants of Hadadezer saw that they had been defeated by Israel, they made peace with Israel, and became subject to them.

(2 Samuel 10:19)

Bringing tribute to overlord (Relief on obelisk of Asshurnasirpal II from Calah)

For he had dominion over all the region west of the Euphrates from Tiphsah to Gaza, over all the kings west of the Euphrates ...

(1 Kings 4:24)

THE ISRAELITE HEGEMONY DURING THE REIGNS OF DAVID AND SOLOMON

CA. 1000 TO 930 B.C.

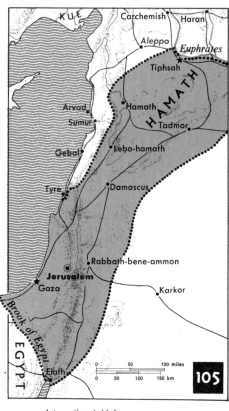

Legend (map 104):
- Judah and Israel
- Conquered kingdom
- Sphere of influence
- •••••• Border of David's empire
- ·········· Interior border

Legend (map 105):
- —— International highway
- Area of sovereignty of king of Israel

the king said to Joab and the commanders of the
[ar]my, who were with him, "Go through all the tribes of
[Isra]el from Dan to Beer-sheba, and number the
[peo]ple ..."

(2 Samuel 24:2)

JOAB'S CENSUS CA. 980 B.C.

The newly established kingdom of Israel is depicted in the census ordered by David. The territory covered represents all of the area directly under control of the monarchy in Jerusalem. Although the text of Joab's itinerary (2 Sam. 24:5-7) is badly preserved in spots, the general course of the census can be discerned. He began at Aroer on the traditional border with Moab (whenever Israel held the tableland). Then he progressed through the territory of Gad (in the western tableland itself according to Mesha's inscription) to Jazer and on through Gilead. The next stage of the journey is obscured by a textual corruption, "tahtim hodshi," but the best Greek version, albeit unclear, suggests that Bashan was the area visited. This makes sense since Joab went from there to Dan and on to "Jaan," a spelling of Ijon with metathesis. Next they moved across Upper Galilee along the border with Sidon, past the "fortress of Tyre," probably the Usu known from Egyptian and Assyrian inscriptions (Hellenistic Palaeotyrus, "Old Tyre"). The next entry is the most tantalizing: "All the cities of the Hivvites and the Canaanites," in other words, all those towns that had initially been unconquered (Judg. 1:27-35). Here we have the tacit admission that those elements of the pre-Israelite population who had maintained their social and political integrity up to now had finally succumbed to the new, united Israel. Specific details about how David subdued those Hivvite and Canaanite cities is not found in any ancient source. The end result can be seen in the dispersal of Levitical settlements (Map 108) and in the Solomonic commissioners' districts (Map 113). The main concentrations of Canaanite towns were on the plain of Acco, in the Jezreel Valley and in the Sharon Plain (including the district of Dor and the hinterland between Gezer and Joppa). The final area to be visited was the Negeb of Judah, the southern frontier zone occupied mainly by subsidiary tribes such as the Kenites and the Jerahmeelites and the Simeonites recently settled there by David. Joab went to the new regional capital, Beer-sheba, located at the center of the Judean Negeb (today's Beer-sheba and Besor Valleys).

106

Route of census-takers   2 SAM. 24:1-9

And the territory of its inheritance included Zorah, Eshtaol, Ir-shemesh, Shaalbin, Aijalon, Ithlah, Elon, Timnah (of) Ekron, Eltekeh, Gibbethon, Baalah, (Beth-dagon), Azor, (Ono), Jehud, Bene-berak, (Lod, Hadid, Zeboim), Gath-rimmon, and on the west the Jarkon with the border facing Joppa.

(Joshua 19:41-46)

THE "INHERITANCE" OF DAN
CA. 980 B.C.

Gezer Levitic city

••••• State boundary

JOSH. 19:40-46   •••••••• Tribal boundary

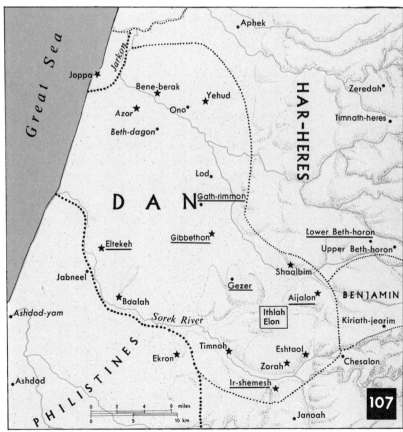

107

THE "INHERITANCE" OF DAN

Although it was acknowledged fact that the tribe of Dan was prevented from descending from the hill country onto the plain (Josh.19:47; Judg. 1:34; 18:1), the Book of Joshua defines the coastal corridor from the valley of Aijalon and the Sorek Valley to the harbor town of Joppa as the "inheritance of Dan" (Josh. 19:41-46). This particular zone was certainly not under Israelite control until the reign of David. There was a Danite enclave around Zorah and Eshtaol and some Benjaminite elements had come to settle in Ono and Lod (1 Chron. 8:13-14) and Gath-rimmon (1 Sam. 7:14; 2 Sam. 4:2-3). Ephraimites were later to be found in the area (Judg. 1:35), even at Gezer where the Canaanites persisted to live among them (Judg. 1:29); this happened at a time when it was possible to subject the non-Israelites to forced labor and that could only have been during the United Monarchy. The Philistines had expanded north of the Sorek as far as Aphek during the 11th century B.C. (1 Sam. 4:1) and by 909 B.C. Gibbethon had reverted to Philistine control (1 Kings 15:27). Therefore, the Danite list could only have existed as a territorial entity under David and Solomon. In fact, it would seem that the list reflects the second of Solomon's administrative districts; though it has some lacunae (especially Ono and Lod and probably also Hadid, Zeboiim, Makaz and Beth-dagon), it is more complete than 1 Kings 4:9. From the best Greek version we get Azor, and the description of the western border is better preserved: "and on the west [literally: from the sea] the Jarkon with the border facing Joppa." The biblical Jarkon must be the brook that forms the western boundary of the Danite settlement area, namely the modern Nahal Ayalon. The modern Yarkon was reckoned in the Bible as the extension seaward of the Brook Kanah (Josh. 17:9). Six Levitical towns were also located in this area and another, Lower Beth-horon, was nearby. The southern border (Josh. 15:10b-11) was Israel's new frontier with Philistia.

THE LEVITICAL CITIES
CA. 975-940 B.C.

The list of Levitical cities should also be ascribed to the period of the United Monarchy. Only under David were all the towns of the list finally brought under Israelite control. After the division of the kingdom, the Levites abandoned their places in the north and migrated to Judah (2 Chron. 11:13-14). Furthermore, even during Solomon's reign, the towns on the plain of Acco were turned over to Hiram of Tyre (1 Kings 9:10-13). Gezer was not conquered but its indigenous population was subjected to forced labor after the Ephraimites had begun to occupy the surrounding territory. A pharaoh, probably Siamon, later conquered Gezer and slew the native Canaanites (1 Kings 9:16); this act of aggression against Israel evidently led to a stalemate and as a condition of the treaty negotiations that followed, Gezer was surrendered as a dowry for pharaoh's daughter when she married Solomon. That military confrontation must have taken place late in David's reign or early in Solomon's, or possibly while the younger man was co- regent with his aging father. The administrative functions of the Levites were still being established in the fortieth year of David's reign (1 Chron. 26:31b).

The forty-eight Levitical cities are listed in two passages, Josh. 21 and 1 Chron. 6:39-66. The latter text is more complex and probably reflects the growth of the prominence and influence gained by the Aaronites and the rest of the tribe of Levi as the Davidic monarchy increased their responsibilities throughout the kingdom. The text in Joshua is linked more schematically to the twelve-tribe system expounded by the book as a whole. Although the neat division among twelve tribes has the appearance of symmetry, the actual distribution of the identifiable towns reflects the varied functions assigned to them in their respective areas. The Aaronite priests were assigned key cities in Judah, Simeon and Benjamin. Hebron was a city of refuge and originally Calebite. Those settlements in the southern Judean hill country could assure the loyalty of the Kenizzites. Libnah and Beth-shemesh guarded the western frontier with Philistia. The towns in Benjamin guarded the key approaches to Jerusalem from the north and northwest. The Kohathites were responsible for the border with Philistia along the Sorek Valley and the main approach route to Jerusalem via Gezer and Beth-horon. They also acquired some key towns on the southern Jezreel Valley and also Jokmeam near the mouth of the great Wadi el-Far'ah, on the route from the ford at Adam to central Samaria. And, of course, the refuge city of Shechem was also theirs. The Gershonites were in Galilee, including the newly organized Issachar territory, and in the Bashan. Eventually, they would lose those towns from Asher to the king of Tyre. The Merarites had some responsibilities in the northern Jezreel Valley but their main settlements were in Transjordan. The Izharite clan of Kohath had special responsibilities as judges and officers of the court throughout Israel (1 Chron 26:29). The Hebronite clan of Kohath had special administrative duties concerning "the work of the Lord and the service of the king" in both Cisjordan and Transjordan (1 Chron. 26:30-32).

It is obvious that the list can hardly be an arbitrary creation by a later writer (although the artificial tribal symmetry certainly is). The assignment of the Levitical towns has clear administrative logic. Some groups were to maintain the defense of political and/or ecological frontiers; others were to establish monarchial control in areas where the indigenous population was largely Canaanite/Amorite or Hivvite. The census by Joab was aimed at the registering of that newly subjugated population, both within the interior of the country and along the frontiers. It will be seen further on (Map 113) that half of Solomon's commissioners were concerned with the same former Canaanite areas. The establishment of the Levitical towns throughout the realm was a major step toward the bureaucratic organization achieved by Solomon. Incidentally, no Levitical towns were established in the Negeb of Judah because Simeon, the brother tribe to Levi, had been settled there by David, undoubtedly for the same motivation. They were to assure the defense of the southern frontier and the loyalty of such diverse groups as the Kenites, the Jerahmeelites and the Cherethites.

The entire cadre of the Levitical tribe was linked functionally with the central religious institution of the new monarchy, the temple being built in Jerusalem. While there were undoubtedly cultic centers at many of the Levitical towns, it was not their responsibility to take over all the places of worship throughout the kingdom. Many others, such as Dan, Bethel, Beer-sheba and Penuel, continued to flourish, not to mention Transjordanian cult centers like Nebo and Ataroth.

All the cities which you give to the Levites shall be forty-eight ...

(Numbers 35:7)

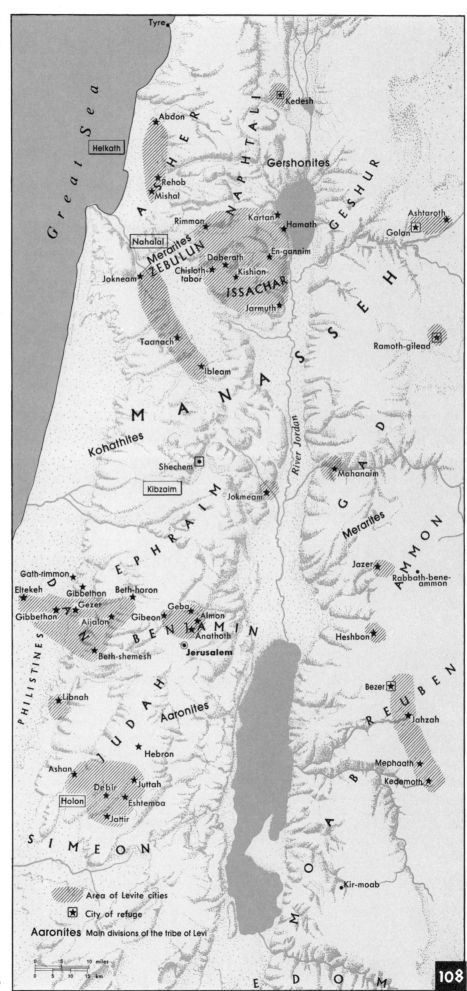

Great Sea

Tyre

Kedesh ✠

A S H E R

Abdon

Helkath

N A P H T A L I

Gershonites

G E S H U R

Rehob
Mishal

Ashtaroth
Golan ✠

Rimmon
Kartan
Hamath

Merarites
Nahalal
ZEBULUN
Daberath
En-gannim

Jokneam
Chisloth-tabor
Kishion

Ramoth-gilead ✠

ISSACHAR

Jarmuth

M A N A S S E H

Taanach

Ibleam

River Jordan

M A N A S S E H

Kohathites

G A D

Shechem ◻

Mahanaim

Kibzaim

E P H R A I M

Merarites

Jokmeam

A M M O N

Jazer
Rabbath-bene-ammon

Gath-rimmon

Eltekeh
Gibbethon
Beth-horon
Gezer
Geba
Almon

Heshbon

Gibbethon
Aijalon
Gibeon
Anathoth

Beth-shemesh

B E N J A M I N

Jerusalem ◉

P H I L I S T I N E S

Libnah

Bezer ✠

R E U B E N

Aaronites

J U D A H

Jahzah

Hebron

Ashan

Mephaath

Debir
Juttah
Kedemoth

Holon
Eshtemoa

Jattir

M O A B

S I M E O N

Kir-moab

▨ Area of Levite cities

✠ City of refuge

Aaronites Main divisions of the tribe of Levi

0   5   10 miles
0   5   10   15 km

E D O M

108

JOSH. 21; 1 CHRON. 6:39-66

So Absalom stole the hearts of the men of Israel.
(2 Samuel 15:6)

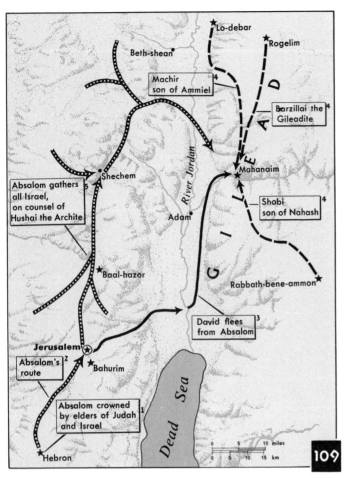

THE REBELLION OF ABSALOM
CA. 978 B.C.

These administrative developments seem to have been felt as a threat to the older tribal leadership. Thus, David's son, Absalom, could play on the sympathies of the leading elders, especially of Judah, and lead them in revolt against his father. Fortunately, David's foreign bodyguards and his elite fighting units maintained their loyalty.

David found refuge in the administrative Levitical center at Mahanaim. The Transjordanians may have felt more strongly the need for a centralized monarchial leadership because of their position on the sensitive eastern frontier and along the major caravan route (the King's Highway) from Arabia to Damascus. The location of Mahanaim, in the deep canyon of the Jabbok, serves to explain how Ahimaaz the son of Zadok outran the Cushite: the Cushite took the more direct route, through the difficult terrain of the "Forest of Ephraim." Ahimaaz ran by a longer but much easier trail along the Jordan Plain and up the course of the Jabbok.

The favorable terms granted by David to the Judahites who had supported Absalom led to a degree of unrest in the north. As a result, Sheba the son of Bichri made an ill-fated attempt at revolt. David's efforts to weld together the diverse tribal and urban elements in his fledgling kingdom were bearing fruit. The institutions that he had fostered, including the Levitical administration and the military establishment, surely felt the need to support the monarchy as the *sine qua non* of their own survival.

2 SAM. 15-19

We have no portion in David, and we have no inheritance in the son of Jesse; every man to his tents, O Israel!
(2 Samuel 20:1)

THE REBELLION OF SHEBA THE SON OF BICHRI CA. 975 B.C.

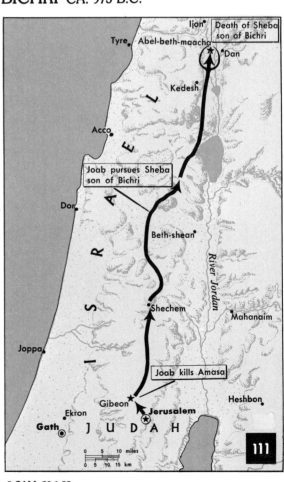

Then Ahimaaz ran by the way of the plain, and outran the Cushite.
(2 Samuel 18-23)

THE BATTLE IN THE FOREST OF EPHRAIM
CA. 975 B.C.

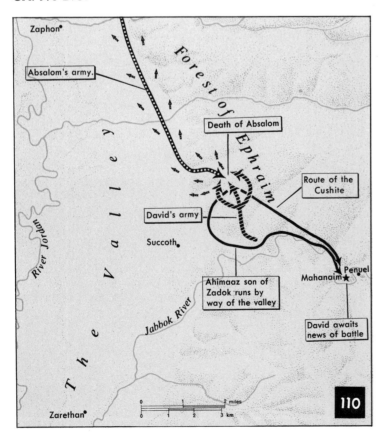

2 SAM. 18

2 SAM. 20:1-22

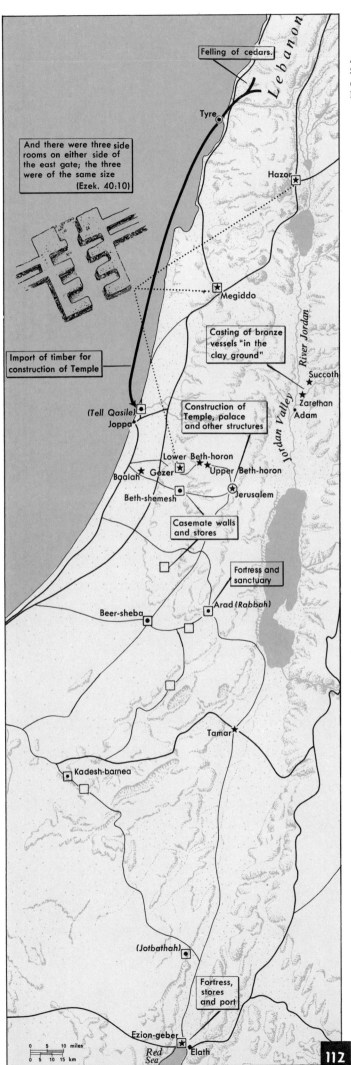

Felling of cedars.

And there were three side rooms on either side of the east gate; the three were of the same size (Ezek. 40:10)

Import of timber for construction of Temple

Casting of bronze vessels "in the clay ground"

Construction of Temple, palace and other structures

Casemate walls and stores

Fortress and sanctuary

Fortress, stores and port

And this is the account of the forced labor which King Solomon levied to build the house of the Lord and his own house and the Millo and the wall of Jerusalem and Hazor and Megiddo and Gezer ...

(1 Kings 9:15)

SOLOMONIC BUILDING PROJECTS
MID-TENTH CENTURY B.C.

King Solomon is credited with being the first major builder in the Davidic dynasty. David is said to have built a palace for himself with Phoenician architects (1 Chron. 14:1-2; 15:2) and there is no reason to doubt that during his long reign he did initiate his own projects. However, the united monarchy reached its apogee after Solomon had assured a steady flow of income from command of the world trade routes. This and a well-organized bureaucracy supported by the military establishment enabled him to harness the manpower now at his disposal. Besides the temple and the royal palace, Solomon built strong fortresses at key points throughout the realm; special mention is made in the Bible of Hazor, Megiddo and Gezer (1 Kings 9:15), where archaeological excavations have revealed almost identical gates, similar in plan to those depicted by Ezekiel as part of the sacred building complex in Jerusalem (Ezek. 40:10). Other sites listed are Lower Beth-horon, Baalath, and Tamar in the wilderness (1 Kings 9:17); there were store cities and cities for the chariotry and the horsemen (vs. 19). The labor force was managed by two separate departments, the levy (*mas*) and the corvée (*sebel*). The levy was imposed upon all the Canaanite and other elements who had only been subdued by David (1 Kings 5:13-14; 9:20; Judg. 1:28, 30, 33, 35); they went in shifts to Lebanon to fell the trees and ship them to Israel. The corvée was recruited from the Israelite tribes; they worked in the hill country of Israel, quarrying stone and transporting it to the building sites; they also provided the labor force for the actual construction (1 Kings 5:15-17; 11:28). Each department had its own cadre of commissioners and overseers.

Solomonic Proto-Aeolian capital from Megiddo

1 KINGS 5-10; 2 CHRON. 2-4; 8-9

☐ Solomonic fortification

ARAM-
DAMASCUS

SIDONIANS

ASHER

NAPHTALI

GESHUR

Argob

Bashan

HAVVOTH-JAIR

Gilead

AMMON

ZEBULUN

ISSACHAR

Mt. Ephraim

(DAN)

BENJAMIN

PHILISTINES

JUDAH

Dead Sea

GAD

(REUBEN)

MOAB

Tyre ⊙

Ijon
Ahlab
Abel-beth-maacah
Dan
Hosah
Kanah
Beth-anath
Kedesh
Hammon
Yiron
Beth-shemesh
Hazor
Achzib • Abdon
Beth-emek
Acco
Rehob
Mishal
Aphek
Cabul
Beten
Hali
Achshaph
Beth-lehem
Helkath
Shimron
Gath-hepher
Sarid
Jokneam
Dor ★

Ramah
Chinnereth
Sea of Chinnereth
Rakkath
Adamah
Hammath
Hannathon
Adami-nekeb
Daberath
Chisloth-tabor
Anaharath
Jabneel
En-haddah
Aphek
Ashtaroth

Megiddo ★
Shunem
Hapharaim
Jarmuth
Lo-debar
Kamon
Beth-arbel
Jezreel ★
Beth-shean ★
Rogelim
Ramoth-gilead ★
Taanach ★
Ibleam
Dothan
Jabesh-gilead
Abel-meholah ★
Socoh ★
Tirzah
Zaphon
Succoth
Mahanaim ★
Shechem
Jokmeam ★
Adam
Ramath-mizpeh
Aphek
Tappuah
Betonim
Joppa
Yehud
Jazer
Rabbath-bene-ammon
Lod
Makaz
Gath-rimmon
Beth-el
Naaran
Beth-nimrah
Gibbethon Lower Beth-horon Mizpeh
Shaalbim
Upper Beth-horon Ramah
Michmash
Mephaath
Gezer ★
Gibeon
Geba
Aijalon ★
Gibeah
Beth-arabah
Beth-haram
Ekron
Heshbon
Ashdod
Beth-shemesh ★
Jerusalem ⊙
Beth-jeshimoth
Beth-peor
Gath ⊙
Kiriathaim
Beth-lehem
Medeba
Bezer
Ashkelon
Beth-baal-meon
Zereth-shahar
Jahzah
Hebron
Ataroth
Kerioth
Dibon
Gaza
Aroer
Mephaath
Kedemoth

Governor of Naphtali is king's son-in-law.

Governor of port-city is king's son-in-law.

Arubboth

LAND OF CABUL

LAND OF HEPHER

Legend:
Border of Solomonic provinces
1 Tribal district
2 Former Canaanite enclave

0   5   10 miles
0 5 10 15 km

113

Solomon had twelve officers over all Israel, who provided
food for the king and his household ...
(1 Kings 4:7)

THE SOLOMONIC COMMISSIONER'S DISTRICTS

The dichotomy between the Israelites of tribal origin and the urban Canaanites was a social and geographical reality of the united monarchy. The non-Israelites who were subjected to the levy lived mainly in the lowland areas such as the coastal plains and the Valley of Jezreel (a notable exception was Beth-shemesh and Beth-anath in Upper Galilee, Judg. 1:32). Solomon's commissioners were assigned territories in accordance with this reality. The old established tribal "inheritances" were recognized and respected; there was no intention to infringe on their integrity. On the other hand, the areas which had remained outside of Israelite tribal occupation until David's reign, were now organized into new districts. The list of Solomon's twelve commissioners and their respective districts (1 Kings 4:7-19) is the most ancient administrative document in the Bible but its text is not well preserved. In spite of some lacunae, it is possible to reconstruct the geographical framework with reasonable certainty. Six of the districts (Nos. 1, 8, 9, 10, 11, 12) are named after tribes and correspond to the areas settled by the Israelites during the Early Iron Age. The town lists for the tribe of Benjamin (Josh. 18:21-27) and for the Galilean tribes, Asher, Naphtali and Issachar (Josh. 19:10-39) may have derived from the records of this Solomonic administration. The Issachar district was settled intensively only in the tenth century B.C. according to recent archaeological survey. The monarchy may have encouraged the Issacharites to move from their original places in the Jezreel Valley up to the tableland, thus freeing them from the onerous levy imposed on the Canaanites down there and also fostering the utilization of this hitherto undeveloped zone. Six other districts (Nos. 2, 3, 4, 5, 6, 7) are defined only by the towns

located in them. They are the areas of the former non-Israelite enclaves of Canaanites, Amorites and others. In two instances, the Solomonic lists are especially defective, namely for districts No. 2 and No. 12. It is highly likely that the original rosters for these two areas are preserved in the Book of Joshua as the tribal inheritances of Dan (Josh. 19:40-46) and Reuben (Josh. 13:15-23) respectively. It must also be noted that there are striking concentrations of Levitical towns in just those lowland and frontier areas of non-Israelite population. There was no attempt to create districts of equal economic potential. Besides sending the monthly provisions for Solomon's palace, the commissioners in the old tribal districts were responsible mainly for the corvée (the best quarries were in those very hill country zones) while the commissioners in the lowland districts were responsible for the levy. Their subjects were mainly Canaanites and others of the pre-Israelite stock. The commissioner in Naphtali evidently had both Canaanites and Israelites to administer. Judah was not included in the twelve but it did have a commissioner. The district divisions of Judah (Map 130) may represent a counterpart to the commissioners' districts but it seems obvious that Judah was considerably favored under the united monarchy.

As Solomon's foreign income began to diminish (due to hostile political elements along the hinterland trade routes), he was compelled to settle a balance-of-payment deficit with Tyre by ceding the "Land of Cabul" to Hiram (1 Kings 9:10-13). Pharaoh Shishak, jealous of Solomon's commercial monopolies, had fostered political refugees from Edom and from Israel, biding his time and looking for an opportunity to end the Israelite hegemony over the Levantine trade routes.

In the fourth year the foundation of the house of the Lord was laid ... He was seven years in building it. Solomon was building his own house thirteen years.
(1 Kings 6:37-7:1)

THE BUILDING AND EXPANSION OF JERUSALEM

MID-TENTH CENTURY B.C.

Solomon extended the limits of Jerusalem, fortifying and embellishing it as befitting the capital of a powerful state. The temple, which took seven years to build, was overshadowed by the royal palace, which took thirteen. The two buildings represented the two leading institutions of the realm, the Aaronic/Levitical religious organization and the monarchy. Each depended upon the other to govern the nation; each had large holdings of land and resources throughout the country.

The threshing floor purchased by David and its hill were converted into a citadel, extending the effective area of the city northward. The technical improvements included massive retaining walls, a sample of which was uncovered in the excavations above the Gihon spring.

On the adjacent hills to the southeast, there were diplomatic missions from Solomon's political allies (as exemplified by his royal marriages, 1 Kings 1:11). Each diplomatic compound had its own shrine for worship of the national deities (1 Kings 11:4-8; 2 Kings 23:13). The wives of Solomon's many political marriages could make offerings at a shrine of their home deity. In his later years Solomon also joined with them in their worship.

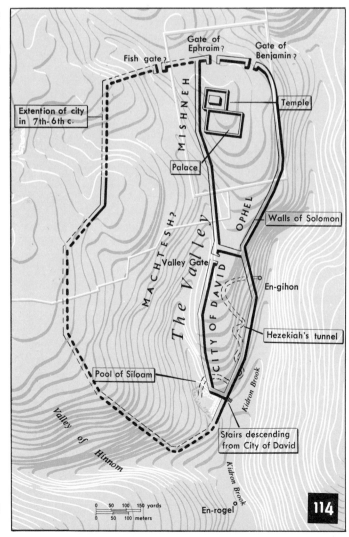

2 SAM. 5:9; 1 KINGS 6-7; 2 KINGS 20:20; 22:14; IS. 22:9-11; 2 CHRON. 2-8; 26:9; 27:3; 32:2-5; 33:14

114

SOLOMON'S TRADE MONOPOLY

Just at a time when there was no great power, either in Egypt or in Mesopotamia, that could dominate the land bridge from Asia to Africa, the newly united nation of Israel gained military and political supremacy over the principal corridors of commerce between the Euphrates and the delta of Egypt (1 Kings 4:21 [Heb. 5:1], 24 [Heb. 5:4]; 2 Chron. 9:26). The small nations adjacent to Israel were politically subordinate, including the Edomites, Moabites, Sidonians (Phoenicians) and the Hittites (Arameans of North Syria); their ties with Solomon's government were symbolized by his marriage alliances (1 Kings 11:1). The population base of the new kingdom had expanded to an extent never before achieved in the country. The fertile grain lands on the plains were joined to the hill regions where orchards and vineyards were under intensive cultivation. Thus, Israel was able to supply the needs of the Phoenician maritime population as well as the needs of the numerous caravans that crossed her territory. In return for fodder and victuals as well as water and military protection, the Israelites received payments in precious metals and in manufactured goods. Some of this income was invested in fortifications, especially of key towns along the leading trade routes (see Map 112). Solomon even launched his own maritime expeditions, with the aid of Phoenician seamen, and brought the exotic products of Somalia and South Arabia to be traded at the seaports of Philistia and Phoenicia. The chief artery of commerce in the Levant, the route from Egypt to Mesopotamia via Jezreel and the Beqa' Valley, or by way of the Jordan fords near Beth-shean to Golan and Damascus, was dominated by Solomon's fortified centers. The "King's Highway" on the Transjordanian plateau, was supervised by Solomon's forces in Bashan, Gilead and the tableland of Moab. The caravans from Ezion-geber to Gaza had to traverse the routes controlled by Solomon's desert and Negeb fortresses. It is no wonder that Hiram of Tyre was so willing to make a treaty of alliance with the kings of Jerusalem.

1 KINGS 5:15-32; 9:26-10:29; 2 CHRON. 1:15-17; 2; 8:17-9:28

A chariot could be imported from Egypt for six hund shekels of silver, and a horse for a hundred and fif they were exported to all the kings of the Hittites the kings of Syria.

(1 Kings 10

KINGS OF ARABIA **115**

THE TRADE OF TYRE 10TH TO 7TH CENTURIES B.C.

The Phoenicians were the unchallenged masters of the sea in Solomon's day though some of the former sea peoples may have shared in the international sea trade. However, Tyre had become the senior power among the city states of the eastern Mediterranean coast. Even Solomon had to depend on Tyrian experts to launch his fleet from Ezion-geber. Phoenician merchantmen were called "ships of Tarshish." Tarsus on the Cilician plain was probably the original Tarshish but, with the spread of Phoenician sea exploration, the name was carried westward; by the ninth century it was applied to Tharros in Sardinia and eventually Tartessos in Spain.

Ezekiel's oracle against Tyre, albeit from the sixth century B.C., must have been based on an older document (related somehow to the Table of Nations in Gen. 10; see Map 15). The role of Phoenicia in ship manufacturing is based on the accessibility of the best woods (Ezek. 27:5-6). Ezekiel recounts the most famous products from the great economic centers of the ancient world. Israel and Judah are known only for their agricultural products, most of which were traded in local markets, especially to feed the population of Phoenicia whose manpower was engaged in the maritime industries. The products from the southern Levant would have had little value as export commodities. But when a strong power such as the united monarchy of Israel, controlled all the caravan routes connecting the main markets with one another, it was possible to reap vast profits from the flow of goods being shipped between the sophisticated societies of Egypt, Mesopotamia, South Arabia, Anatolia and Greece. The partnership between Solomon and Hiram king of Tyre guaranteed an abundant financial harvest for both nations.

Phoenician ship (Relief from palace of Sargon II at Khorsabad)

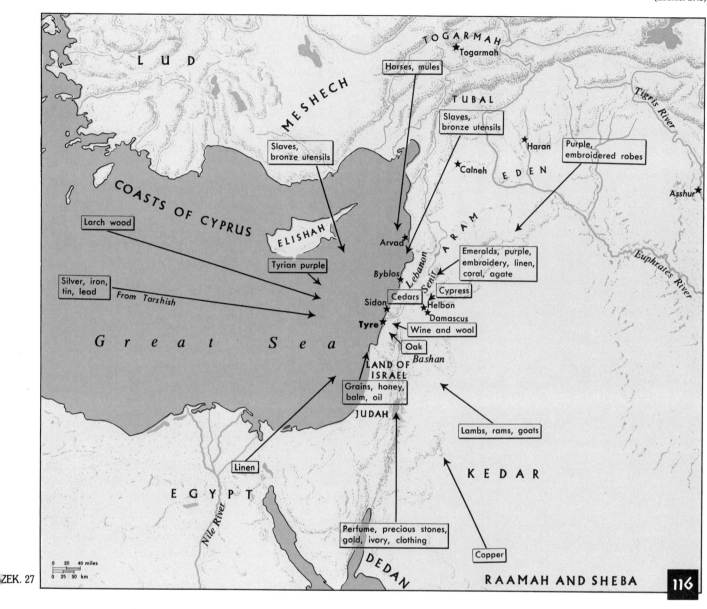

And say to Tyre, who dwells at the entrance to the sea, merchant of the peoples on many coastlands ...
(Ezekiel 27:3)

LUD

MESHECH

TOGARMAH
★ Togarmah

Horses, mules

TUBAL

Slaves,
bronze utensils

★ Haran

EDEN

Purple,
embroidered robes

★ Calneh

Tigris River

★ Asshur

Euphrates River

COASTS OF CYPRUS

Slaves,
bronze utensils

ELISHAH

Larch wood

Tyrian purple

Silver, iron,
tin, lead

From Tarshish

Arvad ★

Byblos ★

Lebanon

ARAM

Senir

Emeralds, purple,
embroidery, linen,
coral, agate

Cedars

Cypress

Sidon ★

Helbon ★

Damascus ★

Great   Sea

Tyre ★

Wine and wool

Oak

Bashan

LAND OF
ISRAEL

Grains, honey,
balm, oil

JUDAH

Lambs, rams, goats

KEDAR

Linen

EGYPT

Nile River

Perfume, precious stones,
gold, ivory, clothing

Copper

0 20 40 miles
0 25 50 km

ZEK. 27

DEDAN

RAAMAH AND SHEBA

116

THE EXPANSION OF THE TYRIANS IN THE MEDITERRANEAN
FROM 9TH CENTURY B.C. ON

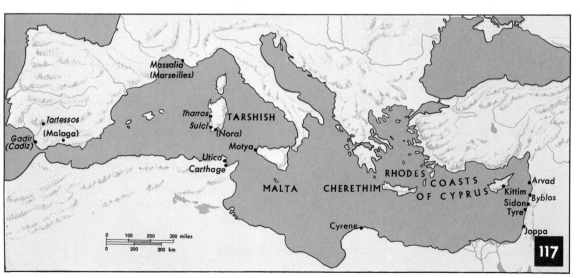

The ships of Tarshish travelled for you with your merchandise. "So you were filled and heavily laden in the heart of the seas."
(Ezekiel 27:25)

Massalia
(Marseilles)

Tharros
Sulci

TARSHISH

Tartessos
(Malaga)

(Nora)

Gadir
(Cadiz)

Motya

Utica
Carthage

RHODES

COASTS
OF CYPRUS

Arvad
Byblos

MALTA

CHERETHIM

Kittim
Sidon
Tyre

Cyrene

Joppa

0 100 200 300 miles
0   200   300 km

117

Then Jeroboam built Shechem ... and he went out from there and built Penuel (1 Kings 12:25)

Royal sanctuary

Coronation of Jeroboam over Israel

Royal sanctuary

118

Rehoboam went to Shechem, for all Israel had come to Shechem to make him king.

(1 Kings 12:1)

THE DIVISION OF THE KINGDOM
931 B.C.

The deep-seated differences between the northern tribes of Israel and the southern alliance of Judah (with Caleb, Kenaz, etc.) were never truly resolved under David and Solomon. The heavy burden of the corvée rankled the people of the north, particularly those of the House of Joseph. Solomon's son, Rehoboam, failed to realize the gravity of their dissatisfaction. His succession in Jerusalem was acknowledged without apparent dissent, but he had to go to Shechem for ratification of his kingship by the tribes of the north. The latter had chosen as their spokesman the recently returned political exile, Jeroboam (who had formerly been in charge of the corvée work carried out by the House of Joseph).

The economic crisis brought about by the external troubles during the latter years of Solomon's reign had made life even more difficult for the citizens of Israel. When Rehoboam haughtily rejected their demands for an easing of their burdens, he foolishly sent an unpopular bureaucrat, Adoniram, to intimidate them. Adoniram was in charge of the hated levy, the forced labor imposed on the formerly non-Israelite enclaves. No wonder that the Israelites expressed their displeasure by stoning him to death! Rehoboam hastened to return to Jerusalem but was dissuaded by the prophet Shemaiah from trying to use armed force against the northern rebels. The population of Benjamin was closely linked with Jerusalem: within its territory there were crown lands, Levitical cities and the Gibeonites did special service at the temple. So Benjamin remained part of the Davidic kingdom.

Damascus and Edom had recently revolted, Ezion-geber was threatened if not lost already; the other neighboring countries were doubtlessly glad to break their ties with the weakened kingdoms of Israel and Judah. The Israelite monopoly over trade and commerce was broken.

Jeroboam I began to organize his new government. Shechem was chosen as the first northern capital and a Transjordan headquarters was set up at Penuel (1 Kings 12:25). Royal worship centers were established at Bethel and Dan, two places with long cultic traditions, one at the southern and the other at the northern extremity of his realm (1 Kings 12:29-30). Other local shrines were also staffed with non-Levitical priests. Shiloh and Tirzah are mentioned (1 Kings 14:4, 17).

1 KINGS 11:26-12:33; 2 CHRON. 10

THE FORTIFICATIONS OF REHOBOAM
CA. 931 TO 926 B.C.

According to the Book of Chronicles, Rehoboam took steps to fortify a network of towns throughout the kingdom of Judah (2 Chron. 11:5-12). There is no reason to doubt the order of events in Chronicles, namely that this attempt to strengthen Judah's defenses came before Shishak's invasion. However, the list of towns in 2 Chron. 11:5-12 may not be complete. On the other hand, the actual work of fortification may not have proceeded at an equal pace at all the sites mentioned. Archaeological investigations at some of the identified towns, Azekah and Beth-zur, have not revealed extensive defense

works from the late tenth century B.C. Yet Lachish (Stratum IV) does have a massive brick wall and triple gate like those at Gezer, Megiddo and Hazor. A certain geographical logic can be seen in Rehoboam's list: protection of the watershed route facing the eastern steppe, Bethlehem, Etam, Tekoa and Ziph; guarding the western approaches, Lachish, Mareshah, (Moresheth-)gath, Azekah, Zorah and Aijalon; and securing internal lines of communication, Socoh and Adoraim. The Levitical cities and some key centers in the Negeb were already fortified.

Rehoboam dwelt in Jerusalem, and he built cities for defense in Judah.

(2 Chronicles 11:5)

Fortified city (Relief from palace of Asshurnasirpal II at Calah)

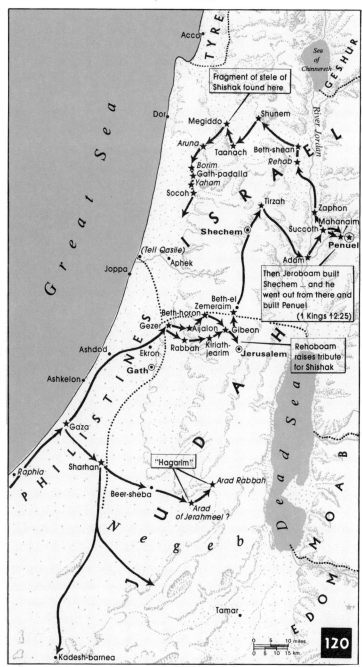

119

—— Road leading into Judah blocked by fortifications

▮▮▮▮ Line of fortifications

░░░░ Road connecting fortresses

2 CHRON. 11:5-12

In the fifth year of King Rehoboam, Shishak king of Egypt came up against Jerusalem ...

(1 Kings 14:25)

THE CAMPAIGN OF PHARAOH SHISHAK
926 B.C.

Egypt was eager to break the Israelite monopoly over commerce and trade in the Levant. In 946 B.C. the twenty-second dynasty was founded by the Libyan Shishak (Sheshonq) I, who ruled from Tanis (Zoan) and Bubastis until 913 B.C. He had encouraged two of Solomon's enemies, Hadad from Edom and Jeroboam from the House of Joseph. Now, five years after Solomon's death, he launched a vigorous attack on the kingdoms of Rehoboam and Jeroboam. The Bible speaks only of an invasion of Judah and of the heavy ransom paid by Rehoboam to save Jerusalem from destruction (2 Chron. 12:2-12; 1 Kings 14:25-28). The Egyptian army comprised Libyans, Sukiim (from the oases of Kharga and Dakhla), and Cushites from Nubia. Only from Shishak's display inscription on the "Bubasite Portal" (which he built on the southwest corner of the Amon temple in Luxor) do we learn that his campaign took him through Jeroboam's realm as well as through the Negeb of Judah. The topographical names are arranged in an upper and a lower register; the upper consists of towns in Israel while the lower contains names from Judah, mainly

1 KINGS 14:25-28; 2 CHRON. 12:2-12; TOPOGRAPHICAL LIST OF SHISHAK — BUBASITE PORTAL, KARNAK, EGYPT

from the Negeb. The course of the campaign as suggested in Map 120 is tentative, based on one method of reconstructing the geographical order of the name (if such really was intended). Other interpretations are equally possible. In spite of the damaged state of the text, there does not seem to be any place where the principal towns of the Judean hill country could have been mentioned. Of Rehoboam's fortified strong points, only Aijalon is named. Kiriath-[jear]im is based on an emendation of q-d-t-m but the name Gibeon is quite clear. It must have been while Shishak was there that he extorted the heavy ransom from Rehoboam. That the list is authentic, and not a copy from earlier pharaohs' inscriptions, is proven by the inclusion of many place names not known before in Egyptian texts and by the use of new spelling conventions for even the well-known places like Megiddo and Beth-shean. At Megiddo the fragment of a statue of Shishak was found showing that he really had occupied the city for a time. His advance into Transjordan against Succoth and Penuel show that he pursued Jeroboam as far as his eastern headquarters. The southern campaign, represented by the lower register of place names, is much more obscure. Few of the names can be identified. Eight places are defined as fortified centers by means of a Semitic term, hqr, corresponding to the late Aramaic Hagra. Besides Patish, only two other "forts" have identifiable names, both of them being Arad. The appearance of two Arads is surprising but not without precedent, especially

in the Negeb. Arad Rabbah is most likely the biblical town at Tel Arad; the "Arad of the House of Yeroham" might be Tel Malhata but this is uncertain. The "fort" of 'brm is hardly a reference to Abram; most likely it is Abelim like the similar usage in Thutmose III's inscriptions. Three areas bear the appellation "The Negeb" and the clans associated with two of these Negebs might be the Eznites (2 Sam. 23:8) and the Shuahites (1 Chron. 4:11). There is a reference to "The Fountains of Geber" which has been taken to represent Ezion-geber but the latter was probably in Edomite hands by now.

Shishak's prime objective was to destroy the key fortified centers of both Israel and Judah. Thus he put an end to their ability to dominate the caravan routes passing through the Jordan and Jezreel Valleys in the north and through the Negeb in the south. Fortunately for Jeroboam and Rehoboam, Shishak was not strong enough to convert his raid into a conquest. Whatever had caused him to use force against Jeroboam, his former protégé, is not known. It would seem that he had been encouraged to come by the Philistines who were weary of being subservient to the power of the united monarchy of Israel.

In his twenty-fifth year (925 B.C.), Shishak issued orders to open a quarry for the production of stone used in building the Bubasite Portal on which he inscribed the proclamation of his successful campaign to Palestine.

Then Abijah stood up on Mount Zemaraim which is in the hill country of Ephraim, and said, "Hear me, O Jeroboam and all Israel!"

(2 Chronicles 13:4)

ABIJAH'S CONQUEST

CA. 911 B.C.

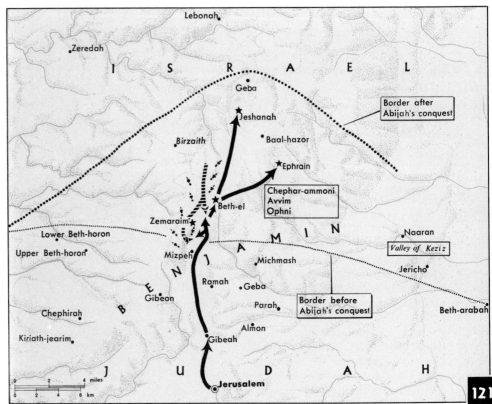

◄▐▥▥▥▥▥▥ Israelite force

◄▬▬▬ Judean force

2 CHRON. 13; JOSH. 18:21-24

A state of belligerence between Judah and Israel continued throughout the reigns of Rehoboam, Abijah and Asa kings of Judah, and the dynasties of Jeroboam and Baasha in Israel. After Shishak's campaign, both kingdoms were doubtless exhausted; the first open conflict we hear about took place in the short reign of Abijah (913-911/910 B.C.). After a bitter confrontation at Zemaraim the Israelites retreated, leaving the towns of Beth-el, Jeshanah and Ephrain (Ophrah) at the mercy of the Judeans. Abijah thus pushed the border between the two nations north of Beth-el, probably encompassing the district of

Benjamin north of the "official" tribal border (see Map 73) as reflected in the tribal town list (Josh.18:22-24).

Jeroboam I died shortly after this crushing defeat and was succeeded by his son Nadab who soon found himself at war with the Philistines. He was assassinated by Baasha son of Ahijah while he and the Israelite army was besieging Gibbethon (1 Kings 15:27; 909 B.C.). Meanwhile, Abijah had also gone to his fate and had been succeeded by his son Asa (911/910 B.C.). Baasha evidently did not pursue the war with Philistia; he may have maintained a belligerent stance towards Judah but probably found it necessary to concern himself with internal affairs. Asa thus enjoyed a decade of peace (ca. 909-899 B.C.) in which to rebuild the strength of Judah (2 Chron. 13:23-14:7).

That peace was shattered by the invasion of Zerah the Cushite with an army of Cushites. Zerah was probably an Arabian leader from the northern Hejaz (cf. Gen. 10:7; Hab. 3:7; 2 Chron. 21:16) (ruled 904-890 B.C.). He may have been invited by the Philistines to attack Judah. He may have begun by destroying some of the newly rebuilt Judean fortresses in the Negeb, such as Beer-sheba. When he tried to penetrate the Shephelah of Judah, Asa routed his forces in the valley "north of Mareshah" (following the Greek version). The army of Judah pursued the enemy back through the western Negeb; there they ravaged and plundered the sedentary population in the towns and the pastoralists in their tent camps, "throughout the vicinity of Gerar" (2 Chron. 14:13-14). In the wake of this victory, Asa capitalized on the national spirit to reform the religious institutions and to strengthen the central temple cult which supported the monarchy. His national convocation took place in 896 B.C., his fifteenth year (2 Chron. 15:10), that is the thirty-fifth year of the separate Judean monarchy (2 Chron. 15:19).

The respite in hostilities between Israel and Judah was rudely interrupted in Asa's sixteenth year, 895 B.C., the thirty-sixth year of the Judean monarchy (2 Chron. 16:1), when Baasha invaded the Benjaminite territory and established a strong point at Ramah. By seizing the junction between the watershed trunk road and the Beth-horon road, Baasha was able to cut Jerusalem off from its most important road link with the coastal plain (1 Kings 15:17; 2 Chron. 16:1). Asa preferred a political maneuver rather than risk another military confrontation with his northern neighbor. He sent a large bribe to Ben-hadad I (a dynastic name), "the king of Aram enthroned in Damascus." The latter invaded northern Israel and occupied most, if not all, of eastern Galilee (1 Kings 15:20; 2 Chron. 16:4).

Baasha withdrew from Ramah and returned to his headquarters at Tirzah. Asa brought out his people and dismantled the fortifications Baasha had built and used the building materials to fortify Mizpeh, on the main trunk road to Beth-el, and Geba, facing the secondary eastern road that skirts the steppe land. It would appear that most of Abijah's territorial gains in the hill country of Ephraim were relinquished at this time. A logical border between Israel and Judah was established between Mizpeh and Bethel; to the west some territory may have remained in dispute (cf. 2 Chron. 25:13).

they smote all the cities round about Gerar...
(2 Chronicles 14:14)

E CAMPAIGN OF ZERAH THE CUSHITE CA. 898 B.C.

BAASHA'S ATTACK ON ASA
CA. 895 B.C.

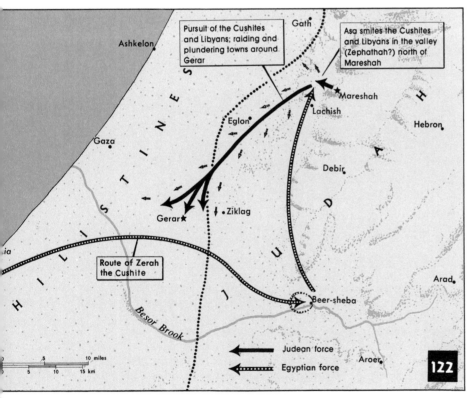

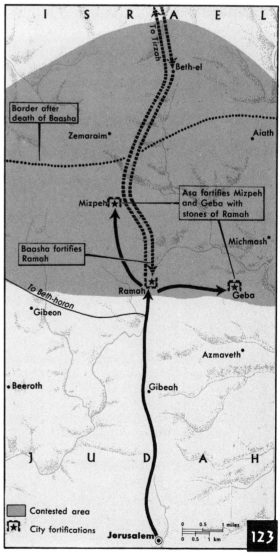

And they carried away the stones of Ramah and its timber, with which Baasha had been building; and with them King Asa built Geba of Benjamin and Mizpah.
(1 Kings 15:22)

HRON. 19:8-14; 15:1-19; 16:8

1 KINGS 16:16-22: 2 KINGS 17:1-6; 2 CHRON. 16:1-10

And Ben-hadad hearkened to King Asa, and sent the
commanders of his armies against the cities of Israel,
and conquered Ijon, Dan, Abel-beth-maacah, and all
Chinneroth, with all the land of Naphtali.

(1 Kings 15:20)

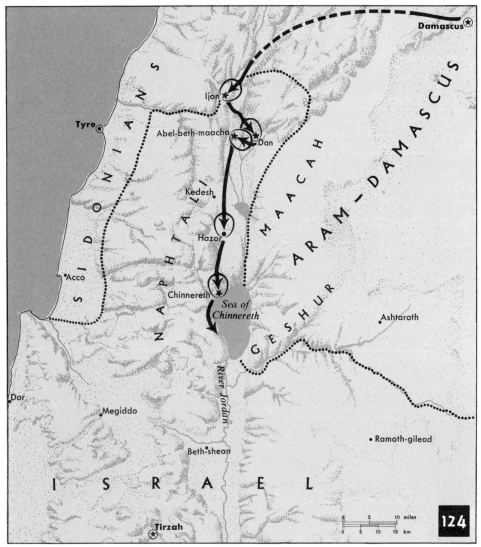

THE CAMPAIGN
OF BEN-HADAD I
895/894 B.C.

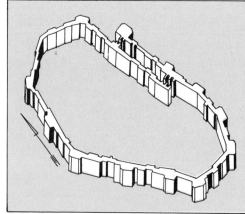

Plan of wall of Mizpeh in the days of Asa

1 KINGS 15:18-21; 2 CHRON. 16:2-5

THE RISE OF OMRI

885/884 B.C.

Baasha's son Elah succeeded his father at Tirzah but soon
found it necessary to renew the war at Gibbethon against the
Philistines. In the second year of his reign he was assassinated
by Zimri. The army at Gibbethon appointed Omri as king and
one week later Zimri had been dispatched. However, a rival
contender, Tibni, plunged the country into a six-year civil
war until Omri and his followers gained the upper hand. For
the next six years (880 to 874/873 B.C.) Omri vigorously went
about the strengthening of his kingdom with an eye to the
ultimate confrontation with Aram-Damascus.

Omri purchased the settlement of Shemer on a hill which

he named Samaria (Heb. *Shomron*) and built a new capital (1
Kings 16:24). The choice of a westward facing site suited his
diplomatic policy of renewing the partnership with Phoenicia.
His son Ahab was united in marriage with Jezebel, daughter
of Etho-baal king of Tyre. A truce was arranged with Judah
and Athaliah married Jehoram son of Jehoshaphat.

As a first step in the war for supremacy over Transjordan,
Omri occupied Medeba and fortified the towns of Ataroth (for
the Gadites living there) and Jahaz facing the steppe land. He
thus regained control over most of the tableland except Dibon
in the south. The stage was set for the clash with Aram.

Ivory carving in Phoenician style from Samaria (Time of Ahab)

All Israel made Omri, the commander of the army, king over Israel that day in the camp.

(1 Kings 16:16)

1 KINGS 16:15-28; 2 KINGS 8:18, 26;
2 CHRON. 21:6; 22:2; MESHA STELE,
LINES 4b-5, 10-11, 18-19

⟵⟵⟵⟵ Aramean force

-◁▯▯▯▯▯▯▯ Israelite force

Ben-hadad the king of Syria gathered all his army together; thirty-two kings were with him, and horses and chariots ...

(1 Kings 20:1)

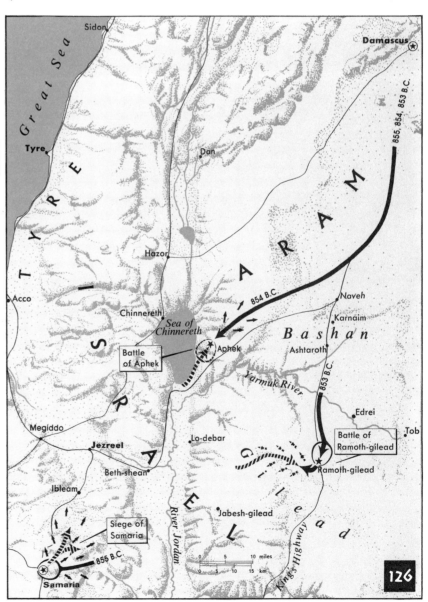

AB'S WARS WITH ARAM

TO 853 B.C.

b pushed ahead with the program launched by his father.
clash of interests with Aram-Damascus was inevitable.
Arameans took the initiative by invading Israel and being Samaria itself but their feudal social structure, a league
vassal kings, made it impossible to exercise a unified
mand; the kinglets were routed in a surprise attack as
lounged in their pavilions (1 Kings 20:1-22). As a result,
king of Damascus reorganized his kingdom and replaced
kings with governors. However, the initiative had passed
Ahab, who carried the battle to Aphek on the heights
ve Chinnereth. His decisive victory won him political and
e concessions from the Aramean (1 Kings 20:23-43). There
wed a three-year armistice between the two countries
ing which time all the states of the Levant banded together
ace the invasion by Shalmaneser III at Qarqar (see Map
). Afterwards Damascus issued another challenge to Israel
Ahab appealed to Jehoshaphat to help him. Jehoshaphat
ed and appointed his son, Jehoram, as co-regent to protect
succession (2 Kings 1:17; 3:1; 8:16). The battle was drawn
Ramoth-gilead; Ahab lost his life and Damascus gained the
er hand in Transjordan (2 Kings 22:1-40; 2 Chron. 18:2-34).

1 KINGS 20:1-34; 22:1-40; 2 CHRON. 18:1-34

THE BATTLE OF QARQAR
853 B.C.

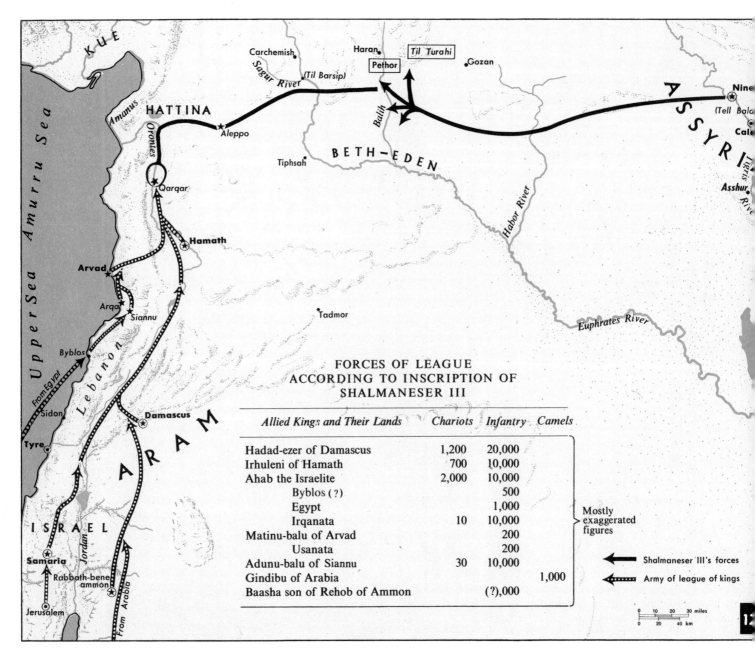

FORCES OF LEAGUE ACCORDING TO INSCRIPTION OF SHALMANESER III

Allied Kings and Their Lands	Chariots	Infantry	Camels
Hadad-ezer of Damascus	1,200	20,000	
Irhuleni of Hamath	700	10,000	
Ahab the Israelite	2,000	10,000	
Byblos (?)		500	
Egypt		1,000	
Irqanata	10	10,000	
Matinu-balu of Arvad		200	
Usanata		200	
Adunu-balu of Siannu	30	10,000	
Gindibu of Arabia			1,000
Baasha son of Rehob of Ammon		(?),000	

Mostly exaggerated figures

→ Shalmaneser III's forces

◄┅┅ Army of league of kings

0 10 20 30 miles
0 20 40 km

1 KINGS 22:1; MONUMENT, SHALMANESER III — CALAH; OTHER INSCRIPTIONS — ASSYRIA

The states of the Levant were rudely shaken by the resurgence of Assyrian might in the ninth century B.C. About 1100 B.C. Tiglath-pileser I, king of Assyria, had reached the "Upper Sea" (the Mediterranean), but under his successors Assyria again reverted to a minor status. Asshurnasirpal II (883-859 B.C.) inaugurated a new expansionist policy. His armies reached Syria and the coastal cities of Phoenicia—Arvad, Byblos, Tyre and Sidon—and extorted heavy tribute. His son, Shalmaneser III (859-824 B.C.), continued this aggressive policy; in his first year his army reached the Amanus Mountains.

The campaign of his sixth year (853 B.C.) saw him march forth from Nineveh to the ford of the Euphrates near Pethor, which he crossed in flood tide. He continued via Aleppo to the territory subservient to the king of Hamath, capturing and plundering. This time the Levantine states had ceased their local quarrels (1 Kings 22:1) and had banded together

to stop the invader. They met him in battle at Qarqar on the Orontes and dealt the Assyrian army a heavy blow. Though Shalmaneser III claimed a victory, he did not return to this area for another four years.

The only detailed report of this battle is a provincial Assyrian stele the text of which is replete with mistakes. The list of the Levantine allies is probably quite authentic but the number of chariots and infantry supposedly brought by each is highly exaggerated. The 500 men from Byblos, the thousand men from Egypt, and the ten chariots from Irqanata may be correct (also the 30 chariots from Siannu, etc.). But the thousands of chariots and troops assigned to Hadad-ezer, Irhuleni, Ahab and others are patently false. This inscription should not be taken as evidence of some mighty chariot force at Ahab's disposal. In reality, he probably had about twenty chariots; compare the chariot forces of Irqanata and Siannu. Judah does not seem to have taken part unless her forces are subsumed under those of Ahab.

Throughout the ninth century, the Assyrian army was making adventurous forays into Syria and other areas, far from their home bases. They were constantly facing a difficult logistic problem. Only by successfully plundering hapless cities and their surrounding countryside could they keep up their momentum. There was always a chance that a well-supplied city could survive unscathed.

After the Assyrian army withdrew, the local states began once again to engage in their local wars. Such was the case between Damascus and Israel. Within a few months at most, Ahab was slain on the field of battle at Ramoth-gilead.

King of Assyria at head of army (Bronze relief of Shalmaneser III from Tell Balawat)

I am Mesha, son of Chemosh, king of Moab, the Dibonite ... I made this high-place for Chemosh ... for he delivered me from all the kings and gave me to prevail over all my enemies.

(Moabite stone, lines 1-4)

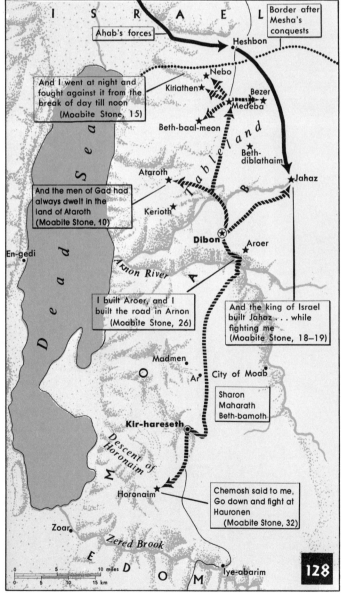

Border after Mesha's conquests

Ahab's forces

And I went at night and fought against it from the break of day till noon (Moabite Stone, 15)

And the men of Gad had always dwelt in the land of Ataroth (Moabite Stone, 10)

I built Aroer, and I built the road in Arnon (Moabite Stone, 26)

And the king of Israel built Jahaz . . . while fighting me (Moabite Stone, 18–19)

Sharon Maharath Beth-bamoth

Chemosh said to me, Go down and fight at Hauronen (Moabite Stone, 32)

←——— Israelite force

-◁|(||||||||||| Moabite force

MOABITE STONE —
DIBON, TRANSJORDAN

THE CAMPAIGNS OF MESHA KING OF MOAB   853-852 B.C.

When Ahab died, Mesha king of Moab saw his chance to regain control of the entire Moabite plateau north of the Arnon. His first move was to attack the Israelite headquarters at Medeba. Then he established new forts at (Beth)-baal-meon and at Kiriathen (Kiriathaim). The Gadite fortress at Ataroth was now cut off from Gilead or the Jordan Valley. Mesha conquered it and slew the entire population. Its "altar hearth of David" was taken as spoil to the Moabite cult center at Kerioth. Mesha settled Ataroth with his own people from Sharon and Maharath. Next he turned his attention to Nebo; Mesha approached it by night and launched his attack at the crack of dawn and by high noon, the place was captured. The population was put to death and the cult vessels of Israel's Lord were taken to be presented as an offering to Chemosh. A king of Israel, most likely Ahaziah, attempted a counterattack from the frontier fort of Yahaz. Again Mesha was victorious.

The Moabite king recounts his building projects at key centers, including Aroer and the highway across the Arnon, Beth-bamoth, and Bezer. He also refortified Medeba, Beth-diblathaim and Beth-baal-meon. He carried out extensive building on the citadel of Dibon and saw to its water supply.

Mesha stele

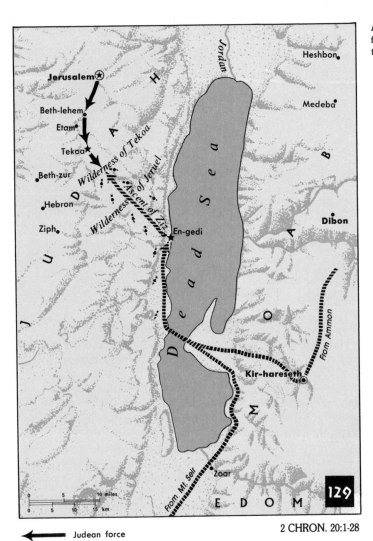

2 CHRON. 20:1-28

⬅️ Judean force

◀‖‖‖‖‖‖ Moabite and allied force

A great multitude is coming against you from Edom from beyond the sea; and, behold, they are in Hazazon-tamar (that is, En-gedi).

(2 Chronicles 20:2)

MOABITES AND THEIR ALLIES ATTEMPT TO INVADE JUDAH

Mesha skips over his ill-fated invasion of Judah (2 Chron. 20:1-28). Jehoshaphat had a powerful, well-fortified kingdom, controlling the trade routes between Arabia and Philistia (2 Chron 17:10-13). His support of Israel posed a threat to Ben-hadad. Mesha, an enemy of Israel, was a natural ally of Damascus. Mesha's invasion force was made up of Moabites, Ammonites and Minaeans (Greek version; probably the Meunites, 2 Chron 20:1, in western Mt. Seir, 2 Chron. 20:10, 23; they were among the Arabians paying tribute to Jehoshaphat for use of the caravan routes to Philistia, 2 Chron. 17:11). At the instigation of Aram (2 Chron. 20:2), they crossed the Dead Sea and established a base camp at En-gedi. Jehoshaphat and his people had come out to the steppe land of Tekoa when they discovered that the invaders were in a turmoil among themselves. The invasion attempt was a failure.

Then he said, "By which way shall we march?" Jehoram answered, "By the way of the wilderness of Edom."
(2 Kings 3:8)

ISRAEL AND JUDAH INVADE MOAB; JEHORAM'S LOSSES

852, 848 B.C.

Failure of the Moabite attack left Jehoshaphat in control of the southern routes, including the base at Ezion-geber. In partnership with Ahaziah, king of Israel, he attempted to launch ships for trade with Ophir but they were wrecked (1 Kings 22:49; 2 Chron. 20:35-37). After the untimely death of Ahaziah, his brother Joram went with Jehoshaphat to invade Moab. The king of Edom, a vassal of Judah, also took part. The allies chose to invade Moab from the south, to avoid the possible danger of a counterattack by the Arameans or the Ammonites. They marched by the "way of Edom," around the southern end of the Dead Sea. On the desert road they suffered from extreme heat and thirst until they were saved by a flash flood, a phenomenon not uncommon in the canyons of the Arabah. Rain had fallen on the plateau above, causing a sudden run-off down below. The invaders wreaked havoc with the southern Moabite countryside. It may be their ascent by the "way of Horonaim" (Isaiah 15:5; Jeremiah 38:3, 5, 34) that Mesha refers to in his inscription, "Then Chemosh said

2 KINGS 1:1; 3:4-24; 8:20-22; 2 CHRON. 21:2-17

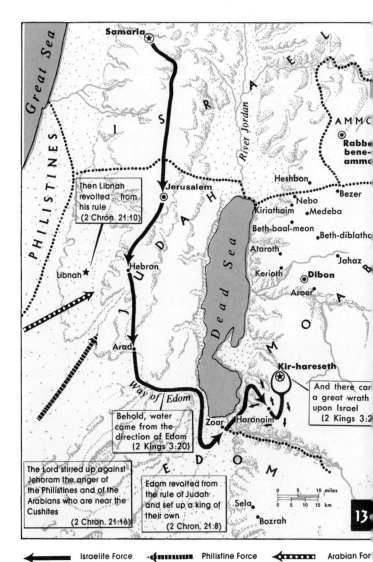

Then Libnah revolted ... from his rule (2 Chron. 21:10)

And there car a great wrath upon Israel (2 Kings 3:2

Behold, water came from the direction of Edom (2 Kings 3:20)

The Lord stirred up against Jehoram the anger of the Philistines and of the Arabians who are near the Cushites (2 Chron. 21:16)

Edom revolted from the rule of Judah and set up a king of their own (2 Chron. 21:8)

⬅️ Israelite Force   ◀‖‖‖‖‖‖ Philistine Force   ◀⟨⟨⟨⟨⟨⟨ Arabian For

to me, 'Go down, do battle at Horonen, so I went down and [fought...]'" (Moabite stone, lines 32-33). Whether or not, Mesha was forced to withstand a siege in his southern capital, Kir-haroseth. The young man sacrificed on the walls of the city was evidently the captured son of the Edomite ruler. This brought about a change in the course of the fighting and the allies were forced to withdraw.

Jehoshaphat died in 848 B.C., leaving Jehoram as sole ruler. His wife was Athaliah from the royal family in Samaria. Jehoram slew all his brothers who had enjoyed positions of authority in the kingdom (2 Chron. 21:2-4). Then Edom broke away and Jehoram tried unsuccessfully to force them back (2 Chron.

21:8-10; also 2 Kings 8:20-22). Because he also established cult centers in the hill country of Judah, in competition with the Jerusalem temple, Libnah the leading priestly-Levitical city in the Shephelah also declared itself in rebellion (2 Chron. 21:10-11). This left his southwestern flank unprotected, inviting an invasion by the Philistines and the Arabians, who sought revenge for the heavy tribute forced on them by Jehoshaphat. They plundered the royal treasury and slew all the king's offspring except the heir, Jehoahaz/Ahaziah (2 Chron. 21:16-17), who became king when Jehoram died of an incurable stomach disease (841 B.C.; 2 Chron. 21:18-20).

THE REBELLION OF JEHU 841 B.C.

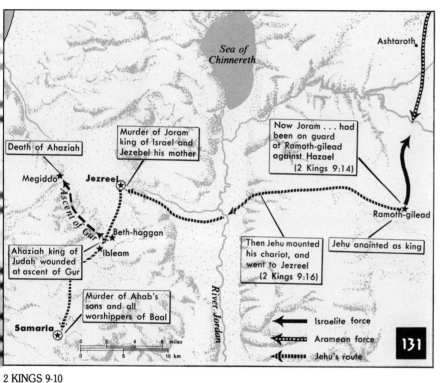

2 KINGS 9-10

Jezebel heard of it; and she painted her eyes, and adorned her head, and looked out of the window. And as Jehu entered the gate, she said, "Is it peace, you Zimri, murderer of your master?"

(2 Kings 9:30-31)

"Woman-in-the-window" on ivory plaque (From Calah)

The hostility between Aram and Israel continued through the reign of Joram; the newly crowned Ahaziah of Judah went with Joram to confront the Arameans at Ramoth-gilead (2 Kings 8:28; 2 Chron. 22:5). Joram was wounded and returned to the royal winter headquarters at Jezreel. Ahaziah came down to visit him. Jehu's revolt, instigated by the prophets,

resulted in the assassination of Joram and his mother, Jezebel. Ahaziah was also mortally smitten and died of his wounds at Megiddo. Jehu launched a wholesale extermination of the Baalistic infrastructure throughout his kingdom. Israel lost her Phoenician ally and was seriously disrupted internally.

THE CAMPAIGN OF SHALMANEZER III 841 B.C.

Shalmaneser III continued his campaigns in Syria in 849, 848, and 845 B.C., though he did not achieve his aims, for in each of these campaigns he came up against the armies of the league of Syrian kings under the leadership of Hadadezer (the son of Hadad) king of Aram-damascus.

Shortly before Jehu's revolt in Israel, Hazael revolted against Ben-hadad and founded a new dynasty in Damascus. In the year 841 B.C. Shalmaneser again came to Syria, this time successfully defeating Hazael at Mount Senir and subsequently laying siege to Damascus, but the city held out. He continued to the mountains of Hauran, destroying many cities, and proceeded westward, destroying Beth-arbel (Hosea 10:14) and probably Hazor (stratum VIII). Reaching the mountain "Baali-rasi" ("Baal-rosh"), on the coast, he set up his statue. The mountain is probably Mount Carmel, a center of the worship

of Baal, known from the accounts of Elijah and other sources. In the Egyptian sources, the Carmel is called "Rosh-kedesh," and the meaning of the name "Baal-rosh" is probably "The Baal of the headland." In this period, the border between Tyre and Israel passed through Carmel, and thus it was here that Shalmaneser received tribute from Tyre and Israel. The kingdom of Israel was known to the Assyrians as the "Land of the House of Omri"; therefore, Jehu, too, is mentioned in their sources as a "son of Omri." He is thus called on the Black Obelisk of Shalmaneser. Shalmaneser moved northward from the Carmel along the Phoenician coast, having an additional victory monument carved into the cliffside at the mouth of Nahr el-Kalb (the Dog River, called the Lycus in Hellenistic times) alongside Assyrian and Egyptian monuments left there before him.

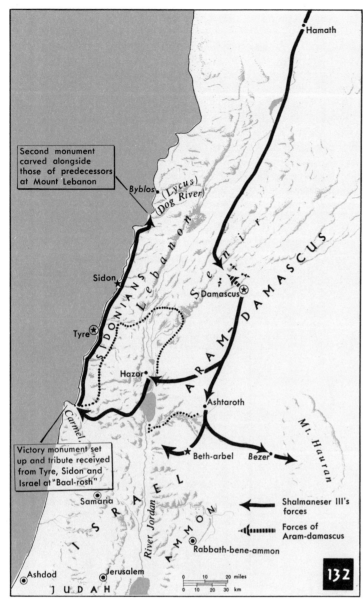

ARAMEAN SUPREMACY CA. 841-798 B.C.

The ensuing years saw Assyria becoming entangled in affairs far removed from the Levant. During the reigns of Jehu (841-814 B.C.) and Jehoahaz (814/813-798 B.C.), Hazael had free rein to conquer Transjordan. The Aramean brutality in Gilead was long remembered (Amos 1:3). Israel's borders were diminished and its military strength curtailed (2 Kings 13:7).

Queen Athaliah of Judah had slain her grandchildren and seized power. One infant, Joash, was rescued and reared in secret by the high priest, Jehoiada. When the child was six (835 B.C.), Athaliah was assassinated during a coup d'état. After Jehoiada died (ca. 800), Joash allowed the princes of Judah to reopen local shrines in competition with the Jerusalem establishment. Zechariah, son of Jehoiada, denounced the king and was summarily executed (2 Chron. 24:17-24).

Near the end of Hazael's long reign but prior to the death of Jehoahaz in Israel and of Joash in Judah, the Aramean army made a foray down the coastal plain (ca. 798 B.C.) and conquered a town named Gath, possibly Gath of the Philistines but more likely Gath(-rimmon)/Gittaim. Hazael's forces then threatened Judah. Though outnumbered, their relatively small strike force defeated the Judean army. After paying a heavy ransom, Joash became desperately ill. Soon afterward, a palace intrigue led to his death (796 B.C.).

THE CAMPAIGN OF SHALMANEZER III

I received tribute from the inhabitants of Tyre, Sidon and from Jehu, son of Omri.
(Annals of Shalmaneser III)

"Jehu the son of Omri" paying tribute to Shalmaneser III
(Black Obelisk, from Nimrud)

In those days the Lord began to cut off parts of Israel. Hazael defeated them throughout the territory of Israel
(1 Kings 10

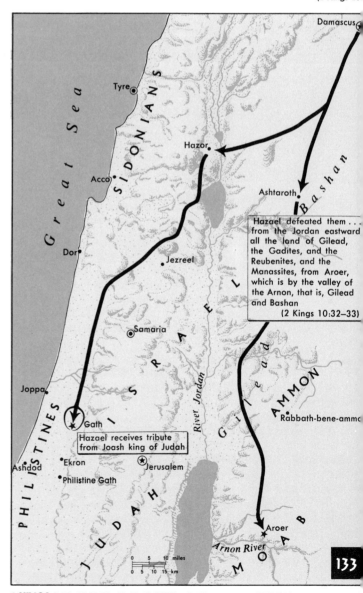

2 KINGS 8:12; 10:32-33; 12:17-18 (HEB. 18-19); 13:3, 7; 2 CHRON. 24:23-24; AMOS 1:3

THE WANDERINGS OF ELIJAH
MID-NINTH CENTURY B.C.

I have been very jealous for the Lord, the God of hosts; for the people of Israel have forsaken thy covenant...
(1 Kings 19:14)

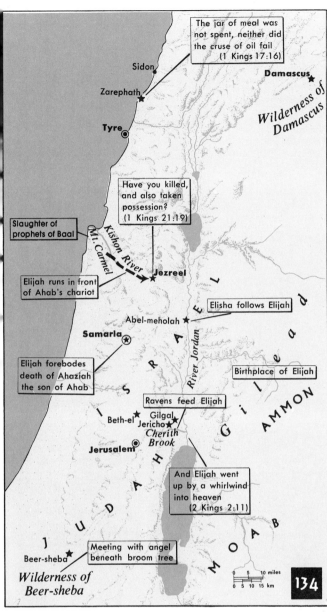

The jar of meal was not spent, neither did the cruse of oil fail (1 Kings 17:16)

Sidon

Zarephath

Tyre

Damascus

Wilderness of Damascus

Have you killed, and also taken possession? (1 Kings 21:19)

Slaughter of prophets of Baal

Mt. Carmel

Kishon River

Jezreel

Elijah runs in front of Ahab's chariot

Elisha follows Elijah

Abel-meholah

Samaria

Elijah forebodes death of Ahaziah the son of Ahab

Birthplace of Elijah

Ravens feed Elijah

Beth-el   Gilgal
Jericho
Cherith
Brook

Jerusalem

And Elijah went up by a whirlwind into heaven (2 Kings 2:11)

River Jordan

ISRAEL   GILEAD   AMMON

JUDAH

MOAB

Beer-sheba

Meeting with angel beneath broom tree

Wilderness of Beer-sheba

0 5 10 miles
0 5 10 15 km

134

1 KINGS 19:16-21; 2 KINGS 2-9; 13

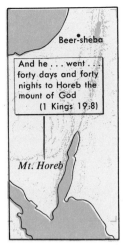

And he . . . went . . . forty days and forty nights to Horeb the mount of God (1 Kings 19:8)

Beer-sheba

Mt. Horeb

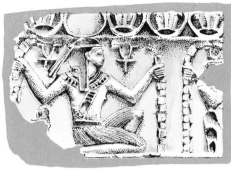

Carved ivory from Samaria (Time of Ahab)

And Jehu the son of Nimshi you shall anoint to be king over Israel; and Elisha the son of Shaphat of Abel-meholah you shall anoint to be prophet in your place.
(1 Kings 19:16)

THE ACTIVITIES OF ELISHA
LATE 9TH CENTURY B.C.

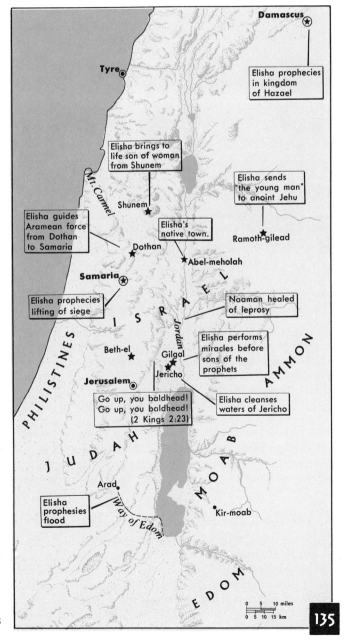

Damascus

Elisha prophecies in kingdom of Hazael

Tyre

Mt. Carmel

Elisha brings to life son of woman from Shunem

Shunem

Elisha sends "the young man" to anoint Jehu

Elisha's native town.

Ramoth-gilead

Elisha guides Aramean force from Dothan to Samaria

Dothan

Abel-meholah

Samaria

Elisha prophecies lifting of siege

Naaman healed of leprosy

ISRAEL

PHILISTINES

Beth-el

Gilgal
Jericho

Elisha performs miracles before sons of the prophets

AMMON

Jerusalem

Go up, you baldhead! Go up, you baldhead! (2 Kings 2:23)

Elisha cleanses waters of Jericho

JUDAH

MOAB

Arad

Elisha prophesies flood

Way of Edom

Kir-moab

EDOM

0 5 10 miles
0 5 10 15 km

135

Prophets had played a role in the public life of Israel and Judah from the days of the united monarchy. After the division, there are numerous references to prophets as political advisors and critics, especially in Judah. During the dark age of Baalism under the Omrides, two prophets stand out as champions of the Lord of Israel against the influences of that Canaanite (Phoenician) religion, namely Elijah from Gilead and his disciple, Elisha from the Jordan Valley. The ties between the royal houses of Omri and Ethobaal of Tyre brought an influx of Phoenician cultural and political influences. The spirit behind Israelite law was beyond the grasp of Jezebel the daughter of the king of Tyre, and she decided to instruct Ahab on how to "govern the kingdom of Israel" (1 Kings 21:7). The murder of Naboth the Jezreelite through a perversion of justice provoked the wrath of Elijah, and his admonition "hast thou killed, and also taken possession?" (1 Kings 21:19) still reverberates in the world today. The activities and missions of Elijah and Elisha extended beyond the borders and included various peoples, for in the view of the prophets these, too, were to be considered a tool in the hands of the Lord.

1 KINGS 17-21: KINGS 1:2-2:18

The Lord gave Israel a saviour, so that they escaped from the hand of the Syrians ...
(2 Kings 13:5)

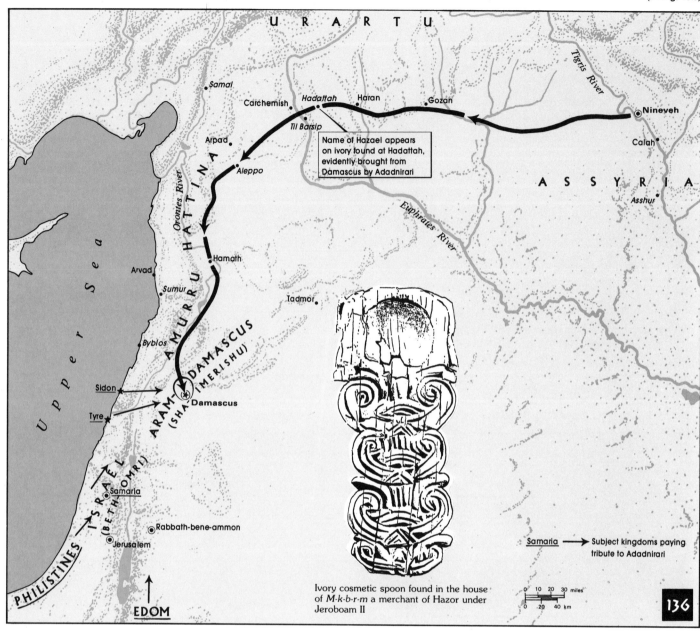

Name of Hazael appears on ivory found at Hadattah, evidently brought from Damascus by Adadnirari

Samaria ⟶ Subject kingdoms paying tribute to Adadnirari

Ivory cosmetic spoon found in the house of M-k-b-r-m a merchant of Hazor under Jeroboam II

0 10 20 30 miles
0 20 40 km

136

MONUMENTS, ADADNIRARI III — CALAH AND SABAA

A new and energetic king arose in Assyria, Adad-nirari III, who once again turned his face westward. The Eponym Chronicle (list of the years, named after Assyrian governors, with significant events) records the following: (805 B.C.) "against Arpad," (804 B.C.) "against Hazazi," (803 B.C.) "against Ba'ali," (802 B.C.) "to the Sea." The next campaign in the west was: (796 B.C.) "against Mansuate," a province just north of Damascus. It must have been during that conflict that Damascus itself was besieged; "Mari" (the Ben-hadad III of 2 Kings 13:3) of Damascus was forced to pay a heavy tribute. Tribute was also received from Jehoash of "the land of Samerina (Samaria),"

called "the land of Omri" in another inscription, as well as Edom and Philistia. Damascus was so crippled by this defeat that it also became embroiled in renewed conflict with its arch-rival, Hamath.

In his later years Adad-nirari III and also his successor, Shalmaneser IV, were fully occupied with a war against Urartu (Ararat), the neo-Hurrian kingdom in eastern Anatolia. This last respite from Assyrian pressure created a power vacuum in the west that permitted the vigorous rulers of Israel and Judah to exert their power and influence throughout the region.

THE WARS OF AMAZIAH AND JEHOASH CA. 793 TO 792 B.C.

Amaziah succeeded Joash in 796 B.C. and sought an alliance with Jehoash of Israel (2 Kings 14:9; 2 Chron. 25:18). Then he set out to conquer Edom accompanied by Israelite mercenaries, whom he dismissed before the battle. He was victorious over the Edomites and reestablished Judean control over it (2 Kings 14:7; 2 Chron. 25:5-13). The angry Israelite troops ransacked Judean towns that had formerly been taken from Israel and Amaziah retaliated by challenging Jehoash to combat. Jehoash appointed Jeroboam II as co-regent before confronting Amaziah

at Beth-shemesh (793 B.C.). He defeated Amaziah and took him prisoner. Part of Jerusalem's defenses were torn down. The people in Jerusalem appointed the sixteen-year-old Azariah (Uzziah) as king (792 B.C.) in place of his captive father (2 Kings 14:21; 2 Chron. 26:2). Amaziah was not released until the death of Jehoash (782 B.C.); he outlived his former captor by fifteen years but died at Lachish (767 B.C.), the victim of a palace plot (2 Kings 14:19-20; 2 Chron. 25:27).

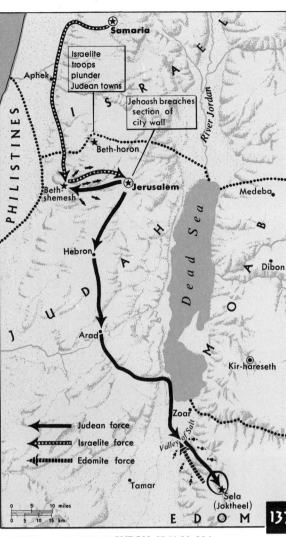

Israelite troops plunder Judean towns

Jehoash breaches section of city wall

Judean force

Israelite force

Edomite force

2 KINGS 14:7-14; 17-21; 2 CHRON. 25:11-26; 26:1

So Jehoash king of Israel went up, and he and Amaziah king of Judah faced one another in battle at Beth-she-mesh, which belongs to Judah.

(2 Kings 14:11)

Seal of "Shema servant of Jeroboam" from Megiddo

He restored the border of Israel from the entrance of Hamath as far as the Sea of the Arabah...

(2 Kings 14:25)

THE CONQUESTS OF JEHOASH AND JEROBOAM II

CA. 790-782 B.C.

Tradition has it that Jehoash defeated Aram-damascus three times (2 Kings 13:18-19). One of these was a decisive victory at Aphek in the Golan (2 Kings 13:17); the others were apparently at Karnaim and Lo-debar (Amos 6:13). Damascus had been too weakened by Adad-nirari and the subsequent conflict with Hamath to prevent Jehoash and Jeroboam II from regaining almost full control over Transjordan (1 Chron. 5:17). Jeroboam "restored the border of Israel from Lebo-hamath as far as the Sea of the Arabah" (2 Kings. 14:25). Though Hamath itself may have become subservient to Israel alongside Damascus (2 Kings 14:28), the tableland of Medeba evidently remained in Moabite hands. Gadites and Reubenites are now found in Bashan and across the eastern steppe land toward the Euphrates (1 Chron. 5:9-11).

With the death of Jehoash (782 B.C.) and the release of Amaziah, it would appear that the royal houses of Samaria and Jerusalem had come to an understanding. Israel now controlled an area almost as large as the northern part of the united monarchy. Vast reaches of productive agricultural land, from the prairies of Bashan (Amos 4:1) to the plantations of Carmel (Amos 1:1), produced abundant harvests of grain, wine and oil (Hosea 1:8). The Transjordanian caravan routes were under Israelite control as well as the Jezreel Valley and the Sharon Plain.

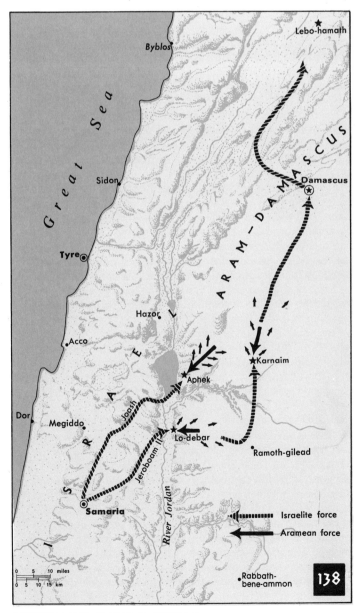

Israelite force

Aramean force

2 KINGS 13:15-19, 25; 14:25, 28; AMOS 6:13

THE SAMARIA OSTRACA

784 TO 783 B.C.

In the ninth year. From Yazith to Ahinoam. A ja[r]
old wine. In the fifteenth year. From Halak to A[...]
Ahimelech. Helez. From Hazeroth.
(Samaria Ostraca Nos. 9 and [...]

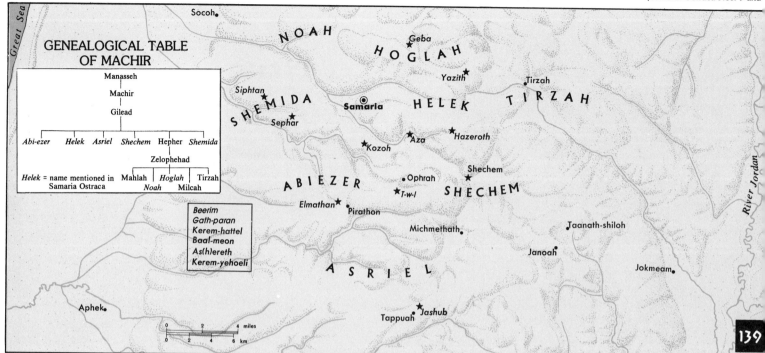

GENEALOGICAL TABLE OF MACHIR

Manasseh
Machir
Gilead

Abi-ezer Helek Asriel Shechem Hepher Shemida

Zelophehad

Mahlah | Hoglah | Tirzah
Noah | Milcah

Helek = name mentioned in Samaria Ostraca

Beerim
Gath-paran
Kerem-hattel
Baal-meon
As(h)ereth
Kerem-yehoeli

139

A collection of more than sixty inscribed potsherds (ostraca) were found during the excavations at ancient Samaria. They were administrative notations of shipments, wine or oil, that had been sent in to various officials from their estates out in the hills of Manasseh. All of the sherds had been discarded and were found in a fill under the floor of a later building. The individual notations had probably been recorded in master lists on papyrus before being thrown away. The formulations on all the texts have the same general format, beginning with the (king's) regnal year and listing the recipient of the shipment. However, the remaining details divide the inscriptions into two groups. One type names the commodity being sent, a jar of either "old wine" or "purified oil." The other group ignores the commodity (apparently all of this group were for either wine or oil) but lists the sender of the shipment. Both groups give the name of the town from which the commodity was being sent, but the same group that omits the commodity adds the name of the clan district in which the town is located. The two groups are also distinguished by their respective dates. Those texts listing wine or oil are dated to "the ninth year," or "the tenth year" (the ordinal number being written out), while those that list the sender are all from "the 15th year" (using Egyptian hieratic numerals). The form of the letters is so similar in both groups of texts that no chronological distinction can be made on the grounds of palaeography. The relative date for the potsherds used as the writing material is in the first quarter of the eighth century B.C. The fact that the texts from the ninth, tenth and fifteenth years were all indiscriminately mixed up together in the same fill raises the question, "What about the eleventh to fourteenth years?"

According to the chronology adopted in this edition of the *Atlas*, Jehoash king of Israel came to the throne in 798 B.C. and his son Jeroboam II was appointed co-regent in 793 B.C. (on the eve of the war with Amaziah). The tenth year of Jeroboam II would thus fall in 783 B.C., the same as the fifteenth year of Jehoash. Therefore, a reasonable conjecture that satisfies all the evidence would be to assign the ninth-tenth year dockets to Jeroboam II and the fifteenth year dockets to Jehoash.

The Samaria Ostraca provide some fascinating sociological

and geographical insights. They contain a corpus of place names unknown from any biblical source but often identifiable with Arabic village names in the Samaria hills. In fact, all the known locations are within the tribal inheritance of Manasseh. The Bible does not give a list of the towns in Manasseh so the information from the Samaria Ostraca is welcome indeed. Furthermore, the clan districts mentioned in the "fifteenth year" dockets are all recognizable as members of the biblical Manasseh/Machir genealogy (see chart above). By means of the locatable towns associated with particular clans, the general locations of the clan districts may be determined. Five of the six principal sons of the tribe appear as districts in the ostraca. The missing son, Hepher, is represented by two daughters of Hepher's son, Zelophohad, whose celebrated case was a precedent in Israel for the inheritance rights of daughters (Num. 26:28-34; 27:1-4(5-11); 36:10-12 (cf. 1-8); Josh. 17:1-6; 1 Chron. 7:14-19). The genealogical information about the tribe is seen to rest on a sociological reality as expressed in the settlement pattern of the towns and districts in Manasseh.

The dozen or so recipients of shipments were evidently living in the capital and having small quantities of wine and oil sent to them from their local estates. Those mentioned in the texts from the fifteenth year were probably serving the old king, Jehoash, while those from the ninth-tenth year texts were serving the co-regent, Jeroboam II. The system of clan districts was followed in the fifteenth year texts, perhaps following a venerable custom in the administration. The other texts ignore the clan system and may represent a departure from the time-honored respect for local social structure. That some recipients got shipments from more than one place suggests that they had acquired other estates in addition to their family patrimony, perhaps as royal grants (cf. 1 Sam. 8:14, "He [the king] will take the best of your fields and vineyards and olive orchards and give them to his servants"). The proliferation of such awards to favored nobles and their ability to foreclose on unfortunate debtors may have been the cause of so much social injustice as denounced by the prophets (Amos 2:6-8; 3:10; 5:10-12).

Samaria Ostraca

He placed forces in all the fortified cities of Judah, and set garrisons in the land of Judah, and in the cities of Ephraim which Asa his father had taken.

(2 Chronicles 17:2)

THE DISTRICTS OF JUDAH

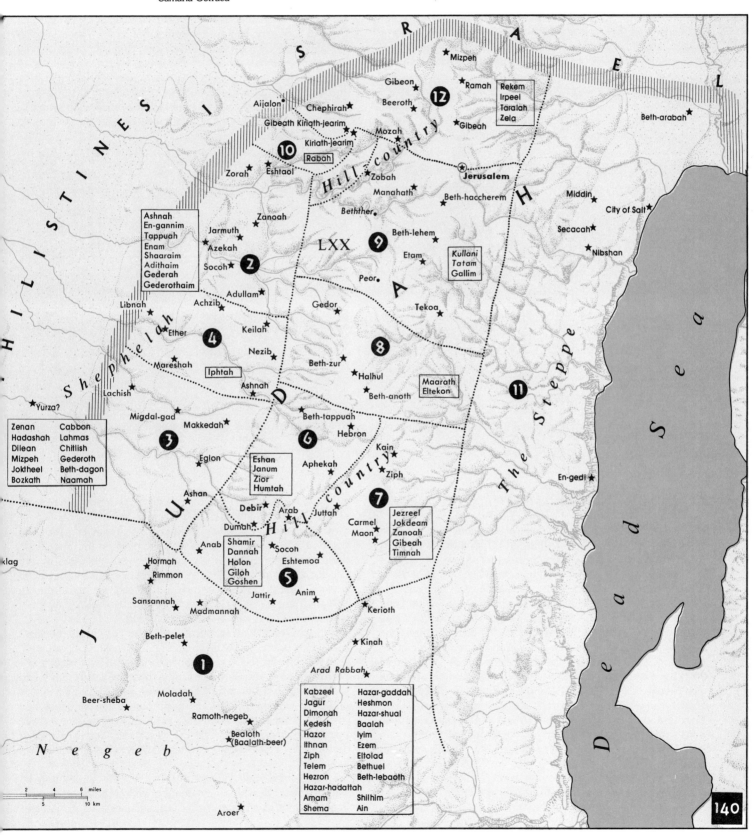

I S R A E L

P H I L I S T I N E S

Mizpeh

Gibeon
Beeroth
⓬
Ramah
Rekem
Irpeel
Taralah
Zela

Aijalon
Chephirah
Gibeath Kiriath-jearim
Gibeah
Beth-arabah

Mozah

Kiriath-jearim
⑩
Rabah

Zorah
Eshtaol
Zobah
★ Jerusalem

Hill country

Manahath
Beth-haccherem
Middin
City of Salt

Bethther
Secacah
Nibshan

Ashnah
En-gannim
Tappuah
Enam
Shaaraim
Adithaim
Gederah
Gederothaim

Zanoah

Jarmuth
Azekah
LXX
⑨
Beth-lehem

Beth-zur

Socoh
②
Peor
Etam
Kullani
Tatam
Gallim

Adullam

Libnah
Achzib
Gedor
Tekoa

Ether
④
Keilah

Shephelah
Nezib
⑧
Mareshah
Iphtah
Beth-zur
Halhul

Ashnah
Beth-anoth
Maarath
Eltekon

Lachish

Yurza?
Migdal-gad
Makkedah
Beth-tappuah
⑪

Zenan   Cabbon
Hadashah   Lahmas
Dilean   Chitlish
Mizpeh   Gederoth
Joktheel   Beth-dagon
Bozkath   Naamah

③
Eglon
Hebron
The Steppe

Eshan
Janum
Zior
Humtah
Aphekah
Kain
En-gedi

Ashan
⑥
Ziph

Debir
Arab
Juttah
Carmel
Maon
Jezreel
Jokdeam
Zanoah
Gibeah
Timnah

Dumah
Hill country
⑦

Anab
Shamir
Dannah
Holon
Giloh
Goshen
Socoh
Eshtemoa

Hormah
Rimmon
⑤
Jattir
Anim

Sansannah
Madmannah
Kerioth

iklag
Beth-pelet
Kinah

①
Arad Rabbah

Beer-sheba
Moladah

Ramoth-negeb
Kabzeel   Hazar-gaddah
Jagur   Heshmon
Dimonah   Hazar-shual
Kedesh   Baalah
Bealoth   Hazor   Iyim
(Baalath-beer) Ithnan   Ezem
Ziph   Eltolad
N e g e b   Telem   Bethuel
Hezron   Beth-lebaoth
Hazar-hadattah
2   4   6 miles   Amam   Shilhim
                   Shema   Ain
5   10 km

Aroer

D e a d   S e a

J U D A H

⓭ 140

15:21-62; 18:25-28

THE DISTRICTS OF JUDAH

The settlement pattern of Judah is reflected in great detail by Joshua 15:20-63. That passage is the most detailed geographical text preserved in the Bible. The date of the original document incorporated by the author of Joshua is disputed. The references to administrative reorganization by Jehoshaphat (2 Chron. 17:1-13) and his appointment of royal sons as local governors (21:3) have led some to suggest that the roster of Judean towns was compiled in the mid-ninth century. Others favor an eighth or seventh century date. In any case the roster is defective as it stands; key towns like Beth-shemesh and Adoraim are missing along with other known settlements from the genealogies of Judah, Caleb and Simeon (1 Chron. 2-4). An entire district is missing from the Hebrew text but can be partially supplied from the Greek version (Josh. 15:59a).

The Joshua list is based on strictly topographical, rather than kinship principles. Comparison with the geographical distribution of clans and families in "Greater Judah" (1 Chron. 2-4) reveals that the pattern of kinship settlement is only partly commensurate with the topographical divisions of Josh. 15:20-63. Here the four principal ecological zones of Judah, namely the Negeb, the Shephelah, the Hill Country and the Steppe ("Wilderness"), are the organizational basis for the list. The towns are grouped into geographical clusters indicated by subtotals; the Negeb and the Steppe each have a subtotal. The Shephelah has three subtotals corresponding to three districts; the Hill Country has six (counting the district preserved in the Greek). This total of eleven may be supplemented by the southernmost district of Benjamin, which had remained under Judean control. Levitical cities are not distinguished. In the Shephelah and the southern Hill Country, the district boundaries correspond to watersheds between wadi systems. In district 2 the roster runs clockwise around the district; in district 4 it is counterclockwise.

Fortress of early 8th century, Arad stratum IX, probably from the reign of Uzziah

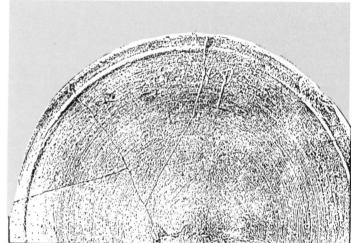

Ritual saucer from beside the altar of Arad stratum X, The inscription is "q-k" for *qodesh kohanim*, "sacred for the priests." Possibly from the reign of Jehoshaphat.

UZZIAH'S SUCCESS 782 TO 750 B.C.

When Uzziah (Azariah) was twenty-six years old, Jehoash of Israel died; Amaziah was returned to Jerusalem, probably as a gesture of good will on the part of Jeroboam II. The two kingdoms embarked on their campaigns of expansion. Uzziah launched a victorious campaign against Philistia. He dismantled the fortifications of Gath, Jabneh and Ashdod and built strong points of his own in the latter's territory (2 Chron. 26:6). Then he warred successfully in the south, gaining the upper hand over the Philistines, the Arabians and the Meunites (2 Chron.26:7). According the the Greek version of 2 Chron. 26:7, the Meunites (*Minaioi*) paid him tribute and his authority was recognized as far as the entry to Egypt. In other words, Uzziah gained control over the caravan routes from Arabia to Philistia and Egypt; the principal element in Sinai, the Meunites, now shared their caravaneer and caravanserai profits with him. Eventually, he was able to rebuild the fortress at Elath, after the death of Amaziah in 767 B.C. (2 Kings 14:22; 2 Chron. 26:2).

This outside income was used to strengthen the internal prosperity of the country. Jerusalem's fortifications were improved (2 Chron. 26:9); towers and water cisterns were constructed in the steppe land ("Wilderness of Judah") for the royal flocks; cultivators farmed the royal holdings in the Shephelah and the coastal plain (especially those lands acquired by the conquest of northern Philistia); and husbandmen tended the royal vineyards "in the hills and in Carmel," i.e. the northern and southern hill country of Judah (2 Chron. 26:10). The army was enlarged and well equipped (2 Chron. 12:11-15).

Jotham, son of Uzziah, became co-regent in 750 B.C. because the king was smitten with an incurable disease (2 Kings 15:5-7; 2 Chron. 26:16-23). Uzziah had attempted to usurp the prerogatives of the Jerusalem priesthood. Jotham continued the building projects of his father, in Jerusalem and throughout Judah (2 Chron. 27:3-4). His one noteworthy conquest was over the Ammonites, whom he forced to pay tribute for three years (2 Chron. 27:5). For the first time, Judah gained a foothold in Transjordan, formerly the exclusive domain of Israel.

Uzziah lived until 740 B.C. In 743 B.C. he is credited by Tiglath-pileser III with having led a coalition of western states in an attempt to stop the Assyrians' advance into the Levant.

And his fame spread far, for he was marvelously helped, till he was strong.

(2 Chronicles 26:15)

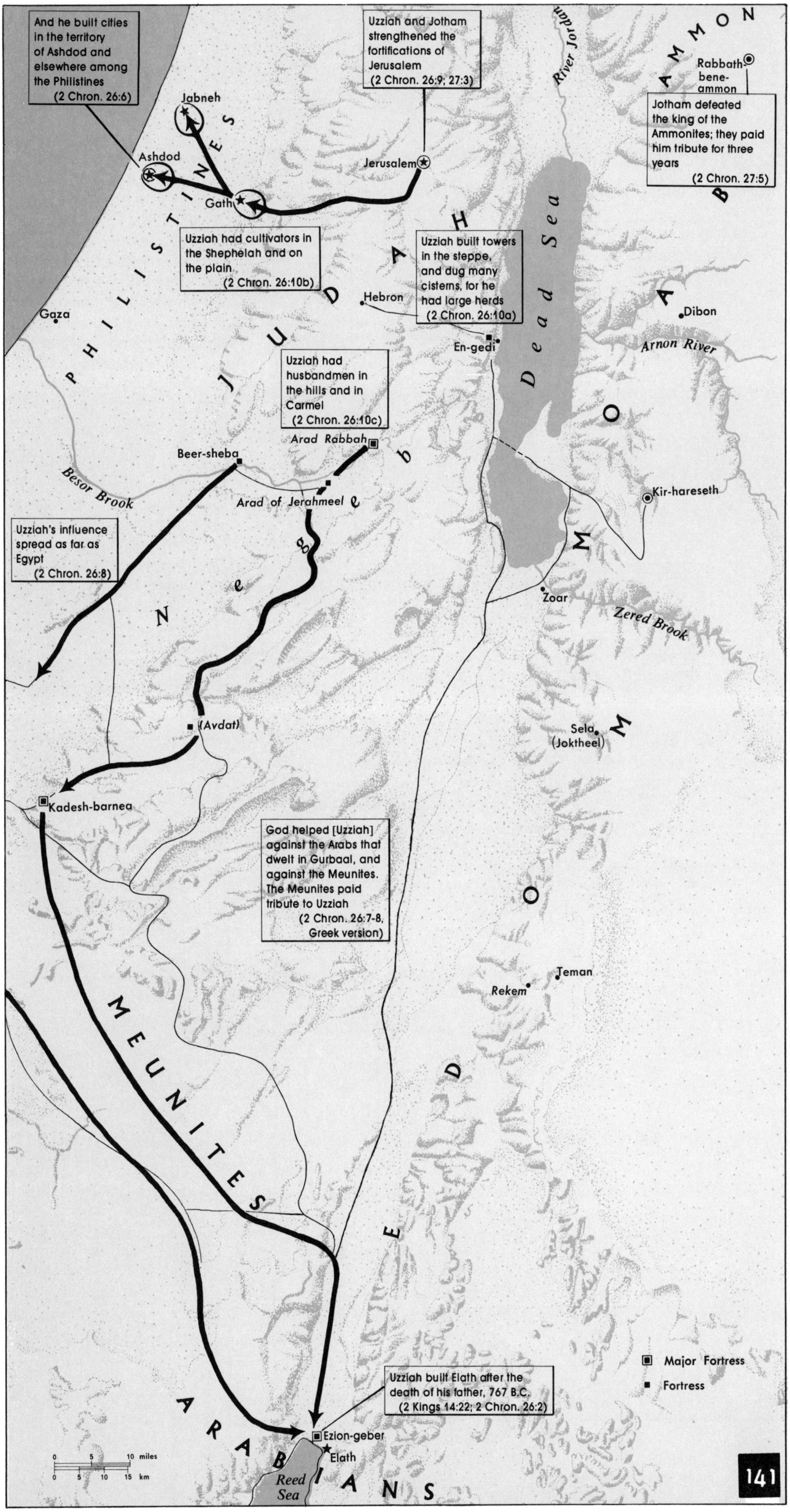

And he built cities in the territory of Ashdod and elsewhere among the Philistines (2 Chron. 26:6)

Uzziah and Jotham strengthened the fortifications of Jerusalem (2 Chron. 26:9; 27:3)

Jotham defeated the king of the Ammonites; they paid him tribute for three years (2 Chron. 27:5)

Uzziah had cultivators in the Shephelah and on the plain (2 Chron. 26:10b)

Uzziah built towers in the steppe, and dug many cisterns, for he had large herds (2 Chron. 26:10a)

Uzziah had husbandmen in the hills and in Carmel (2 Chron. 26:10c)

Uzziah's influence spread as far as Egypt (2 Chron. 26:8)

God helped [Uzziah] against the Arabs that dwelt in Gurbaal, and against the Meunites. The Meunites paid tribute to Uzziah (2 Chron. 26:7-8, Greek version)

Uzziah built Elath after the death of his father, 767 B.C. (2 Kings 14:22; 2 Chron. 26:2)

2 KINGS 14:22;
2 CHRON. 26:2-15; 27:3-5

AMMON

Rabbath bene-ammon

P H I L I S T I N E S

Jabneh

Ashdod

Gath

Jerusalem

Gaza

J U D A H

Hebron

En-gedi

Dead Sea

Dibon

Arnon River

M O A B

Kir-hareseth

Beer-sheba

Arad Rabbah

Arad of Jerahmeel

Besor Brook

Zoar

Zered Brook

N e g e b

(Avdat)

Sela (Joktheel)

E D O M

Kadesh-barnea

Teman

Rekem

M E U N I T E S

A R A B I A N S

Ezion-geber

Elath

Reed Sea

◨	Major Fortress
◼	Fortress

0   5   10 miles
0   5 10 15 km

141

How he recovered for Israel Damascus and Hamath,
which had belonged to Judah ...

(2 Kings 14:28)

ISRAEL AND JUDAH IN THE DAYS OF JEROBOAM II AND UZZIAH MID-EIGHTH CENTURY B.C.

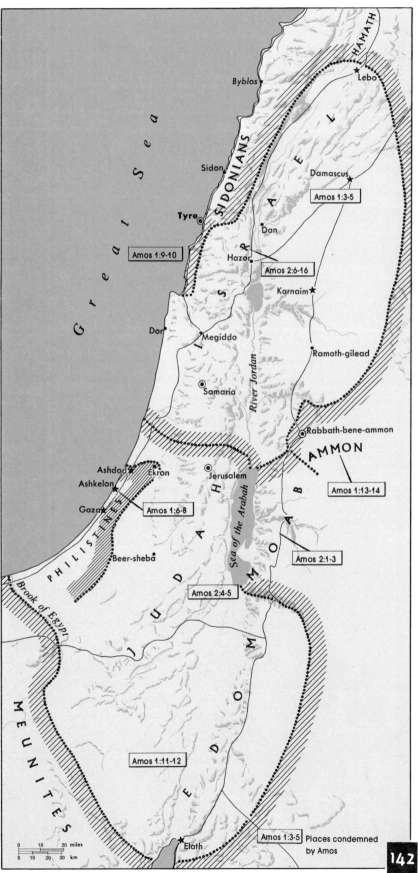

Amos 1:3-5 Places condemned by Amos

0 10 20 miles
0 10 20 30 km

142

2 KINGS 14:22; 2 CHRON. 26:2-15

The kingdoms of Israel and Judah achieved their last zenith of real prosperity and power during the second quarter of the eighth century B.C. Together they once again dominated the major arteries of world commerce across the southern arm of the Fertile Crescent. The success of Jeroboam II was acclaimed by Jonah, son of Amittai, a prophet from Gath-hepher in Galilee (2 Kings 14:25). The prophetic schools of the ninth century continued to flourish in the eighth; their critique of ethical and moral affairs was directed at both the international and the internal scene. Amos, from Tekoa, issued his pronouncements at Beth-el, the royal cult center of Israel (Amos 7:10-17). In the name of the Lord of Israel he proclaimed judgment on Israel's principal enemies: Damascus for its aggressions in Gilead (Amos 1:3-5), Philistia (Gaza, Ashdod, Ashkelon, Ekron) for helping the Edomites to enslave Judeans (vs. 6-8), Tyre for sharing in that enterprise (vs. 9-10), Edom for his cruelty against the Judeans (vs. 11-12), Ammon for its atrocities in Gilead (vs. 13-14), and Moab for desecrating the bones of a rival king (2:1-3). Then Amos turned his wrath upon Judah for not keeping the Law of the Lord (vs. 4-5), and upon Israel for gross violations of social justice (vs. 6-16).

Amos saw that the defense of walled cities (as practiced by Samaria and Damascus in the ninth century) would not succeed against a determined conqueror like Tiglath-pileser III, who would advance inexorably from province to province never mounting a major campaign without adequate logistic support from an Assyrian governor close by (Amos 3:11).

Hoshea, whose city is unknown, reveals a deep love for the countryside of Samaria alongside an abhorrence for its religious corruption.

I will raise up for them a prophet like you from among their brethren; and I will put my words in his mouth.
(Deuteronomy 18:18)

THE CITIES OF THE PROPHETS
9TH TO 7TH CENTURIES B.C.

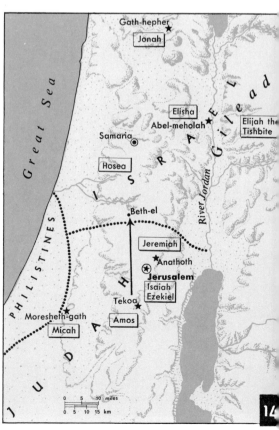

0 5 10 miles
0 5 10 15 km

Because Syria, with Ephraim and the son of Remaliah, has devised evil against you, saying, "Let us go up against Judah and terrify it, and let us conquer it for ourselves, and set up the son of Tabel as king in the midst of it" ...

(Isaiah 7:5-6)

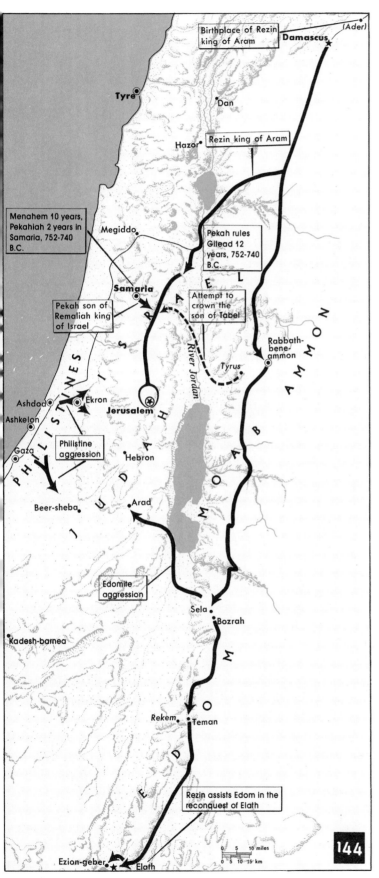

Birthplace of Rezin king of Aram

(Ader)

Damascus

Tyre

Dan

Rezin king of Aram

Hazor

Menahem 10 years, Pekahiah 2 years in Samaria, 752-740 B.C.

Megiddo

Pekah rules Gilead 12 years, 752-740 B.C.

Samaria

Attempt to crown the son of Tabel

Pekah son of Remaliah king of Israel

River Jordan

AMMON

Rabbath-bene-ammon

Tyrus

Ashdod

Ekron

Ashkelon

Jerusalem

PHILISTINES

Gaza

Philistine aggression

Hebron

MOAB

Beer-sheba

Arad

Edomite aggression

Sela

Bozrah

Kadesh-barnea

EDOM

Rekem

Teman

Rezin assists Edom in the reconquest of Elath

144

0   5   10 miles
0 5 10 15 km

Ezion-geber   Elath

THE CAMPAIGN OF REZIN AND PEKAH AGAINST JUDAH

735 B.C.

The Kingdom of Israel began its disintegration with the assassination of Zechariah, son of Jeroboam II, after only six months in office (752 B.C.). His successor, Shallum, lasted only one month (2 Kings 15:8-14). Menahem, the new usurper, reigned in Samaria for ten years and was followed by his son, Pekahiah, for two more years (752-742/741 B.C.; 2 Kings 15:17-26). Meanwhile, Pekah the son of Remaliah began a twenty-year rule in Gilead (see Hosea 5:3-5); he apparently had a presumed reconciliation with Pekahiah but assassinated him and took power over all of Israel for another eight years (740-732 B.C.; 2 Kings 15:25-31). Jotham had taken advantage of the divided rule in the north to exert Judean military power against the king of Ammon, thus gaining a foothold in Transjordan.

However, Tiglath-pileser III renewed Assyria's expansionist policy. Unlike most of his predecessors, he was not satisfied with the submission of local kings and the payment of tribute; rather he initiated the annexation of conquered territories, reducing them to provinces under Assyrian governors. Opposition to Assyrian permanent rule was squelched by exiling the upper classes and resettling deportees from some other part of the empire. Tiglath-pileser III avoided long campaigns far from his supply bases. The newly-appointed governors provided logistic support for the Assyrian army when it pushed out in the next step of conquest.

In 743 B.C. Tiglath-pileser III was faced by a coalition of western states surprisingly led by Azariah of Judah. The effort was unsuccessful and Menahem of Israel paid tribute to the Assyrians (2 Kings 15:19-20). The heavy burden that this payment imposed on the nobility of Israel may have engendered the unrest that led Pekah to power in Samaria three years later.

While Tiglath-pileser III was engaged elsewhere, especially in Urartu (Ararat), Pekah made an alliance with Rezin, king of Damascus. They hoped to organize a strong united front against the Assyrians. Jotham apparently shared his late father's anti-Assyrian bias but the leadership in Jerusalem did not. After sixteen years of reign, Jotham was effectually deposed in favor of his son, Ahaz (735 B.C.), who refused to join Pekah and Rezin against Tiglath-pileser III. Jotham actually lived to his twentieth year (732/731 B.C.; 2 Kings 15:30).

Pekah and Rezin immediately declared war on Ahaz in an attempt to depose him in favor of a certain Tabal (probably Tabel, from a Judean noble family recently settled in Transjordan, ancestors of the later Tobiads). Rezin assisted the Edomites in the reconquest of Elath (2 Kings 16:6) and the Edomites attacked Judah from the south (2 Chron. 28:17). Meanwhile, the Philistines invaded the western Negeb and the northern Shephelah of Judah and occupied many towns on the key approaches to the hill country (2 Chron. 28:5-15). Pekah was unable to force his will upon Jerusalem and the prisoners taken during his foray were returned (2 Kings 16:5b; 2 Chron. 28:17-19; Isaiah 7:1-6). Ahaz promptly turned to Tiglath-pileser III for help.

2 KINGS 16:5-9; IS. 7-9; 2 CHRON. 28:16-21

And the Philistines had made raids on the cities in the Shephelah and the Negeb of Judah ...

(2 Chronicles 28:18)

PHILISTINE CONQUESTS IN THE DAYS OF AHAZ

735 B.C.

In the days of Pekah king of Israel Tiglath-pileser king of Assyria came and captured Ijon, Abel-beth-maacah, Janoah, Kedesh, Hazor, Gilead, and Galilee, all the land of Naphtali; and he carried the people captive to Assyria.

(2 Kings 15:29)

THE CAMPAIGNS OF TIGLATH-PILESER III

734 TO 732 B.C.

Tiglath-pileser III responded with alacrity. The dates of his campaigns in the southern Levant are determined in accordance with his annals and the Eponym Chronicle. In 734 B.C. he marched against Philistia. Since the northern Shephelah had recently fallen into Philistine hands (see Map 145), the siege of Gezer depicted on one of Tiglath-pileser's reliefs must have taken place during this campaign. Gaza was conquered next after its king, Hanun, had fled to Egypt. The Assyrian army proceeded into northern Sinai where the Meunites were also forced to submit; a garrison was left at the Brook of Egypt. The kings of Palestine were cut off from any possible help on the part of the Egyptians.

The following year, 733 B.C., saw the invasion of northern Israel. The main course of the campaign can be deduced from 2 Kings 15:29. Tiglath-pileser III launched the attack from the Lebanese Beqaʻ Valley, first taking Ijon and Abel-beth-maachah. Then he turned westward across Upper Galilee to Janoah, in the foothills above Tyre. Thus he assured his lines of communication with Tyre. Marching back across Upper Galilee, he conquered Kedesh. Yiron and Merom appear in an Assyrian list of prisoners from this campaign, so they were evidently taken at this time. He could now concentrate on the siege of Hazor without fear of harassment from Upper Galilee. Forces were sent into Gilead and to "Galilee, all the land of Naphtali." Isaiah describes these territories, the first to fall under a conqueror's heel, as "The way of the sea, the land beyond Jordan, and Galilee of the nations." Biblical semantics require that "way of the sea" be a route leading to the sea; this fits perfectly the road from Abel-beth-maacah to Janoah. Gilead is, of course, the "land beyond Jordan," and "Galilee of the nations" is literally the "Region of the goiim," mainly the Jezreel Valley (the equivalent of Harosheth-ha-goiim in Judges 4:2).

Damascus was now completely isolated. The following year, 732 B.C., saw its downfall before the victorious army of Tiglath-pileser III. An Assyrian relief from Calah shows the exile of inhabitants from Ashtaroth, chief city of Bashan, one of the cities taken at this time.

In the wake of this crushing defeat, Pekah was assassinated by Hoshea, son of Elah (732 B.C.). Tiglath-pileser III says that he appointed Hoshea as king of Israel and received a heavy payment of tribute from him. This was also the twentieth, and last, year of Jotham (2 Kings 15:30); Ahaz's sole reign of sixteen years is reckoned from this date (2 Kings 16:2; 2 Chron. 28:1).

Exile of inhabitants of Ashtaroth (Relief from palace of Tiglath-pileser III at Calah)

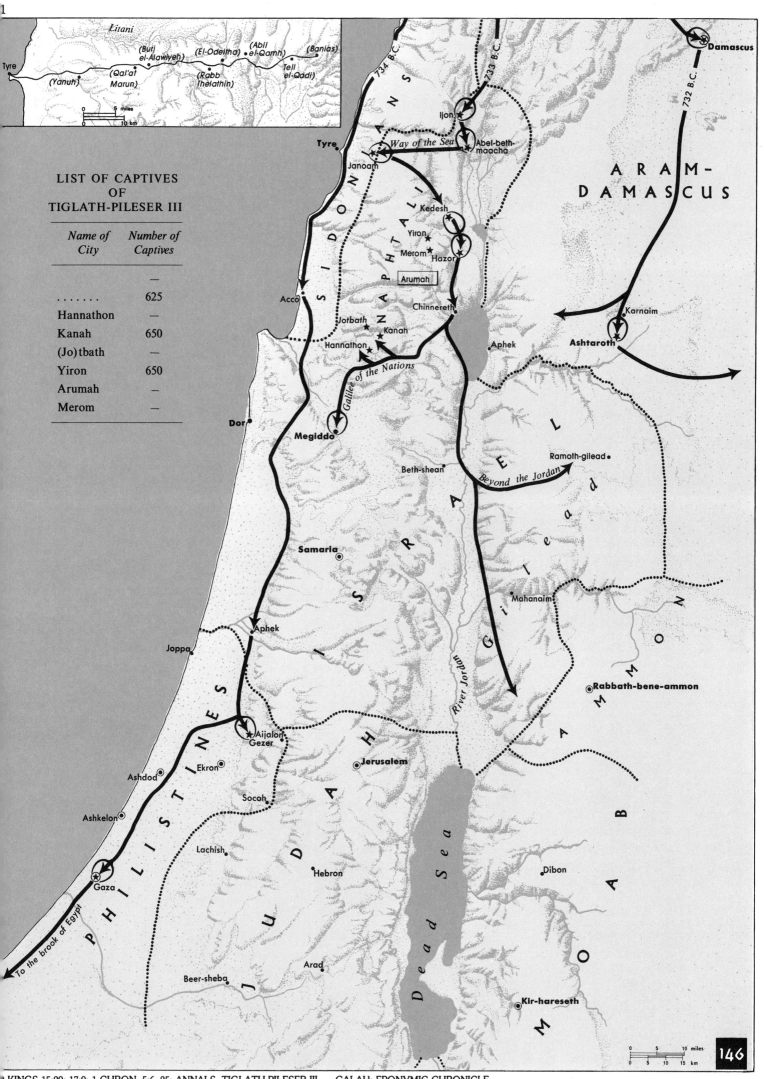

LIST OF CAPTIVES
OF
TIGLATH-PILESER III

Name of City	Number of Captives
	—
....	625
Hannathon	—
Kanah	650
(Jo)tbath	—
Yiron	650
Arumah	—
Merom	—

Litani

(Butj el-Alawiyeh) (El-Odeitha) (Abil el-Qamh) (Banias)

Tyre (Yanuh) (Qal'at Marun) (Rabb Thelathin) (Tell el-Qadi)

0 — 5 miles
0 — 10 km

734 B.C. 733 B.C. 732 B.C.

Damascus

Ijon

Way of the Sea Abel-beth-maacha

Tyre Janoam

A R A M –
D A M A S C U S

Kedesh

Yiron

Merom Hazor

Arumah

Acco

Chinnereth

S I D O N I A N S

N A P H T A L I

Karnaim

Jotbath Kanah

Hannathon

Aphek

Ashtaroth

Galilee of the Nations

Dor

Megiddo

Ramoth-gilead

I S R A E L

Beth-shean

Beyond the Jordan

Samaria

G i l e a d

Mahanaim

A M M O N

Rabbath-bene-ammon

Aphek

Joppa

River Jordan

Aijalon
Gezer

Ekron

Jerusalem

Ashdod

Socoh

J U D A H

Lachish

Hebron

Dibon

Ashkelon

Dead Sea

M O A B

Gaza

To the brook of Egypt

P H I L I S T I N E S

Beer-sheba Arad

Kir-hareseth

0 — 5 — 10 miles
0 — 5 — 10 — 15 km

146

KINGS 15:29; 17:9; 1 CHRON. 5:6, 25; ANNALS, TIGLATH-PILESER III — CALAH; EPONYMIC CHRONICLE

With my many chariots I have gone up the heights of
the mountains, to the far recesses of Lebanon ...
(Isaiah 37:24)

THE RISE OF THE KINGDOM OF ASSYRIA
9TH TO 7TH CENTURIES B.C.

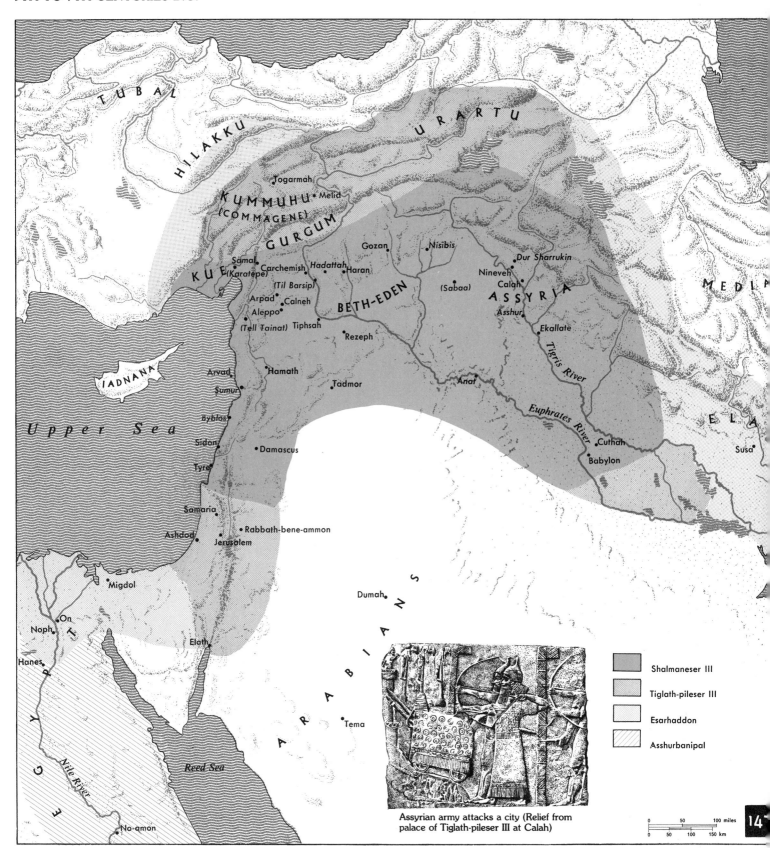

TUBAL

HILAKKU

KUMMUHU
(COMMAGENE)

URARTU

Togarmah

Melid

GURGUM

Samal
(Karatepe)
KUE
Carchemish
(Til Barsip)
Arpad
Aleppo
(Tell Tainat) Tiphsah

Hadattah
Haran

Gozan

Nisibis

Dur Sharrukin

Nineveh
(Sabaa) Calah

ASSYRIA

MEDIA

Calneh
BETH-EDEN

Rezeph

Asshur
Ekallate

IADNANA

Arvad
Sumur

Hamath

Tadmor

Anat

Tigris River

Euphrates River

ELA

Upper Sea

Byblos

Sidon
Tyre

Damascus

Cuthah
Babylon

Susa

Samaria
Ashdod
Jerusalem

Rabbath-bene-ammon

Migdol

Dumah

A R A B I A N S

On
Noph

Hanes

Elath

Tema

E G Y P T

Nile River

Reed Sea

No-amon

Assyrian army attacks a city (Relief from
palace of Tiglath-pileser III at Calah)

	Shalmaneser III
	Tiglath-pileser III
	Esarhaddon
	Asshurbanipal

0   50   100 miles
0   50   100   150 km

14

In the former time he brought into contempt the land of Zebulun and the land of Naphtali, but in the latter time he will make glorious the way of the sea, the land beyond the Jordan, Galilee of the nations.

(Isaiah 9:1)

THE ASSYRIAN DISTRICTS IN THE DAYS OF TIGLATH-PILESER III

732 B.C.

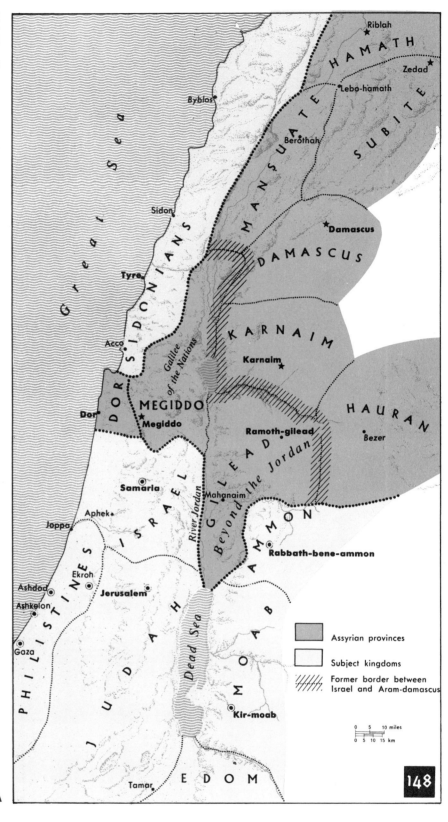

IS. 9:1; EZ. 47:16-18; EPONYMIC LISTS,
ADMINISTRATIVE DOCUMENTS — ASSYRIA

Assyrian policy called for the organization of the newly conquered territories into districts under loyal governors. This did not preclude the continuation of some local dynasties in key states such as Tyre and the four main Philistine cities: Gaza, Ashkelon, Ashdod and Ekron. Ahaz in Judah and Hoshea in Israel were tributaries and were charged with maintaining the loyalty of their subjects. But Damascus had caused too much trouble for its dynasty to survive. Its territory was divided into four provinces. The territory taken from Israel had a similar fate. Upper Galilee, or most of it, was probably assigned to Tyre. An Assyrian governor was installed in the newly rebuilt administrative center at Megiddo. The Megiddo province was mainly the Jezreel and Beth-shean Valleys and probably Lower Galilee as well. Transjordan became the province of Gal'azi (=Gilead). The Sharon Plain was evidently still part of Samaria, especially the key city of Aphek. Dor may have already been a dependent of Tyre though its territory (Naphoth-dor) might have been assigned provisionally to the governor at Megiddo. It is mentioned in Assyrian records but never as the seat of a governor.

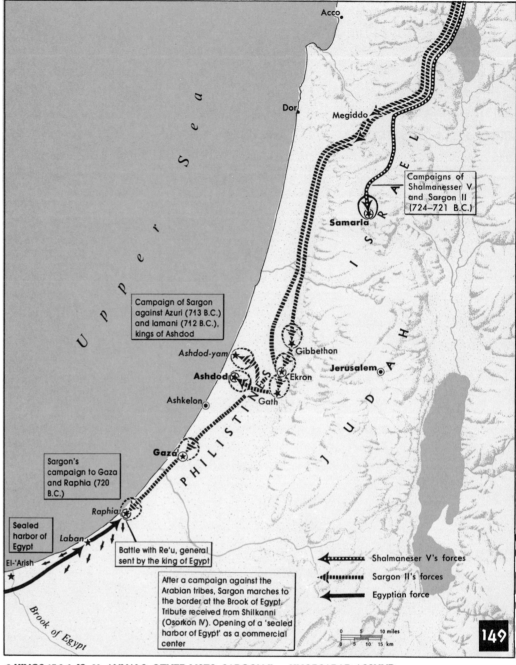

Against him came up Shalmaneser king of Assyria...

(2 Kings 17:3)

THE CAMPAIGNS OF SHALMANESER V AND SARGON II TO PALESTINE
724 TO 712 B.C.

Campaigns of Shalmanesser V and Sargon II (724–721 B.C.)

Campaign of Sargon against Azuri (713 B.C.) and Iamani (712 B.C.), kings of Ashdod

Sargon's campaign to Gaza and Raphia (720 B.C.)

Sealed harbor of Egypt

Battle with Re'u, general sent by the king of Egypt

After a campaign against the Arabian tribes, Sargon marches to the border at the Brook of Egypt. Tribute received from Shilkanni (Osorkon IV). Opening of a 'sealed harbor of Egypt' as a commercial center

Acco·
Dor·
Megiddo
Samaria
Ashdod-yam
Ashdod
Ashkelon
Gibbethon
Ekron
Gath
Jerusalem
Gaza
Raphia
Laban·
El-'Arish
Brook of Egypt

U p p e r S e a
I S R A E L
J U D A H
P H I L I S T I N E S

⟵····· Shalmaneser V's forces
⟵⟨····· Sargon II's forces
⟵ Egyptian force

0   5   10 miles
0 5 10 15 km

149

2 KINGS 17:3-6; IS. 20; ANNALS, OTHER LISTS, SARGON II — KHORSABAD ASSHUR

With the death of Tiglath-pileser III in 727 B.C., his successor, Shalmaneser V, found it necessary to campaign in the west. Hoshea paid his tribute when the Assyrian threat approached (2 Kings 17:3). However, Hoshea turned to "So king of Egypt" (Osorkon IV or 'Tefnakhte' ruler of Sais) for help and ceased paying his tribute to Shalmaneser. The Assyrian king arrested Hoshea and launched his attack on the disloyal kingdom of Samaria in Hoshea's seventh year (725/724 B.C.). The city succumbed to the siege in Hoshea's ninth year (723/722 B.C.), and its population was taken into exile. Shalmaneser V died shortly thereafter and was succeeded by Sargon II. Years later, Sargon's scribes assigned the conquest of Samaria to their master.

Conquest of Ekron (Relief from palace of Sargon II at Khorsabad)

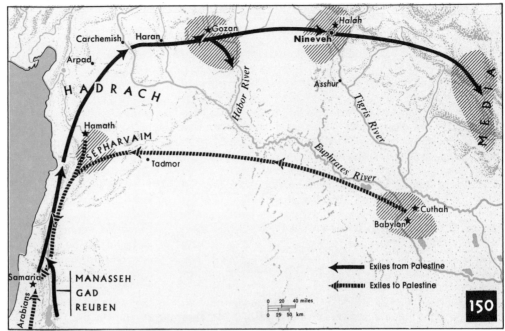

the king of Assyria brought people from Babylon,
[C]ah, Avva, Hamath, and Sepharvaim, and placed
[...]h in the cities of Samaria instead of the people of
[...]...

[T]HE EXILE OF PEOPLES
[T]O AND FROM ISRAEL
[U]NDER THE ASSYRIANS
[...] TO 712 B.C.

[...] KINGS 17:6, 24; 30-31; 1 CHRON. 5:26;
[A]NNALS, TIGLATH-PILESER III, SARGON II

I reorganized these cities. I settled there people from
the lands of the west, whom I had captured. I appointed
my officer over them as governor, and counted them
as Assyrians, and they bore my yoke.

(Annals of Sargon II)

THE DISTRICTS
OF ASSYRIA IN THE
DAYS OF SARGON II
733 TO 716 B.C.

Sargon II (Relief from palace of Sargon II
at Khorsabad)

▨ Assyrian provinces
☐ Subject kingdoms

ANNALS, OTHER LISTS,
SARGON II — KHORSABAD, ASSHUR

People from Geder
attacked a Moabite
town

THE DISTRICTS OF ASSYRIA IN THE DAYS OF SARGON II

Sargon II did have to put down a rebellion in the Levant led by the ruler of Hamath and supported by the remaining population of Samaria (720 B.C.). He then marched southward for a confrontation with the Egyptian army. On the way, he may very well have had to take Gibbethon and Ekron, two Philistine towns whose conquest is portrayed on reliefs from his palace. The decisive battle was fought at Raphia; the Egyptian general, Re'u, fled from the scene and Hanun, king of Gaza, was captured.

Four years later (716 B.C.), Sargon II conducted a campaign against the northern Arabians. After defeating them and forcing them to pay tribute, he came to the Egyptian border at the Brook of Egypt. Sargon's control over the trade routes from Arabia and Philistia was now recognized by Shilkanni, king of Egypt (Osorkon IV), who sent him a rich payment. The "Sealed Harbor of Egypt" was inaugurated as a center for trade and commerce.

While Arabian exiles were being settled in Samaria, Hezekiah succeeded Ahaz on the throne of Judah (715 B.C.). That same year, Piye, king of Cush, campaigned in the Egyptian delta. Since there was no longer a kingdom in Samaria, Hezekiah invited the remaining Israelites to share in his renewed Passover celebrations in Jerusalem (2 Chron. 30:5-6, 10-11). To strengthen the position of the Jerusalem temple, he then initiated a campaign against the rival cultic centers throughout Judah and Samaria.

Egyptian-inspired unrest continued to fester in Philistia. The disloyal king of Ashdod, Azuri, was replaced by his brother, Ahimitti, in 713 B.C. The following year, a popular revolt broke out in Ashdod, led by a pretender named Iamani (a personal name that might be equated with Hebrew Yavan, Greek Ion). Judah, Edom and Moab seem to have been involved but they evidently paid their tribute in a hurry when Sargon's general arrived with the army. Hezekiah had also been warned by Isaiah not to take part (Isaiah 20). The cities of Gath and Ashdod were conquered. Iamani fled to Egypt; he got as far as Syene but was refused political asylum by the Cushite king (Shabako, brother of Piye). Shabako was already in control of Egypt but he was not willing to insult the Assyrians. The Assyrian province of Ashdod was now established although local dynasties continued to rule the city-states.

Meanwhile, an Assyrian commissioner reported to Calah that a certain Ayanur of the land of Tab'el had brought news about people of the land of Geder who had attacked a Moabite town. The capital of Tab'el was called Tyre; it is known later as the estate of the Tobiads.

In 710 B.C., Sargon defeated Merodachbaladan, the Chaldean pretender to the throne of Babylon. Five years later, Sargon met his death while on a campaign against the Cimmerians in the north.

HEZEKIAH'S PREPARATIONS FOR REBELLION
705 TO 701 B.C.

Hezekiah and other local kings in the southern Levant saw the death of Sargon II as an opportunity to throw off the Assyrian yoke. Shabako, the Cushite ruler of the twenty-fifth dynasty, promised support to the rebels (Isaiah 30:1-5; 31:1-3). Sennacherib, Sargon's successor, was busy for the next few years with conflicts in the east and especially in Babylonia. Merodachbaladan, the Chaldean chieftain, laid claim to the throne of Babylon, but the Assyrian army drove him into exile in Elam.

His policy of obedience under Sargon II had allowed Hezekiah to reap tremendous profits from the caravan trade (2 Chron. 32:27-29). Now he used these resources to make Judah an armed camp, with newly-fortified towns and fresh weapons (2 Chron.32:5). Silli-baal, king of Gaza, refused to cooperate, so Hezekiah sent his troops to occupy Philistine strong points in the western Negeb (2 Kings 18:8). The Simeonites were encouraged to settle there (1 Chron. 4:39-41) and also to take (western) Mount Seir from the Amalekites (1 Chron. 4:42-43). The king of Ashkelon gained control of Joppa and its agricultural hinterland. The people of Ekron supported the anti-Assyrian plot but their ruler, Padi, did not. He was deposed and handed over to Hezekiah to be imprisoned in Jerusalem. Gath and Gezer apparently became Judean strongholds; Azekah was another. Lachish and Libnah were the chief centers in the southwestern Shephelah.

Provisions were stored in the fortresses throughout the kingdom (2 Chron. 32:27-30). Especially prominent were four-handled wine jars from the royal wineries, found in nearly every site of military importance in the north and west of Judah. The jars were stamped with seals bearing an official symbol, either a four-winged scarab or a two-winged sun disk. The inscription above reads: "(Belonging) to the king;" below was written the name of the town where the wine was processed, Hebron, Ziph, Socoh or Memshath. Since the royal vineyards were in the hill country (2 Chron. 26:10c), three of these centers are each in one of the southern districts of the Judean hills. The fourth, *Memshath*, is unidentified and unknown from the town lists. It may have been in the Bethlehem district (preserved only in the Greek text) or perhaps it was an abbreviated form of Hebrew *memshe(le)th*, "government," and stood for the capital city, Jerusalem. Officials responsible for the administration of the wineries often stamped their personal seals on one or more of the handles. The clay of all the jars derived from some spot in the Shephelah; it was probably extracted and delivered to the four centers where potters made the jars for the wine.

Engineering projects for assuring the water supply in the fortified cities were also undertaken (2 Chron. 32:3-4), in particular the Shiloah tunnel from the Gihon spring (2 Kings 20:20; 2 Chron. 32:30).

During the frantic preparations for war, Hezekiah fell ill, but Isaiah assured him he would recover and live fifteen more years (2 Kings 20:1-11; Isaiah 38:1-22; i.e. from 701 to 686 B.C.). An embassage also arrived from Merodachbaladan who was still plotting against Sennacherib even though he was a political refugee in Elam (2 Kings 20:12-19; Isaiah 39:1-8).

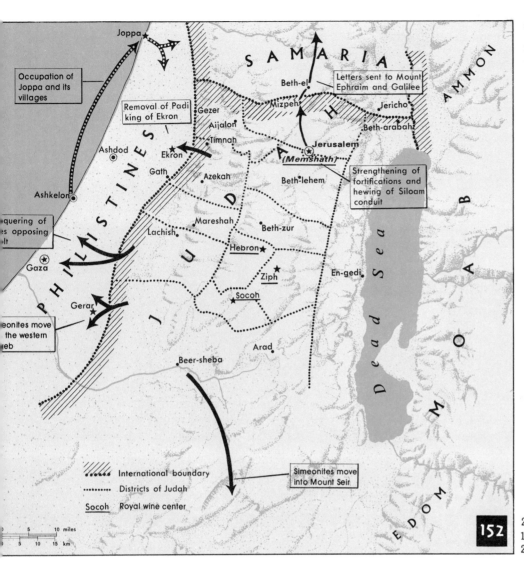

Map 152 labels:

- Joppa
- Occupation of Joppa and its villages
- SAMARIA
- Beth-el
- Mizpeh
- Letters sent to Mount Ephraim and Galilee
- Jericho
- AMMON
- Removal of Padi king of Ekron
- Gezer
- Aijalon
- Timnah
- Beth-arabah
- Ashdod
- Ekron
- Gath
- Jerusalem (Memshath)
- Azekah
- Strengthening of fortifications and hewing of Siloam conduit
- Ashkelon
- Beth-lehem
- ...quering of ...es opposing ...lt
- Mareshah
- Beth-zur
- Lachish
- Hebron
- Gaza
- En-gedi
- Dead Sea
- Gerar
- Ziph
- ...eonites move ...the western ...eb
- Socoh
- M O A B
- Beer-sheba
- Arad
- PHILISTINES
- J U D A H
- International boundary
- Districts of Judah
- Socoh Royal wine center
- Simeonites move into Mount Seir
- E D O M
- 0 5 10 miles
- 0 5 10 15 km

152

Storehouses also for the yield of grain, wine, and oil
... He likewise provided cites for himself ... This same
Hezekiah closed the upper outlet of the waters of
Gihon and directed them down to the west side of
the city of David. And Hezekiah prospered in all his
works.

(2 Chronicles 32:28-30)

Conquest of Lachish by Assyrian army (Relief from
palace of Sennacherib at Nineveh)

2 KINGS 18:6-8; 20:12-20; IS. 22:8-11;
1 CHRON. 4:38-43; 2 CHRON. 30; 32:3-8,
27-31; ANNALS, SENNACHERIB

SENNACHERIB'S RECONQUEST OF PHOENICIA

701 B.C.

Sennacherib, now on his third military campaign, arrived with
his army in 701 B.C. The first objective was conquest of the
Phoenician coast; the rebellious leader, Luli (Elulaios) of Sidon,
fled to Iadana (Cyprus) where he met his death. Ethobaal was
appointed in his place. The fall of the Phoenician cities inspired
fear in many of Hezekiah's erstwhile allies; they rushed to Acco
to pay their tribute and renew their allegiance to Sennacherib
(see Map 153).

Sennacherib then marched against Philistia and Judah. Joppa
and its hinterland towns, occupied by the rebellious Sidqia
of Ashkelon, were taken, thus assuring logistic support by
sea from Phoenicia. Here the Assyrian scribes mention two
logically, but not chronologically, related events, namely the
deposing of Sidqia and the defeat of the Egyptian-Cushite
army that had come to the aid of Sidqia and Hezekiah.
The biblical chronology of events shows that the battle at
Eltekeh came after the fall of Lachish and during the siege
of Libnah (2 Kings 19:9; Isaiah 37:9). The next conquest was
Timnah in the Sorek Valley; Ekron was thus cut off from
immediate support by Hezekiah. Ekron was taken and the
rebels punished by impalement. A fragmentary "Letter to the
god (Asshur)" reporting the king's victory may supplement
the account in Sennacherib's Annals. Its reference to the
capture of Azekah, a lofty Judean fortress, is followed by a

Map 153 labels:

- Luli king of Sidon flees to Iadnana (Cyprus)
- Sidon
- Beth-zaith
- PHOENICIA
- Zarephath
- Litani River
- Mahalab
- Tyre
- Usu
- Sennacherib receives tribute from kings of: Samsimuruna, Sidon, Arvad, Byblos, Ashdod, Ammon, Moab, Edom
- Achzib
- Acco
- Sea of Chinnereth
- 0 5 10 miles
- 0 5 10 15 km

153

Philistine town taken over by Hezekiah, most likely Gath. The seizure of Azekah would leave Gath unprotected. The two main approaches to Judah from the west were now blocked. Lachish, the largest city conquered on this campaign, would have been next, followed by Libnah. Micah's dirge over the towns of the Shephelah suggests the fate of other towns in the area (Mic. 1:8-16). Isaiah defines the march of a hostile force from the north to threaten Jerusalem (Isaiah 10:28-32). Sennacherib claims the capture of forty-six walled cities and

their surrounding villages. Excavations have found remains of severe destruction at this time at Lachish, Beer-sheba, Arad, Debir, Beth-shemesh and elsewhere. It was a blow from which Judah never fully recovered. But Jerusalem was saved. After defeating the Egyptians, led by Tirhaka (Taharka) Shabako's younger brother and possibly co-regent, the Assyrian army was smitten — in biblical terms by "the Angel of the Lord." Sennacherib accepted Hezekiah's promise of heavy tribute payments and withdrew.

SENNACHERIB IN PHILISTIA AND JUDAH   701 B.C.

Therefore thus says the Lord concerning the k
Assyria: He shall not come into this city...
(Isaiah

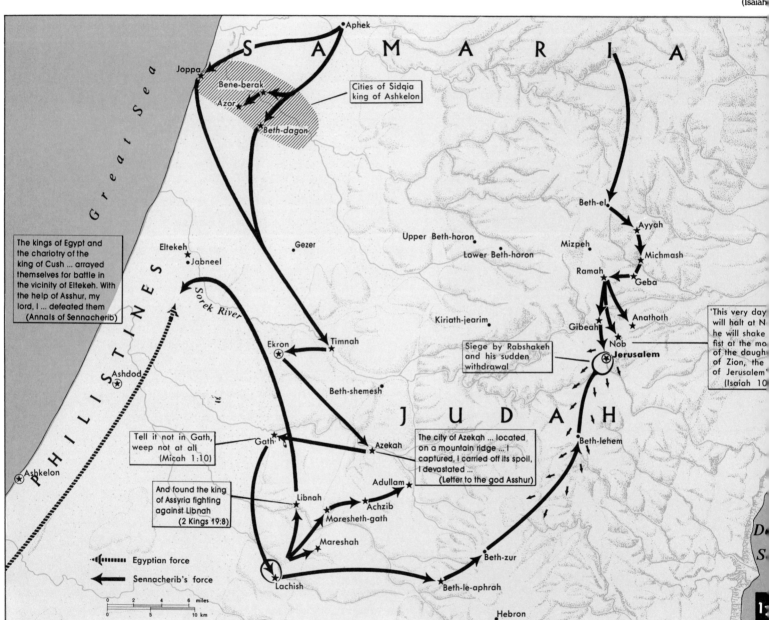

The kings of Egypt and the chariotry of the king of Cush ... arrayed themselves for battle in the vicinity of Eltekeh. With the help of Asshur, my lord, I ... defeated them
(Annals of Sennacherib)

Tell it not in Gath, weep not at all
(Micah 1:10)

And found the king of Assyria fighting against Libnah
(2 Kings 19:8)

The city of Azekah ... located on a mountain ridge ... I captured, I carried off its spoil, I devastated ...
(Letter to the god Asshur)

Siege by Rabshakeh and his sudden withdrawal

'This very day will halt at N he will shake fist at the mo of the daugh of Zion, the of Jerusalem'
(Isaiah 10

Egyptian force

Sennacherib's force

2 KINGS 18-10; IS. 10:28-32; 36-37; MIC. 1:8-16; 2 CHRON. 32:1-23; RELIEFS, SIEGE OF LACHISH — PALACE OF SENNACHERIB, NINEVEH; LETTER TO THE GOD ASSHUR, NIN

JUDAH AND HER NEIGHBORS DURING THE REIGN OF MANASSEH   701 TO 642 B.C.

Judah's territory was greatly reduced by Sennacherib as punishment for leading the revolt. The towns and areas in question were given to the loyal kings of Gaza, Ashdod and Ekron. Hezekiah may have enjoyed a certain notoriety because of his deliverance from Sennacherib (2 Chron. 32:23), but he continued to pay a heavy indemnity to the Assyrians. Mean-

while, because of his recent illness, he appointed his son, Manasseh, co-regent as soon as the latter became twelve years of age (2 Kings. 21:1; 2 Chron. 33:1; 697 B.C.). In Egypt, the Cushite Taharka (biblical Terhaka) came to the throne in 690 B.C. and engaged in an active policy of interference in Asia. The Phoenicians leaned strongly to the Egyptian

e. When Esarhaddon became king of Assyria after the sassination of Sennacherib (681 B.C.), he was soon faced th a rebellion by Tyre and Sidon (679 B.C.). That year he sured his control of the southern coast by seizing the town Arza at the "border of the Brook of Egypt." Two years er, Esarhaddon conquered Sidon and ended its hegemony Phoenicia. A treaty was made with Baal, king of Tyre, in ich the Assyrian coastal towns along the coast were given Tyre, down to the border of Philistia; Dor and Acco were luded.

During that same year (677 B.C.), the rulers of twelve states the Land of Hatti — Beyond the River, provided corvée or to cut and deliver trees from Lebanon to Esarhaddon's w palace being built at Nineveh.

Manasseh was now sole ruler of Judah with its heavy eco- mic burdens. He turned to his neighbors, especially to Tyre, w Assyria's favored state, which meant reintroduction of the Canaanite cult practices that Hezekiah had removed, luding worship of Baal, Asherah and the host of heaven. us, he is compared with Ahab of Israel (2 Kings 21:3). e many foreign cults, Sidonian, Moabite and Ammonite, presented diplomatic and economic as well as religious links th the neighboring states; their shrines (and embassies) were ated "east of Jerusalem, to the south of the mount of rruption" (2 Kings 23:13). These religious forms were not quired by Assyria; the imperial god Asshur was not even orshipped in Jerusalem. The Assyrians did not generally ake a policy of forcing their vassals to worship the Assyrian ds.

During the years after 676 B.C., Esarhaddon was engaged in ilitary and diplomatic efforts towards the Arabians. A hostile rabian leader was deposed and a man loyal to Assyrian terests was installed. The Assyrian monarch intended to vade Egypt; for this he needed Arab support. In return they ijoyed control of the caravan routes. From the first successful vasion of Esarhaddon (671 B.C.) to Asshurbanipal's conquest No-ammon (664/663 B.C.), the Levantine states, including idah, were involved in the war effort. Manasseh, along with s neighbors, sent troops to Egypt (667 B.C.).

Judah's fortunes changed radically after the great civil war at rocked the Assyrian empire. Shamash-shum-ukin, Asshur- inipal's younger brother, was not content to be king of abylon only; he challenged his brother's imperial throne (652 c.). The Tyrians and the Arabians supported Babylon. An rabian army was caught and demolished by the Assyrians it tried to enter the Euphrates Valley (650 B.C.). Babylon ll and its young king died in 648 B.C. While reorganizing abylonia, Asshurbanipal had the western leaders brought ere for interrogation. Manasseh was among them; he man- ied to convince the Assyrian king of his loyalty and was turned to Judah with permission (and probably funds) to build Jerusalem and to reestablish the fortified cities of Judah Chron. 33:11-17). Later on, Asshurbanipal carried out an tensive campaign against the Arabians (644/643 B.C.); on the turn march he also attacked Usu and Acco as punishment r Tyre's support of his erstwhile brother.

Manasseh died in 642 B.C., leaving his successors with an pportunity to capitalize on this extraordinary turn of events.

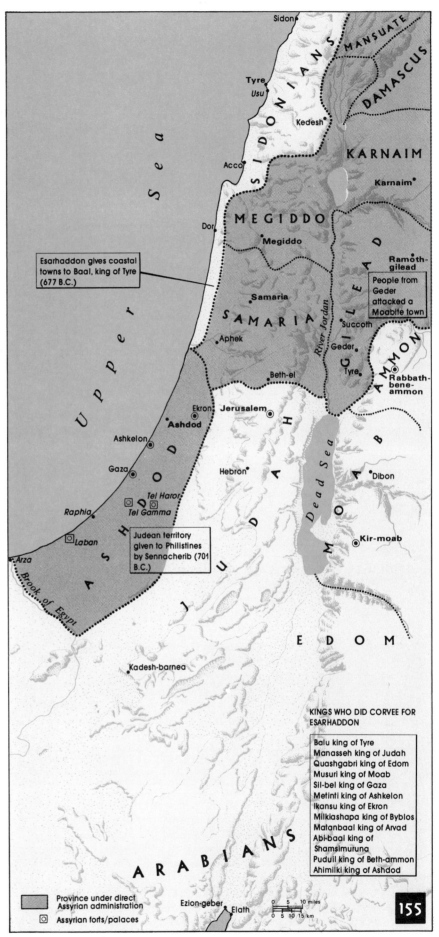

Esarhaddon gives coastal towns to Baal, king of Tyre (677 B.C.)

People from Geder attacked a Moabite town

Judean territory given to Philistines by Sennacherib (701 B.C.)

KINGS WHO DID CORVEE FOR ESARHADDON

Balu king of Tyre
Manasseh king of Judah
Quashgabri king of Edom
Musuri king of Moab
Sil-bel king of Gaza
Metinti king of Ashkelon
Ikansu king of Ekron
Milkiashapa king of Byblos
Matanbaal king of Arvad
Abi-baal king of Shamsimuruna
Puduil king of Beth-ammon
Ahimilki king of Ashdod

Province under direct Assyrian administration

Assyrian forts/palaces

155

2 KINGS 21:1-18; 2 CHRON. 33:1-20; ANNALS OF SENNACHERIB AND ESARHADDON; TREATY BETWEEN ESARHADDON AND BAAL OF TYRE; LETTER FROM NIMRUD

From the city of Aphek in the Land of Samaria to the
city of Raphia in the region of the Brook of Egypt, there
exists no river!

(Annals of Esarhaddon)

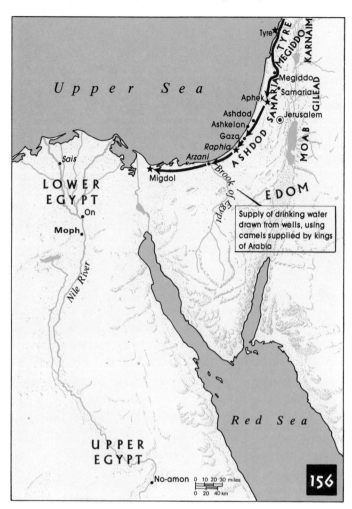

ANNALS OF ESARHADDON AND ASSHURBANIPAL; OTHER
ASSYRIAN DOCUMENTS; BABYLONIAN CHRONICLE

THE CONQUEST OF EGYPT BY ASSYRIA
669 TO 663 B.C.

The failure of Esarhaddon's first attempted invasion of Egypt
(674 B.C.) may have been due to lack of Arabian assistance.
During the second invasion (671 B.C.), the Arabs gave Esarhaddon their active support in transporting the Assyrian army
safely across the desert. The delta was freed of the Cushite
yoke and local pro-Assyrian rulers installed, in particular Neco
I of Sais. The twenty-fifth dynasty Cushites had meddled in
the Levant. Now Esarhaddon was determined to drive them
out of Egypt itself. In 669 B.C., the Assyrian king died on
his way to another Egyptian campaign. Taharka returned to
Memphis (Moph) but Asshurbanipal defeated his army and
drove him back to No-ammon (667/666 B.C.). Finally, in 664/663
B.C., Asshurbanipal took No-ammon and appointed Psammeticus I, son of Neco I of Sais, as ruler of the delta.

Psammeticus installed his daughter as high priestess in No-
ammon in 655 B.C., thus uniting Egypt under the twenty-sixth
dynasty. He gained independence from Assyria with the aid
of mercenaries sent by Gyges, king of Lydia. But Gyges lost
thereby the support of Assyria against the Cimmerians, and
lost his life during their invasion of Lydia (654 B.C.).

Conquest of Egyptian town by Assyrian army (Relief from
palace of Asshurbanipal at Nineveh)

THE DECLINE AND FALL OF THE ASSYRIAN EMPIRE
LATE 7TH CENTURY B.C.

The reign of Asshurbanipal was the high-water mark in Assyrian
power. Yet there were signs of internal stress and external
danger that eventually spelled its downfall. Psammeticus I
gained independence for a united Egypt in 655 B.C. The Cim-
merian threat from the north was deflected towards Lydia
(654 B.C.). A serious attack by the Medes was thwarted
by the death of their king, Phaortes, in battle (653 B.C.).
The conflict with Shamash-shum-ukin, king of Babylon (652-
648 B.C.), revealed just how fragile was the loyalty of some
client peoples such as the Phoenicians and the Arabians.
Asshurbanipal wore the crowns of Assyria and Babylon until
630 B.C., when he handed the empire over to Asshur-etil-ilani.

He may have kept the throne of Babylon (under the name
Kandalu) until his death in 627 B.C. Rivalry between usurpers
in Babylon eventually affected the imperial throne in Nineveh
and permitted Nabupolassar, a Chaldean, to claim Babylon. By
623 B.C. he was firmly in control of an independent Babylonia
allied with the Medes against Assyria. In 616 B.C. Psammeticus
I sent an expeditionary force to help the Assyrians but they
were beaten by the Medes and Chaldeans. Cyaxares the
Mede captured Asshur in 614 B.C. and Nabupolassar rushed
to Nineveh in 612 B.C. to join in the conquest. The Assyrians
retreated to Haran but were driven out in 610 B.C. and forced
to fall back to Carchemish.

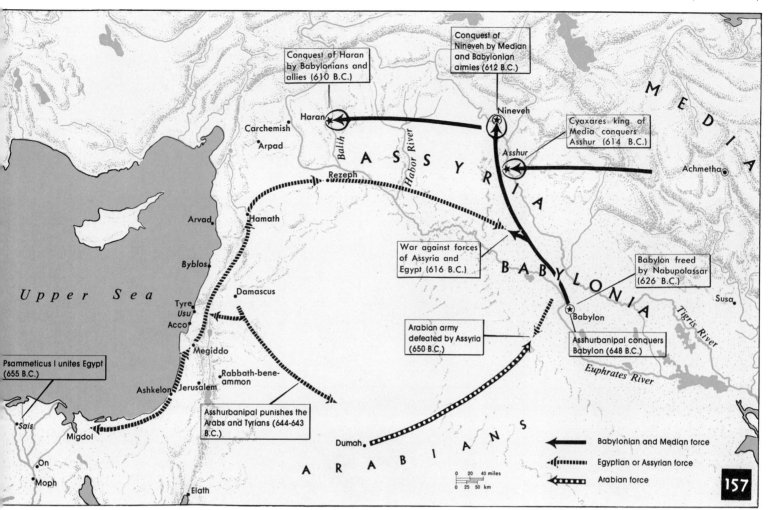

Conquest of Haran by Babylonians and allies (610 B.C.)

Conquest of Nineveh by Median and Babylonian armies (612 B.C.)

Cyaxares king of Media conquers Asshur (614 B.C.)

War against forces of Assyria and Egypt (616 B.C.)

Babylon freed by Nabupolassar (626 B.C.)

Arabian army defeated by Assyria (650 B.C.)

Asshurbanipal conquers Babylon (648 B.C.)

Psammeticus I unites Egypt (655 B.C.)

Asshurbanipal punishes the Arabs and Tyrians (644-643 B.C.)

Babylonian and Median force

Egyptian or Assyrian force

Arabian force

0 20 40 miles
0 25 50 km

157

BABYLONIAN CHRONICLE, DAYS OF NABUPOLASSAR KING OF BABYLON

THE KINGDOM OF JOSIAH

628 TO 609 B.C.

Amon son of Manasseh reigned only two years (642-640 B.C.) before he was slain in a palace plot. The "people of the land," that is the landed nobility, executed the regicides and crowned the eight-year old Josiah as king (2 Kings 21:23-22:1; 2 Chron. 33:24-34:1). At age fourteen he was already a father (634 B.C.); Jehoiakim was born to him by Zebidah, daughter of Pedaiah from Rumah in Lower Galilee (2 Kings 23:36; 2 Chron. 36:5). Two years later Hamutal, daughter of Jeremiah from Libnah, bore him Jehoahaz. In this, his eighth year (632 B.C.), he began to seek "the god of David his father" (2 Chron. 34:3), under the influence of his father-in-law from the priestly city of Libnah in the Shephelah.

News of Asshurbanipal's retirement (in 630 B.C.) may have inspired Josiah to launch his campaign against all the cult places rivaling Jerusalem, not only in Judah but also in "the towns of Manasseh and Ephraim and Simeon and as far as Naphtali in the hill country" (2 Chron. 34:6). Simeon is the city of Zebulon on the Jezreel Plain called Shimron in the Book of Joshua (Josh. 11:1; 19:15) but known as Shim'on in the Execration Texts, the list of Thutmose III, and the Amarna Letters. Its name in the Second Temple period was Simonia as attested by Josephus and Talmudic sources. It was the leading Israelite

town in the Jezreel Valley after Megiddo became an Assyrian headquarters. Even Megiddo was abandoned by the Assyrians by 609 B.C. when Josiah chose to do battle there with Neco II.

Josiah was following the example of Hezekiah in drawing the northern Israelites back to Jerusalem. The Assyrian governors were apparently unable to oppose him. In the year of Asshurbanipal's death (627 B.C.), Jeremiah began his twenty-three years of prophecy (Jer. 1:2; 25:1-3) and by the time Nabupolassar was firmly established in Babylon (623 B.C.), the kingdom of Judah was ready to seal its covenant of independence. Josiah's great covenant ceremony and national reform were inaugurated in 622 B.C. (2 Kings 22:3-24:28; 2 Chron. 34:8-35:39). Only the Jerusalem-oriented cadre of priests and Levites was allowed to function (2 Kings 23:9).

The chance find of a small fort on the shore north of Ashdod-yam brought to light some inscriptions in good Judean Hebrew script and language, proving that Josiah's authority had been extended to the seacoast. Just how firm was his control over "all of Israel" is uncertain but he seems to have been well on the way to reestablishing the Israelite kingdom with Jerusalem as the capital.

Behold a son shall be born to the house of David, Josiah by name ...

(1 Kings 13:2)

THE KINGDOM
OF JOSIAH

May my lord, the officer, hear the word of his servant. Your servant is a harvester ... and your servant harvested and measured and stored as always before the Sabbath ... and Hoshayahu son of Shobai came and took your servant's cloak after I had measured my harvest ...

(From the Hebrew letter from Mesad Hashavyahu)

Hebrew letter from Mesad Hashavyahu

2 KINGS 22:1-23:30; 2 CHRON. 34-35

THE CAMPAIGN OF NECO II TO HARAN

609 B.C.

Psammeticus died in 610 B.C. and was succeeded by his son, Neco II. The new pharaoh continued the policy of his father and marched forth towards Carchemish to help the last Assyrian king, Asshur-uballit, in the reconquest of Haran. Josiah realized that his own kingdom could not maintain its newly won independence if Neco should succeed. He tried to stop the Egyptian advance by giving battle at Megiddo, but he paid for his daring attempt with his life. Jehoahaz, the prince whose mother came from Libnah, was anointed by the "people

of the land," but three months later Neco deposed him and appointed his older brother Jehoiakim (2 Kings 23:30-35).

Neco's attempt to drive the Babylonians out of Haran failed miserably. Nevertheless, this did not prevent him from behaving as master of the Levant. His action in removing the chosen Judean king, appointing his own candidate and imposing a heavy tribute payment on the country proves that he fully expected to control the eastern Mediterranian littoral even if the Assyrians did survive the Babylonian onslaught.

...days Pharaoh Neco king of Egypt went up to the
...f Assyria to the river Euphrates. King Josiah went
...et him; and Pharaoh Neco slew him at Megiddo.

(2 Kings 23:29)

Concerning the army of Pharaoh Neco, king of Egypt,
which was by the river Euphrates at Carchemish and
which Nebuchadrezzar, king of Babylon, defeated in
the fourth year of Jehoiakim the son of Josiah, king of
Judah ...

(Jeremiah 46:2)

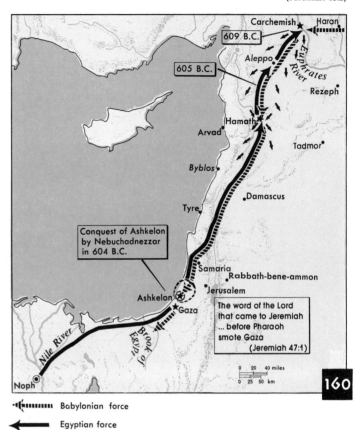

Carchemish

Haran

609 B.C.

Aleppo

605 B.C.

Euphrates River

Rezeph

Hamath

Arvad

Tadmor

Byblos

Damascus

Tyre

Conquest of Ashkelon
by Nebuchadnezzar
in 604 B.C.

Samaria

Rabbath-bene-ammon

Jerusalem

Ashkelon

Gaza

The word of the Lord
that came to Jeremiah
... before Pharaoh
smote Gaza

(Jeremiah 47:1)

Brook of Egypt

Nile River

0   20   40 miles
0   25   50 km

160

Noph

◀┫▓▓▓▓   Babylonian force

◀━━━━   Egyptian force

JER. 46:2; 47:1; BABYLONIAN CHRONICLE; HERODOTUS II, 159

THE CAMPAIGNS OF NEBUCHADNEZZAR
605 TO 601 B.C.

Egypt controlled the Levant for four years until the Babylonians
conquered Carchemish. Nebuchadnezzar, the crown prince of
Babylon, got word of his father's death, rushed to Babylon
and returned as king to finish the siege. When Carchemish
fell (605 B.C.), he pursued the retreating Egyptians to the land
of Hamath and ravaged the countryside (Jer. 46:1-2). The
following year, he marched south and took Ashkelon (604 B.C.),
causing such fear in Judah that a fast was proclaimed (Jer.
36:9). Jehoiakim became his servant, paying tribute for three
years (2 Kings 24:1; 2 Chron. 36:6 Greek version). In 603 the
Babylonian army took another important city, Gaza or perhaps
Ekron. In 602 B.C. there was another campaign, mainly a show
of force to collect tribute. In 601 B.C., Pharaoh Neco came
forth. According to the Greek historian Herodotus, Neco
encountered "the Syrians" at Migdol and defeated them; then
he conquered Kadytes (Gaza), an act confirmed by Jeremiah
47:1. The Babylonian account says that the kings of Babylonia
and Egypt "smote one another on the breast," meaning that
the battle was a draw. At any rate, Nebuchadnezzar retired
to Babylon and did not come forth the following year. At this
time, Jehoiakim probably felt safe in withholding his tribute (2
Kings 24:1).

Carchemish

Haran

Aleppo

Siege of Haran fails;
Euphrates becomes
border between
Babylon and Egypt

Euphrates River

Rezeph

Orontes River

H A M A T H

Hamath

Arvad

Tadmor

Riblah

Byblos

Necho installs
Jehoiakim in place of
Jehoahaz his brother

Litani

Damascus

Tyre

Plain of Megiddo

Megiddo

...o comes
...id of
...ur-uballit

Josiah killed
near Megiddo

Rabbath-bene-ammon

Jerusalem

Ashdod
Ashkelon

Gaza

◀━━━━   Necoh

◀┫▓▓▓▓   Josiah

0   10   20   30 miles
0   20   40 km

159

...GS 23:29-30; JER. 47; 2 CHRON. 35:20-24; BABYLONIAN CHRONICLE

Stone window railing (From the palace of
Jehoiakim at Ramat Rahel)

And the king of Egypt did not come again out of his land, for the king of Babylon had taken all that belonged to the king of Egypt from the Brook of Egypt to the river Euphrates.

(2 Kings 24:7)

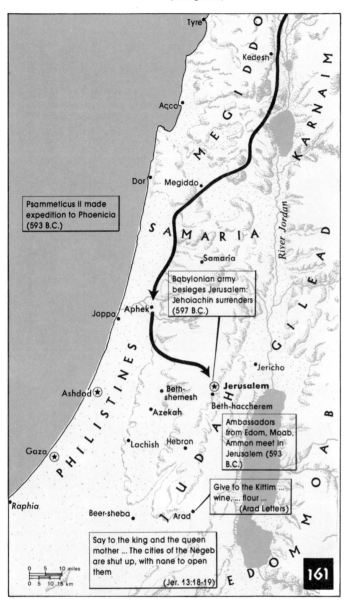

Psammeticus II made expedition to Phoenicia (593 B.C.)

Babylonian army besieges Jerusalem: Jehoiachin surrenders (597 B.C.)

Ambassadors from Edom, Moab, Ammon meet in Jerusalem (593 B.C.)

Give to the Kittim ... wine, ... flour ... (Arad Letters)

Say to the king and the queen mother ... The cities of the Negeb are shut up, with none to open them

(Jer. 13:18-19)

2 KINGS 24; 2 CHRON. 36:6a, 8-10a, 6b-7, 10b-13; JER. 13:18-19; 22:1-30; 27:3, 12; 28:1; 51:1; BABYLONIAN CHRONICLE; ARAD LETTERS; HERODOTUS

When the army of the king of Babylon was fighting against Jerusalem and against all the cities of Judah that were left, Lachish and Azekah; for these were the only fortified cities of Judah that remained.

(Jeremiah 34:7)

THE FINAL CAMPAIGN OF NEBUCHADNEZZAR AGAINST JUDAH
15 JANUARY, 588 TO 19 JULY, 586 B.C.

Psammeticus II was followed by Hophra in 589 B.C. who renewed the policy of interference in Syria. Zedekiah was induced to revolt from Babylon. The Chaldean response was swift; Jerusalem came under siege on the tenth day of the tenth month in Zedekiah's ninth year (2 Kings 25:1; Jer. 39:1; 52:4; cf, Ezekiel 24:1-2), 15 January, 588 B.C. Hophra's army did come into the field causing the Babylonians to raise the siege temporarily, but

THE CLOSING YEARS OF THE KINGDOM OF JUDAH
599 TO 586 B.C.

Nebuchadnezzar (Nebuchadrezzar) stayed in Babylon in 600 B.C.; in 599 Babylonian troops attacked the Arabians while local Chaldean, Aramean (or Edomite?), Moabite, and Ammonite troops were sent to harass Judah (2 Kings 24:2). The Babylonian army was sent to besiege "the city of Judah" (Jerusalem) in 598 B.C. They set out from Babylon in Kislev (17 Dec. 598 to 15 Jan. 597); meanwhile, Jehoiakim had already died on 21 Marcheshvan (8 Dec.) 598 B.C. and his young son, Jehoiachin, assumed the throne under the tutelage of his mother, Nehushta. The Edomites, and perhaps others, attacked Judah from the south, "the cities of the Negeb are closed and there is no one to open" (Jer. 13:19). The Babylonian army laid siege to Jerusalem and Nebuchadnezzar arrived shortly thereafter; on 2 Adar (Sat., 16 March) 597 B.C. the city was taken. A little over a month later, on 10 Nisan (22 April) 597 B.C., Nebuchadnezzar sent orders to bring Jehoiachin and his entourage as prisoners to Babylon. Zedekiah, another son of Josiah, was appointed king (2 Kings 24:10-17; 2 Chron. 36:10a, 6b-7, 10b).

The Chaldean army was sent once again to the Levant in 596 B.C.; in 595 the king had to crush a rebellion in Babylon itself. The next two years saw him back in the west. Egypt was apparently stirring up diplomatic ferment; ambassadors from Edom, Moab and Ammon were conferring in Jerusalem (Jer. 27:3, 12; 28:1) and Psammeticus II, successor of Neco, made a trip to Phoenicia. Zedekiah was taken to Babylon (Jer. 51:1) but managed to convince Nebuchadnezzar of his loyalty. He returned to Jerusalem and his government remained loyal to Babylon for a time. Kittim, probably Cypriote mercenaries in Chaldean service, patrolled the Negeb and received supplies from Judean fortresses such as Arad.

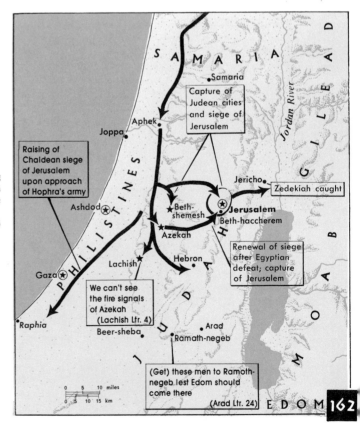

Capture of Judean cities and siege of Jerusalem

Raising of Chaldean siege of Jerusalem upon approach of Hophra's army

Zedekiah caught

Renewal of siege after Egyptian defeat; capture of Jerusalem

We can't see the fire signals of Azekah (Lachish Ltr. 4)

(Get) these men to Ramoth-negeb lest Edom should come there

(Arad Ltr. 24)

the Egyptians were soon routed and the siege renewed (Jer. 37:3-15); all this took place before the end of 587 (Jer. 32:1). The other towns throughout Judah were also ravaged. The Edomites invaded the Negeb; reinforcements were ordered from Arad and Kinah to Ramoth-negeb, "Lest Edom should come there." At one stage only Lachish and Azekah remained (Jer. 34:7); soon a soldier, Hoshayahu, reported to Ya'ush, his commander at Lachish, that fire signals could not be seen from Azekah. Lachish itself must have fallen soon thereafter. Jerusalem's defenses finally collapsed on 19 July, 586 B.C. (2 Kings 25:2-3; Jer. 39:2; 52:5-6). Zedekiah fled but was captured near Jericho.

This is the number of the people whom Nebuchadrezzar [Nebuchadnezzar] carried away captive: in the seventh year, three thousand and twenty-three Jews; in the eighteenth year of Nebuchadrezzar he carried away captive from Jerusalem eight hundred and thirty-two persons; in the twenty-third year of Nebuchadrezzar, Nebuzaradan the captain of the guard carried away captive of the Jews seven hundred and forty-five persons; all persons were four thousand and six hundred.
(Jeremiah 52:28-30)

THE EXILE FROM JUDAH

597 TO 582 B.C.

The epilogue to the book of Jeremiah gives what seem to be fairly accurate figures for three stages of exile from Judah (Jer. 52:28-30). They took place in 597, 586 and 582 B.C. The latter seems to have been carried out during Nebuchadnezzar's campaign in the west against "Coele Syria" and the Moabites and Ammonites (Josephus, Antiq., X, 181-182). Neo-Babylonian cuneiform tablets, especially the archive of the banking house of Murashu at Nippur, contain many references to Judeans as well as other exiled peoples.

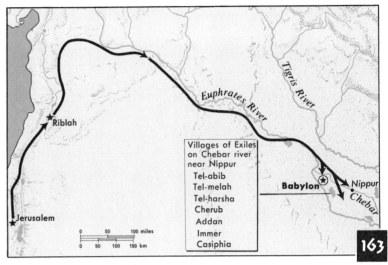

Villages of Exiles on Chebar river near Nippur
Tel-abib
Tel-melah
Tel-harsha
Cherub
Addan
Immer
Casiphia

2 KINGS 24:11-16; 25:11; JER. 52:28-30; EZEK. 3:15; EZRA 2:59; 8:17

THE FLIGHT TO EGYPT

CA. 586 B.C.

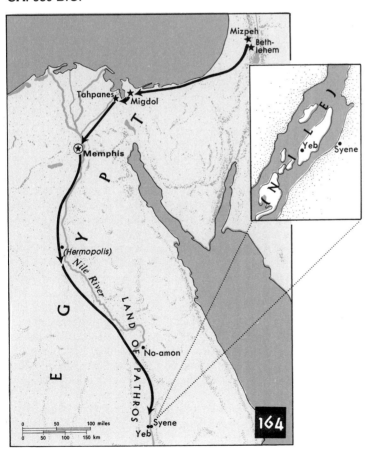

Gedaliah son of Ahikam, the former "Steward of the royal palace," was appointed governor of Judah by the Babylonians. He made his headquarters at Mizpah. Other Judeans who had fled to neighboring countries such as Moab, Ammon and Edom, gathered to him there. Ishmael, son of Nethaniah, of the royal house, was incited by Baalis, king of the Ammonites, to assassinate Gedaliah. This deed was perpetrated in the seventh month (October, 586 B.C.). Afterwards, a band of leading Judeans chose flight to Egypt for fear of Babylonian reprisals. They settled in Tahpanes (where Baal-zephon was worshipped) and eventually entered service as mercenaries. Their one attested colony is at Yeb (Elephantine) where family and community documents in Aramaic have been found.

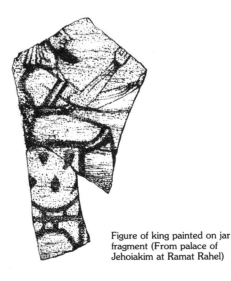

Figure of king painted on jar fragment (From palace of Jehoiakim at Ramat Rahel)

2 KINGS 25:25-26; JER. 39:11-44:30

So you shall divide this land among you according to the tribes of Israel.

(Ezekiel 47:21)

EZEK. 47:13-48:29

EZEKIEL'S VISION OF THE RESTORED TRIBES   573 B.C.

Return to the homeland was a hope kept alive by the exiled community. On the tenth day of Nisan in the twenty-fifth year of captivity (counting from 597 B.C.) i.e. 28 April, 573 B.C., Ezekiel received his vision of the restored temple (Ezek. 40:1) with an appended vision of the restored tribes of Israel (Ezek. 47:13-48:29). The visionary distribution of tribes, in east-west territorial bands across the country, is set in a realistic geographical framework. The origin of the northern border tradition is seen in the explicit reference to "the border between Damascus and Hamath" (Ezek. 47:16). This border description had been acquired during the Israelite monarchy. From the Late Bronze to the Hellenistic Age there is evidence that it was the recognized limit of "Canaan." The southern border comes from the kingdom of Judah. The author of Num. 34 used them to define the hypothetical inheritance in Joshua's day; Ezekiel projects them into the visionary future.

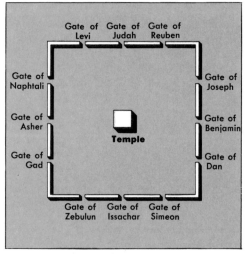

EZEK. 48:30-35

THE RISE AND FALL OF THE KINGDOM OF BABYLON
626 TO 539 B.C.

Chaldean rule over Babylon began officially with Nabopolassar's claim to kingship in 626 B.C.; his hold on the city was consolidated by 623 B.C. Previously, he had been the chieftain of the Chaldean tribes who had long struggled to free southern Mesopotamia from the Assyrian yoke. The ensuing decade saw an alliance between Nabopolassar and Cyaxares II of Media against the Assyrians. The fall of Asshur to the Medes (614 B.C.), and of Nineveh to the combined forces of Media and Babylonia (612 B.C.) and Haran (610 B.C.) marked the expulsion of the Assyrian government from Mesopotamia. From 609 to 605 B.C., the Babylonians continued the war against the Assyrian government-in-exile (supported by Neco II of Egypt) at Carchemish; Nebuchadnezzar reduced that city shortly after the death of his father, Nabopolassar. Henceforth, Cyaxares concentrated on the conquest of Armenia (formerly Urartu) and Cappadocia while Nebuchadnezzar fought to establish firm control over "Hatti land" (the eastern Mediterranean littoral). Egypt tried by military (601 and 587 B.C.) and diplomatic (593 and 587 B.C.) means to challenge Babylonian supremacy in the Levant but to no avail. Destruction of the small territorial states of Judah (586 B.C.), Ammon and Moab (582 B.C.) and the thirteen-year siege of Tyre (585 to 572 B.C.) show that the subject peoples in this area did not readily acquiesce

to Babylonian domination. After the troublesome pharaoh Hophra was deposed by Amasis (570 B.C.), Nebuchadnezzar invaded the delta and plundered it (568 B.C.) but established no foothold there.

Nebuchadnezzar was succeeded by Evil-merodach (Amel-Marduk) in 562 B.C. Just before the New Years Festival in the first of Nisan, the new king released Jehoiachin from prison (thirty-seventh year of exile, twelfth month, twenty-seventh day = 2 April, 561 B.C.). Two years later Evil-merodach was slain in a revolt and his brother-in-law, Neriglissar (Nergal-shar-user), became king. After a serious defeat on a campaign into Cappadocia, he died (assassinated?) in Babylon and was followed by his son, Labashi-Marduk, who was shortly dispatched by a coup d'état in March, 556 B.C. A military junta appointed as king Nabonidus (Nabu-naid) the son of a high priestess of the moon god Sin at Haran. His mother may have been of royal Assyrian lineage. Nabonidus, perhaps in collusion with Cyrus II, took Haran from Astyges, king of Media, while the latter was engaged in the struggle with Cyrus.

To rescue the failing economy of Babylonia, Nabonidus took his army to Hamath where he recruited large numbers of troops from the western provinces (Hatti land) and launched a campaign into northern Arabia. He established his headquarters t Tema and appointed his son, Belshazzar (Bel-shar-usur), egent in Babylon. During the next ten years he campaigned outhward, going as far as Yathrib (Moslem Medina). He stablished garrisons at six identifiable oases using native abylonians and peoples from Hatti land. (In Muhammad's day, ve of those oases were occupied by Jews!) This ten-year stay the desert was considered madness by many; it is the subject f an Aramaic text found among the Jews at Qumran and rovides the background for Daniel 4:28-37 where the story is ttached to the more famous Nebuchadnezzar.

Meanwhile, Cyrus II (the Great) had not been idle. He sacked e Median capital at Ecbatana (Achmetha) after defeating his ther-in-law, Astyges (550 B.C.). A march across the Halys led the defeat of Croesus and the conquest of Sardis, capital of Lydia. Croesus had appealed in vain for help from Sparta, from Amasis of Egypt, and from Labynetus (Nabonidus).

In 542 B.C. Nabonidus returned to Babylon, perhaps because Cyrus had occupied northern Assyria. The temple to Sin at Haran was rebuilt and that at Ur was refurbished. Sin was elevated at the expense of Marduk, god of Babylon. The enmity thus engendered among the priesthood of Marduk and other Mesopotamian communities (probably including the Jews), encouraged Cyrus to invade Babylonia. After two victories along the Tigris, Cyrus occupied Sippar without a fight. A turncoat governor, Gobyrus, joined Cyrus and led troops into Babylon on 13th Oct., 539 B.C. On the 29th of that month, Cyrus made his triumphant entry into the city.

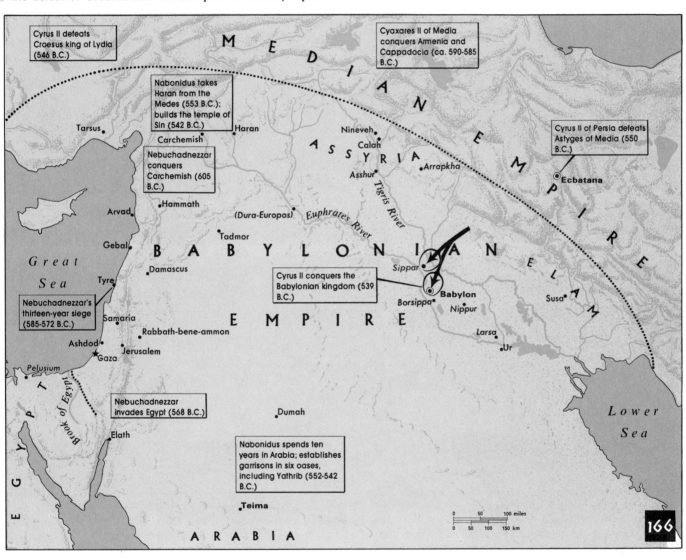

THE RETURN TO ZION 538 TO 445 B.C.

Cyrus the Great won the allegiance of his subject peoples by tolerance of their religious and national feelings. Upon entering Babylon he issued a decree permitting the return of cult statues to their home temples (Nabonidus had dragged them nto the capital). A similar decree from his first year of reign over the empire) is preserved in the Bible (2 Chron. 36:22-23; Ezra 1:1-5) granting permission for Jews to return home and to ebuild the temple in Jerusalem. The first wave of returnees, ed by Sheshbazzar (probably Shenazzar, son of Jehoiakim, Chron. 3:18), arrived in 538 B.C. The altar was set up and n the second year the foundations were laid (Ezra 5:14 [Heb.

17]), but due to opposition from the neighboring peoples, the temple was not built until the reign of Darius I. In his second year (520 B.C.), Darius ordered that the work be completed. The temple was finished in his sixth year on the 3rd of Adar (13 March, 515 B.C.).

Though contacts with Babylonian Jewry were frequent (e.g. Zech. 5:9), the returnees were relatively few. More came with Ezra in the seventh year of Artaxerxes I (458 B.C.; Ezra 7:7). The Law of the Lord was certified by the Persian king as the official code of the Jewish community in the satrapy "Beyond the River" Ezra 7:25-26).

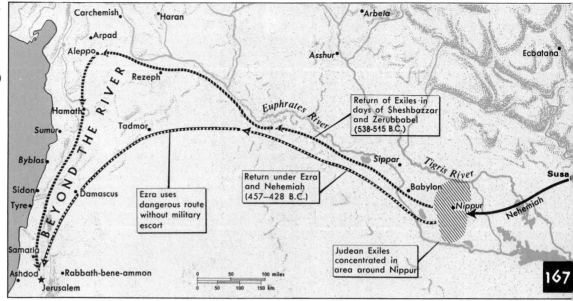

In the first year of Cyrus king of Persia ... his kingdom ... Whoever is among you of all his people, may his God be with him, and let him go up to Jerusalem, which is in Judah, and rebuild the house of the Lord, the God of Israel...

(Ezra 1:1-3)

THE RETURN TO ZION

Return of Exiles in days of Sheshbazzar and Zerubbabel (538-515 B.C.)

Return under Ezra and Nehemiah (457-428 B.C.)

Ezra uses dangerous route without military escort

Judean Exiles concentrated in area around Nippur

EZRA 1-2: NEH. 1-3

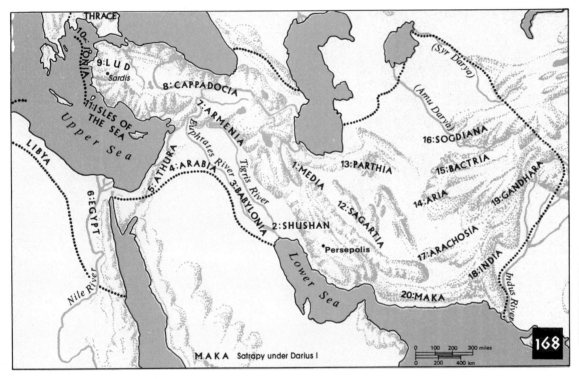

Who reigned from India to Ethiopia over one hundred and twenty-seven provinces (Esther 1

THE PERSIAN EMPIR
538-332 B.C.

Darius enthroned (Relief from Persepo

MAKA Satrapy under Darius I

The Achaemenid dynasty ruled the ancient Near East for two centuries. Its founder, Cyrus II (the Great), appointed his son, Cambyses, king of Babylon, to assure the succession. Cambyses achieved the conquest of Egypt (525 B.C.). To cross the Sinai desert he gained the support of the Arabian king who ruled over the coast from Kadytes (Gaza) to Ienysus. Upon Cambyses' death, his cousin, Darius, rushed home to slay a false claimant to the throne. By 520 B.C. he had quelled insurrections in Babylon and elsewhere and was strong enough to make a state visit to Egypt (519 B.C.). His wars in Thrace (513 B.C.) and Macedonia (492 B.C.) carried Persian rule to its farthest extent. Herodotus described the Persian Empire as consisting of twenty satrapies; these were summarized as "one hundred and twenty-seven provinces" (Esther 1:1). Each satrapy could include several "provinces," with various ethnic and national groups.

Two geopolitical issues dominated Achaemenid history: control over the Greek cities of the eastern Aegean and over Egypt. To achieve these aims and to assure supremacy in the eastern Mediterranean, the Persians depended upon the Phoenician

fleet. During the fifth century B.C. Egypt revolted three times: 484-483, 463-454 and 404-343 B.C. (under the twenty-seventh through the thirtieth dynasties). A brief resurgence under the thirty-first dynasty (338-334 B.C.) was soon followed by Alexander's conquest (332 B.C.).

Another serious problem that developed was the tendency of local satraps to behave like independent monarchs and sometimes to revolt against the emperor. Megabyzus, brother-in-law of the king, rebelled over a political matter and inflamed his satrapy, "Beyond the River" (449 B.C.). Cyrus the Younger, satrap of Lydia, even tried to overthrow his brother the king with the aid of Greek mercenaries (404 B.C.). The "Satraps' Revolt" (367-362 B.C.) involving Asia Minor and the Levant, nearly destroyed the empire.

The various ethnic groups were allowed maximum cultural autonomy (language, script, religion) so long as they paid their taxes. The Persian emperors took pride in the multiracial nature of their realm as witnessed by reliefs and inscriptions from their main capital cities, Persepolis and Susa.

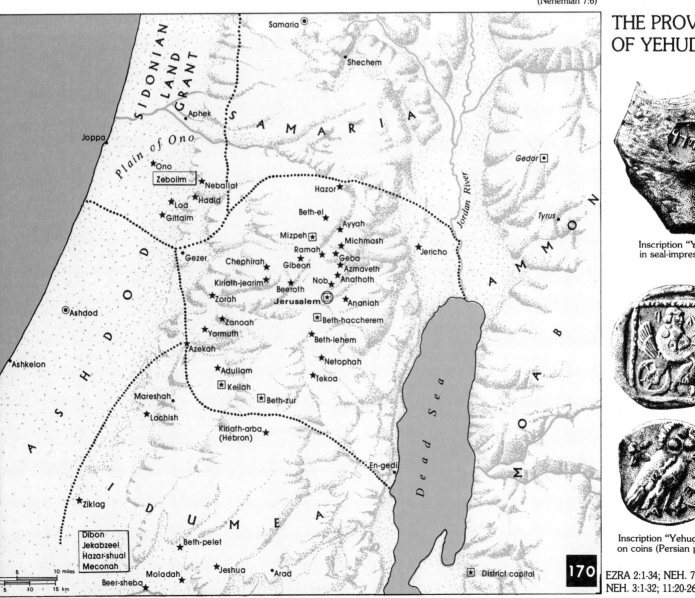

Map 169 — Post-Exilic Jerusalem

Tower of the Hananel
Tower of the hundred
Fish gate?
Sheep gate?
Upper chamber of the corner
Muster gate?
House of the temple servants and the merchants
Temple
Chamber of Meshullam son of Berechiah
East gate?
House of Zadok son of Immer
Houses of the priests
Horse gate?
House of Jedaiah son of Harumaph
OPHEL
Great projecting tower
Older wall
En-gihon
Valley gate
Water gate?
1 2 3 4 5 6 7 8
Nehemiah continues on foot.
Fountain gate?
Nehemiah's night walk.
Stairs descending from city of David

0 50 100 150 yards
0 50 100 meters

169

Then I arose in the night, I and a few men with me; and I told no one what my God had put into my heart to do for Jerusalem.

(Nehemiah 2:12)

POST-EXILIC JERUSALEM CA. 440 B.C.

The Jews who had come from Artaxerxes in the mid-fifth century (Ezra 4:12, 7:7) took steps to refortify Jerusalem, doubtless in the face of the tumultuous events of that time, e.g. the rebellion of the satrap Megabyzus. The local officials and regional leaders protested to the Persian king and were ordered to halt the construction (Ezra 4:21-22). This state of affairs was reported to Nehemiah (Neh. 1:3) who got an appointment as governor of Judea with authority to fortify Jerusalem. The narrative of his nocturnal inspection of the walls (Neh. 2:12-15) and his account of the construction teams (Neh. 3:1-32) depict the gates, the towers and many buildings adjacent to the city wall. Archaeological research has shown that the post-exilic city was considerably smaller than in the days of the monarchy. Only the eastern spur was occupied and the walls were higher up the slope.

NEH. 2:12-15; 3:1-32

1 Upper house of the king
2 House of Azariah
3 House of Benjamin and Hasshub
4 House of Eliashib the high priest
5 Ascent to the armory
6 House of the mighty men
7 Artificial pool
8 Sepulchres of David

These were the people of the province who came up out of the captivity of those exiles ... they returned to Jerusalem and Judah, each to his town.

(Nehemiah 7:6)

THE PROVINCE OF YEHUD

Inscription "Yehud" in seal-impression

Inscription "Yehud" on coins (Persian period)

Samaria
Shechem
SIDONIAN LAND GRANT
Aphek
SAMARIA
Joppa
Plain of Ono
Ono
Zeboim
Neballat
Hazor
Gedor
Lod
Hadid
Beth-el
Ayyah
Jordan River
Tyrus
Gittaim
Mizpeh
Michmash
Gezer
Chephirah
Ramah
Geba
Jericho
Gibeon
Azmaveth
Kiriath-jearim
Nob
Anathoth
AMMON
Beeroth
Zorah
Jerusalem
Ananiah
Ashdod
Zanoah
Beth-haccherem
ASHDOD
Yarmuth
Beth-lehem
Azekah
Netophah
Ashkelon
Adullam
Tekoa
Keilah
Mareshah
Beth-zur
MOAB
Lachish
Dead Sea
Kiriath-arba (Hebron)
En-gedi
Ziklag
IDUMEA
Dibon
Jekabzeel
Hazar-shual
Meconah
Beth-pelet
Moladah
Jeshua
Arad
Beer-sheba

5 10 miles
5 10 15 km

District capital

170

EZRA 2:1-34; NEH. 7:6-38; NEH. 3:1-32; 11:20-26

THE PROVINCE OF YEHUD CA. 440 B.C.

Jewish communities in the Post-exilic period fall into two categories, those within the Judean province known officially by the Aramaic name, Yehud, and those living outside it (Neh. 4:12). Ezra was sent to enforce the Law as the binding code for all the Jews in the province Beyond the River (Ezra 4:25-26). The Jerusalem leaders were strict about who should participate in building the temple (Ezra 4:1-3) but Nehemiah recognized settlements in Kiriath-arba (Hebron), the Negeb, the Shephelah, and the "Plain of Ono" (Neh. 11:25-36). In the list of returnees (Ezra 2:1-34; Neh. 7:6-38) many towns are recorded, some of which can hardly have been in Yehud. Society was comprised of three groups: Israel, priests and Levites (Ezra 9:1), the former including people from Judah, Benjamin, Ephraim and Manasseh; Shilonites; and Netophathites (1 Chron. 9:1-16).

The list of those who rebuilt the city's defenses mentions geographic communities (Neh. 3:1-32). Certain men in this roster bore the title "officer of (half) the work crew (pelekh) of (place)." The distribution of these towns may be compared to that of the official "Yehud" seal impressions, found on jar handles from Mizpah in the north, Jericho in the east, Engedi in the south and Gezer in the west. The jars represent the official wine industry; other seals mention "Mozah," or governor with his title, pahwa. The settlement pattern from the Hellenistic age confirms this picture; below Beth-zur the Edomites (Idumeans) have come in.

Nehemiah refused to meet with the other governors on the "Plain of Ono" (Neh. 6:2-3). At that time it was part of the land grant awarded to Eshmunazer, king of Sidon, by Artaxerxes II, "Dor and Joppe, the rich grain lands in the territory of Sharon." In spite of its Jewish population, it would have been an ideal venue for an assassination plot against the governor of Yehud.

THE SATRAPY "BEYOND THE RIVER" 539 TO 332 B.C.

From the river of Egypt to the great river, the river Euphrates (Gen.15:18), all the region west of the Euphrates from Tiphsah to Gaza (1 Kings 4:24), this is the geographical entity that formed a key satrapy in the Persian Empire. Known as Hatti Land or Amurru in Assyrian and Babylonian sources, it was called "Beyond the River" from the days of Esarhaddon and this became its official Aramaic name in Persian documents. Because the last Assyrian government had been located at Carchemish, the province also acquired the name Athura/Ashura in royal inscriptions (in Persian and Elamite respectively). The clipped form of Athura (Assyria) became Syria among the Greeks, such as the historian Herodotus (mid-fifth century B.C.).

Its role as the land bridge to Egypt and as the home of the Phoenician fleet gave it singular importance in Persian geopolitics. Every expeditionary force to Egypt followed the land route across Sinai with the support of Phoenician ships along the coast. At times Cyprus was joined to the satrapy "Beyond the River." Herodotus gives only a description of the satrapy's coast; its northern border point was Posideon (Basit), its southern was the Serbonic lake with Pelusium as the key Egyptian border town. A stretch of the coast was "Syrian," then came the Phoenicians followed by the "Syrians of Palestine (Philistia)." From Gaza to Ienysos (el-'Arish) was controlled by an Arabian king; the last stretch to Egypt was again "Syrian."

When Cyrus took Babylon he appointed a governor over "Babylon and Beyond the River," i.e. the entire Chaldean kingdom. But there was also a local governor of "Beyond the River." Tattenai (Ezra 5:3,6; 6:6) is known to have served from 520 to at least 502 B.C. "Beyond the River" was an independent satrapy at least by 482 B.C. after a serious revolt in Babylon was brutally suppressed.

Cambyses marched down the coast towards Egypt and got the assistance of the Arabians holding the Gaza-Ienysos coastal strip (525 B.C.) in return for special economic status. The Arabians controlled the caravan trade from Arabia to Egypt and to the Mediterranean sea ports. They are evidently the Kedarites, whose king, Gashmu (biblical Geshem) is named on inscribed silver bowls dedicated at an Arabian temple on the Egyptian border (Tell Mashkhuta).

It is hardly a coincidence that troubles with Egypt coincided with accusations against the Jews of Yehud. The satrap of Egypt was minting coins without permission in the second year of Darius when Tattenai tried to stop Zerubbabel's building the temple (Ezra 4:24-6:15). Egypt was in revolt during Xerxes' accession year (486 B.C.; Ezra 4:6). Again, early in the reign of Artaxerxes, Egypt declared its independence (cf. Ezra 4:7-23). That revolt lasted from 459 to 454 B.C. when Artaxerxes' brother-in-law, Megabyzus, who had been appointed satrap of "Beyond the River," led an army supported by a Phoenician fleet to the delta and defeated the Athenian fleet that had ably supported the Egyptians. The emperor had rewarded Eshmunazer of Sidon with a land grant of the coast from Dor to Joppa and their associated grain-producing hinterlands in the Sharon Plain. Ezra's commission in Artaxerxes' seventh year was aimed at stabilizing the Jewish population and assuring their loyalty. Because his word of safe-conduct to the captured Egyptian leaders was broken by the emperor's wife, Megabyzus himself led his satrapy into revolt (448-447 B.C.). He repulsed an invading army sent from Egypt and another sent from Babylon. Finally, he agreed to retire and return to Persia. Those upheavals account for the accusations against the Jews who sought to refortify Jerusalem (Ezra 4:7-23). Nehemiah arrived two years later with permission to rebuild Jerusalem's walls (445 B.C.).

Biblical sources are silent about the next century and a half but the province had a checkered history nonetheless. Egypt revolted successfully in 404 B.C. and Abrokomus, the satrap of "Beyond the River," organized an invading force; he was diverted by the attempt of Cyrus the Younger to unseat his brother, king Artaxerxes II (401 B.C.). Pharaoh Achoris made an alliance with king Evagorus of Salamis on Cyprus. While the Persians invaded Egypt, Evagorus landed in Phoenicia, occupied Tyre and ravaged other Phoenician towns (386 B.C.). A naval force was assembled at Acco under Straton I ('Abdashtart) of Sidon (373 B.C.) to support another unsuccessful invasion of Egypt. When the western satraps revolted against the emperor (368-360 B.C.), the "Syrians" and Phoenicians joined in. Tachos, king of Egypt, marched into the Levant (362 B.C.). Artaxerxes III regained control over the empire (358 B.C.) and made another unhappy attempt to invade Egypt (351 B.C.). His failure inspired Tennes, king of Sidon, to revolt. Sidon was finally taken by Artaxerxes himself in 345 (B.C.). Sidon was severely punished but under Straton II was able to support Artaxerxes' successful reconquest of Egypt in 343 B.C. Egypt revolted again during the reign of Darius III but was again subdued (between 338 and 334 B.C.). Where the satrap made his headquarters is not known. Under Alexander, the capital of "Syria" was Damascus. The provinces within the satrapy are generally those inherited from the Assyrians. In addition to Yehud, the Bible mentions Samaria, Ammon and Ashdod. Geshem the Arab controlled the southern caravan routes and the coastal strip of Gaza. When the Edomites settled in the central Judean hills and the Negeb is not clear. Edomite names appear along with Jews and others in the Aramaic ostraca from Arad and Beer-sheba.

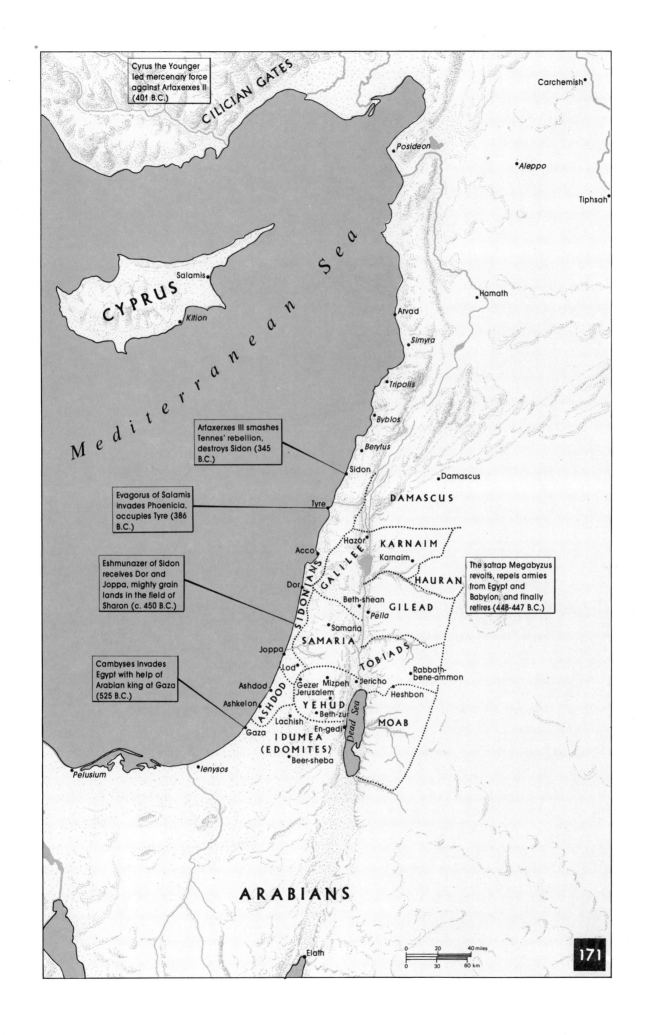

Cyrus the Younger
led mercenary force
against Artaxerxes II
(401 B.C.)

CILICIAN GATES

Carchemish•

•Posideon

•Aleppo

Tiphsah•

•Hamath

Salamis•

CYPRUS

•Arvad

•Kition

•Simyra

Mediterranean Sea

•Tripolis

•Byblos

Artaxerxes III smashes
Tennes' rebellion,
destroys Sidon (345
B.C.)

•Berytus

•Sidon

•Damascus

Evagorus of Salamis
invades Phoenicia,
occupies Tyre (386
B.C.)

•Tyre

DAMASCUS

•Hazor

KARNAIM

Acco•

•Karnaim

Eshmunazer of Sidon
receives Dor and
Joppa, mighty grain
lands in the field of
Sharon (c. 450 B.C.)

Dor•

GALILEE

SIDONIANS

HAURAN

•Beth-shean

GILEAD

The satrap Megabyzus
revolts, repels armies
from Egypt and
Babylon, and finally
retires (448-447 B.C.)

•Pella

•Samaria

SAMARIA

Joppa•

TOBIADS

Cambyses invades
Egypt with help of
Arabian king at Gaza
(525 B.C.)

•Lod

•Jericho

•Rabbath-
bene-ammon

Ashdod•

•Gezer •Mizpeh

•Jerusalem

•Heshbon

Ashkelon•

ASHDOD

YEHUD

•Beth-zur

MOAB

•Lachish

Dead Sea

•En-gedi

Gaza•

IDUMEA
(EDOMITES)

•Beer-sheba

•Pelusium

•Ienysos

ARABIANS

•Elath

0   20   40 miles
0   30   60 km

171

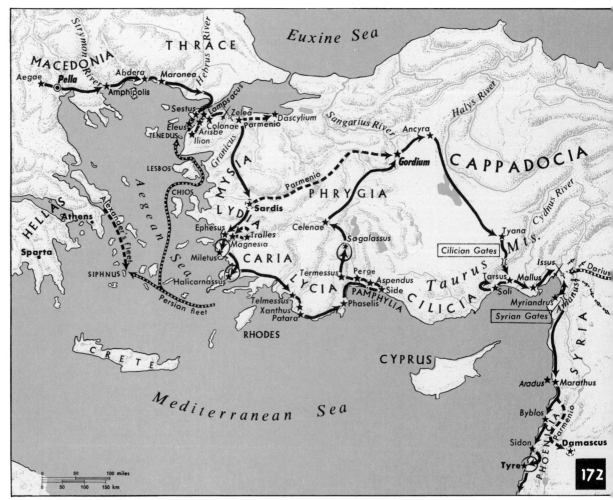

ARRIAN: ANABASIS; PLUTARCH: LIFE OF ALEXANDER; DIODORUS 17; CURTIUS RUFUS; JUSTIN 11:12.

Behold, a he-goat came from the west across the face of the whole earth.

(Daniel 8:5)

THE CAMPAIGN OF ALEXANDER DOWN TO THE SIEGE OF TYRE

334 TO 332 B.C.

In 334 B.C., Alexander, son of King Philip II of Macedonia, set out against Persia at the head of an army of 35,000 men. He took the same route as had Xerxes in 480 B.C., but in the reverse direction. Alexander crossed the Dardanelles at Eleus and fought his first battle against the Persian satraps who governed Asia Minor, routing their armies on the banks of the river Granicus. After this victory, Alexander ordered his general, Parmenio, to secure the royal treasury at Dascylium; he himself proceeded south and captured Sardis and then the coastal cities of Ionia, after besieging Miletus and Halicarnassus. The strong Persian navy attacked the coastal towns, but did not succeed in halting Alexander's advance into Caria and Lycia. From Side in Pamphylia Alexander turned inland toward the centers of opposition, Aspendus and Sagalassus. He took the latter by storm. After this he reached Gordium, the ancient capital of Phrygia, and continued on his way to Ancyra.

Meanwhile, it had come to Alexander's knowledge that Darius III, king of Persia, was amassing an army in Assyria. At Gordium Alexander joined forces with Parmenio, who had arrived from Sardis. The combined armies moved south, passing unopposed through the narrow Cilician Gates in the Taurus Mountains, and reached Tarsus, capital of Cilicia. From there, the king set out on a punitive expedition in the Cilician mountains until he reached Soli. After breaking all resistance there, Alexander marched eastward through the Syrian Gates, a pass in the Amanus Mountains, and came to Myriandrus. Here he learned that Darius and his army had arrived at Issus,

at his rear. He hastened back and, by a daring cavalry attack (333 B.C.), defeated his foe; Darius escaped with his life, but lost his family and treasury to the victor.

Alexander did not pursue the fleeing king, but headed south, to capture the Phoenician cities. As long as their fleets remained loyal to Persia, they might cut him off from Macedonia and even incite the Greek cities to revolt. Aradus, Sidon, and Byblos surrendered without resistance. Alexander proceeded along the coast to Tyre, while Parmenio marched on Damascus to seize the royal treasury. Tyre was Phoenicia's major city and Greece's most serious competitor in Mediterranean trade. The Tyrians refused to surrender their city, relying on its location on an island off the coast and on the help of their colony Carthage. Alexander's army labored and fought for seven months, until they had completed a mole joining the island to the coast. The Tyrian fleet was defeated and the city fell in July, 332 B.C.

The amazing success of Alexander stemmed from the tactical superiority of his forces, mainly the Macedonian cavalry, and his own strategic brilliance; he well knew how to inspire his soldiers and urge them on to ever greater exertions. In contrast, Persia, mighty in the days of Darius I, now suffered from feeble leadership; ironically only the Greek mercenaries in the Persian army showed courage and military ability.

In the course of his early conquests, Alexander retained the Persian forms of administration, merely substituting Macedonians for the Persian satraps. In some instances, he even appointed native Persians to high office.

ALEXANDER IN PALESTINE

332 TO 331 B.C.

After the surrender of Tyre, Alexander proceeded along the coast toward Egypt. While he was still besieging Tyre, Syrian and Palestinian delegations arrived, offering peaceful submission.

According to tradition, Sanballat, satrap of Samaria, and his army of 8,000 men joined Alexander; the king, however, placed little trust in reinforcements of this kind. There was, however, some resistance, and Alexander sent cavalry units into the mountains of Lebanon to suppress rebellious tribes. Acco, the royal fortress in northern Palestine, surrendered without a fight and the army advanced south, most probably along the coast, to Strato's Tower. Here it was undoubtedly forced to swerve east, for the coastal area was at that time still covered by swamps and sand dunes. From Lod the Macedonian army probably turned again to the coast, there to accept the surrender of Azotus and Ascalon. At Gaza the eunuch Batis, commander of the fortress, aided by Arab mercenaries, refused to surrender and Alexander once more started a siege. The fierce resistance of Gaza can be explained by the apprehension of its citizens and their Nabatean allies, who feared the domination of their Greek competitors in this important port city, their outlet to the Mediterranean. Alexander captured Gaza in September, 332 B.C., after a siege of two months, by means of earthworks and siege machinery brought from Tyre. Most male captives were killed on the spot; the women and children were sold into slavery. The city was repopulated with people from the neighboring areas. While the siege was still in progress, Greek cavalry proceeded against the Nabateans. It is possible that troops were also sent to Lachish, the capital of the province of Idumea.

With Gaza fell the last obstacle on Alexander's way to Egypt, where he wintered in 332-331 B.C. He crossed Palestine once more on his return to Tyre. Two traditions are connected with this journey: Samaritan allegiance to the Greeks was, according to some sources, short-lived, and they rose against their governor Andromachus and burned him alive. In revenge, Alexander destroyed Samaria and, on its lands, settled Macedonian veterans. According to another version, it was not Alexander but the regent Perdiccas who founded this colony. However, archaeological evidence proves that the city was destroyed at about that time. In a cave in Wadi Daliah papyrus documents were found belonging to refugees from Samaria. They took refuge here from the advancing Macedonian army and brought with them their personal documents. The Macedonians had trapped them there and smothered them by building fires at the mouth of the cave. The Macedonian colony in Samaria resulted in the revival of Shechem as a Samaritan center for future generations. The Macedonians seem to have penetrated as far inland as Jericho, and it can be presumed that some troops, and maybe the king himself, forayed into the interior. These units then rejoined the main force, which must have marched along the coastal road, probably at Acco.

Of a more legendary nature is the story of Alexander's visit to Jerusalem and his meeting with the high priest Jaddua. Josephus ascribes this to the time of the siege of Gaza (Ant. 11:325-339). Talmudic sources repeat this tradition, but refer it to the high priest Simon the Just.

Dium and Gerasa, two cities beyond the Jordan, were thought to have been founded by Alexander, but this story also lacks foundation.

ARRIAN: ANABASIS; PLUTARCH: LIFE OF ALEXANDER; DIODORUS 17; CURTIUS RUFUS; JUSTIN 11:12.

Alexander the Great (From a mosaic found at Pompeii)

And [he] made many wars, and won many strongholds.
(1 Maccabees 1:2)

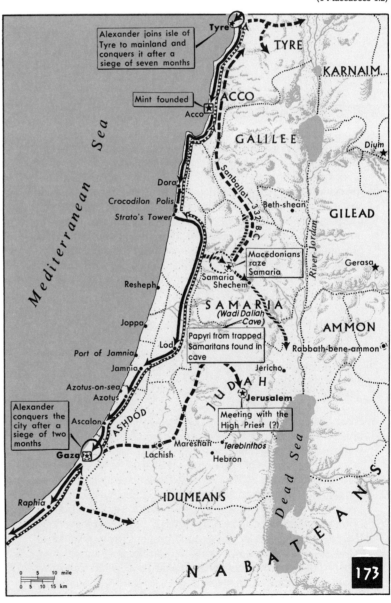

Alexander joins isle of Tyre to mainland and conquers it after a siege of seven months

Mint founded

Macedonians raze Samaria

Papyri from trapped Samaritans found in cave

Alexander conquers the city after a siege of two months

Meeting with the High Priest (?)

Campaign to Egypt—332 B.C.

Secondary movements

Campaign to the north—331 B.C.

Secondary movements

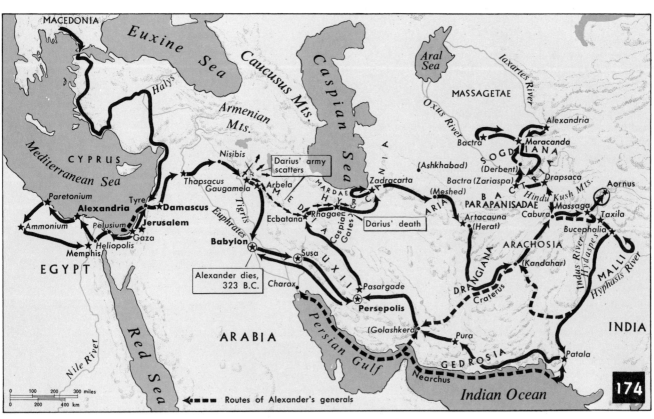

ARRIAN: ANABASIS; PLUTARCH: LIFE OF ALEXANDER; DIODORUS 17; CURTIUS RUFUS; JUSTIN 11:12.

From Tyre and Damascus, Alexander advanced to Thapsacus, crossing the Euphrates there. On his way along the foot of the Armenian mountains, he passed the Tigris and reached Gaugamela. Between this village and the town of Arbela waited the last of Darius' armies, and here in 331 B.C. came the decisive battle. Darius was defeated and fled to Media and then to the Caspian Sea, where he was put to death by his own followers a few hours before Alexander reached the Persian camp. The Macedonians had by then already captured the administrative centers of Persia: Babylon, Susa, and Persepolis. After Darius' death, Alexander continued his campaign through eastern Persia. He advanced into the steppes of Central Asia and crossed the Hindu Kush mountains into the valley of the Indus. In India, on his way to the Ganges valley — close to the end of the earth as Alexander conceived it — his army mutinied and refused to go any farther. Alexander turned south to the mouth of the Indus River and returned to Babylon after much suffering, mainly in the desert of Gedrosia. The Macedonians returned in three corps: the force of Craterus; the naval forces under Nearchus; and the king's army. In the month of June, 323 B.C., Alexander died in Babylon at the age of thirty-two.

The great horn was broken, and instead of it there came up four conspicuous horns ...
(Daniel 8:8)

PTOLEMY I IN PALESTINE

320 B.C.

Alexander's heirs were Philip, his half-witted brother, and his unborn child, who later became Alexander IV. Real power devolved upon his generals, who soon set aside the dynastic heirs and began to fight among themselves. The main struggle was between those wishing to keep the empire intact (such as the regent Perdiccas or Antigonus Monophthalmus) and those provincial governors who wished to divide it. Ptolemy, the son of Lagos, who had obtained the satrapy of Egypt, was among the principal leaders of this second group. Firmly established in Egypt, he defeated an attempt by Perdiccas to unseat him; then, to safeguard his Egyptian realm, he coveted Palestine, which he proceeded to occupy with his land forces, led by Nicanor, while he himself advanced by sea.

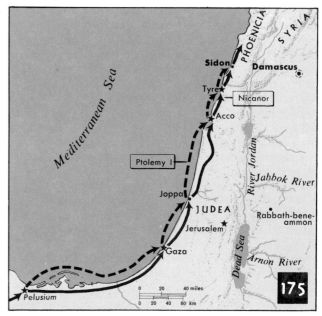

DIODORUS 18:43; 19:58-59, 79-80, 90-92, 100-105, 20:73-76; APPIANUS: SYRIACA 52; ANT. 12:1-9

Now Ptolemy, after taking many captives both from the hill country of Judea and the district round Jerusalem and from Samaria...

(Antiquities 12:7)

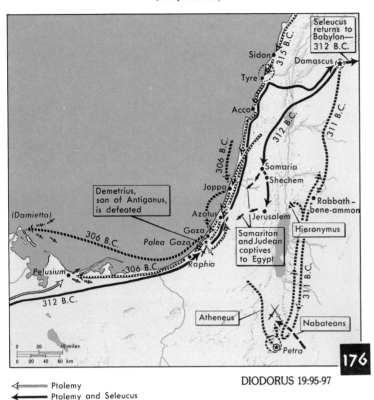

Ptolemy
Ptolemy and Seleucus
Demetrius
Antigonus

DIODORUS 19:95-97

THE STRUGGLE OF THE DIADOCHI IN PALESTINE   315 TO 306 B.C.

After the death of Perdiccas, the central power of Alexander's empire rested with Antigonus Monophthalmus ("one-eyed"), who was ably assisted by his son Demetrius Poliorcetes ("taker of towns"). Antigonus first suppressed the last supporters of Alexander's dynasty (in particular, Eumenes of Cardia) and then, assuming the title of king, he turned against his fellow generals. Seleucus, governor of Babylonia, fled to Ptolemy, ruler of Egypt, who was the main support of the divisive tendency. In the years 315-306 B.C., the forces of Antigonus and Ptolemy played seesaw with the eastern approaches to Egypt. Antigonus and Demetrius thrice advanced to the borders of the Nile valley. The first time, in 315, Ptolemy retreated without a fight; the second, 312 B.C., he defeated Demetrius, but retreated before the superior forces of Antigonus, dismantling the fortresses of Palestine and taking with him many prisoners from Jerusalem, Judea, and Samaria, whom he settled in Egypt. In the same year, Seleucus returned to Babylon to stir the East against Antigonus. In 311 B.C. Atheneus, the general of the Antigonids, and then Demetrius himself twice attempted to seize Petra, the Nabatean stronghold, with its riches, and also to obtain control of the Dead Sea and its valuable asphalt resources; but they failed both times. A combined sea and land assault by Antigonus and Demetrius in 306 B.C. failed before Pelusium and the Damietta branch of the Nile. Finally, in 301 B.C., Ptolemy joined forces with Seleucus and a third general, Lysimachus. With the help of Seleucus' Indian elephants (for which he had traded the province of India), the allies triumphed over Antigonus and his son at Ipsus in Asia Minor. With this battle, the dream of a united Hellenistic Empire came to an end.

THE TRAVELS OF ZENON IN PALESTINE

259 TO 258 B.C.

After the defeat of Antigonus, the Ptolemies were in the ascent, and Palestine was integrated into the complex administration of their empire. The forms of administrative division and institutions established at this time continued to exist until the Roman period, and many of them lasted until the destruction of the Second Temple. The Ptolemaic Empire was distinguished by its economic activity. Agents of the royal monopolies traveled to the far corners of the Land, in search of goods required by Egypt, mainly olive oil (Egyptian oil was inferior), wine, timber, and slaves. One such agent was Zenon, son of Agreophon from Caria, a subordinate of Apollonius, minister of finance under Ptolemy II.

Zenon's archives were discovered at Philadelphia in the Fayum, where he had settled after his retirement from government service. These archives contain documents that are an important source for the Ptolemaic administration in Palestine. Zenon traveled there in 259-258 B.C. He landed at Strato's Tower (Herodian Caesarea, see Map 223) and proceeded to Jerusalem, most likely by way of Pegae. He then went to Jericho, where large-scale irrigation works were started in the Hellenistic period, and to Abila, city of vineyards, beyond the Jordan. He visited Tyrus, the capital and military colony of the Tobiads, founders of an ancient Jewish principality. Zenon then reached Lacasa (Kisweh, near Damascus); it is doubtful whether Damascus itself was at that time under Ptolemaic rule. He returned to Eeitha (Hit), and then continued to Beth-anath where there was a wine-producing estate of a Greek officer. (Alternative identifications have been suggested for both Eeitha and Beth-anath. This would somewhat change the route described on the map.) From Beth-anath he went to Cadasa and embarked at Ptolemais (Acco). Apart from this journey, the archives contain evidence of the many contacts Zenon had with agents and officials at various administrative centers, mainly in the south, e.g., Marisa and Joppa.

Strato's Tower ... Jerusalem ... Jericho ...
(Zenon, Papyrus Cairo 59004)

Azotus City with agent of Zenon

ARCHIVE OF ZENON

And the daughter of the king of the south shall come to the king of the north to make peace ... a branch from her roots shall arise in his place; he shall come against the army and enter the fortress of the king of the north ...

(Daniel 11:6-7)

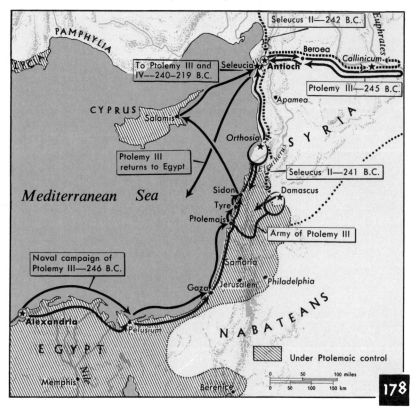

DIODORUS 19; PLUTARCH: DEMETRIUS; JUSTIN-TROGUS 13-15

THE THIRD SYRIAN WAR
246 TO 240 B.C.

After the battle of Ipsus, Ptolemy III kept Palestine and Phoenicia for himself, contrary to an agreement made with Seleucus Nicator prior to the battle. When Seleucus became king of Asia, he refrained from fighting Ptolemy, his old comrade-in-arms. Seleucus' successors were less hesitant, and the result was a series of conflicts — the Syrian Wars. In the First and Second of these, the Ptolemies were on the offensive. Temporary peace was restored in 255 B.C., and Antiochus II wed Berenice, sister of Ptolemy III, and repudiated his previous consort, Laodice.

The deposition of Berenice, after the death of Antiochus II, and her subsequent death at the hand of Laodice, caused the renewal of war between Syria and Egypt.

The king of Egypt attacked Antioch and Seleucia in a combined land and sea operation; both cities surrendered. He then invaded Babylonia but decided to turn back on hearing rumors of a revolt in Egypt. The Syrians, who at first had welcomed Egyptian rule, soon turned their backs on the Ptolemies. Seleucus II, the son of Laodice, returned to his capital in 242 B.C. and reconquered Mesopotamia, where he founded the town of Callinicum on the banks of the Euphrates. He also relieved the besieged garrisons of Orthosia and Damascus. Peace was made in 240 B.C. Of all his conquests, Ptolemy III held on only to Seleucia, the port of Antioch, which remained in Egyptian hands until 219 B.C.

The king of the north shall come and throw up siege-works and take a well-fortified city. And the force of the south ... and he shall stand in the glorious land.

(Daniel 11:15-16)

THE FIRST CAMPAIGN OF ANTIOCHUS III
219 TO 217 B.C.

In the year 223-222 B.C., two young rulers ascended the thrones of Syria and Egypt, almost simultaneously; Antiochus III began to reign at Antioch and Ptolemy IV at Alexandria. The Seleucid was the stronger of the two and almost at once set out to realize an ambition of his predecessors — to wrest Palestine from the rival dynasty. Invading the valley of Lebanon in 221 B.C., he was brought to a stop between Brocchoi and Gerrha at the strong line of fortifications erected by Theodotus, Ptolemy's general. In 219 B.C. Antiochus had better luck: he captured Seleucia, and Theodotus and his second in command, Panetolus, went over to Antiochus in 218 B.C. With their help he defeated the new Egyptian commander Nicolaus at the river Damuras, south of Beirut. Sidon, Tyre, and Ptolemais surrendered. While Nicolaus was blockaded in Dora, the king himself proceeded from Tyre inland. The first cities to surrender were Philoteria, an administrative center on the shores of the Sea of Galilee, and Scythopolis; he captured Itabyrium (Mount Tabor) by a ruse (a feigned retreat), and took Pella, Gephrus, and Camus. He then advanced to Abila and Gadara, which opened their gates without resistance. At the same time the Nabateans, allies of Antiochus III, attacked Philadelphia (Rabbath-bene-ammon). He rushed to their aid and, after

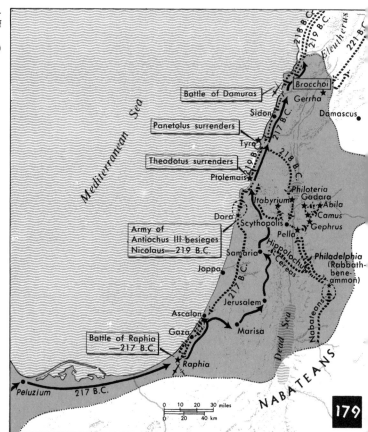

POLYBIUS 5:54-86

◄┅┅┅┅ Antiochus III
◄──── Ptolemy IV
▨ Under Ptolemaic control—219 B.C.

penetrating by way of the city's water system, he captured it. From Philadelphia, Antiochus returned to Ptolemais and wintered there during 218-217 B.C. Hippolochus and Cereas, two commanders who had earlier deserted Ptolemy, were ordered into Samaria with five thousand horses.

Meanwhile, the Egyptians mobilized all their forces and, for the first time in Ptolemaic history, even recruited local auxiliaries. Ptolemy IV set out at the head of an army numbering seventy thousand soldiers, five thousand horsemen, and 73 war elephants, crossed the desert and, in the spring of 217 B.C., reached Raphia. Waiting for him there was Antiochus III with sixty-two thousand foot-soldiers, six thousand horses, and 102 elephants. The Egyptians prevailed and Antiochus retreated from Palestine. Ptolemy IV then embarked on a triumphal march throughout the country; he visited Marisa, Jerusalem, Ptolemais, and Tyre, and proceeded to the borders of his empire. It seemed as if Egyptian rule in Palestine had once more been stabilized.

THE FINAL CONQUEST OF PALESTINE BY ANTIOCHUS III   201 TO 198 B.C.

Antiochus returned to his capital after having quelled a major rebellion in Asia Minor, and after a prolonged campaign in the interior of Asia, he again invaded Palestine. In 201 B.C. his army penetrated as far as Gaza, which remained loyal to Ptolemy and held out bravely. In the end Antiochus III captured the town, but he retreated in the face of the advancing Egyptian army led by Scopas. Scopas headed for the interior, reached the gates of Jerusalem (the Jews there may have favored Antiochus III), and occupied the city. He then proceeded to Panias (Banyas near Dan); there Antiochus lay in wait for him. The armies of Ptolemy IV were defeated in a decisive battle; their remnants and Scopas himself fled to Sidon, where they were besieged.

Antiochus and his army then passed through Batanea, Abila, and Gadara to Jerusalem. The Jews received him willingly, supplied the needs of his army, and fought alongside him when he attacked the garrison left by Scopas at the Acra of Jerusalem. Antiochus in turn granted them many favors: he provided ritually-clean cattle, as well as wine, oil and frankincense, wheat, flour and salt for sacrifices, and timber for the maintenance of the Temple. He allowed the Jews to live according to their ancestral laws, and exempted the Gerousia (Council of Elders), the priests, and the scribes of the Temple from paying head and salt taxes. The other citizens of Jerusalem enjoyed the same privilege for three years and were also remitted one-third of their bond service. He ordered prisoners released and forbade import into the city of ritually-unclean meat. For thirty-one years Judea remained tranquil under Seleucid rule.

While the Hellenistic kingdoms were frittering away their strength in internecine fighting, a new power arose in the West: Rome had first united Italy, and then, in the Second Punic War (218-201 B.C.) defeated Carthage. Mistress of the western Mediterranean, she struck down the Macedonian monarchy in 197 B.C.; then she turned upon the Seleucids.

Antiochus III tried to forestall the danger threatening his kingdom. His victories over Egypt had rendered his southern border safe; he therefore turned northward, occupying large parts of Asia Minor. In 196 B.C. he crossed the Hellespont and occupied Thrace. The Romans declared war upon him in 192 B.C., whereupon Antiochus landed in Greece, accompanied by Hannibal, the inveterate foe of the Romans. However, the Syrian army was not equal to the Roman legions; Antiochus was defeated at the Thermopylae in 191 B.C. and had to evacuate Greece. His final defeat came in 190 B.C. at Magnesia in Asia Minor. In the peace signed at Apamea, Antiochus gave up all Asia Minor, disarmed most of his army, and paid a huge indemnity.

POLYBIUS 15:13, 25; 16:18-19, 22, 39; ANT. 12:133-146

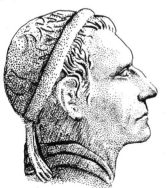

Antiochus III, king of Syria

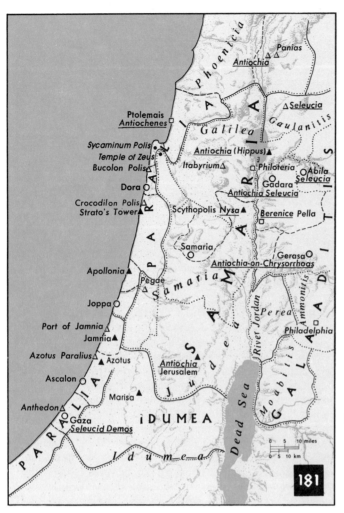

THE GREEK CITIES IN PALESTINE

312 TO 167 B.C.

To the Greeks, the city (polis) was the only form of political organization fit for a civilized people. The founding of new cities was, therefore, the best way to spread Hellenic culture. Nevertheless, the Ptolemies were circumspect in the granting of municipal rights to the settlements within their boundaries because these involved a large measure of autonomy. They honored existing privileges, but gave dynastic names to only two cities: Philadelphia and Ptolemais. Similar in status were Pella, for a time called Berenice after a Ptolemaic queen, another Berenice — Elath — on the shores of the Red Sea, and Philoteria, named after the sister of Philadelphus. The Seleucids, in contrast, relied heavily on the cities for support of their rule. Antiochus III and his heirs were therefore very generous to the cities under their control. They gave them dynastic names and the freedom to organize in the Greek manner, with archons, a boulé (council), and a demos (all citizens, but not all the population).

————	Border of Seleucid eparchy
– – – –	Border of Ptolemaic city
··········	Border of Ptolemaic hyparchy
PARALIA	Seleucid eparchy
Judea	Ptolemaic hyparchy
<u>Seleucia</u>	City given Seleucid dynastic name
□	City given Ptolemaic dynastic name
O	City with municipal rights under Ptolemaic rule
△	Town given Greek name
▲	City given Greek name

THE JEWISH DIASPORA IN THE PTOLEMAIC KINGDOM

3RD TO 1ST CENTURIES B.C.

LEONTOPOLIS (TELL EL-YAHUDIYEH) CITY AND TEMPLE

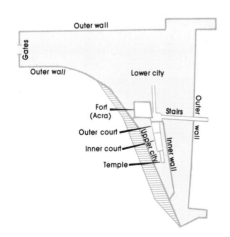

The small land of Judea could not feed its entire population. Already in the Hellenistic period we find, side-by-side with the ancient forms of population movement (exile and military colonies), the emigration of individual families attracted by the material prosperity of the surrounding world. Thus there appear in Egypt, in addition to the military colonies of Pelusium-Migdol, Daphne, Elephantine and Cyrene, many Jews who earned their bread by farming or government service. They were concentrated in Alexandria the capital and in the Arsinoite District (Fayum), which had been resettled through the initiative of the Ptolemies. Many others lived in Thebes (Diospolis Magna), in Upper Egypt and its vicinity. Evidence exists of Jewish settlements throughout Egypt. Of special interest is the temple built by Onias, the deposed high priest, at Leontopolis in the Delta in the second century B.C., known in Talmudic literature as the "House of Onias." It stood until after the destruction of the Second Temple, but it too was destroyed soon after. In the hundreds of papyri discovered in ancient Egyptian cites there is information about the Jewish population and its organizational structure.

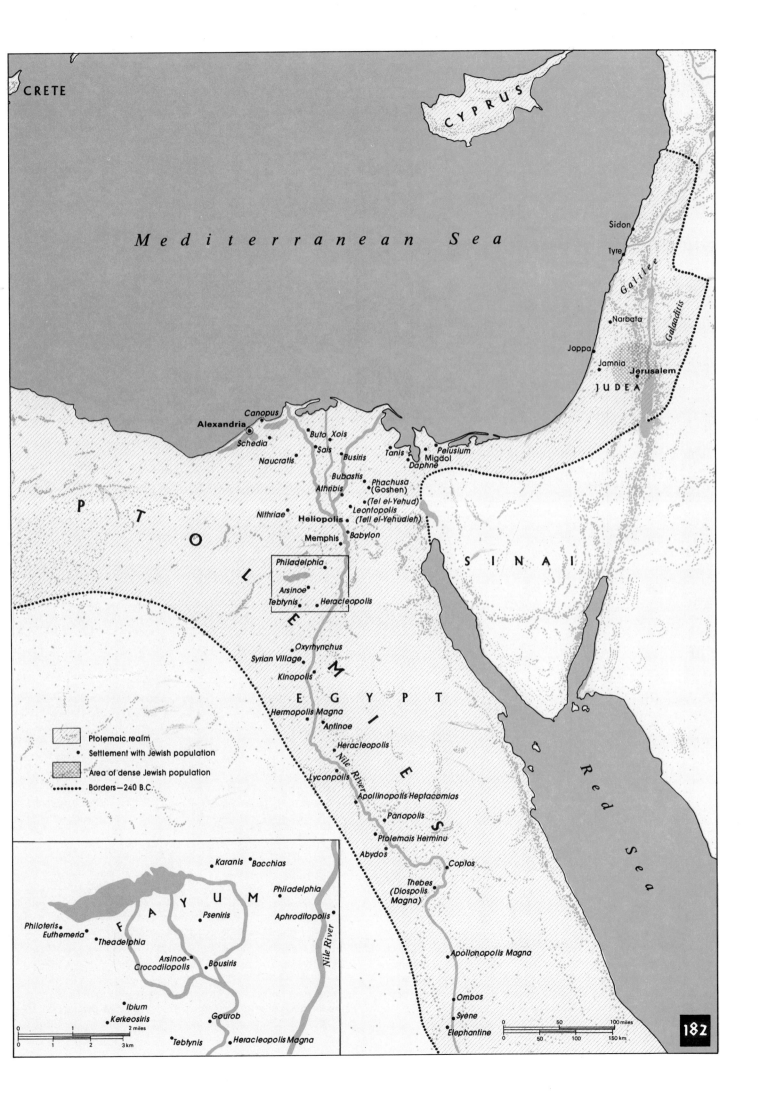

CRETE

CYPRUS

Mediterranean Sea

Sidon

Tyre

Galilee

Narbata

Galaaditis

Joppa

Jamnia

Jerusalem

JUDEA

Canopus

Alexandria

Buto *Xois*

Schedia

Sais

Naucratis

Busiris

Tanis

Pelusium

Migdol

Daphne

Bubastis

Phachusa

(Goshen)

Athribis

(Tel el-Yehud)

Nithriae

Leontopolis

Heliopolis

(Tell el-Yehudieh)

Memphis

Babylon

P T O L E

Philadelphia

Arsinoe

Tebtynis

Heracleopolis

SINAI

Oxyrhynchus

Syrian Village

Kinopolis

M I D D L E

Hermopolis Magna

E G Y P T

Antinoe

Heracleopolis

Nile River

Lyconpolis

S

Apollinopolis Heptacomias

Panopolis

Ptolemais Herminu

Abydos

Coptos

Thebes

(Diospolis

Magna)

Red Sea

☐ Ptolemaic realm

• Settlement with Jewish population

▨ Area of dense Jewish population

⋯⋯ Borders—240 B.C.

Apollonopolis Magna

Ombos

Syene

Elephantine

Karanis *Bacchias*

Philadelphia

F A Y U M

Pseniris

Aphroditopolis

Philoteris

Euthemeria

Theadelphia

Arsinoe-

Crocodilopolis

Bousiris

Nile River

Ibium

Kerkeosiris

Gourob

Tebtynis

Heracleopolis Magna

0   1   2 miles

0   1   2   3 km

0   50   100 miles

0   50   100   150 km

182

THE JEWISH DIASPORA IN BABYLONIA, ASIA MINOR AND GREECE   3RD TO 1ST CENTURIES B.C.

For I believe that they [the Jews] will guard our well-wishers from the wrath [in their hearts].
(Letter of Antiochus III to the governor of Phrygia)

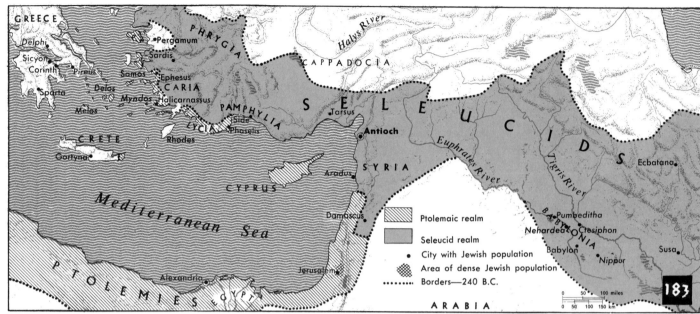

INSCRIPTIONS; ANT. 12:148-153; 1 MACC. 15:22-23

While the relative abundance of papyri found in Egypt enables us to reconstruct the map of Jewish settlement there with reasonable detail, there are few sources for the Jews in other parts of the Hellenistic world. The Diaspora there falls into three groups: the early Babylonian exiles, agricultural-military settlements established by the Seleucids in Asia Minor — mainly in Caria, Pamphylia and Phrygia — and isolated communities in the commercial centers of Greece and Asia Minor. These are known mainly from 1 Macc. 15:22-23.

Epitaph mentioning the "all-highest god" found at Rhenea near Delos

When the kingdom was established before Antiochus, he thought to reign over Egypt, that he might have the dominion of two kingdoms.

(1 Maccabees 1:16)

THE EGYPTIAN CAMPAIGNS OF ANTIOCHUS IV EPIPHANES
170 TO 167 B.C.

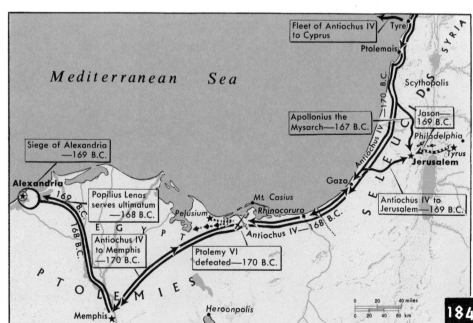

1 MACC. 1:17-24; POLYBIUS 28:18; DIODORUS

Antiochus III and his sons, Seleucus IV and Antiochus IV, saw the necessity of preparing their country for the coming struggle with Rome. Antiochus IV, a man of vision, desired to strengthen his kingdom through religious unity, integrating all its gods with Olympian Zeus at their head. In this context, Antiochus Epiphanes violated the promise of his father Antiochus III to the Jews, to respect their religious autonomy, and

supported Menelaus, a Hellenized high priest.

Antiochus IV also thought the time ripe to conquer Egypt, then at its lowest ebb, under the rule of Ptolemy VI Philometer. Invading Egypt in 170 B.C. he defeated its army between Mount Cassius and Pelusium, and reached Memphis, where he proclaimed himself king of Egypt. Antiochus then proceeded to Alexandria and besieged the city (169 B.C.); however, he turned back to Asia before its fall. While beleaguering Alexandria, Antiochus learned that Jason, a former high priest dismissed by the king, had tried to capture Jerusalem with the aid of the Tobiads, thus endangering the lines of communication of his army in Egypt. Antiochus proceeded against Jerusalem and appropriated the Temple treasure. In 168 B.C. Antiochus set out once more against Egypt, while he sent his fleet to Cyprus. Again he advanced to within four miles of Alexandria, but was now met by the Roman Popilius Laenas ("the commander" in Dan. 11:18) who ordered him to withdraw from Egypt. When the king requested time for consideration, the Roman drew a circle on the ground around him and forced him to "decide before leaving this circle"; Antiochus submitted. On his return, he sent Apollonius, commander of the Mysian mercenaries, with twenty thousand of his men to Jerusalem; this is probably what is intended by the "Forces from him" in Dan. 11:31.

THE SELEUCID EMPIRE

After the battle of Magnesia in 189 B.C., the Seleucids were forced to retreat from Asia Minor, and subjected to stringent peace conditions. Nonetheless, the Seleucid Empire remained large and powerful, encompassing all of present-day Israel and Syria, most of Iraq and almost all of Iran. The Seleucid army remained powerful and, except for Rome, none of the neighboring powers could contend with its technological superiority. Its combat technique was based on the phalanx, a battle formation consisting of sixteen or more rows of soldiers arrayed in close order, with the number of soldiers in each row dependent on the extent of the battlefield. The phalangite was armed with a long spear and shield. The densely-packed phalanx arrayed for battle with spears bristling in all directions must have been an awesome sight for less well-equipped opponents. The phalanx was flanked by light and heavy cavalry and units of "challengers" carrying pikes, and by archers and spear throwers. The aim of these auxiliary forces was to exhaust the opposing forces and inflict as many casualties as possible.

Sometimes the Seleucids used elephants to demoralize the enemy and as firing platforms, but they were mainly used for defensive purposes. Tactics were rigid and never changed. The majority of the men were recruited from the settlers of the colonies set up by the Seleucid kings. The young men served in the regular forces and their fathers made up the reserve force that was called to arms in times of emergency.

The Seleucid troops also included mercenaries, and young boys were also conscripted from among the subjugated peoples. Altogether, the Seleucid armed forces numbered between 60,000 and 100,000 combatants.

To control and rule its farflung empire, the Seleucid army had to be highly mobile. Thus its commanders depended on quick and decisive victories. These then were the realities facing the Maccabees and influencing their strategy.

DEPLOYMENT OF HELLENISTIC ARMIES

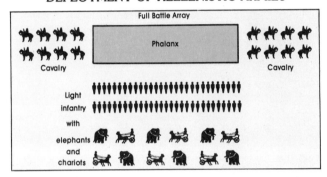

And they distributed the beasts among the phalanxes; with each elephant they stationed a thousand men armed with coats of mail, and with brass helmets on their heads; and five hundred picked horsemen were assigned to each beast.

(1 Maccabees 6:35)

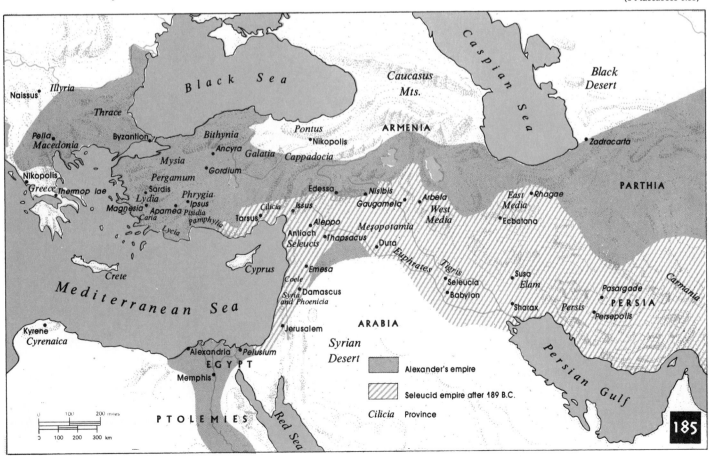

In those days arose Mattathias in Modiin ... the king's
commissioner, who compelled men to sacrifice, he killed
... so he and his sons fled into the mountains ...
(1 Maccabees 2:1, 25, 28)

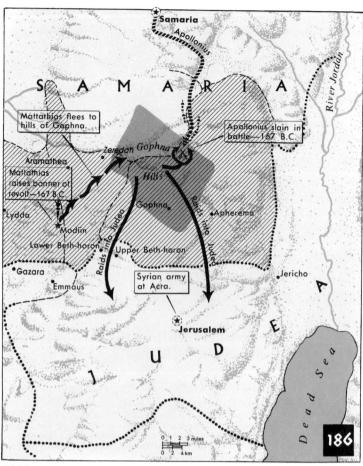

Area transferred from Judea to Samaria

1 MACC. 2:1-3:13; 2 MACC. 8:1-7

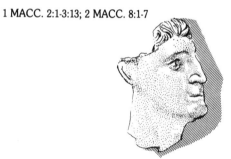

Antiochus IV (From bronze statue)

THE BEGINNINGS OF THE MACCABEAN REVOLT 167 B.C.

Antiochus and his advisers, heeding the more extreme of the Hellenized Jews, believed that the majority of the Jewish nation was ready to accept Greek culture. Being impatient with the slow progress of Hellenization, Antiochus decided to turn the House of God into a Greek temple of Zeus or Dionysius, whom he equated with the God of Israel. The strong resistance of the people led to the first known instance of religious persecution in history: worship of God was forbidden and the Jews were forced to sacrifice to other gods. The Hellenists built a fortress, the "Acra," to secure their position in Jerusalem, and next to it a new city, in the Greek style (see Map 205).

The persecution led to a revolt that broke out not in Jerusalem, but in the Jewish townlet of Modiin, in the district of Lydda. Some of the leaders came from neighboring villages, such as Yose ben Joazer of Zeredah, leader of the Hasidim, pious Jews who rallied to the defense of the Law. Mattathias, priest of the Hasmonean family, and his sons refused to obey the royal order to sacrifice to Zeus. Mattathias killed a Jew who was about to obey the order, as well as the king's representative, and destroyed the altar there. Modiin itself was close to Lydda, the district capital, and thus exposed to reprisals. Mattathias and his sons fled, probably to the mountains "around Samaria" (Gophna). There they were joined by the Hasidim. From their refuge Mattathias and his men went forth, overturned the altars of the foreign gods, and roused the Jewish villages against the Hellenizers living in Jerusalem under the protection of the Seleucid army. Apollonius, commander of the troops at Samaria and governor of the region near Gophna, went out to crush the rebellion. Judas Maccabeus, who had assumed command on the death of his father Mattathias, attacked the royal troops, probably at the ascent of Lebonah, and destroyed them. Apollonius was killed in the fighting and Judas took his sword "and fought with it thereafter" (1 Macc. 3:12). In response, the Seleucid authorities removed the regions of Lydda and Gophna from Judea and annexed them to Samaria.

But we fight for our lives and our laws
(1 Maccabees 3:21)

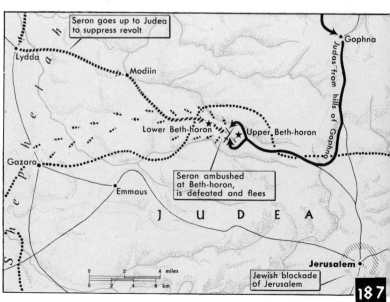

THE BATTLE OF BETH-HORON

166 B.C.

News of Apollonius' crushing defeat, and the increasing distress of the Hellenizers isolated in Jerusalem, moved Seron, a Seleucid commander, to suppress the growing rebellion. To relieve Jerusalem he chose the traditional route from Lydda by way of the ascent of Beth-horon. While Seron's men labored up the steep ascent, Judas Maccabeus unexpectedly attacked and Seron and his men were swept before him. The remnants of the defeated army fled back to the coastal plain and retreated to "Philistia." The second attempt to break the blockade of Jerusalem had also ended in failure.

1 MACC. 3:13-24

THE BATTLE OF EMMAUS   165 B.C.

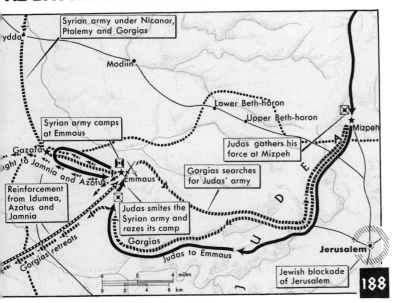

Syrian army under Nicanor, Ptolemy and Gorgias

Modiin

Lower Beth-horon

Upper Beth-horon

Mizpeh

Syrian army camps at Emmaus

Judas gathers his force at Mizpeh

Gazara

ight to Jamnia and Azotus

Emmaus

Gorgias searches for Judas' army

Reinforcement from Idumea, Azotus and Jamnia

Judas smites the Syrian army and razes its camp

Gorgias

Judas to Emmaus

Gorgias retreats

Jerusalem

Jewish blockade of Jerusalem

188

MACC. 3:38-4:25; 2 MACC. 8:8-29

Hellenistic tomb painting at Marisa

Behold our enemies are crushed; let us go up to cleanse the sanctuary and dedicate it.

(1 Maccabees 4:36)

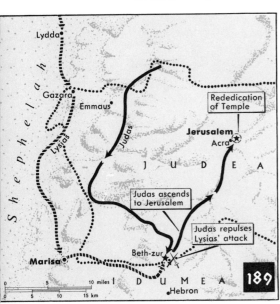

Lydda

Shephelah

Gazara

Emmaus

Rededication of Temple

Jerusalem

Acra

Judas

J U D E A

Lysias

Judas ascends to Jerusalem

Judas repulses Lysias' attack

Beth-zur

Marisa

189

I D U M E A

Hebron

1 MACC. 4:28-61

Antiochus IV, at this time warring against Persia and Media, had entrusted the administration of the empire west of the Euphrates to Lysias, the superior of Seron. Upon Seron's defeat, Lysias raised a strong army and put it under the command of Ptolemy, Dorimenes, Nicanor, and Gorgias. The army camped at Emmaus, as the commanders feared entanglement in the mountain passes leading to Jerusalem. They were reinforced by troops from Idumea and the district of Jamnia and Azotus ("Philistia").

Judas Maccabeus rallied his men at the ancient holy site of Mizpeh. Here he was strategically placed in relation to both Jerusalem and the coast. In the end the Seleucid generals decided to seek out the rebels; Gorgias with five thousand soldiers and one thousand horsemen went out under cover of night and, guided by men from the Acra, proceeded toward the rebel camp in order to capture Judas in a surprise attack. On hearing of the division of the enemy forces, Judas Maccabeus left Mizpeh and bivouacked probably south of Emmaus. At dawn, Judas and his men (three thousand in all) advanced toward the Syrian camp. The Seleucid army formed for battle but was defeated and pursued to Gazara, the strong royal fortress at the approaches to Jerusalem. Judas restrained his men from an ill-considered chase, and while the enemy was still fleeing in the direction of Jamnia and Azotus, he returned to Emmaus to face Gorgias.

At the end of his night march, Gorgias found Judas' camp abandoned; he had worn out his men in vain. Returning to Emmaus, he saw from a hilltop that his camp was aflame. He retreated to the coast without having made contact with the rebels, and thus failed in the third attempt to free the Hellenizers encircled in Jerusalem.

THE BATTLE OF BETH-ZUR AND THE REDEDICATION OF THE TEMPLE

165 B.C.

Lysias made one last attempt against the Jews. He chose the route along the watershed in Idumea, rather than endangering his forces in the narrow passes and on the steep ascents, which thrice had been the undoing of the Seleucid army. The new campaign passed along the coast to Marisa, inhabited at the time by Hellenized Sidonians and Idumeans — enemies of the Jews. From Marisa they marched with ease and arrived opposite Beth-zur, the border fortress of Judea.

The Maccabean, who surely used his interior lines of communication to follow the movements of the enemy, went forth from Beth-zur to face the invader and succeeded in repulsing the attack. Lysias retreated and Judas and his men, rejoicing, went up to Jerusalem. The fortress of Acra was still in the hands of their enemies, but the Temple Mount was regained by the Jews. Judas and his men now cleansed the Temple and repaired it after the long period of neglect. The service of God was restored after having been interrupted for three and one-half years, and they lit the lamps of the menora to light up the temple.

Thus, the feast of Hanukkah was observed for the first time on the twenty-fifth of Kislev, 165 B.C. Judas fortified Mount Zion (the "Mount of the Temple") and Beth-zur, "that the people might have a fortress against Idumea."

They [the heathen] determined to destroy the descendants of Jacob who lived among them.

(1 Maccabees 5:2)

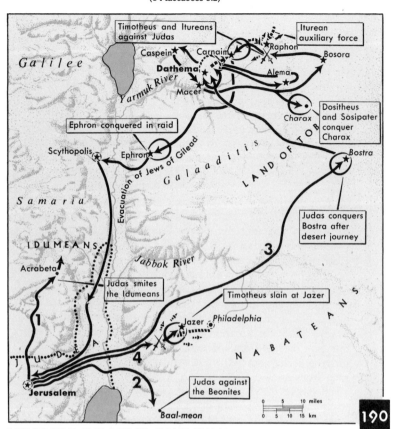

1 MACC. 5:3-13, 24-55; 2 MACC. 10:24-37, 12:10-11

JUDAS MACCABEUS' EARLY CAMPAIGNS 163 B.C.

Judas' successes aroused the ire of the neighboring peoples and he undertook several defensive campaigns. He first attacked the Idumeans in Acrabeta who were oppressing the Jews living among them; he mounted a similar operation against the tribe of the Beonites beyond the Jordan.

His most difficult military feat, however, was the relief of the Jewish population of Gilead. Disturbing news from there told about the persecution of the Jews, in Bostra, Bosora, Alema, Caspein, Macer, and Carnaim, all fortified cities, and in the Land of Tob. Many of the Jews fled to the fortress of Dathema and were besieged there. Judas, with his brother Jonathan and eight thousand men, set out to relieve them. Instead of going straight to Gilead, they utilized their good relations with the Nabateans east of Gilead, cut across the desert in a three-day march, and appeared, quite unexpectedly, at the gates of Bostra.

After capturing Bostra, Judas and his men marched all night, arriving at Dathema in the morning, at the very moment the enemy was about to storm the city. Judas launched a three-pronged attack on the army of Timotheus, commander of Gilead; the enemy fled on recognizing their attacker. Judas continued on to Alema, Caspein, Macer, and Bosora, everywhere relieving the beleaguered Jewish populations. Soon thereafter, Dositheus and Sosipater, commanders under Judas, overcame Charax in the Land of Tob.

Timotheus had meanwhile reorganized his army and reinforced it with auxiliary Arab troops (probably Itureans, for the Nabateans sympathized with the Jews); he confronted Judas near Raphon. In this battle too the enemy was vanquished. Judas took Carnaim and burned down the temple of Atargatis. From Carnaim Judas and the Jewish evacuees began their long march, passing through Ephron (which refused them entrance, but was taken by storm) and Scythopolis (Beth-shean), whose inhabitants received Judas cordially. The caravan finally ascended Zion with song and dance. There was one more confrontation with Timotheus, at Jazer; here too the Jews were victorious. Timotheus fell on the battlefield, and Jazer was captured.

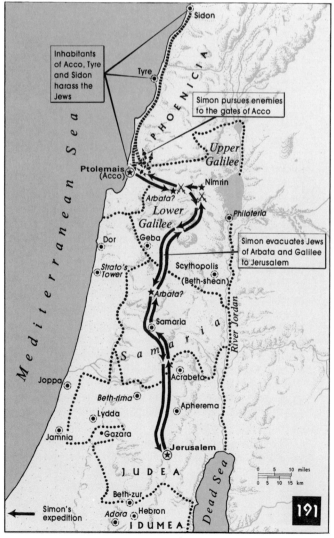

So Simon went to Galilee and fought many battles against the Gentiles, and the Gentiles were crushed before him.

(1 Maccabees 5:21)

SIMON'S EXPEDITION TO WESTERN GALILEE

While Judas campaigned in Gilead, his brother Simon at the head of three thousand men proceeded to Galilee, where the Jews had been attacked from Ptolemais, Tyre, and Sidon. Simon scattered the enemy and pursued them from Nimrin to the gates of Ptolemais. He took with him the Jews of Galilee and Arbata (several suggestions have been put forward for the identification of this city) and brought them safely to Jerusalem. It must be noted that even after this campaign Jews remained settled in the Esdraelon Valley and in Galilee.

1 MACC. 5:14-15, 20-23

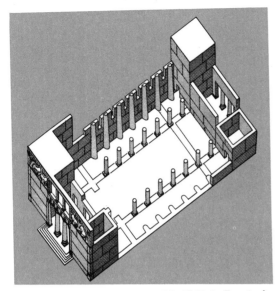

Plan of palace at Tyrus, capital of the Tobiads, Transjordan

Afterward went Judas forth with his brethren, and
fought against the children of Esau.

(1 Maccabees 5:65)

JUDAS IN THE COASTAL PLAIN AND IDUMEA
163 B.C.

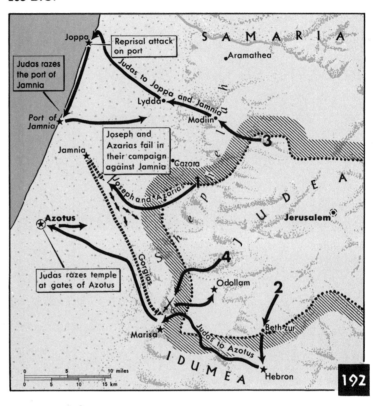

While Judas and Simon were occupied in Gilead and Galilee, Joseph (the son of Zacharias) and Azarias, two commanders who had remained in Judea, tried their luck against Jamnia. Here camped Gorgias (of the battle of Emmaus), who had probably remained behind as governor of Idumea. This action failed utterly. After Judas' return from Gilead, he himself went against Idumea. He attacked Hebron and Marisa, and even reached the gates of Azotus, and there destroyed a pagan temple.

In another campaign Judas avenged the Jews of Joppa, after their fellow townsmen had drowned them, in an act of atrocious deceit. He destroyed the port of Joppa and burned the ships. He repeated this deed at the port of Jamnia upon learning that the inhabitants of the city intended to imitate Joppa. In yet another campaign near Marisa, Gorgias was almost taken prisoner, but in the end Judas disengaged his forces and retired to Odollam in the Judean Shephelah.

1 MACC. 5:1-2, 37-60, 65-68; 2 MACC.12:1-15. 32-38; ANT. 12:353

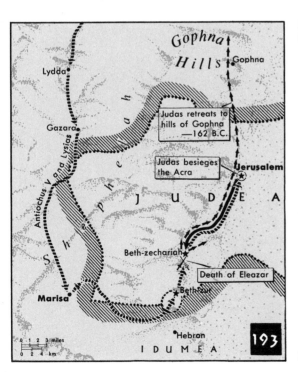

Seeing the strength of the king, and the violence of his
forces, (they) turned away from them.

(1 Maccabees 6:47)

THE BATTLE OF BETH-ZECHARIAH
162 B.C.

Notwithstanding all the victories of Judas in remote places, Jerusalem remained divided between Mount Zion (the Temple Mount), which was in the hands of the rebels, and the Acra, which was held by the Hellenizers (see Map 205). On his return from campaigning, Judas beleaguered the Acra, whose inhabitants appealed to the young king Antiochus V (Antiochus IV had died in Persia in 163 B.C.). In response to their call, Lysias arrived from Syria with a vast army. Having learned from experience, the Syrians took the longer but easier route through Idumea and attacked Beth-zur. Judas left Jerusalem and encamped at Beth-zechariah, north of Beth-zur. The royal army advanced toward Judas and a great battle ensued.

Eleazar (also called Avaran), the youngest of Judas' brothers, fell in this battle; in the belief that a war elephant, richly

1 MACC. 6:28-63; 2 MACC. 13:1-23

caparisoned with the king's arms, carried the king in person, he slew the animal but was thus crushed to death — the first to die of the five sons of Mattathias. This act of valor had no influence on the outcome of the battle. The Jews "turned away from them" (1 Macc. 6:47). Beth-zur surrendered for lack of food (it was a Sabbatical year, when fields were left fallow). Antiochus and Lysias arrived at the Temple Mount and breached its fortifications. However, remembering the fierce Jewish reaction in the days of Antiochus IV, they did not interfere with the religion as such or with the Temple services. The Hasidim abandoned the revolt and Judas was forced to retreat to his original refuge in the mountains of Gophna.

Seleucid war elephant

When Alcimus saw that Judas and those with him had grown strong, and realized that he could not withstand them ...

(1 Maccabees 7:25)

THE BATTLE OF CAPHARSALAMA
162 B.C.

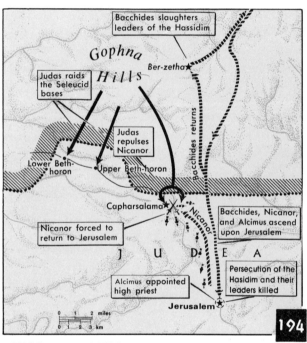

1 MACC. 7:19-31; 2 MACC. 14:15-18

THE BATTLE OF ADASA
161 B.C.

Infuriated, Nicanor at once renewed the struggle. This time he succeeded in reaching Beth-horon, where he was joined by Syrian auxiliaries from the coast. On his way back, however, he was attacked near Adasa, south of the main highway; Nicanor, apparently, was expecting an attack from the north. On the thirteenth of Adar (the "Day of Nicanor" of Jewish tradition) the enemy was vanquished. Nicanor himself fell in battle; his army, cut off from Jerusalem, fled in the direction of the royal fortress at Gazara, being pursued to its very gates by Judas, and by the villagers who were stirred into action by the sounding of trumpets. The day of battle was declared a holiday and was celebrated by future generations.

1 MACC. 7:39-49; 2 MACC. 15:25-28

In 162 B.C. Demetrius I, the son of Seleucus IV, landed at Tripolis on the Syrian coast, thus starting a chain of fraternal wars within the House of Seleucus, ending in the destruction of their rule. Antiochus V was taken prisoner and put to death. The new king sent to Judea his general, Bacchides (who was in charge of the countries west of the Euphrates), with one Alcimus (Eliakim), whom he made high priest. The pious majority ("Hasidim") acknowledged in Alcimus a descendant of the high priest Aaron; they believed his promises of peace and abandoned the Maccabees, who alone persisted in their struggle for freedom.

In Jerusalem, Bacchides enthroned Alcimus, who began by slaying several leaders of the Hasidim. Bacchides, too, on his way back to Antioch, killed many of them at Beth-zetha (Berzetha). Judas Maccabeus continued the struggle with reduced forces, and Alcimus once more had to ask for help. King Demetrius I sent Nicanor, one of the commanders in the battle of Emmaus. In one of his first actions, Nicanor tried to open the Beth-horon road connecting Jerusalem with the Seleucid bases in the coastal plain. This attempt failed at Capharsalama (near Gibeon), and Nicanor, shamefaced, returned to Jerusalem.

On the thirteenth [day] of Adar, the day of Nicano
(Scroll of Fastin[g]

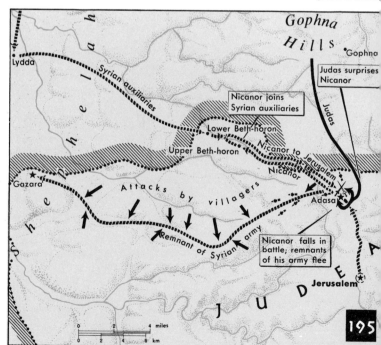

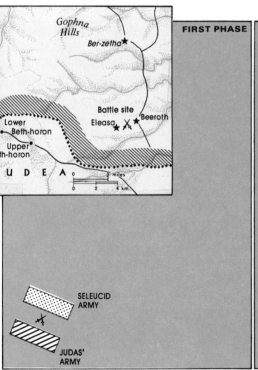

1 MACC. 9:1-4; ANT. 12:420-422

He sent Bacchides and Alcimus into the land of Judea
the second time ...

(1 Maccabees 9:1)

THE CAMPAIGN OF BACCHIDES 161 B.C.

Tidings of Nicanor's defeat impelled Demetrius I again to dispatch Bacchides, with a first-class army — the so-called right wing — to Judea. The suppression of the revolt had now become urgent to the Seleucid king, for Judas in the meantime had entered into an alliance with the Romans, who were ready to support all enemies of the Seleucids. Endeavoring to surprise Judas, Bacchides, on his march from Damascus, passed through the desert and the Jordan Valley and ascended by the dangerous Gilgal route. Bacchides took vengeance on the Jewish inhabitants of "Arbela." He encamped at Eleasa, thereby cutting off both Judas and Jerusalem from the main forces of the rebels in the Gophna Hills and in the area of Modiin.

Seleucid coin with Apollo on reverse

THE BATTLE OF ELEASA AND THE DEATH OF JUDAS 161 B.C.

Then Judas said, God forbid that I should do this thing, and flee away from them: if our time be come, let us die manfully.

(1 Maccabees 9:10)

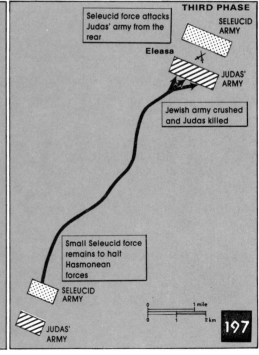

1 MACC. 9:5-19: ANT. 12:426-434

The appearance of Bacchides on the outskirts of Jersualem surprised Judas, who had failed to realize what was happening and had not mobilized his forces in time. He was faced with three difficult choices; he could face up to the Seleucid siege of Jerusalem (with the Hellenized Jews in open support of the Syrian army), or he could retreat to the hills and abandon Jerusalem and the Temple, or he could stand and fight despite his numerical inferiority.

Judas chose the third option despite the advice of his men. The Seleucid army encamped at Beeroth (El-Bira) and Judas camped next to Eleasa (next to Ramallah). The battle took place between these two towns on a plain which was suitable to maneuvers by the cumbersome Seleucid forces. The two armies rallied against each other; on the right flank the choice troops were arrayed and were commanded by Bacchides himself on the one side and Judas on the other.

The book of Maccabees tells us that Judas' force numbered only three thousand soldiers whereas the Seleucid force had twenty thousand infantry and two thousand cavalry. The course of battle, however, proved that Judas' army could not have been that small even though it was certainly outnumbered by the Seleucids.

Initially it seemed that Judas faired better in the battle. The Seleucid right flank began to retreat to Mt. Baal-hazor, some seven miles from the battle site, and Judas' right flank pursued them. In the second stage the battle turned. The left flank of the Seleucids split in two; one part stopped the remnants of the Jewish force and the other pulled back to aid the retreating

forces. In the third stage of the battle, the retreating Seleucids managed to consolidate their ranks and thus Judas' army was captured between the two prongs of the Seleucid army. After a heroic battle the Jewish force was destroyed; Judas himself was killed.

It is difficult to understand how the retreating Seleucid force managed to organize its troops into a phalanx formation. It is therefore believed that the retreat was a ploy, in order to trap Judas' force and destroy it.

After the battle, the Jewish revolt was ostensibly crushed. Bacchides took control of Jerusalem without a battle. The remnants of the Maccabeans, with Jonathan at their head, escaped to the hills of Modiin and rekindled the flame of the revolt.

Jonathan took the governance upon him at that time, and he rose up instead of his brother Judas.

(1 Maccabees 9:31)

JONATHAN IN THE WILDERNESS OF JUDEA, AND THE FORTIFICATIONS OF BACCHIDES   160 TO 155 B.C.

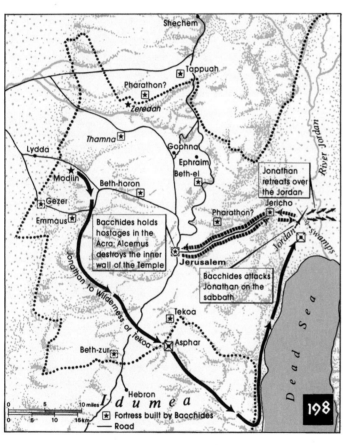

After the defeat at Eleasa, the Maccabeans could no longer maintain their stronghold in the mountains of Gophna. They elected Jonathan as their leader and promptly repaired to the wilderness of Tekoa, in the Judean desert, encamping near the well of Asphar.

The wilderness of Judea has served as a refuge for the oppressed and as a hideaway for insurgents since time immemorial (see Map 92); it was here that Jonathan rallied his supporters. It appears that Jonathan retreated and entrenched himself in the desert near Jericho on the River Jordan. Here he was confronted by Bacchides. After heavy fighting Jonathan escaped with his men by swimming across the Jordan, hoping to find sanctuary there. Before the battle with Bacchides, Jonathan had been at odds with the tribes across the Jordan and in a hostile encounter with them his brother John had been killed. Jonathan retaliated by destroying a desert caravan of one of the tribes.

To strengthen his hold on Judea, Bacchides built two tiers of fortifications, a northern and a southern line. The northern line ran north along the boundary of Judea and included Tapuah (Sh. Abu Zarad), Tekoa according to Josephus; Pharathon (Farka), identified by some scholars to be in the Judean desert; and Thamna. The southern line ran through the heartland of Judea and included Gezer, Emmaus, Beth-horon, Beth-el and Jericho. The area to the south was under the control of the fortress of Beth-zur. These and the royal fortresses at the Acra, Gazara and Beth-zur formed a system of defense considered adequate to safeguard rule in rebellious Judea.

1 MACC. 9:28-33, 50; ANT. 13:5-8, 15

Then went he and laid siege against Beth-basi; and they fought against it a long season, and made engines of war.

(1 Maccabees 9:64)

THE SIEGE OF BETH-BASI, JONATHAN AT MACHMAS   156 TO 152 B.C.

Alcimus the high priest died in 159 B.C., after he had offended the Hasidim by opening the lattice surrounding the Temple in the outer court, the limit beyond which Gentiles were not allowed to enter. Bacchides returned to Antioch, and the country remained at peace for two years. Bacchides then returned with his army, but his attempt to capture Jonathan and his men, who apparently lived in peace in Modiin, came to

nothing. The Maccabeans occupied Beth-basi, an abandoned fortress southeast of Bethlehem. This was a daring move because it occurred in a settled region, even if on the outskirts of the desert. Jonathan and his men thus gained a foothold in populated Judea, not far from the road which passes along the water divide.

Thus challenged, Bacchides assaulted Beth-basi with heavy

siege machinery. Remains of the siege works were discovered near Khirbet Beth-basi in the Judean Desert. Jonathan, however, was too experienced a fighter to let the enemy entrap him. He charged his brother Simon with the defense of Beth-basi and went forth to harass Bacchides. Traveling through the desert, Jonathan came across two wandering tribes, called Odomera and Phasiran in 1 Maccabees; they are not known from any other source. Odomera resembles the name of a Bedouin tribe, the Beni Ta'amare, who live in the area of Khirbet Beth-basi to this day. Jonathan's forcefulness persuaded the tribesmen to join his attack on Bacchides. At the same time, Simon sallied forth from the city and burned the siege works. This induced Bacchides to negotiate.

The internal situation in the Seleucid kingdom had become unsettled and many plots against Demetrius I were contrived by rivals. Jonathan received permission in the agreement made, probably in 155 B.C., to settle in Machmas, while the Hellenizers continued to hold Jerusalem. However, after Bacchides' army had left Judea, Jonathan extended his rule over the whole country, except for the capital and the fortress of Beth-zur: "And (Jonathan) began to govern the people; and he destroyed the ungodly men out of Israel" (1 Macc. 9:73).

Hellenistic cavalryman (Painted tombstone from Sidon)

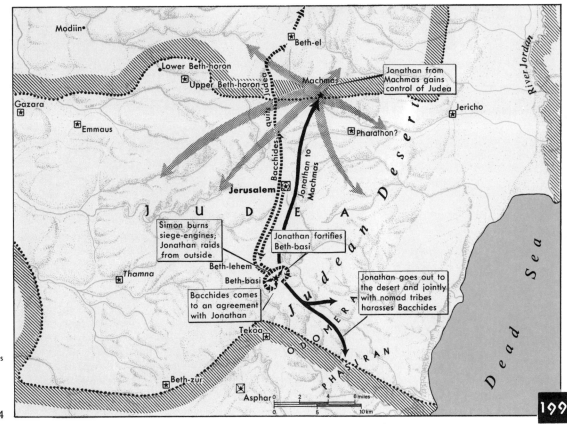

Fortress held by Bacchides
— Jonathan's army
∙∙∙∙∙∙∙∙ Bacchides' army

1 MACC. 9:62-73; ANT. 13:26-34

And sent him a buckle of gold, as the use is to be given to such as are of the king's blood: he gave him also Accaron with the borders thereof in possession.
(1 Maccabees 10:89)

THE EXPANSION OF JUDEA IN THE DAYS OF JONATHAN 152 TO 142 B.C.

Jonathan exploited the decline of Seleucid rule to raise the prestige of Judea. When Demetrius I learned that Alexander Balas, who claimed to be the son of Antiochus IV, had invaded Ptolemais, he felt endangered and granted Jonathan the privileges of a royally appointed commander. He permitted the Hasmonean to recruit an army and to forge weapons. He also returned the Jewish hostages held in the Acra. These concessions enabled Jonathan to establish himself in Jerusalem

and repair the fortifications of the Temple Mount. Except for the Acra and Beth-zur, Jonathan was the de facto ruler of Judea.

Alexander Balas, who also wanted Jonathan's support, appointed him high priest. Jonathan wore the finery of this office for the first time during the feast of Tabernacles in the year 152 B.C. Demetrius in turn tempted Jonathan by offering him the three districts with Jewish populations, still

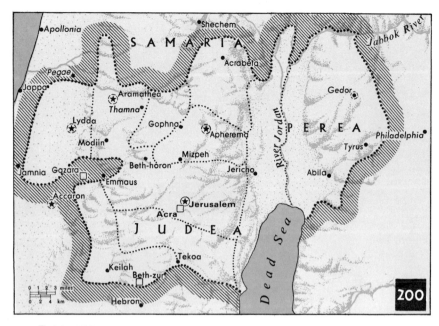

Key (map 200):
- □ Seleucid fortress
- \\\\\\ Judean border after Jonathan's conquests
- .... District border

1 MACC. 11:33. 57-74: ANT. 13:102, 128

under the administration of Samaria. Jonathan, however, supported Alexander, the weaker of the two rivals; and Alexander defeated Demetrius I in 150 B.C.

At a meeting in Ptolemais between Alexander and Ptolemy VI in the same year, Jonathan was also present and the Syrian king granted him the title "Strategos and Meridarches" (commander and governor) of Judea. After Jonathan had overcome the forces of Demetrius II in the battle of Jamnia (see Map 202), Alexander gave him the district of Accaron and an estate (147 B.C.). Demetrius II then also realized that it was preferable to have Jonathan as an ally rather than an enemy and approved the transfer of three districts (Lydda, Aramathea and Apherema) from Samaria to Judea. When Tryphon, regent for Antiochus VI, rose against Demetrius II, he too wished to remain in the good graces of Jonathan and, in 144 B.C. endorsed his annexation of the "four districts." From the phrasing of the endorsement we can infer that Jonathan had meanwhile added the Perea — Jewish "Transjordan" — legacy from the Tobiads, to his dominions (see Map 177): it is possible that the fourth district was Accaron or Acrabeta

Coin ot Demetrius I

And east darts at the people, from morning till evening.
But the people stood still, as Jonathan had commanded
them and so the enemies' horses were tired.
(1 Maccabees 10:80-81)

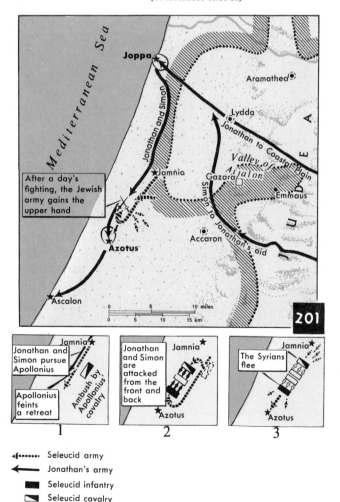

Key (map 201):
- ◄······· Seleucid army
- ← Jonathan's army
- ▬ Seleucid infantry
- ◣ Seleucid cavalry
- □ Seleucid fortress

THE FIRST CONQUEST OF JOPPA AND THE BATTLE OF JAMNIA
147 B.C.

In 147 B.C., when Demetrius II had triumphed over his rival Alexander Balas, he appointed one Apollonius as commander of Coele-Syria and instructed him to take strong measures against Judea, which had supported Alexander Balas. Apollonius, encamped at Jamnia, challenged Jonathan to a contest "in the valley, where there is no stone, no rock, no place to flee to." He believed that the Jewish army could win only by irregular warfare in the mountains. But the Maccabean army had grown stronger and Jonathan, at the head of ten thousand men, went to war in the plain, joined by Simon and a further battalion. As a start to their campaign, the Maccabeans forced Joppa to open its gates to them.

Apollonius had meanwhile prepared an ambush between Jamnia and Azotus. He concealed a regiment of horsemen along the road between the two towns and feigned a retreat. Jonathan followed him and when the two armies clashed, the Jewish forces were attacked from the rear. In the ensuing battle the Jewish army proved its prowess; "the people" stood fast for a whole day until the enemies' horses wearied. At eventide Simon attacked the cavalry, who fled toward the coast. The remainder of Apollonius' army retreated to Azotus, with Jonathan pursuing them. Azotus was captured, and the Jewish force proceeded to Ascalon, which received Jonathan cordially.

The Maccabean army emerged from the battle as the strongest military power in the whole Land of Israel. According to the description of the battle, the Jewish military force was organized in a phalanx formation and included cavalry.

1 MACC. 10:69-87; ANT. 13:88-101

Afterward Jonathan returned to Jerusalem with peace and gladness.

(1 Maccabees 10:66)

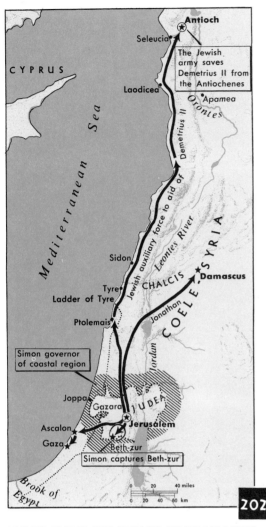

1 MACC. 10:57-65; ANT. 13:103-105, 133-142, 146, 148-153

Afterward turning again to battle, he put them to fight, and so they ran away.

(1 Maccabees 11:72)

THE BATTLE OF HAZOR   144 B.C.

The daring exploits of Jonathan in Coele-Syria made Demetrius' commanders suspicious for, in theory at least, Jonathan was acting for his rival, Antiochus VI. To curb his activities, Demetrius' troops advanced beyond Damascus and camped at Cadasa on the boundary of Galilee. Jonathan left Gennesaret and went up to the plain of Hazor (near ancient Hazor; see Map 10). Demetrius' generals again tried the ruse used by Apollonius at Jamnia (see Map 201). They hid part of their army in the hills of Cadasa and attacked Jonathan from the rear after he had joined battle with the main force. A large part of the Maccabean army panicked; only Jonathan and his generals, Mattathias son of Absalom and Judas son of Hilphai, stood fast and finally defeated the enemy, chasing them to Cadasa and capturing their camp.

◁∎∎∎∎∎∎∎∎∎∎ Seleucid army

◀━━━━━ Jonathan's army

1 MACC. 11:63-74; ANT. 13:158-162

THE CAMPAIGN OF JONATHAN IN COELE-SYRIA   150 B.C.

The position of Demetrius II was further weakened when he dismissed his Cretan mercenaries. The king was forced to seek the aid of Jonathan in suppressing Tryphon's rebellion. Jonathan sent three thousand men to defend Demetrius from the Antiochian mob besieging him in his palace. The Jews gained the upper hand and — for a time — saved the throne of Demetrius II. The latter, as soon as he felt himself secure, forgot his promises to Jonathan.

Meanwhile, the power of Tryphon and Antiochus VI increased steadily. To win Jonathan's support, Tryphon appointed Simon royal governor of the coastal plain, from the Ladder of Tyre to the brook of Egypt. Jonathan and his army passed through the whole region of Coele-Syria at their pleasure, arrived once more at Ascalon, and there were received with great pomp. The residents of Gaza, however, kept their gates shut. Jonathan devastated the outskirts of the city and forced the citizens to conclude a treaty with him. Again Jonathan crossed the country to Damascus. At the same time, Simon captured Beth-zur. In all Judea, only the Acra of Jerusalem remained in alien hands.

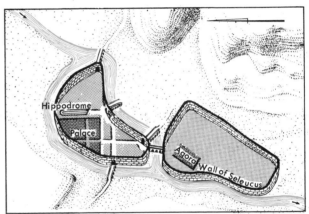

Plan of Antioch in the Hellenistic period

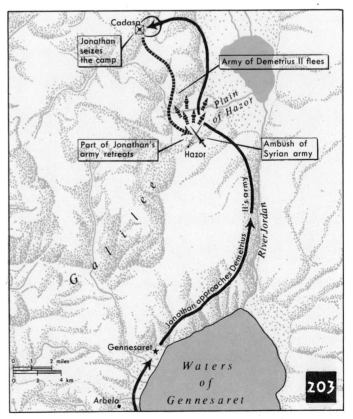

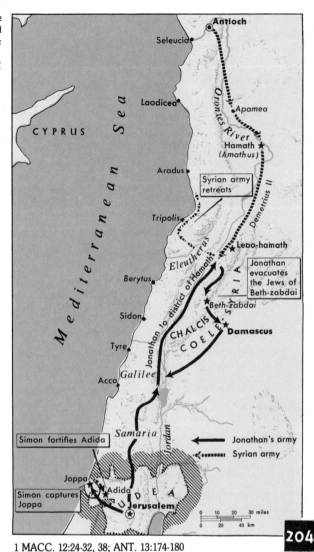

1 MACC. 12:24-32, 38; ANT. 13:174-180

204

On the seventeenth (day of Adar) the Gentiles arose against the remainder of the scribes in the country of Chalcis and Beth-zabdai; and there was a salvation for the children of Israel.

(Scroll of Fasting)

THE HAMATH CAMPAIGN   143 B.C.

Jonathan felt the tide turning in his favor and sent delegations to Rome and Sparta to renew old alliances. Again the armies of Demetrius started out against him, but for once the fight did not take place in the Land of Israel, for Jonathan "gave them no opportunity to come into the land" (1 Macc. 12:25). The armies deployed in the district of Hamath in the valley of Lebanon. When Demetrius' armies saw no chance to defeat Jonathan, they secretly retired across the river Eleutherus, which marked the boundary of Coele-Syria. Jonathan turned toward Beth-zabdai, in the land of Chalcis (where the remnants of the Jewish population were being persecuted), freed his brethren and took booty from the enemy. From there he proceeded to Damascus and crossed the breadth of Coele-Syria. Simon had meanwhile captured Joppa for the second time, and fortified Adida, overlooking the coastal highway near Lydda.

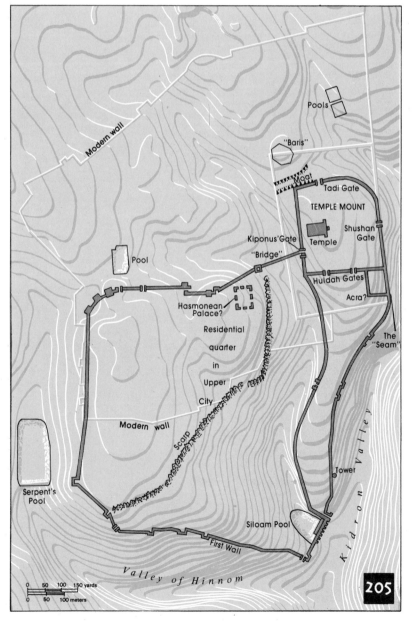

205

Let Jerusalem also be holy and free ...

(1 Maccabees 10:31)

JERUSALEM OF THE MACCABEES

164 TO 141 B.C.

At the beginning of Hellenization, the more "progressive" citizens felt that the old city on the eastern hill, surrounded by ancient walls (restored by Nehemiah, and again in the days of Antiochus III), was hardly fit to be the new "Antiochia." They probably decided to build a city in the Hippodamic tradition: straight streets intersecting at right angles. They started to construct this city on the western hill between the valley of Hinnom and the Tyropoeon valley. A hillock at the eastern end of this new Hellenistic city, protected by a small valley to the west, served as its fortress. In the Maccabean period it was called Acra — not to be confused with the old Acra, the citadel (Baris) of the days of Nehemiah, which was situated north of the Temple Mount. (There have been several suggestions as to the location of the Acra.)

With the capture by Judas Maccabeus of the Temple Mount (see Map 189) and the renewal of worship in the Temple, in 164 B.C., the city was divided into two parts, a division which lasted till 141 B.C. The Maccabeans held Mount Zion in the days of Judas, and again in the days of Jonathan and Simon

1 MACC. 4:37-60, 6:61-62, 10:10-12, 12:36-37, 13:49-53

— always in opposition to the Hellenizers' fortress. By raising a siege wall, the "Caphenatha," and rebuilding a quarter named after it, Jonathan and Simon tried to cut off the garrison of the Acra from the market place (the Hellenistic "Agora") and to force its surrender through starvation.

After the final conquest of the Acra in 141 B.C., the Jews razed the part of the fortress commanding the Temple (Ant. 13:217). The Maccabeans, now lords of the entire city, built a wall around the western hill, constructed a bridge across the Tyropoeon valley, between the Temple Mount and the western hill, and built a palace for themselves on the ruins of the Acra. They also strengthened the "Citadel" by adding towers, one of which was called Strato's Tower in the days of Aristobulus I.

TRYPHON'S CAMPAIGN AGAINST JONATHAN 143 TO 142 B.C.

And they answered with a loud voice, saying, Thou shalt be our leader instead of Judas and Jonathan thy brother.

(1 Maccabees 13:8)

When Tryphon had the upper hand (while his rival Demetrius II was occupied with the preparation of his campaign against the Parthians) he decided to cut Jonathan down to size, the ruler of Judea seemingly having become too independent. Tryphon and his army set out for Judea, but Jonathan met him at Beth-shean with so strong a force that it was obvious to the Seleucid regent that he could not overcome the Jews in battle. Tryphon therefore decided to ensnare Jonathan by leading him on with promises of turning over Ptolemais, the royal fortress. He persuaded Jonathan to send home most of his forces, which he did but for a guard of three thousand. Both men marched toward the coast. Near Ptolemais, Jonathan was induced to leave an additional two thousand men in western Galilee and Esdraelon (where Jewish settlement had apparently been renewed). Thus, only one thousand men accompanied him to within Ptolemais. The inhabitants, who had conspired with Tryphon, closed the gates of the city and slaughtered the Jewish troops; thus Jonathan was taken captive by his enemies.

Tryphon wished to exploit the confusion now reigning among the Jews, in order to subdue them, but his attack on Jonathan's troops remaining in Galilee was repelled, and Simon assumed command and encouraged the dejected people. Tryphon then went up against Judea, with Jonathan a prisoner in his camp. Simon ordered his general, Jonathan son of Absalom, to capture Joppa and resettle it with Jews. He then positioned his army near the new fortress of Adida. Tryphon dared not meet the Jewish army face to face, but tried Lysias' old ruse: he passed through Idumea near Adora to the road along the watershed. The Hellenizers beleaguered in the Acra, in their despair, called for his help and Tryphon tried to reach Jerusalem in a forced march through the Judean desert. Caught by a snowstorm, however, he was forced to retreat to the warmth of the Jordan Valley.

After his failure, Tryphon returned by way of Gilead, putting Jonathan to death at Bascama (Beth-shikma). Jonathan was buried with great pomp in the family tomb in Modiin. Simon was elected to lead the people in his brother's stead.

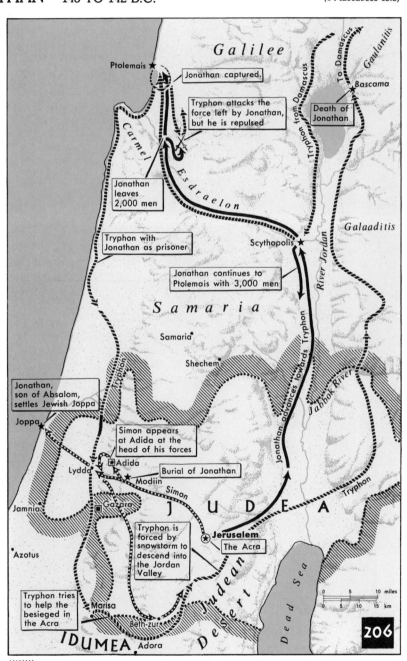

////// Judean border at succession of Simon

1 MACC. 12:39-54, 13:1-30; ANT. 13:187-212

Cavalry and infantry battle (On sarcophagus from Sidon)

Then did they till their ground in peace ...
(1 Maccabees 14:8)

THE CONQUESTS OF SIMON   142 TO 135 B.C.

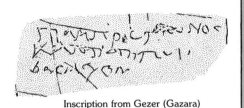

Inscription from Gezer (Gazara)
cursing the "House of Simon"

1 MACC. 13:42-48, 14:5; ANT. 13:215; WAR 1:50

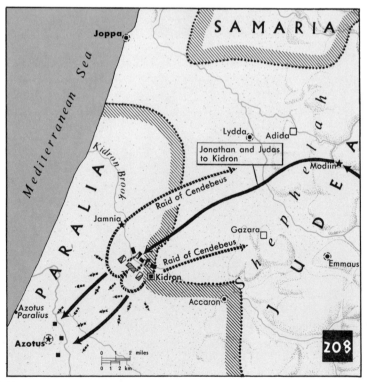

Gazara conquered
and made a
Hasmonean fortress

The Acra
conquered

☐ Maccabean fortress

▒ Areas conquered by Simon

207

Tryphon's treachery drove Simon to side with Demetrius II, who granted independence to Judea in 142 B.C. Now "the yoke of the foreigners was removed from Israel, and the people began to write: 'In the first year of Simon the high priest ...' "

But Simon was not satisfied with Judean independence within its existing boundaries. Already in the days of Tryphon he had added Joppa (see Map 206): "He took Joppa for a harbor and made it an entrance to the islands of the sea." He also took Gazara (Gezer) with the aid of a siege machine (helepolis), and then built there a fortress and a palace, and turned the city into a Jewish military center second only to Jerusalem. And finally, he forced the people of the Acra to surrender, and "a great enemy was annihilated in Israel."

He himself advanced with his force in another direction
... came through without losing a single engagement.
(1 Antiquities 13:227)

Jonathan and Judas
to Kidron

Raid of Cendebeus

Raid of Cendebeus

208

☐ Maccabean fortress   ◣ Maccabean cavalry

◼ Seleucid fortress   ▨ Seleucid infantry

▪ Forts of Azotus   ◪ Seleucid cavalry

▬ Maccabean infantry

1 MACC. 15:38-16:10; ANT. 13:223-235

THE BATTLE OF KIDRON   137 B.C.

In 137 B.C., Antiochus VII succeeded in evicting the pretender Tryphon from Dora. He now found himself in Judea with a strong army and tried to wrest from Simon the districts that, in his opinion, the Jews held unlawfully — in particular, Joppa and Gazara. Th Seleucid king appointed his general, Cendebeus, as commander of the "Paralia" district and put at his disposal both mounted and foot soldiers. Cendebeus was ordered to build a fortress at Kidron (near modern Gedera) on the Judean border. He then transferred his headquarters to Jamnia, whence he proceeded to harass the population of Judea.

To counter this new danger, John Hyrcanus, the son of Simon, moved to Gazara, facing Kidron. From there John and Judas, his brother, went forth with twenty thousand soldiers to surprise the Seleucid forces (passing a night in Modiin). At dawn they advanced to Kidron until only the river in the lower part of the valley of Sorek separated the opposing forces. The Seleucids were deployed in their usual manner — infantry in the center and horse flanking. However, John — with little cavalry — scattered his horses among his foot soldiery. In spite of the difficult terrain, which required crossing the river, the Maccabeans prevailed; the Syrians fled, first to Kidron and later to forts in the territory of Azotus. Judas was wounded at Kidron, but John doggedly pursued his enemy to Azotus and destroyed the forts there.

Simon was not for long to enjoy the victory of his sons; Ptolemy son of Abubus, his own son-in-law, whom he had appointed as governor of Jericho, treacherously killed him together with his sons Judas and Mattathias, during a banquet at Docus (135 B.C.). But the murderer's scheme, to hand Judea over to Antiochus VII, failed. John Hyrcanus, who at the time was at the fortress of Gazara, escaped the assassin. Thus perished Simon, the last surviving of Mattathias' five sons — none of whom died a natural death.

This brings to a close the history of the Hasmoneans in the first book of Maccabees. It is written there (16:23-24): "As concerning the rest of the acts of John, and his wars ... behold, these are written in the chronicles of his priesthood ..."; but this latter book has not come down to us. Frcm here on we rely upon Josephus' *Antiquities* as the main source of Jewish history.

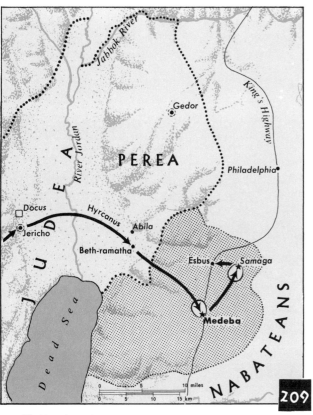

Maccabean fortress
Judean border at succession of Hyrcanus
Hyrcanus' conquests

And he captured Medeba ... next he captured Samaga ...
(Antiquities 13:255)

THE CONQUESTS OF HYRCANUS BEYOND THE JORDAN 128 B.C.

In 129 B.C. Antiochus VII was killed warring against the Parthians. With his death, the power of the once mighty Seleucid dynasty came virtually to an end. Hyrcanus was now completely free from the interference of Syria. His army was the most powerful in the region, and he began to reacquire what he considered to be the patrimony of the Israelites from the days of David. His first conquests were beyond the Jordan near Perea, where the Jews had had a foothold since the days of Jonathan and the Tobiads (see Map 200). Hyrcanus attacked Medeba and captured it after a prolonged siege; he then took Samaga, a town in the region of Esbus. With this, the Maccabeans acquired a strong position straddling the "King's highway," the important international route from Aila on the Red Sea to Damascus following the edge of the desert. This, together with possession of a section of the coastal route between Lydda and Pegae, gave Hyrcanus control of the two major commercial routes crossing the Land of Israel.

ANT. 13:255; WAR 1:63

He further took numerous cities in Idumea, including Adora and Marisa.
(War 1:63)

THE CONQUESTS OF HYRCANUS IN IDUMEA 112 B.C.

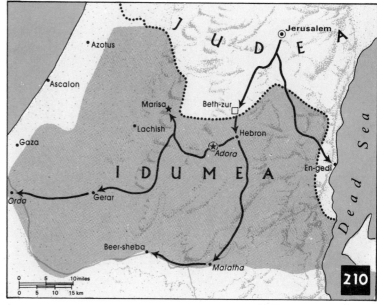

Maccabean fortress
Judean border at succession of Hyrcanus
Hyrcanus' conquests

ANT. 13:257-258; WAR 1:63

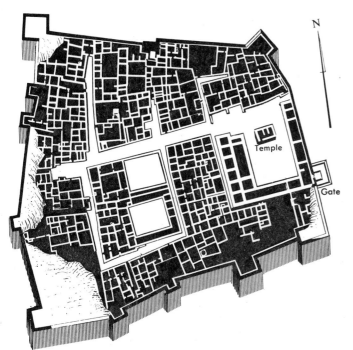

Plan of Hellenistic Marisa

THE CONQUESTS OF HYRCANUS IN IDUMEA

Hyrcanus next turned against two small peoples isolated between emerging Judea and the Greek cities: the Samaritans (see Map 211) and the Idumeans. The latter had previously lived in southern Transjordan, but were drawn to the fertile parts of southern Judea following the depopulation brought about by the exile under Nebuchadnezzar (see Map 163). These Idumeans had lost contact with their Arab neighbors and offered little resistance. Their conquest gained Hyrcanus Hebron and Adora. The semi-Hellenized Marisa was completely destroyed. According to Josephus, the Idumeans were forced to convert to Judaism in order to assure their loyalty; but some scholars nowadays doubt whether in fact the Idumeans were converted forcibly or by choice. In any event, within a few generations they were integrated into the Jewish nation, as witnessed by their great bravery in the war against the Romans. The conquest of Idumea extended the borders of Judea to Beersheba and Orda.

On the twenty-fifth (day of Heshvan) the wall of Samaria was taken.

(Scroll of Fasting)

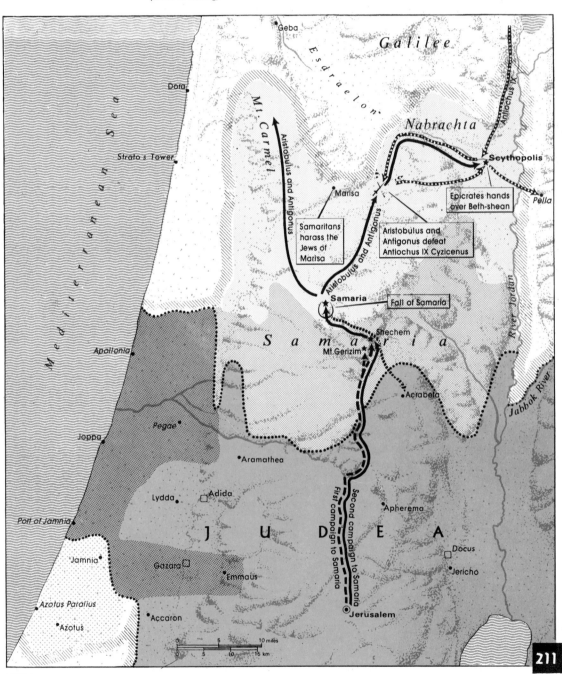

THE CONQUESTS OF HYRCANUS IN SAMARIA AND THE COASTAL PLAIN
126 TO 104 B.C.

Statue of Hercules found at Samaria

211

ANT. 13:255-256, 275-283; WAR 1:63-66; SCROLL OF FASTING, 21 KISLEV, 25 HESHVAN, 15-16 SIVAN

Area of Judea—129 B.C.

Area conquered during first campaign to Samaria

Area conquered during second campaign to Samaria

Hyrcanus' conquests in Coastal Plain

Before setting out against the Idumeans (see Map 210), Hyrcanus embarked on a campaign against the Samaritans. This people lived isolated in the mountains of Ephraim. Hyrcanus captured Shechem and destroyed the temple and the little town on Mount Gerizim. Their temple gone, the Samaritans henceforth focused their religion on an edition of the Pentateuch inscribed in an archaizing script like that used on Hasmonean coins. They did not join the mainstream of Judaism but continued (to this day) to preserve their unique identity. Hyrcanus extended his domain in the coastal plain, too. Shortly after the death of Antiochus VII, he recaptured the districts temporarily lost in 132 B.C.: Joppa, Gazara, Pegae, and "the harbors" (Apollonia and the port of Jamnia); before he died, he also held Jamnia and Azotus with its harbor.

After the annexation of Idumea and Samaria, Hyrcanus set out for his primary objective: the string of Greek cities that prevented Judea's expansion to the north and its union with Galilee. These were Strato's Tower, Samaria, and Scythopolis — forming a line from the sea to the River Jordan. In 108-107

B.C., Hyrcanus began to beleaguer Samaria, whose inhabitants had provoked him and were further harassing the Jews of Marisa in the district of Nabrachta (mentioned in the Scroll of Fasting).

The siege of Samaria was protracted and difficult, the Greeks defending themselves valiantly. They appealed to Antiochus IX Cyzicenus for aid; he came to Scythopolis, but while proceeding to Samaria, a heavy defeat was inflicted upon him by Aristobulus I and Antigonus, the sons of Hyrcanus. The latter pursued him and captured Scythopolis (according to Josephus' *Antiquities*). In Josephus' *War*, however, they are reported to have purchased the city from the local commander, Epicrates. At the same time the brothers had also invaded the Carmel area and possibly conquered the region of Narbata. Samaria was finally captured and partially destroyed by Hyrcanus (as evidenced in archaeological excavations) and its citizens exiled. The site, however, was resettled soon thereafter under Janneus. Thus, the way to Galilee was opened to the Jews.

THE BOUNDARIES OF JUDEA ACCORDING TO THE BOOK OF JUDITH 108 TO 107 B.C.

A story that is not historical in content often reflects the historical reality at the time of its writing. The Book of Judith seems to have been composed in the days of the siege of Samaria, although some scholars see it as an account of a war at the close of the Persian period. The Hebrew original is lost and only a Greek translation survives. This dating is based not only on the national-religious spirit permeating the book, but mainly on the boundaries of an imaginary "Israel" outlined by its author.

The Book of Judith, as a story, takes place in the days of "Nebuchadnezzar, king of Assyria" and relates of a town, "Bethulia," (similar to Beth-el, the "House of God," a synonym for Judea or Meithalun in northern Samaria), besieged by Holophernes, commander of the Assyrian army. Holophernes (a name appearing in the list of Persian satraps) was killed by the heroic Jewess Judith, after which his army dispersed in confusion. Both from what is included and from what is omitted in the story, we learn of the extent of Jewish rule within the historic reality of the period of the author. Thus, Nebuchadnezzar turns to the "nations of Carmel, Gilead and Upper Galilee" (Judith 1:8), and also to Sidon, Sur (Tyre), Ocina (Ptolemais), and Jemnaan (Jamnia), Azotus and Ascalon (2:28), indicating perhaps that these cities were not under Judean rule. Also, Holophernes encamped "against Esdraelon, near unto Dothaim. And he pitched between Geba and Scythopolis" (3:9-10), and from "Belmen [Abel-maim] ... unto Cyamon [Jokneam]." He sent troops of the "Sons of Esau" (Edomites) and Ammonites to Ekrebel (Acrabeta) which is near Chusi (Kuzi) on the brook Mochmur (Wadi Ahmar between Acrabeta and Jericho Valley; 7:18). To counter this danger, the "children of Israel that dwelt in Judea" sent messages to "the coasts of Samaria," Cola (Qa'un), "Bethoron [Beth-horon] and Belmen [Abel-maim] and Jericho and to Choba and Esora [Jazer] and to the Valley of Salem" (4:4). This serves to define a boundary of Judea, from Samaria to Jokneam and the Valley of Salem, south of Scythopolis, but excluding the latter itself, Geba, the Carmel, Jamnia, Azotus and Ascalon. The whole Jordan Valley and Transjordan up to Jazer were included. Ptolemais, Tyre, Sidon, Philadelphia, and Ascalon were independent cities.

JUDITH 1:8-9, 2:28, 3:1-6, 10, 4:4, 6, 7:4

After this time every one returned to his own inheritance.
(Judith 16:21)

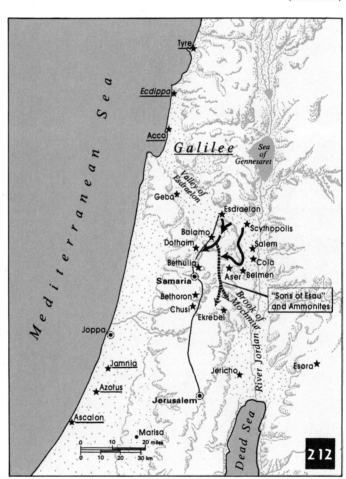

Azotus City or region invaded by Holofernes

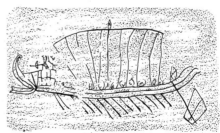

Warship (Depicted in Jason's Tomb, Jerusalem)

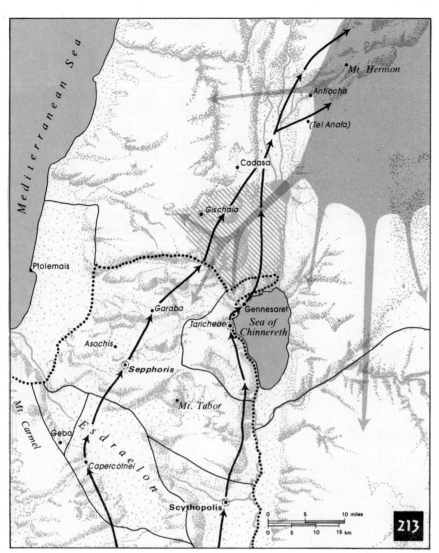

ANT. 13:319; WAR 1:76

This man was a kindly person and very serviceable to the Jews ...
(Strabo, quoted by Josephus, Antiquities 13:319)

ARISTOBULUS CONQUERS UPPER GALILEE 104 TO 103 B.C.

John Hyrcanus lived to a ripe old age; when he died left a prosperous kingdom, in spite of the split between rival Sadducees and Pharisees, a dissension that forebode days for Judea. His successor, Judas Aristobulus I, reig for only one year, but in this short period he succeede conquering Upper Galilee. During his brief reign Aristob fought against the Itureans and, according to a sources cr of the Hasmoneans, forced them to convert to Judaism. Itureans were a group of tribes of Arab origin which banded together into a kingdom in the Beqa' valley in Leba and on Mt. Hermon. The extent of their territory car discerned from the pottery finds characteristic of these tri The Itureans apparently exploited the fall of the Sele empire and spread into the Upper Galilee and the Tibe valley. (Lower Galilee was Jewish at the time.) Aristob took control of the Upper Galilee and raided the Itu' strongholds, but did not conquer their kingdom. The s of their forced conversion seems exaggerated like tha conversion of the Idumeans. Apparently Hasmonean p was not that strident. It seems that social expedience many decades eventually made the inhabitants of the U Galilee part of the Jewish people.

Coin of Alexander Janneus

A song for the welfare of Jonathan the King (Alexander Janneus)

THE KINGDOM OF ALEXANDER JANNEUS 103 TO 76 B.C.

Aristobulus' successor, his brother Alexander Janneus (103-76 B.C.), completed the conquest of almost the whole of the Land of Israel. Although generally unlucky in the field, he succeeded through his perseverance in a series of campaigns, and added to the Maccabean domains Dora and Strato's Tower, together with the Carmel cape; Gaza and her satellite towns down to Rhinocorura on the brook of Egypt; the lands surrounding the Dead Sea; and most of the lands east of the Jordan from Panias at the source of the river southward — only Philadelphia remained unconquered. Alexander also succeeded in staving off various enemies — Ptolemy Lathyrus, king of Cyprus; the Seleucids Demetrius III and Antiochus XII; and the Nabatean kings. He was less successful in the interior; dissension between the ruling dynasty and its Sadducee followers, and the Pharisees (who first rose under Hyrcanus) waxed under Janneus into a rebellion, subsequently suppressed with great cruelty. Under Janneus, the Maccabean state reached its apogee.

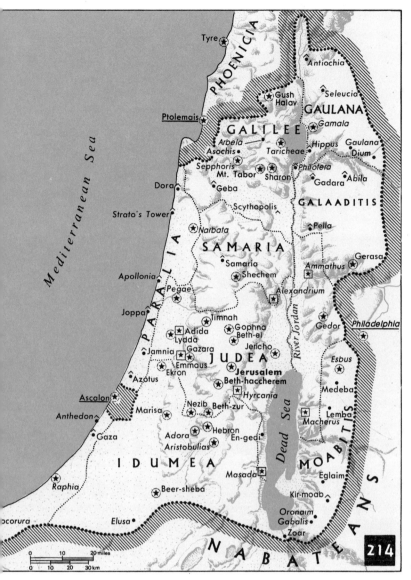

13:395-404; WAR 1:106

Now at this time the Jews held the following cities of Syria ...

(Antiquities 13:395)

THE KINGDOM OF ALEXANDER JANNEUS

.... District border

★ Fortress

⌃ Greek city held by Janneus

✪ Local administrative center

Philadelphia City not conquered by Janneus

Pompey ... took the army ..., and the auxiliaries ... as well as the Roman legions already at his disposal, and marched against Aristobulus.

(Antiquities 14:48)

POMPEY'S CAMPAIGN IN PALESTINE
63 B.C.

After Janneus' death (76 B.C.), his widow Alexandra reigned till 67 B.C. Upon her death, civil war broke out between her sons, Hyrcanus II and Aristobulus II. The former was weaker and, prompted by Antipater the Idumean (the evil genius of the Hasmonean dynasty), called Aretas, the Nabatean king, to his aid. The invaders besieged Jerusalem, but the Romans finally intervened.

Rome had gradually annexed the entire Hellenistic East after defeating the Seleucids. From 88 to 64 B.C. she fought Mithradates king of Pontus, her most dangerous enemy in the East. In 64 B.C., Pompey, who finally defeated Mithradates, came to Damascus, annexed the Seleucid kingdom (which then became the province of Syria) and turned his attention toward Judea.

⟵ Aristobulus' army

⫞⫞⫞⫞⫞⫞ Pompey's army

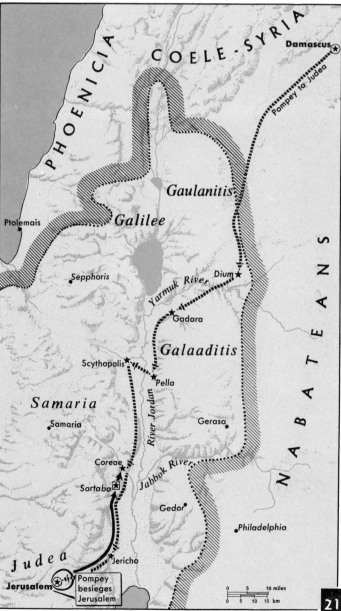

ANT. 14:48-55; WAR 1: 133-139

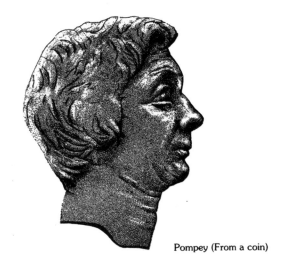

Pompey (From a coin)

At first he sent Scaurus, one of his commanders, to Judea and ordered a truce. Aretas and Hyrcanus retreated (on their way back they were soundly defeated by Aristobulus at Papyron near the Jordan). Pompey next ordered the two rivals to appear before him; seeing that Hyrcanus was the weaker personality of the two, he chose him to rule over the Jews. Aristobulus retired to the fastness of Alexandrium, overlooking the Jordan Valley. Pompey followed him with his army, passing Dium (and probably also Gadara), Pella, and Scythopolis. At Coreae the Roman army entered Judea proper. Aristobulus negotiated from weakness and finally surrendered. Pompey then advanced to Jericho, where he learned that Aristobulus' adherents refused to surrender the capital; thereupon the Roman army — now in high spirits, for at Jericho news had arrived of the death of Mithradates of Pontus, Pompey's old foe — marched upon the Holy City.

> For we lost our freedom and became subject to the Romans, and the territory which we had gained by our arms ... we were compelled to give back ...
> (Antiquities 14:77)

POMPEY'S SIEGE OF JERUSALEM
63 B.C.

When the Roman army approached the gates of Jerusalem, it encamped to the south of the city. The Upper City and the King's palace were in the hands of Hyrcanus' partisans, who opened the gates to Pompey. Aristobulus' supporters demolished the bridge connecting the Upper City with the Temple and prepared their resistance from the Temple Mount and the nearby Baris. The Romans put a dike around the Temple fortifications and built a camp to the north. They prepared a two-pronged assault: across the fosse next to the "towers" of the Baris in the north and at the ruined bridge in the west. They built a ramp and positioned their siege engines and catapults. Work was facilitated by taking advantage of the Jews' reluctance to fight on the Sabbath: on this day, the Jews hesitated to interfere with the building of the ramps, unless physically attacked. The assault finally came on the Sabbath, of course. The towers and the wall gave way, and the Romans invaded the Temple, but the priests continued the service as if nothing had happened. According to Josephus, twelve thousand people died on this one day. Pompey entered the Holy of Holies, but did not touch the Temple or its treasures.

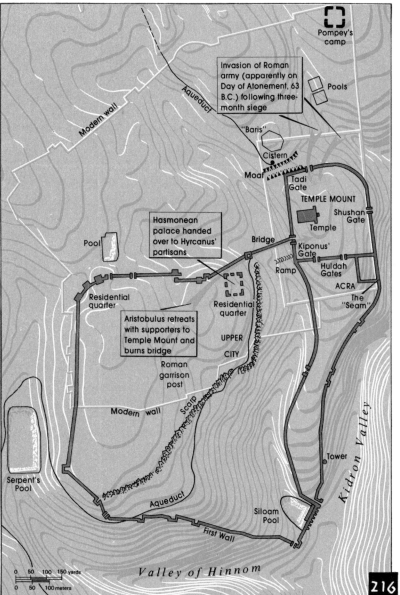

ANT. 14:57-71; WAR 1:141-151

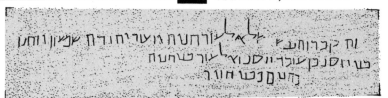

Inscription on tomb of the sons of Hezir, Jerusalem

He also set up five councils and divided the nation into
as many districts.

(Antiquities 14:91)

POMPEY'S TERRITORIAL ARRANGEMENTS   63 TO 55 B.C.

Judean border before Pompey's arrangements

Border of synedria of Gabinius

District/municipal boundary

★ Independent city under proconsul of Syria

⊛ Gabinius' synedria

⊛ District capital

▨ Area of Jewish settlements

▨ Decapolis

▨ Autonomous Samaritan region

ANT. 14:74-76, 88; WAR 1:156-166, 169-170

The arrangements of Pompey after the conquest, completed by Gabinius (proconsul of Syria in 57-55 B.C.) were relatively easy on the Nabateans, harder on the Itureans, and very harsh on the Jewish state. Pompey "liberated" the Greek and Hellenized cities occupied by the Jews since the days of Hyrcanus and subjugated their rural populations to these Greek cities. Thus, there again rose autonomous units (under the supervision of the Roman proconsul in Syria) such as: Gaza, Azotus, Jamnia, Joppa, Apollonia, Arethusa (Aphek), Strato's Tower, and Dora on the coast; in the interior: Marisa, Sebaste, and Scythopolis. Beyond the Jordan, Gadara, Hippus, Abila, Dium, Pella, and Gerasa were "reestablished." The Jews kept Judea proper, the eastern part of Idumea, Perea, and Galilee. The Samaritans became independent, and the plain of Esdraelon was detached from Galilee. Esbus was returned to the Nabateans who, except for being removed from Damascus, hardly suffered any diminution of the area under their control. The area of Lake Semechonitis, Panias, and Gaulanitis were given to the Itureans, but they lost their possessions on the Mediterranean coast.

Pompey joined the majority of the cities beyond the Jordan into a "League of Ten Cities" — the Decapolis, including also Scythopolis west of the Jordan, to minimize the danger of their being isolated. The Carmel was returned to Ptolemais. The Jews held on to those areas that were densely populated by them, except Joppa and its neighborhood and the plain of Esdraelon.

In all the Greek cities reestablished by Pompey and Gabinius, the populations exiled by the Maccabeans were returned. Hyrcanus II again became high priest in Jerusalem, but administration was entrusted to Antipater. Aristobulus II and his family were exiled to Rome.

During the rule of Gabinius, an attempt was made to split the Jewish State into five synedria (districts), a tactic applied by the Romans in Macedonia. The seats of the synedria were in Sepphoris (Galilee), Ammathus (Perea), Jericho, Jerusalem, and Adora (eastern Idumea). But the unity of the people could not be destroyed by such means, and the synedria were dissolved after a short time.

Judea profited from the civil war between Pompey and Julius Caesar. When Caesar emerged victorious, he pursued Pompey to Egypt and there became entangled in fighting at Alexandria.

In the ensuing events, Antipater was of great assistance to the relieving army of Mithradates of Pergamum and was duly rewarded by Caesar.

Hyrcanus II was appointed ethnarch by Caesar, and Antipater as the effective administrator of the State. In appreciation of the help he had received from the Jews, Julius Caesar returned to them Joppa and the plain of Esdraelon. From then on Antipater was the actual ruler of the land. He appointed Phasael, his firstborn, as governor over Jerusalem, and his younger son Herod, who was yet a boy, as governor of Galilee.

Coin of Mattathias Antigonus

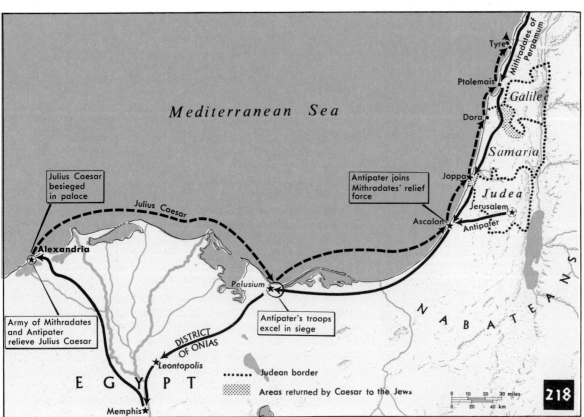

It was to please him (Antipater) that Caesar confirmed the appointment of Hyrcanus to the office of high priest.
(War 1:194)

JULIUS CAESAR AND JUDEA
47 B.C.
ANT. 14:127-143, 205, 207

Julius Caesar

Mattathias the high priest and the community of the Jews.

(Coin of Antigonus)

THE PARTHIAN INVASION AND THE ESCAPE OF HEROD   40 B.C.

The assassination of Julius Caesar in Rome (44 B.C.) caused the renewal of the civil war, but Antipater and his sons succeeded in keeping the reins of government by submitting to the various Roman rulers. One of these was Cassius, proconsul of Syria, who tyrannized the population of Judea. He sold into slavery the inhabitants of Lydda, Thamna, Gophna, and Emmaus, and razed their towns when they were late in paying taxes. In 43 B.C., Antipater was murdered by one of his opponents, but Herod avenged his father and suppressed the unrest; and he, together with his brother Phasael, was appointed ruler over all Judea (42 B.C.).

When the Parthians invaded Syria two years later, they were joined by Antigonus (Mattathias), the son of Aristobulus II. He accompanied Pacorus, son of Ordes king of the Parthians, along the coast; simultaneously the satrap Barzapharnes invaded Galilee from Damascus. When Pacorus came up to Jerusalem, he was joined by the Jews of Carmel and of the Drymus (the great forest in the Sharon plain). In Jerusalem, the people revolted against Phasael and Herod, who were forced to open the gates to the Parthians. Phasael submitted to Barzapharnes, but was imprisoned near Ecdippa, together with Hyrcanus II; he committed suicide in captivity, and Hyrcanus was maimed to make him unfit for the priesthood. Mattathias Antigonus was thereupon crowned in Jerusalem.

Herod and his family (including his betrothed, Mariamme the Hasmonean, daughter of Alexander and granddaughter of Aristobulus) fled south. At Tekoa, where the fortress Herodium was later to rise, he overcame his pursuers and continued on his way to Idumea. He was joined by his brother Joseph at Orhesa, and together they proceeded to Masada, where

ANT. 14:330-362; WAR 1:248-268

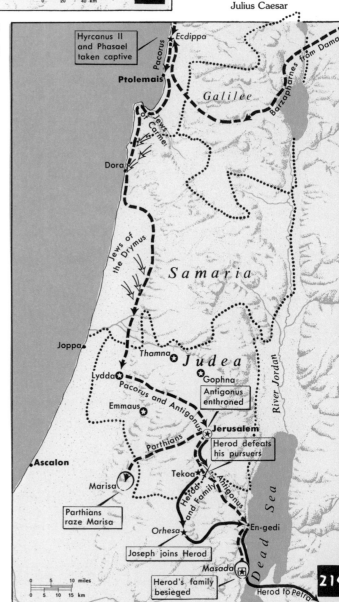

Town oppressed by Cassius
Herod
Parthians and Antigonus

Herod's family was later besieged by Antigonus. Herod himself crossed the Dead Sea and went to the Nabateans. When Malchus II, king of the Arabs, refused to come to his aid, Herod continued to Alexandria in Egypt and thence to Rome. The siege of Masada was meanwhile carried on in a most lethargic manner; at one time the defenders were saved from thirst only by a sudden cloud-burst. The Parthians, allies of Antigonus, returned beyond the Euphrates after invading Judea.

But they [the Hasmoneans] lost their royal power through internal strife, and it passed to Herod, son of Antipater ...

(Antiquities 14:end)

THE RISE OF HEROD
40 TO 37 B.C.

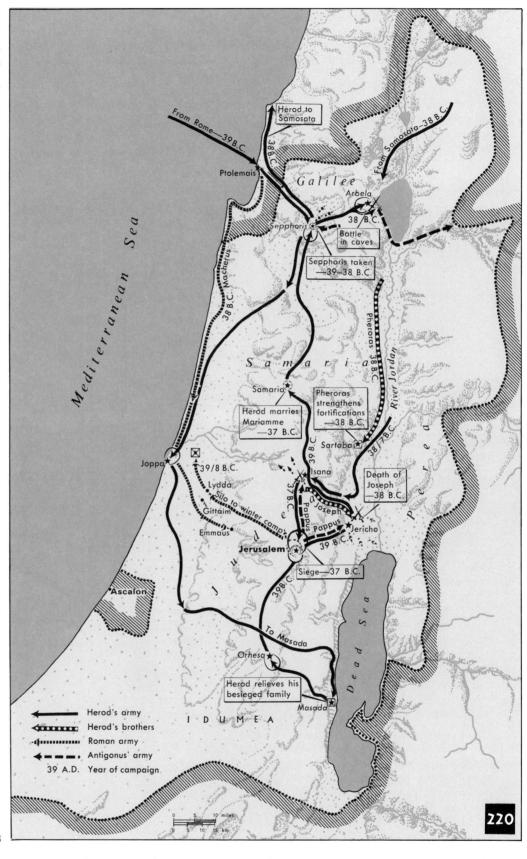

ANT. 14:394-491; WAR 1:290-353

Herod was received in Rome with great honors. Octavian (Caesar's nephew and successor) and Mark Antony persuaded the Senate to appoint him king of the Jews. They also added western Idumea and the lands of the Samaritans to his kingdom. The new king, however, had to fight for every inch of the land, for not only was the country destined for him in the hands of Antigonus, his rival, but the people hated the "Idumean slave"; even his Roman allies deserted him at times. But Herod overcame all these difficulties.

He landed at Ptolemais, for Joppa the port of Jerusalem was

in hostile hands. In the winter of 39 B.C. he set out to establish his rule in Galilee, and from there proceeded to capture Joppa, then continuing on to Masada. He freed his family, returned to Idumea, where he took Orhesa and went up against Jerusalem. Together with the Roman commander, Silo, he attacked the city, but the Romans broke off the siege having been bribed by Antigonus, and departed for their winter camp on the coast. Herod returned to Galilee, took Sepphoris during a snowstorm (winter 39-38 B.C.), pursued his opponents to the river Jordan, and stormed their fortified caves at Arbela, where the Jews put up a stout resistance.

In the summer of 38 B.C. Macherus, a Roman leader, was sent to Herod's aid; he attacked Emmaus while Pheroras, Herod's youngest brother, advanced through the Jordan Valley and rebuilt the fortifications of Alexandrium. Herod himself sent to meet Mark Antony who, at the time, was besieging Samosata on the Euphrates. On Herod's return he learned of his brother Joseph's defeat and death at the hands of Pappus, general of Antigonus. Herod left Jericho for the Judean mountains, routing Pappus near Isana. He and his allies again turned toward Jerusalem in the winter of 38-37 B.C. While the siege was in progress, Herod married Mariamme in Samaria. Jerusalem fell in the summer of 37 B.C. and many of the citizens were slaughtered. Antigonus, too, was executed, by order of Mark Antony. Herod was now undisputed ruler of Judea.

THE GROWTH OF HEROD'S KINGDOM 40 TO 4 B.C.

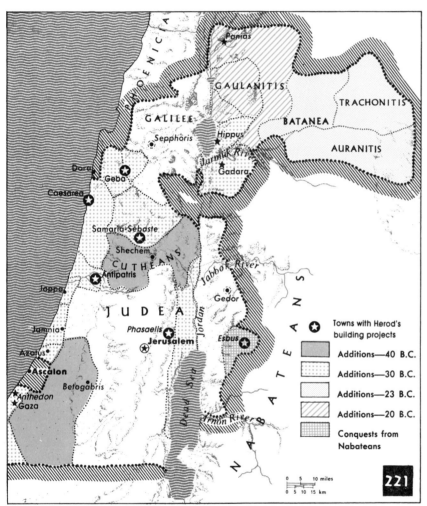

Towns with Herod's building projects

Additions—40 B.C.
Additions—30 B.C.
Additions—23 B.C.
Additions—20 B.C.
Conquests from Nabateans

0   5   10 miles
0 5 10 15 km

221

ANT. 15:217, 343, 344, 360; WAR 1:396, 398, 400; APPIAN: CIVIL WARS 5:75

Herod maintained his position under Cleopatra, and when the battle of Actium (31 B.C.) made Octavian — now the emperor Augustus — undisputed master of the Roman world, Herod quickly gained the favor of his new overlord. He was confirmed in his kingdom, to which Augustus in 30 B.C. added Gaza and the coastal cities (except Ascalon and Dora) as well as Gadara and Hippus. In 23 B.C., Herod received the task of pacifying the unruly Batanea, Trachonitis, and Auranitis, and in 20 B.C., Panias and Gaulanitis were placed under his rule. By then Herod's kingdom had reached its greatest extent.

Apart from the conquest of his own kingdom (see Map 220) Herod made only one conquest by arms: having in 32 B.C. defeated the Nabateans in the field, he annexed Esbus and settled veterans there.

The thought could not but occur both to Caesar himself and to his soldiers that Herod's realm was far too restricted, in comparison with the services which he had rendered them.

(War 1:396)

Coin of Herod the Great

Whoever has not seen Herod's Temple has never seen a beautiful building.

(Baba Bathra 4a)

HEROD'S BUILDING IN JERUSALEM

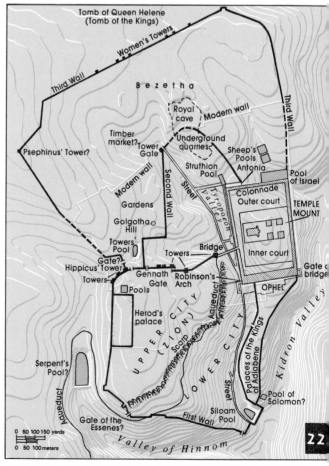

0 50 100 150 yards
0 50 100 meters

22

ANT. 15:318, 380-425; WAR 1:401, 5:108, 161, 238, 246, 507, 7:172-177

Herod's love of pomp, his wish to immortalize his name, to secure his rule, and to appease the hostile population and provide it with work — these were the main motives for fortifying and embellishing Jerusalem. His revenues derived from trade and from taxes allowed him to build a magnificent palace in the northwestern corner of the Upper City; it was guarded on the north by three strong towers that he named Phasael (after his brother), Mariamme (in honor of his wife), and Hippicus (after his friend). He also built a theater in the part of the city inhabited by wealthy Hellenizers, and strengthened the North Gate in the Second Wall. South of the Temple Mount he built a stadium, probably in the Tyropoean Valley.

Herod was even more active on the Temple Mount: doubling the area of the Temple esplanade, he girdled it with walls and porticoes. Its most prominent feature was the "royal portico" (basilica) in the south of the square. The king also rebuilt the Temple proper and to secure control over the Temple rebuilt the old Baris, at the northwestern corner of the Temple Mount, into a huge fortress, which he called "Antonia" in honor of Mark Antony.

Herod was also active as a builder outside his capital: he founded the harbor city of Caesarea in place of Strato's Tower and rebuilt Samaria, calling the new city "Sebaste" in honor of the emperor Augustus. He also built at Geba, Phasaelis and Antipatris. He built fortresses at Herodium and near Jericho, and entirely reconstructed Macherus and Masada on the two opposing shores of the Dead Sea.

Reconstruction of Herod's Temple

Border of Herod's realm
To Philip
To Herod Antipas
To Archelaus
To Province of Syria
Julias City founded by Herod's sons

... Caesar ... appointed Archelaus not king indeed but ethnarch of half the territory ... Antipas received ... Perea and Galilee ... Batanea, Trachonitis, Auranitis ...
(Antiquities 17:317-318)

THE DIVISION OF HEROD'S KINGDOM
4 B.C. TO A.D. 6

After much hesitation, the emperor Augustus decided in 4 B.C. to divide Herod's kingdom among his three surviving sons, as recommended by the dead king. Archelaus, the son of Malthace the Samaritan, was appointed ethnarch ("ruler of the nation") over Judea, Idumea, and Samaria. The cities of Caesarea and Sebaste were included in his domain, which included Jews and non-Jews in about equal proportions. Herod Antipas, the second son, received two purely Jewish, but widely separated, areas: Galilee and Perea (Jewish Transjordan). The third son, Herod Philip, was endowed with the newly settled lands of the Gaulanitis, Batanea, Trachonitis and Auranitis, as well as Caesarea Panias. Most of his subjects were probably non-Jews, but as the Jews in his lands had been settled by Herod the Great, they were loyal to the dynasty. Salome, Herod's sister, was given Jamnia and Azotus, and Phasaelis in the Jordan Valley. The cities of Gaza, Gadara, Geba and Hippus, which had borne Herod's rule with much dissatisfaction, were attached to the province of Syria.

All of Herod's sons tried to emulate their father in building cities; Archelaus even called a new settlement in his own name: Archelais. Antipas built Tiberias (named in honor of the emperor Tiberius), Sepphoris and Livias (in honor of the emperor's mother). Philip added to Caesarea Panias, which was from this time called Caesarea Philippi, and built Julias (also in honor of Livia) near Bethsaida.

Archelaus had a short and turbulent reign and was banished in A.D. 6, his lands being handed over to a Roman procurator. Herod Antipas remained till A.D. 39 (see Map 254). Only Philip died in possession of his tetrarchy, in A.D. 34.

> Well, ours is not a maritime country: neither commerce nor ... We devote ourselves to the cutivation of the productive country with which we are blessed.
>
> (Against Apion 1:60)

THE ECONOMY OF JUDEA

4TH CENTURY B.C. TO A.D. 1ST CENTURY

Thanks to its agricultural wealth, Judea was prosperous in the days of the Second Temple, a prosperity that began with the Hellenistic period mainly during the reign of Janneus. The areas suitable for wheat-growing were indeed few, and their extent limited: the Esdraelon Valley, parts of the coastal plain and some of the larger mountain valleys. In the south, barley took the place of wheat. Olives and vineyards thrived in the mountains. Dates were grown mainly in the hot Jordan Valley and balsam on the royal estate near Jericho. Wool from the mountains of southern Judea served to clothe the population. The western slopes of the mountains, on both sides of the Jordan, were still covered with extensive forests, and a good part of Sharon was wooded with oaks. These regions also served as pasture lands for sheep and cattle.

Various industries connected with the Temple and life in the metropolis in general existed in Jerusalem. Pottery, tied as it was to sources of raw material, was probably the country's one major industry; the others (mainly spinning and weaving) were home industries. Fishing boats plied the Sea of Galilee and the Mediterranean, and murex shells yielding purple were collected and processed at Azotus, Dora, and farther north. The name Taricheae, "place of salted fish," is evidence of a fish-preserving industry, which probably exported its produce. Copper from the Arabah, iron from the mountains of Gilead, and bitumen from the Dead Sea were the main natural resources; to these must be added the hot springs at Callirrhoe and Baaras as well as those near Pella, Gadara, and Tiberias.

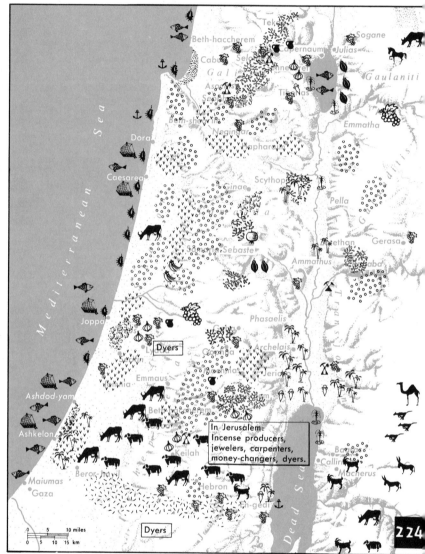

Coin of Herod Antipas, struck at Tiberias

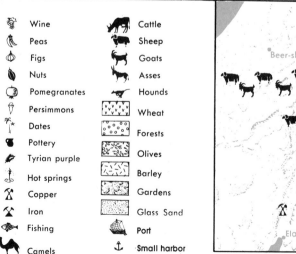

Wine	Cattle
Peas	Sheep
Figs	Goats
Nuts	Asses
Pomegranates	Hounds
Persimmons	Wheat
Dates	Forests
Pottery	Olives
Tyrian purple	Barley
Hot springs	Gardens
Copper	Glass Sand
Iron	Port
Fishing	Small harbor
Camels	
Horses	

THE ESSENES

Toward the end of the Second Temple period sectarianism with its attendant rivalries and antagonisms was on the rise. Josephus lists three major sects: the Pharisees, the Sadducees and the Essenes. In addition there were the Zealots who were not a religious sect but held nationalistic religious views which were also held by some Pharisees and Essenes. We learn of the Pharisees mainly from the Oral Law which was handed down and recorded during the second and third centuries A.D. We know somewhat more about the Essenes due to contemporary finds discovered in the Judean desert during the late 1950s and 1960s. The Essenes apparently developed their creed and teachings in the days of Hasmonean rule. During the reign of Janneus they isolated themselves from the rest of the population; many adherents and their leader, possibly the founder of the sect himself, the "Teacher of Righteousness," took voluntary refuge in the Judean desert. Living in the desert, with its messianic inspirations, the Essenes were cut off from the world around them and devoted themselves to a fundamental and ascetic existence. Some members of the sect remained in various towns and villages. Part of their writings have survived to the present-day owing to the dry desert climate. From their scrolls we can deduce much about their way of life and culture. The term Essenes refers to many different sects and offshoots, and the scholars themselves are in dispute as to whether all the documents found in the Judean desert caves belonged to the Essenes. It appears that at least part of them belonged to the Pharisees; some of the Essene groups were indeed very similar to the Pharisees.

In general, the Essenes did not not attach great importance to the Oral Law. True, their teachings contained addenda to and interpretations of the Written Law, but nothing in these writings points to a belief that their leaders had the authority to interprete or change the holy writ.

The Essene sect was messianic in nature, and their fervent belief in the coming of the Messiah is evidenced in many of their writings. At first theirs was an active and political messianism; later it became less strident. In the Revolt against Rome the Essenes sided with the rebels and as a result their centers (Khirbet Qumran) in the Judean desert were destroyed by the Romans.

And all who come into the order of the community shall pass over into the covenant before God ...
(Manual of Discipline 1:16)

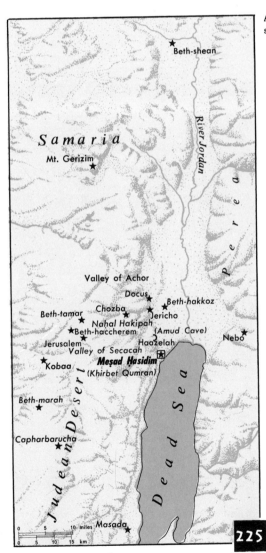

★ Alleged treasure caches
 of the Dead Sea Sect

COPPER SCROLL; MANUAL OF DISCIPLINE;
THANKSGIVING HYMNS;
THE DAMASCUS COVENANT

QUMRAN

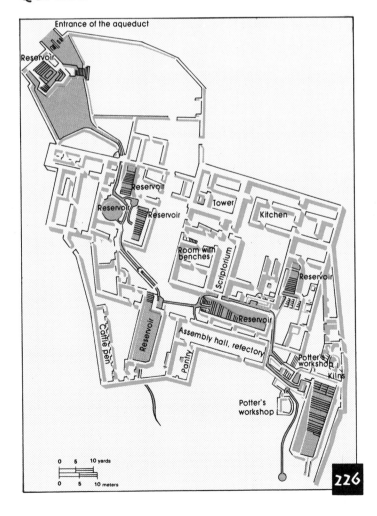

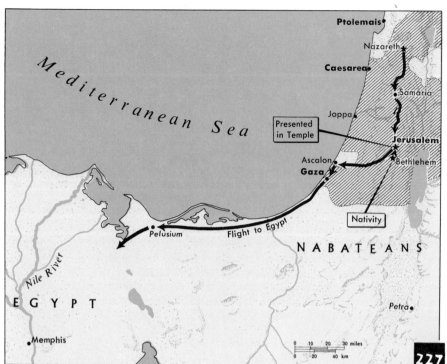

And she gave birth to her first-born son ... and laid him in a manger, because there was no place for them in the inn.

(Luke 2:7)

THE BIRTH OF JESUS AND THE FLIGH INTO EGYPT

The story of Jesus is set out in the four gospels of Matth Mark, Luke, and John. The first three are called the "synop gospels, because they are studied together owing to th similarity; the fourth gospel, that of John, contains m details not found in the others and is different in many of ways also. According to Christian tradition, Jesus was b at Bethlehem in the days of King Herod (who died in spring of 4 B.C.); Jesus' birth probably occurred in Decemb 5 B.C. According to Luke (2:22-24), the child was presen at the Temple. Menaced by Herod, Joseph and Mary decic to flee to Egypt by night. The shortest way to leave Herc domain was seemingly by way of Ascalon, which lay on main route to Egypt; the safer way of the desert would ha been too arduous for a woman and a newborn babe. T family arrived unharmed in the land of the Nile, where th found shelter and sustenance among the many Jews th living in Egypt (see Map 243).

MT. 1:18-2:15; LK. 2:4-38

And Jesus increased in wisdom and in stature and in favor with God and man.

(Luke 2:52)

MT. 2:19-23; LK. 2:41-52

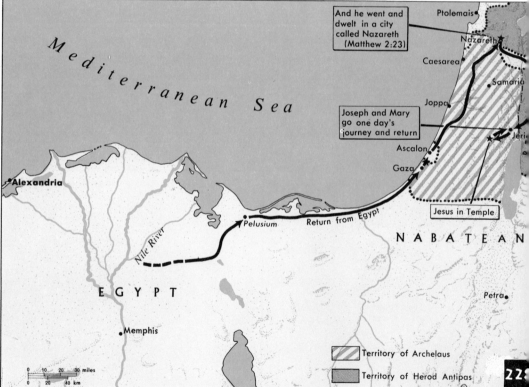

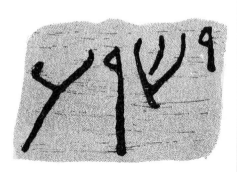

The name "Jesus," as written in Hebrew on an ossaury

THE RETURN FROM EGYPT; THE BOY JESUS IN THE TEMPLE

After the death of Herod, Joseph had a vision in which he was told to return to the Land of Israel. Fearing Archelaus, the ethnarch of Judea, Joseph decided to return to his native Nazareth, then under the milder rule of Herod Antipas (see Map 223). Nazareth was a small Jewish village about seven miles southeast of Sepphoris, the capital of western Galilee. There Jesus grew into manhood. The only story of these "hidden years" in the gospels is that related by Luke (2:41-51),

according to which Jesus went with his parents to Jerusalem when he was twelve years old. Jesus stayed behind in Jerusalem when his parents went a day's journey on their way back to Nazareth (presumably down to Jericho, so as to return by way of Jewish Perea rather than through Samaria). Missing the boy, they returned to the Holy City and there found him debating with the teachers in the Temple. They then returned with him to Nazareth.

THE BAPTISM OF JESUS AND THE SOJOURN IN THE DESERT

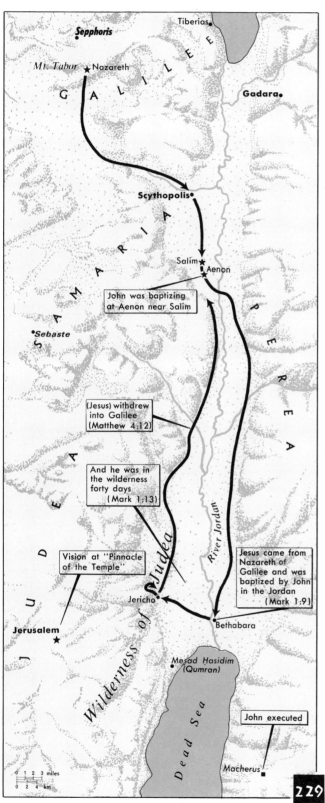

The beginning of Jesus' public activity, the "fifteenth year of the reign of Tiberius Caesar" (that is, A.D. 27-28), was also when John the Baptist began to preach "a baptism of repentance for the forgiveness of sins" (Luke 3:1-3). Combining the Gospel story with other historical sources of the period (in particular Josephus and the Qumran documents), we see the activity of John as part of a deep spiritual ferment pervading the whole of Judea at that time. John's activity was concentrated in the Jordan Valley, either at Beth-abara at the fords of the Jordan near Jericho, or higher up the river at Aenon (identified in the 4th century as lying two miles south of Salim; today at Khirbet ed-Dir), south of Scythopolis (Beth-shean). Among the multitudes who flocked to be baptized was Jesus, who came from Nazareth in Galilee. This was the beginning of his ministry. According to the Gospels, his baptism was followed by forty days of seclusion in the wilderness, most probably the wilderness of Judea above Jericho. This has from time immemorial been a refuge for those who have wished to isolate themselves from the world. The sequence of baptism and seclusion in the wilderness was common at the time, especially among the Dead Sea sect (the Essenes), whose headquarters were at Mesad Hasidim (Khirbet Qumran, see Map 226) not far away; no positive evidence, however, has been found to connect John or Jesus with the sect. Gospel tradition has it that Jesus was tempted by Satan in the desert and carried by the evil spirit to the "pinnacle of the Temple" in Jerusalem — presumably the southeastern corner of the Temple Mount — which had a sheer drop of 130 feet. Having overcome temptation, Jesus returned to Galilee. John continued to preach and baptize and was ultimately arrested by order of Herod Antipas, kept in prison for some time (traditionally at Macherus in southern Perea), and executed when Herod succumbed to the wiles of his wife, Herodias, who hated the prophet because he denounced her evil ways (Mark 6:14-29; Matthew 14:1-12; Luke 3:19-20). According to Christian tradition John was buried in Samaria (Sebaste) although it was outside the kingdom of Herod Antipas. These events occurred during Jesus' ministry, but they cannot be chronologically fixed on the evidence available.

Tiberius Caesar

MT. 3-4:12, 14:1-2; MK. 1:4-14, 6:14-29; LK. 3:1-22, 6:18-30, 9:7-9;
JN. 1:6-8, 15-42, 3:22-24

FROM NAZARETH TO CANA AND CAPERNAUM

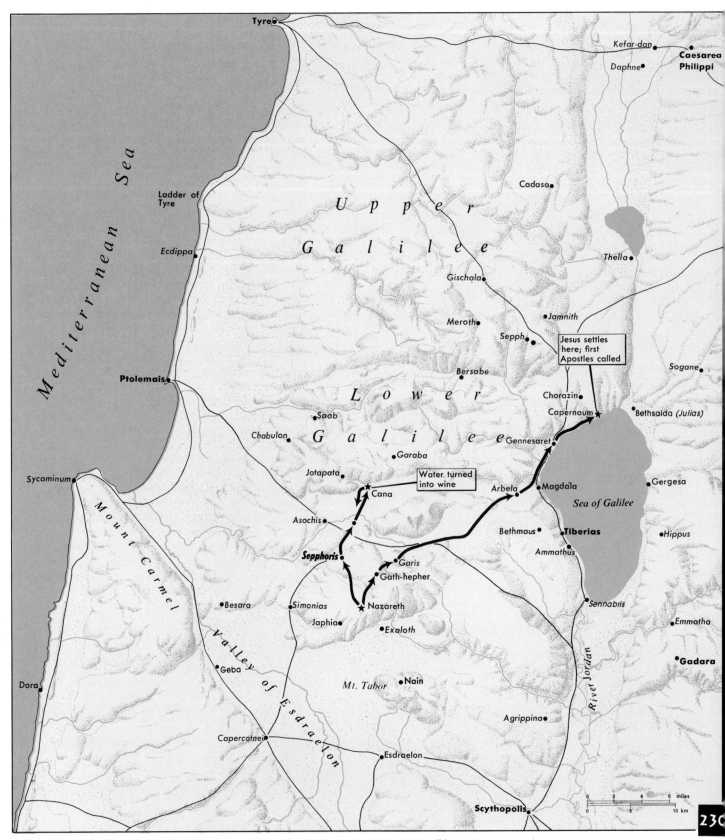

Mediterranean Sea

Tyre

Kefar-dan •
Daphne •
Caesarea Philippi

Ladder of Tyre

Upper Galilee

Cadasa •

Thella •

Ecdippa •

Gischala •

Meroth •

Sepph •

Jamnith •

Ptolemais

Lower

Bersabe •

Sogane •

Saab •

Galilee

Chorazin •

Jesus settles here; first Apostles called

Chabulon •

Garaba •

Gennesaret

Capernaum ★

Bethsaida (Julias)

Jotapata •

Water turned into wine

Arbela •

Magdala •

Gergesa •

Sycaminum •

Cana ★

Sea of Galilee

Asochis •

Bethmaus •

Tiberias

Hippus •

Sepphoris

Garis •

Ammathus •

Mount Carmel

Gath-hepher •

• Besara

Simonias •

Nazareth ★

Japhia •

Exaloth •

Sennabris •

Emmatha •

• Geba

Mt. Tabor

Nain •

Valley of Esdraelon

Dora •

River Jordan

Gadara

Agrippina •

Capercotnei •

Esdraelon •

| 0 | 2 | 4 | 6 miles |
| 0 | | 5 | 10 km |

Scythopolis

230

MT. 4:12-22, 8:5-17. 9:9-10, 18-20; MK. 1:16-34. 2:1-17, 5:22-43; LK. 4:31-41, 5:27-32, 7:1-10, 8:40-56; JN. 2:1-12

According to Luke 3:23, Jesus was about thirty years old when he began his ministry. It appears that his first preaching at Nazareth was unsuccessful, and he left the town to settle at Capernaum on the shores of the Lake Gennesaret. Capernaum (in the original Hebrew, Kefar-nahum, "Village of Nahum") was a prosperous townlet whose inhabitants engaged mainly in fishing (a great haul of fish is recorded in Luke 5:6). Being a frontier town between the domains of Antipas and Philip, it had a custom post (the apostle Matthew may have been called from his duty there as a tax-collector; Matthew 9:9;

Mark 2:3-14; Luke 5:27). A centurion commanding the local garrison, though a Gentile, had built the local synagogue (Luke 7:5), where Jesus often preached. It was at Capernaum that Jesus called his first disciples, the fishermen Simon, Peter, and Andrew, men of nearby Bethsaida east of the Jordan (John 1:44), as well as James and John, the sons of Zebedee; and here he invested the Twelve Apostles (Mark 3:13-19; Matthew 10:1-4). It was here also that he performed many of the miraculous deeds reported in the Gospels. From then on Capernaum was called "his own city" (Matthew 9:1). As Capernaum had a more varied population and was nearer the borders of the Decapolis than landlocked Nazareth, it is likely to have been more receptive to the new teachings. Yet Jesus did not entirely sever his ties with the town of his youth. John 2:11 continues, after the story of his baptism, with a miracle performed by Jesus at Cana in the presence of Mary and the disciples. Therefore, if we follow John's Gospel, the visit to Cana occurred at the beginning of Jesus' ministry.

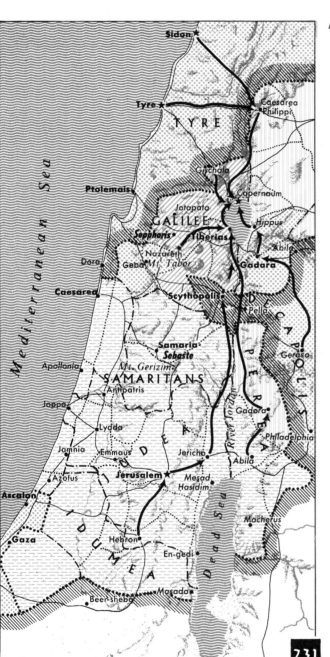

Territory of Herod Philip

Cities under the Proconsul of Syria

Territory of Herod Antipas

Territory of the Procurator of Judea

Herod's kingdom at its greatest extent

MT. 4:25; MK. 3:7-8; LK. 6:17

A great multitude, hearing all that he did, came to him.
(Mark 3:8)

THE HOLY LAND AND COELE-SYRIA IN THE TIME OF JESUS

The Gospels tell that the teachings of Jesus, which mainly took place around the Sea of Galilee, drew crowds from Galilee, Judea, Jerusalem, Idumea, the lands beyond the Jordan, Tyre, and Sidon (Mark 3:7-8; Matthew 4:25 [adding "the Decapolis"] and Luke 6:17). The list of countries and towns reflects the area of Jewish settlement in the Holy Land at the time. In Judea, Jerusalem is singled out as the only "city" proper in the land; Idumea had been a separate administrative unit since the days of Alexander Janneus, although its inhabitants were merging more and more with the rest of the Jews. The lands "beyond the Jordan," or Perea, were Jewish from the days of the Tobiad dynasty (see Map 214). There were Jewish communities in the cities of the Decapolis which were, however, predominantly Gentile. Finally, the territories of Tyre and Sidon, although predominantly Phoenician (see Map 231), had considerable Jewish populations. Though politically split up between various territories and rulers (all of which were subject to Roman suzerainty), the Jews of the Holy Land were one spiritually and any wave of religious feeling rising in one community could sweep them all. It is significant that Samaria and the coastal cities are absent from the list, though later (see Map 264) Christianity made much progress there.

Inscription honoring Philip, son of Herod

A prophet is not without honor, except in his own country.

(Mark 6:4)

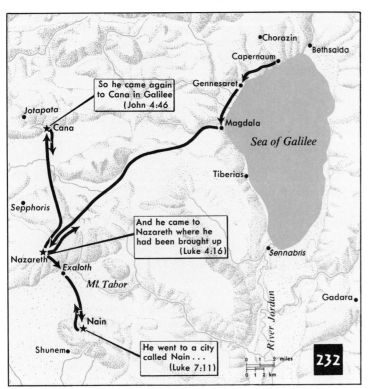

So he came again to Cana in Galilee (John 4:46

And he came to Nazareth where he had been brought up (Luke 4:16)

He went to a city called Nain . . . (Luke 7:11)

232

CANA AND NAZARETH REVISITED

Mark (6:1-6) inserts, within the story of Jesus' teaching around the Sea of Galilee, an episode of a visit to Nazareth. Jesus preached in the synagogue there, but was rejected by the worshipers who refused to believe that "the carpenter" was an inspired prophet. In Matthew 13:53-58 the episode is placed in the same context, though Jesus is here called "the carpenter's son." Luke, on the other hand (4:16-30), places the incident at the very beginning of Jesus' ministry. It is in connection with this visit to Nazareth that we may perhaps place Jesus' second visit to Cana, during which (according to John 4:46) he healed the son of an "official" (the original Greek has "basilikos," "the king's man"). Cana was situated at the border of the plain of Asochis, where there were royal estates and the "king's man" was probably the royal steward administering this domain.

During another of Jesus' visits in the neighborhood, he healed the widow's son at Nain (Luke 7:11-17). Although called "a city," Nain was a mere village five miles southeast of Nazareth; situated on a hilly slope, it had a gate and wall. In later times Nain was the capital of a separate district. Remains of the cemetery of this ancient village are still visible in the rocky area by the side of the road leading from Nain to the central trunk route.

MT. 13:53-58; MK. 6:1-6; LK. 4:16-30, 7:11-17; JN. 4:46-54

AROUND THE SEA OF GALILEE

Who is this, that even wind and sea obey him?
(Ma▶

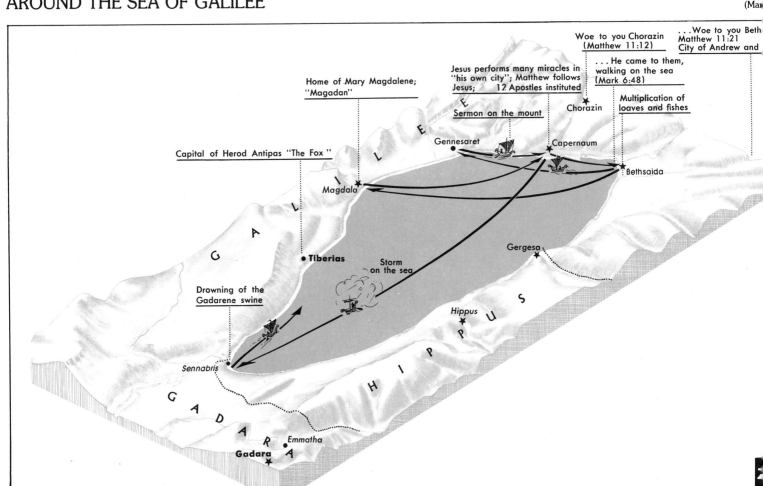

MT. 4:18, 5:1, 8:18, 23-24, 9:1, 13:1, 14:13-34, 15:29-39; MK. 2:16-20. 2:13, 4:1, 35-41, 5:1-21, 6:32-53, 8:1-10, 22; LK. 5:1-11. 8:22-39. 9:10-17; JN. 6:1-25

Apart from several journeys, Jesus' entire activity before his final departure for Jerusalem was concentrated around the Sea of Galilee (Matthew 15:29; Mark 1:16, 6:31), also called Lake Gennesaret (Luke 5:1) and Lake Tiberias (John 6:1, 21:1), and usually just "the sea" in the Gospels. Gennesaret seems to be an earlier name, for it replaces the biblical "Sea of Chinnereth" (Numbers 34:11), because the city of Gennesaret was located on the site of Chinnereth (Tell Ureime). "Sea of Tiberias" is clearly posterior to the foundation of that city in A.D. 18-19 (see Map 223). The first Apostles were fishermen; sometimes Jesus taught while standing in a boat, with the crowds listening on the shore. The Sermon on the Mount was delivered according to tradition near Capernaum (Matthew 8:1 and 5); the site is said to be located on the height just behind Capernaum. Only occasionally did Jesus upbraid the cities that refused to repent ("Woe to you Chorazin, woe to you Bethsaida, Capernaum shall be brought down to Hades" — Matthew 11:21-23; Luke 10:13-15).

On the Sea of Galilee there are frequent storms. During one such storm, Jesus slept while sailing across to the Gadarenes (Mark 5:35-41; Matthew 8:23-27; Luke 8:22-24) and upon his awakening the sea was suddenly becalmed. The location of the incident of the "Gadarene swine" has been much disputed (the usual version "Gerasene" is quite impossible, for there was no territory of Gerasa on the lake shore); the two possibilities are "Gergasene" — pointing to Gergasa (Kursi) on the eastern shore of the lake in the territory of Hippus — and "Gadarene"; Gadara might have possessed a stretch of the shore that lay between the river Jordan and Kefar-semah. The shore there is steep; thus the plunging of the herd of swine into the waters of the lake is plausible. The inhabitants of Gadara, being Gentiles, did not share Jewish scruples regarding the raising of swine. In any event, the name Gergasa appears in an ancient Jewish source as the name of a village east of the Jordan river and is thus evidence that a village by this name existed. In the sixth century a large monastery was founded in the area.

Other events recorded in the Gospels pertaining to the Sea of Galilee and its surrounding are the Multiplication of Loaves and Fishes at a lonely spot near the town of Bethsaida, the story of Jesus' walking on the water, and Peter's attempt to follow his example (Mark 6:45-51; Matthew 15:22-23; and John 6:15-21). Other journeys of Jesus include a visit to "Magadan" ("Dalmanutha," in Mark 8:10); in both cases we should read Magdala, the most important townlet on the sea shore after Tiberias, and famous for its fish-curing industry. This locality was the home of Mary Magdalene, who followed Jesus to Jerusalem; she was one of a group of women "who had been healed of evil spirits and infirmities ... who provided for him out of their means" (Luke 8:2-3).

And from there he arose and went away to the region of Tyre and Sidon.

(Mark 7:24)

THE VISIT TO TYRE, SIDON, AND CAESAREA PHILIPPI

Gold glass from Rome depicting carpenters at work

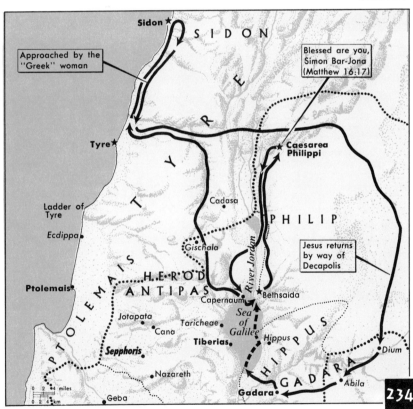

MT. 15:21-29, 16:13-20; MK. 7:24-31, 8:27-30

The only time Jesus left the traditional boundaries of the Holy Land proper was during his journey to Tyre and Sidon. Mark 7:24 and Matthew 15:21 define this journey as one to the "region" or "district" of these two cities; we are not told whether he entered the cities themselves. Both had extensive territories; that of Sidon had a common border with the city of Damascus, far inland. The region of Tyre reached Cadasa in the mountains overlooking the Huleh valley (Ulatha).

During this journey Jesus healed the daughter of a "Greek" or "Syrophoenician" woman; that is to say, a Phoenician woman who had adopted the Hellenistic culture then common in the Roman East. According to Mark (7:31), Jesus passed through the region of the Decapolis on his return to the Sea of Galilee — possibly detouring inland through Gaulanitis to the territories of Abila, Dium, Hippus, and Gadara.

Another, shorter, journey took Jesus and his disciples to

the district of Caesarea Philippi, Hellenistic Panias, rebuilt by Herod and his son Philip. The outstanding feature of the region was the high cliffs near the city with a cave dedicated to the god Pan and many rock-cut niches holding dedicatory statues of the Nymphs. The sight of this great rock-cliff may have inspired the naming of Peter, "The Rock," on which the church was to be built.

These journeys between Tyre and Caesarea Philippi were probably associated by Matthew (Mt. 4:15) with the "way of the sea" mentioned by Isaiah (Isa. 9:1). The route intended by the prophet was evidently the road from Tyre to Panias via Abel-beth-maacah (see Map 147).

And after six days Jesus took with him Peter and James and John and led them up a high mountain ...

(Mark 9:2)

THE TRANSFIGURATION

A Phoenician woman (On a sarcophagus from Sidon)

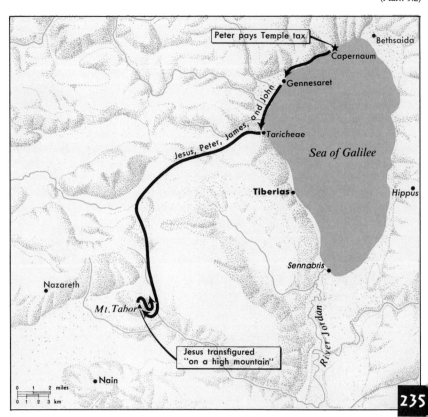

MT. 17:1-8; MK. 9:2-8; LK. 9:28-36

After the return to the Sea of Galilee, the Gospels relate the visit of Jesus, together with the Apostles Peter, James, and John, to "a high mountain" — where the Transfiguration is said to have taken place. This mountain is not named in the sources, but tradition connects the event with Mount Tabor, a prominent landmark that had served in biblical times as a boundary point between the territories of three tribes; it had been a Hellenistic fortress and later it was a Jewish one. Owing to its shape and isolated position, it is visible from practically the whole of Lower Galilee and the Valley of Esdraelon.

After the Transfiguration Matthew tells of a significant incident at Capernaum: Jesus had Peter pay the half-shekel tax to the Temple for both of them, so as "not to give offense" (Mt. 17:24-27).

JESUS' VISIT TO JERUSALEM

The Gospel according to John records several more journeys of Jesus to Jerusalem, about which the other Gospels are silent. Thus, in John 2:13-3:21 there is the story of a visit to Jerusalem at Passover, during which Jesus cleansed the Temple of moneychangers and sellers of animals, an event placed by the other Gospels in his last days in Jerusalem (Mark 11:15-17; Matthew 21:12-13; Luke 19:45-46). During this stay Jesus was baptizing in Judea while John was doing the same in the well-watered plain of Aenon, near Salim (John 3:22-24). It was on his return from this ministry in Judea that Jesus passed through Samaria and met the Samaritan woman at the well of Sychar, staying two days with the Samaritans, many of whom believed in him.

One more journey to Jerusalem, during which a paralytic was healed at the pool of Bethesda in the Holy City, is recorded in John 5.

John (chapter 7) gives a slightly different version of Jesus' last journey than that found in the three other Gospels. According to John, he went secretly to Jerusalem at the Feast of Tabernacles (in the autumn); and was still there at the Feast of Dedication (in early winter, John 10:22), after which he returned beyond the Jordan, probably to Bethabara (John 10:40). He then came back to Bethany, raised Lazarus from the dead (John 11:1-46), and retired once again into the wilderness of Ephraim, northeast of Jerusalem (John 10:54).

The Passover of the Jews was at hand, and Jesus went up to Jerusalem.

(John 2:13)

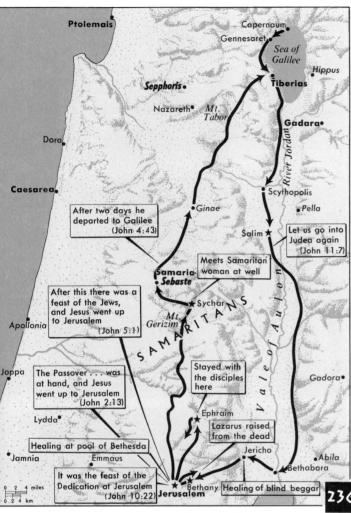

After two days he departed to Galilee (John 4:43)

Meets Samaritan woman at well

Let us go into Judea again (John 11:7)

After this there was a feast of the Jews, and Jesus went up to Jerusalem (John 5:1)

The Passover . . . was at hand, and Jesus went up to Jerusalem (John 2:13)

Healing at pool of Bethesda

It was the feast of the Dedication at Jerusalem (John 10:22)

Stayed with the disciples here

Lazarus raised from the dead

Healing of blind beggar

236

JN. 2:13-2:22, 3:22, 4:1-42, 5:1-18, 7:1-10, 10:40, 11:1-44, 54

Remains of ancient boat retrieved from the Sea of Galilee

When the days drew near for him to be received up, he set his face to go to Jerusalem.

(Luke 9:51)

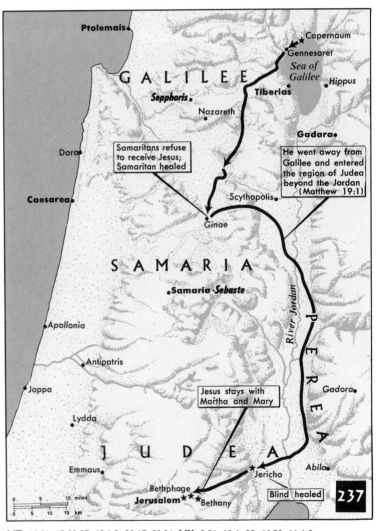

Samaritans refuse to receive Jesus; Samaritan healed

He went away from Galilee and entered the region of Judea beyond the Jordan (Matthew 19:1)

Jesus stays with Martha and Mary

Blind healed

237

JESUS' LAST JOURNEY TO JERUSALEM

When the days drew near for him "to be received up" (Luke 9:51), at the end of his stay in Galilee, Jesus began to foretell of his fate in Jerusalem to his disciples, "and they were greatly distressed" (Matthew 17:23).

We may possibly insert into the story of Jesus' last journey to Jerusalem the incident mentioned in Luke 9:52-56. Perhaps Jesus intended to take the shorter route to Jerusalem by way of Samaria but, as the people would not receive him, he turned eastward and went through Perea, the "Judea beyond the Jordan." From there, he and his disciples crossed the Jordan and continued by way of Jericho, where he stayed at the house of Zacchaeus, a chief tax-collector (probably of the imperial estates in the Jordan Valley, inherited by the emperor from the Herodian dynasty). Two blind beggars were healed outside the town. Then Jesus continues along the pilgrim road, which went up to the Mount of Olives and so to Bethphage on the mount and to Bethany, where he stayed at the house of Martha and Mary, the sisters of Lazarus.

MT. 16:21, 17:22-27, 19:1-2, 20:17, 29-34; MK. 8:31, 10:1, 32, 46-52, 11:1-2; LK. 9:51-56, 10:38-42, 13:22, 18:31-42, 19:1-10, 28-35; JN. 12:1-8

THE AREA OF JERICHO

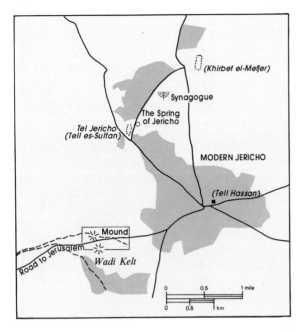

THE AREA OF JERICHO

(Khirbet el-Mefjer)

Synagogue

The Spring of Jericho

Tel Jericho (Tell es-Sultan)

MODERN JERICHO

(Tell Hassan)

Mound

Road to Jerusalem

Wadi Kelt

| 0 | 0.5 | 1 mile |
| 0 | 0.5 | 1 km |

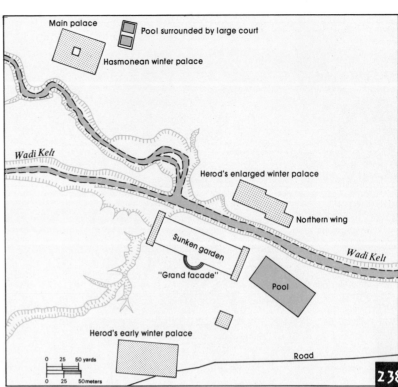

Main palace

Pool surrounded by large court

Hasmonean winter palace

Wadi Kelt

Herod's enlarged winter palace

Northern wing

Sunken garden

"Grand facade"

Wadi Kelt

Pool

Herod's early winter palace

Road

| 0 | 25 | 50 yards |
| 0 | 25 | 50 meters |

238

O Jerusalem, Jerusalem, killing the prophets and stoning those who are sent to you!

(Matthew 23:37)

JESUS' TRIAL, JUDGMENT AND CRUCIFIXION

Modern wall

Jesus' triumphal entry from Bethany

Tower Gate

Jesus condemned

Sheep's Pools

Third Wall

Modern wall

Second Wall

Via Dolorosa

Struthion Pool

Pool of Israel

Antonia

To Antipas and back

Street

Tyropoeon Valley

Preaching

TEMPLE MOUNT

Crucifixion and burial

Gardens

Golgotha Hill

Jesus arrested

Towers' Pool

Gennath Gate

Bridge

Temple cleansed

Gethsemane

Gate? Tower

Tower

OPHEL

Hippicus' Tower

Tower

Herod Antipas palace

Pools

To Pontius Pilate

UPPER CITY (ZION)

Brought to Caiaphas

Kidron Valley

From Bethany

Herod's palace

Scarp

Jesus before high priests; Peter's denial

LOWER

House of Caiaphas

To Gethsemane

Street

CITY

Pool of Solomon?

Last Supper

Serpent's Pool?

Gate of the Essenes?

Aqueduct

First Wall

Siloam Pool

| 0 | 50 | 100 | 150 yards |
| 0 | 50 | 100 meters |

Valley of Hinnom

239

RIBERIEVM
IVSPILATVS
ECTVSMDA

Inscription of Pontius Pilate, found at Caesarea

MT. 21-27; MK. 11-15; LK. 19:28-23; JN. 12-19

JESUS' TRIAL, JUDGMENT AND CRUCIFIXION

Jesus began his stay in Jerusalem with what is invariably referred to as the triumphal entry, riding on the colt of a she-ass found at a village opposite Bethphage. He was received by the people with cries of "Hosanna" ("Save now!"); they spread their garments on the road and waved palm branches in blessing. After teaching in the Temple he returned to Bethany. The synoptic Gospels place the cleansing of the Temple courts during this second visit (see also Map 236). Next day he and his disciples held the Last Supper at a house, the large upper room of which was "furnished and ready" (Mark 14:15 and Luke 22:12); we may assume that it took place in the rich Upper City of Jerusalem, at the home of one of Jesus' followers. This supper has been held to correspond with the Pascal meal and certainly is colored by Passover motifs. After the Supper, Jesus and the disciples descended to the Kidron Valley, to Gethsemane (the "Oil Press") at the foot of the Mount of Olives. There he was arrested by a crowd armed with swords and clubs, led by Judas Iscariot, one of the Twelve, who had betrayed his master. According to the Gospels Jesus was led to the house of the high priest Caiaphas, there to be interrogated first by the former high priest Annas and then by an informal tribunal presided over by the high priest himself. It was during these events that Peter, who was waiting outside in the courtyard of the palace, thrice denied Jesus.

Jesus was interrogated as to his beliefs; but though his inquisitors regarded his utterances as blasphemous, they were not, in the judgment of most scholars, empowered to inflict the death penalty. They decided therefore to accuse Jesus before the governor, Pontius Pilate, of a political offense — rebellion against the emperor, implied in Jesus' claim to be "King of the Jews." According to Luke (23:6-12) Pilate sent Jesus to Herod Antipas (as "he belonged to Herod's jurisdiction") who sent him back to Pilate. Antipas most probably resided in the old Hasmonean palace, which was the residence of the Herodians on their visits to Jerusalem. Pilate, as governor, would have resided either at the palace of Herod on the western side of the city, or at the fortress of Antonia north of the Temple. As his main reason for staying in Jerusalem was to supervise the Temple during the mass pilgrimage at Passover, we can accept the tradition that the judgment on Jesus was passed at the praetorium set up in Antonia. From there, Jesus was led by Roman soldiers to Golgotha, traditionally a place outside the Second Wall of Jerusalem; here he was executed according to Roman practice, by being affixed to a cross. According to the same tradition he was buried nearby, in a tomb belonging to Joseph of Arimathaea.

And they found the stone rolled away from the tomb, but when they went in they did not find the body.
(Luke 24:2-3)

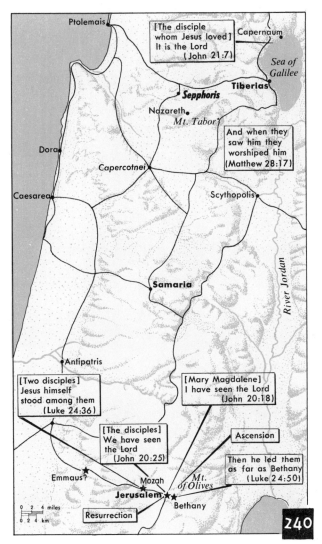

THE RESURRECTION AND ASCENSION

The Gospels are unanimous in continuing the story of Jesus after the Crucifixion. According to Christian belief, Jesus rose from the dead on the third day after his crucifixion. The Gospels record appearances of the risen Christ in Galilee (Matthew and Mark) and in Judea, at Emmaus (possibly Mozah), Bethany, Jerusalem (John, Luke and Matthew by inference). Finally, we are told (Acts 1:2-12), he ascended to heaven from the Mount of Olives.

The rolling stone in Herod's family tomb, Jerusalem

MT. 28; MK. 16; LK. 24; JN. 20-21; ACTS 1:1-8; 1 COR. 15:7

... and he went to the synagogue, as his custom was, on the sabbath day. And he stood up to read ...

(Luke 4:16)

Ancient synagogues:

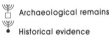 Archaeological remains

Historical evidence

•••••• Border of Herod's realm

SYNAGOGUES IN THE SECOND TEMPLE PERIOD

The synagogue was the main public institution for the Jewish community. Here the leadership conducted its business and here the community gathered to discuss matters of importance.

During the week the synagogue served as a place of study for boys only. On the sabbath and holy days the community met here to read from the Torah, to pray and to listen to sermons. At first prayer was not the main event at such meetings. Usually there were readings from the Torah and sometimes from the prophetical writings (*Haftorah*) and if there was a scholar or teacher in the community he would deliver a homily (*drasha*).

Whenever Jesus visited a Galilean village, such as Capernaum, he would be invited to deliver a sermon in the synagogue. Jesus used these occasions to spread his message.

Little is known of the antecedents of the synagogue as an institution. In Egypt synagogues existed as early as the third century B.C. In Israel the earliest synagogues found date from the first century A.D. Synagogues dating from the second century A.D. have been discovered at Masada, Herodium, Gamla and possibly Arbel, where one structure could well have served as a synagogue. A synagogue inscription was found in Jerusalem. From New Testament sources and from the writings of Josephus we learn that synagogues existed in many villages.

Moses received the Torah on Mt. Sinai and gave it to Joshua and Joshua ... to the people of the Knesset ha-Gedolah.

Avoth 1:a

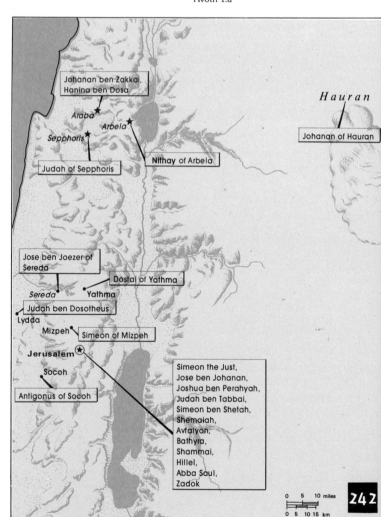

THE "HAKHAM" IN THE DAYS OF THE SECOND TEMPLE

Hakham, literally wise man or sage, was the title given to spiritual leaders of the Pharisees. This title is best rendered as "rabbi" or "teacher" because teaching the Law was one of their main functions at the time. These teachers derived their authority from the prestige attached to their knowledge of the Law (Torah) and their ability to pass on the Oral Law from generation to generation.

The teacher usually worked within a small circle of students (*habura*) whom he taught without reward. He derived his livelihood from other work or in some cases from income from his property. Studies were conducted mainly in the evenings so as not to interfere with daytime work, particularly intensive seasonal agricultural work. Such study groups existed in many villages, but the main center of study of the Law was, of course, Jerusalem. Here groups congregated in city squares and in the Temple court. Apart from local groups there was the itinerant teacher who, together with his students, traveled from village to village bringing the Law to the masses. Jesus was one such teacher.

The close of the Second Temple period saw an increase in the power of the teachers. The most prominent among them became national leaders and administrators of the Temple. There was a constant struggle between Pharisees and Sadducees over who would conduct the divine services in the Temple. Knowledge of the Law was a prestigious accomplishment and source of community power. According to Josephus the Pharisees wielded great influence over the people, while the Sadducees held the more important positions in the community and the Temple. Initially, teachers had no official standing and the title "rabbi" signified respect rather than rank in the hierarchy. In the Avot Tractate "Pairs" of scholar-teachers are mentioned, but it is not clear what their function and official standing was at the time of the Second Temple. Even though many of the teachers were "priests," they always believed that the Law should be revealed to one and all. Slogans such as "they raised many scholars" and "they were guardians of the Torah" served as guidelines for teachers for many generations.

Now there were dwelling in Jerusalem Jews, devout men every nation under heaven.

(Acts 2:5)

HE JEWISH DIASPORA IN THE TIME OF JESUS

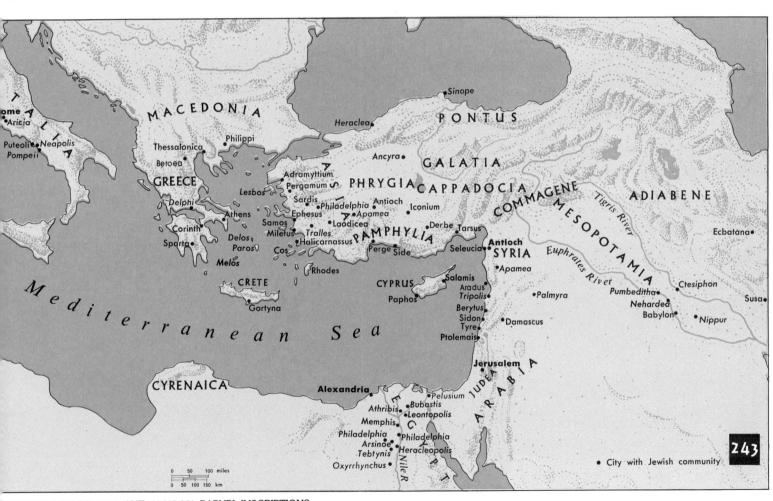

ACTS 2:8-11; 1 MACC. 15-23; ANT. 14:213-264; PAPYRI; INSCRIPTIONS

At the beginning of the Christian era, the Jewish communities were mainly concentrated in the Eastern, Greek-speaking half of the Roman Empire. Two outlying areas were central Italy, where Jews had been brought as slaves after Pompey's campaign and where conditions became favorable under Julius Caesar, and Babylonia, where the communities grew strong under Parthian rule. But the bulk of the Jewish diaspora was still confined to the Greek world; the largest and most affluent community was in Egypt (see Map 182). There the Jewish communities were centered around the synagogue, with full internal autonomy, their own archons and elders, communicating with each other and with Jerusalem. This state of affairs goes far to explain the context of Paul's missionary activity (see Maps 247-252). The communities were on the whole prosperous, but dependent on Gentile authorities and anxious to preserve good relations with them.

THE PENTECOST

The Jewish diaspora was linked to Jerusalem by strong religious bonds; as long as the Temple stood, thousands of pilgrims came every year from outlying communities to fulfill the duty of "going up to the mountain of the Lord" on one of the three main festivals. At these times Jerusalem assumed a strangely cosmopolitan air, people from West and East jostling one another, speaking a rich variety of languages. According to the story as told in Acts, many of the pilgrims came to hear the Apostles and were astounded to be addressed in their own languages. On this occasion, the author of Acts gives (Acts 2:9-10) an extensive survey of the diaspora of his time (which possibly looks back symbolically to the tower of Babel and the

giving of the Law), beginning with the East, which was beyond the boundaries of the Roman Empire — Parthia, Media, Elam, and Mesopotamia. He then gives Judea and, going north, lists Cappadocia and Pontus; from the shores of the Black Sea he turns westward to the province of Asia, then inland to Phrygia and Pamphylia. From there he moves on across the sea to Egypt and its neighbor, Cyrene. Rome, with its Jews and proselytes, represents the western diaspora; Crete and Arabia (the "Nabatene") round off his survey. The variety of coins found in Jerusalem from the late Second Temple period testifies to the extensive trade carried on between Jerusalem and various countries.

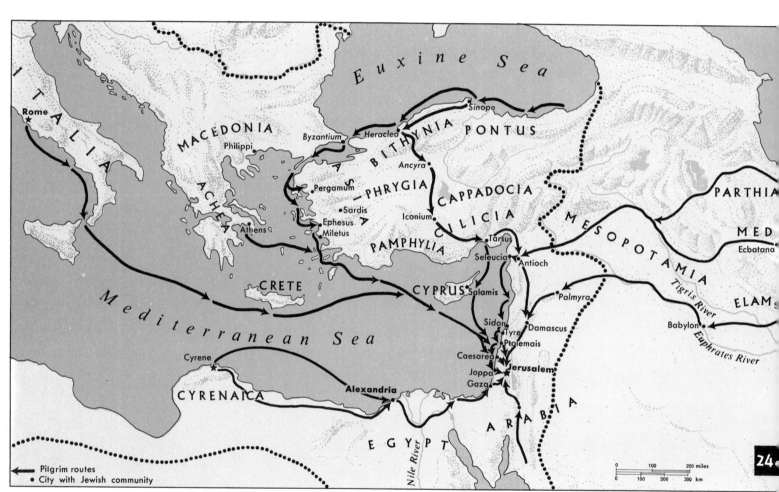

ACTS 2:9-11

PETER AND PHILIP TO SAMARIA AND THE COASTAL PLAIN

The success of the Apostles' preaching at Jerusalem provoked a reaction. Some of the Apostles were arrested and then freed on the sage advice of the Pharisee Gamaliel; but when the men of the synagogue of the freedmen (former slaves) accused Stephen, a deacon of the Christian community, he was tried for "blasphemy" and stoned to death or lynched. The Apostles now turned further afield: Philip preached in Samaria, and even converted a certain Simon Magus, who joined the Church from impure motives and was confounded

by Peter and John, who also preached in the villages of Samaria. Peter then went to Lydda and healed Aeneas, and continued to Joppa where he healed Tabitha and stayed with Simon the tanner. It was at Joppa that he had a vision which led him to accept the invitation of Cornelius, the centurion (a Gentile), to come to Caesarea. Thus Peter, who in general represented a conservative attitude, accepted the extension of the teachings of the church beyond Jewry.

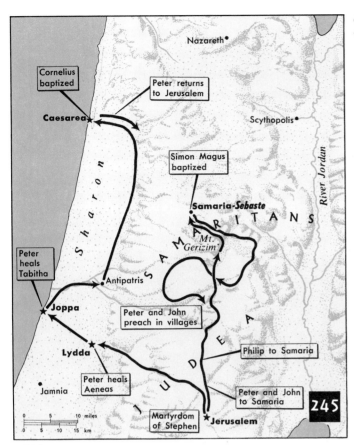

ACTS 8:4-25, 9:32-11:2

PETER AND PHILIP TO SAMARIA AND
THE COASTAL PLAIN

A Roman carriage for interurban travel of
the type probably used by the Ethiopian
eunuch

THE JOURNEY OF PHILIP

A.D. 36

The Apostle Philip, after preaching the gospel in Samaria, was
called to go to Gaza, "the Desert." This was the city that
had once been destroyed by Alexander Janneus, but after
having lain desolate for many years, was rebuilt — in contrast
to "Old Gaza" (Beth-eglaim) and "New Gaza" (Neapolis) on
the coast. The Apostle set out in the direction of Betogabris
(Beth-govrin) but, before having gone far, he met a eunuch, a
proselyte in the service of the Ethiopian queen Candace. Philip
converted him and baptized him in a spring by the roadside.
The Ethiopian continued on his way home (probably by way
of Gaza) whereas Philip went on to preach the gospel along
the coast from Azotus to Caesarea.

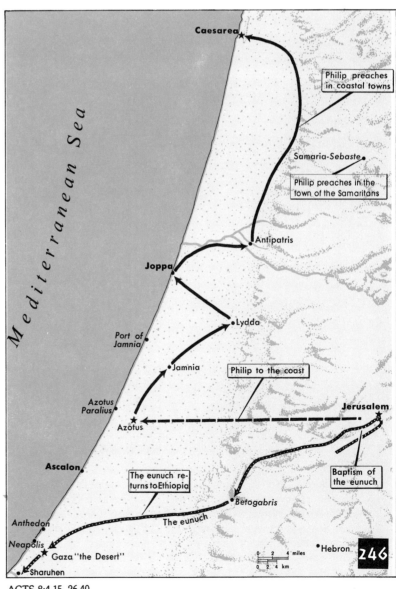

ACTS 8:4-15, 26-40

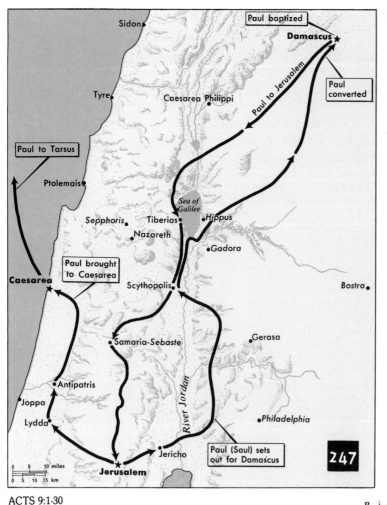

ACTS 9:1-30

He is a chosen instrument of mine to carry my name
before the Gentiles.

(Acts 9:15)

PAUL'S JOURNEY TO DAMASCUS
A.D. 36 TO 38

One involved in the martyrdom of Stephen, the deacon (see Map 245), was Saul, a Pharisee of Tarsus. He asked to be sent to Damascus to seek out Christians, and was dispatched by the high priest. On approaching Damascus, Saul had a vision of Jesus and was converted. Temporarily blinded, he arrived in the city and was received by a certain Judas. A disciple called Ananias was sent to meet Saul, who recovered his sight and was baptized. His zealous preaching in the synagogues of Damascus enraged some of the Jews; to save his life he was smuggled out of the city. He came to Jerusalem, where the local community accepted him only after some hesitation. When his life again became endangered at the hands of the Hellenists, Paul went down to Caesarea and departed thence to his native Tarsus.

Rise and go to the street called Straight.

(Acts 9:11)

DAMASCUS
IN THE TIME
OF PAUL

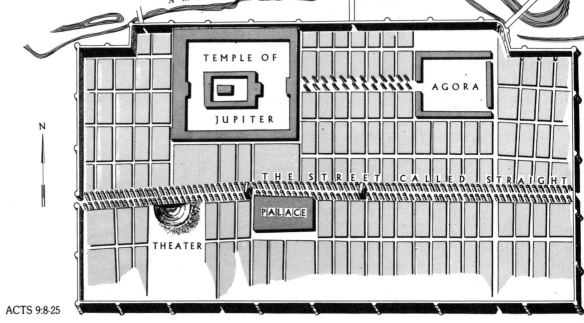

ACTS 9:8-25

The ancient city of Damascus, situated in an oasis irrigated by the rivers Amana and Parphar, was entirely replanned in Hellenistic times, when it was one of the main towns of the Seleucid empire. Today's city still bears traces of the Hippodamic town of classical times, surrounded by a wall with gates. (It is recalled that Paul was lowered over the wall in a basket, as the gates were guarded.) Rectangular in shape, the city had two parallel main streets running along its length. One of these is "the street called Straight" of Acts 9:11, running past the theater and the former royal palace, in Paul's day the residence of the city's Nabatean governor (2 Corinthians 11:32). The second parallel street connected the agora (market place) with the temple of Jupiter, once the sanctuary of Haddad and later the Church of St. John (now the Ummayyad mosque).

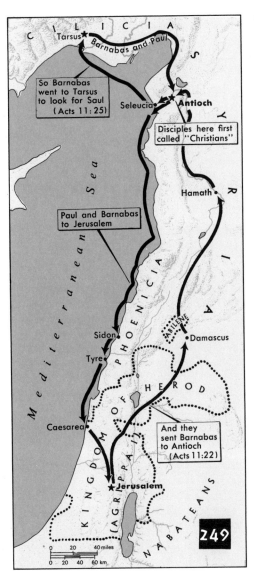

ACTS 11:22-30

The disciples were for the first time called Christians.
(Acts 11:26)

PAUL'S JOURNEY TO ANTIOCH AND HIS RETURN TO JERUSALEM
A.D. 40 TO 46

Antioch, the capital of Syria and the third largest city of the Roman empire, had an old established Jewish community that we may conjecture became a base for Christian preaching. The first Apostle to be sent there was Barnabas. It was at Antioch that the disciples were first called "Christians," that is, followers of Christos, "the anointed one," or the Messiah. The community there was able to succor the Church of Jerusalem at a time of famine in the days of emperor Claudius (Acts 11:27-30). With the Christian community at Antioch safely established, Barnabas went to Tarsus, and returned with Paul to Antioch, where they labored for a year, setting the Church on a firm basis.

It is related in Acts that at that time "Herod the king" (Agrippa I) took strong measures against the Christian community. Sometime after Agrippa's death (A.D. 44) Barnabas and Paul returned to Jerusalem, bringing with them John, "whose other name was Mark" (Acts 12:12).

By my mouth the Gentiles should hear the word of the gospel and believe.
(Acts 15:7)

THE FIRST MISSIONARY JOURNEY OF PAUL
A.D. 46 TO 48

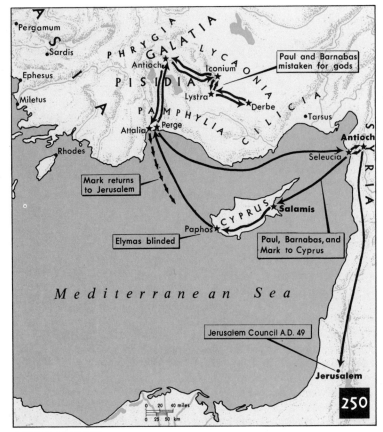

ACTS 13-14, 15:1-30

From Jerusalem Paul returned to Antioch. From there he, Barnabas and Mark set out upon the missionary journeys which are divided into three stages in the Acts of the Apostles. From Seleucia, the harbor of Antioch, they sailed to Cyprus, preaching first at Salamis and then at Paphos, the capital. There they confounded a Jewish magician called Elymas, greatly impressing the proconsul Sergius Paulus. From Paphos they continued to Perge in Pamphylia (where Mark left them, much to Paul's displeasure — Acts 15:38). Barnabas and Paul continued on to Antioch in Pisidia, preaching on the sabbath in the synagogue of that locality and causing great dissension in the community. Those of the Jews who clung to the religion of their forefathers appealed to the rulers of the city and forced the Apostles to leave; the same occurred at Iconium. Paul and Barnabas continued to Derbe and Lystra; in the latter town they healed a cripple and narrowly escaped being worshiped as gods. They returned to Pamphylia and took ship from Attalia to Antioch in Syria.

The area covered in this journey through south-central Asia Minor was part of the province of Galatia. It was to the communities visited on this trip that Paul's Epistle to the Galatians was addressed, probably from Antioch before Paul and Barnabas went to Jerusalem for the "Jerusalem Council" (Acts 15:1-30)

Men of Athens, I perceive that in every way you are
very religious.

(Acts 17:22)

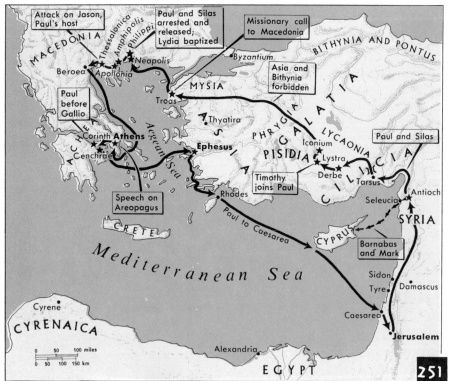

THE SECOND MISSIONARY JOURNEY OF PAUL   A.D. 49 TO 52

On his second journey Paul took Silas as his companion (t
were joined by Timothy at Iconium), while Barnabas
Mark went to Cyprus. Paul returned by land to the cities
viously visited in Pisidia and traversed Phrygia until he reac
Alexandria Troas on the Aegean Sea. There he was calle
a vision to go to Macedonia. Arriving at Philippi, he conver
many Gentiles, including Lydia of Thyatira, "a seller of pu
goods who was a worshiper of God" (a semiproselyte) (A
16:14). Paul and Silas were arrested there, but were relea
with apologies when the authorities realized that Paul wa
Roman citizen. They continued to Thessalonica where Jas
Paul's host, was attacked, and then continued by ship
Athens. In this capital of the Hellenic spirit, Paul is repor
to have made his famous speech to the philosophers at the
of Areopagus, beginning with a reference to the altar of
unknown god." From Athens Paul went to Corinth, the ca
of the province of Achaia, where he was arrested and brou
before the proconsul Gallio (who, however, refused to interf
in matters of religion). From Corinth Paul sailed to Ephe
and then to Caesarea in Palestine. After he had "greeted
church" at Jerusalem, he returned to Antioch.

251   ACTS 15:39-18:22

An altar dedicated to "the unknown gods" (From Pergamum)

THE THIRD MISSIONARY JOURNEY OF PAUL   A.D. 53 TO 57

Departing from Antioch, Paul went by way of the provinces of
Galatia and Phrygia (a region divided between the provinces
of Galatia and Asia) to Ephesus, the metropolis of Asia, a land
he had not previously been allowed to visit. He settled there
for two years, teaching in the "hall of Tyrannus" and laying
the foundations for the churches of Asia. From Ephesus he
dispatched Timothy and Erastus to Macedonia. His success in
the end enraged the worshipers of Artemis "of the Ephesians,"
who rioted in the city and theater, till calmed down by the
magistrates. Paul then left for Macedonia and Greece. Finally,
he departed from Philippi, passing Troas where he miraculously
saved a young man called Eutychus, and sailed by way of
Assos, Mitylene, Chios, Samos, and Miletus to Cos, Rhodes,
and Patara. From there he took a ship to Phoenicia, passing
south of Cyprus, and landed at Tyre. The Apostles returned
to Jerusalem via Ptolemais and Caesrea.

And argued daily in the hall of Tyrannus.

(Acts 19:9)

ACTS 18:22-21:16   **252**

PAUL'S VOYAGE TO ROME

A.D. 59 TO 62

ACT 27-28:16

Upon his return to Jerusalem, Paul was recognized by a "Jew from Asia" and was accused of profaning the Temple. He escaped with difficulty and was taken into protective custody by the Romans. From the fortress of Antonia he was sent to Caesarea under military guard, to be judged by the procurator, Felix. After a spirited defense, the governor decided to keep Paul in open confinement; and thus the Apostle remained for two years. Brought again before the new governor, Festus, Paul appealed to the emperor as a Roman citizen, and the governor, bound by law, sent him to Rome. The first part of the voyage was via Sidon to Myra in Lycia. There, the party embarked on a ship carrying wheat from Alexandria to Rome. Though late in the season, the captain decided to brave the weather. After passing Crete, the ship was caught by a tempest near the Adriatic Sea and was shipwrecked at Malta. Paul and his companions spent the winter there, continuing the voyage in the spring. After touching at Syracuse and Rhegium, they landed at Puteoli and proceeded to Rome, where Paul continued his missionary activity.

Ancient merchant ship represented on a sarcophagus from Sidon

THE KINGDOM OF AGRIPPA I A.D. 37 TO 44

Agrippa was the grandson of king Herod and the son of Aristobulus, whose mother was Mariamme, the last of the Hasmoneans. After an adventurous youth, passed mostly at Rome, he became the favorite of Caius Caesar (Caligula), the successor of Tiberius as emperor. In A.D. 37 Caligula endowed him with Philip's tetrarchy, and in A.D. 39 when Antipas had fallen out of the emperor's favor, with that of his other uncle. Caligula was assassinated at Rome in A.D. 41. Agrippa, who was then on a visit to the imperial capital, rendered such services to the emperor Claudius, on his accession, that the grateful ruler gave him the lands of Archelaus. Thus Agrippa united under his hand almost the whole of his grandfather's kingdom. Once established in Jerusalem, Agrippa became the favorite of the people by his observance of Jewish laws: his reign was regarded as the last peak in the Second Temple period, before disaster overcame the nation. As part of his orthodox policy, Agrippa was severe with the Christians in his domain (see Map 249). Agrippa I died suddenly at Caesarea during a performance in the theater.

ANT. 18:237, 252, 19:274-275; WAR 2:181, 183, 215

To his compatriots he was proportionately more generous ... and he scrupulously observed the traditions of his people.

(Antiquities 19:331)

THE KINGDOM OF AGRIPPA I

- Caligula's grant—37 A.D.
- Caligula's grant—39 A.D.
- Claudius' grant—41 A.D.
- Kingdom of Herod of Chalcis
- Agrippa I's kingdom—44 A.D.

After the death of Herod ... Claudius presented h[is] kingdom to his nephew Agrippa, son of Agrippa.

(War 2:22[3])

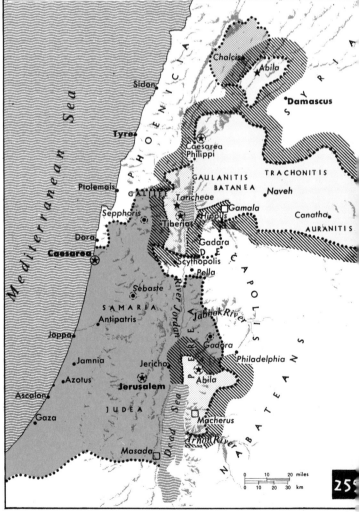

ANT. 20:104, 138, 159; WAR 2:223, 247, 252

THE KINGDOM OF AGRIPPA II A.D. 44 TO 66

On his death Agrippa I left only an adolescent son; the emperor Claudius therefore decided to return Judea to the rule of Roman procurators. Four years later, however, he granted Agrippa II the land of Chalcis in Lebanon, and in A.D. 53 exchanged this area for Abila (near Damascus) and the tetrarchy of Philip (Gaulanitis, Batanea, Trachonitis, Auranitis, and Caesarea Philippi). Under Nero, Agrippa II also received Tiberias and Taricheae, as well as Abila in Perea, with its surrounding villages. The revolt against the Romans prevented Agrippa II from enlarging his kingdom as had his father before him, but he remained in power until his death (about A.D. 95).

Among the procurators ruling Judea after A.D. 44 were Tiberius Alexander (scion of a patrician Jewish family from Egypt, a nephew of Philo, who had forsaken his religion, and joined the Romans) and Felix, a slave freed by Claudius. Felix, and after him Albinus (A.D. 62-64) and Gessius Florus (A.D. 64-66), were corrupt and cruel, and by their acts helped spark the revolt.

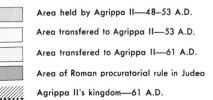

- Area held by Agrippa II—48–53 A.D.
- Area transferred to Agrippa II—53 A.D.
- Area transferred to Agrippa II—61 A.D.
- Area of Roman procuratorial rule in Judea
- Agrippa II's kingdom—61 A.D.

This action laid the foundation of the war with the
Romans; for the sacrifices offered on behalf of that
nation and the emperor were in consequence rejected.
(War 2:409)

THE OUTBREAK OF THE FIRST REVOLT AGAINST ROME

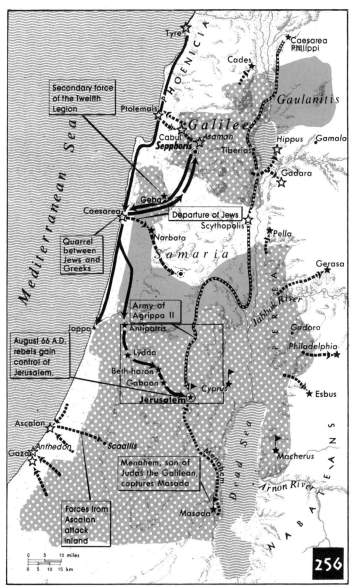

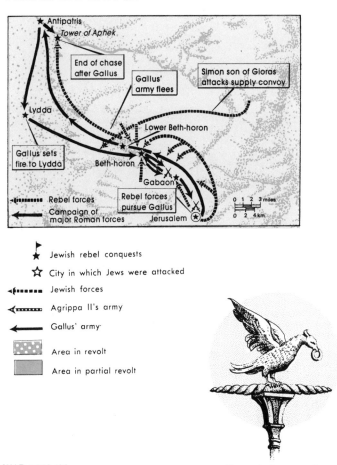

WAR 2:278-486   Roman legionary eagle

Fearing the recurrence of Caligula's attempt to desecrate the Temple by putting up his statue there and inspired by messianic hopes, the majority of Pharisees joined the Zealots, who had been fighting Rome relentlessly since the days of Herod; thus the revolt of the people against Rome became general. After a clash at Caesarea between Jews and Greeks, the Jews were forced to leave Caesarea for Narbata. When news of this reached Jerusalem, riots broke out there too; the appearance of the hated procurator, Gessius Florus, together with his soldiers, only served to fan the flames. Agrippa II tried to calm the people but his efforts came to nought.

Menahem, son of Judas the Galilean, arrived in Jerusalem with his men, after he had secured Masada with its stores of arms. Eleazar, son of Ananias, one of the chief officials in the Temple, with the support of a few "teachers" who were close to the Pharisees, ordered the sacrifice for the emperor to cease, thereby giving the signal for open revolt. One by one, the strongholds of Jerusalem were captured and in the month of August the entire city was in the hands of the Jews. Though Menahem was put to death by his aristocratic rivals among the Jews, the revolt continued. The Jews captured the fortresses of Cyprus and Macherus and the rebellion spread throughout the entire country. Jews attacked the Greek cities in the vicinity of Judea, these in turn revenging themselves on the Jews living in their midst. Most cruel were the inhabitants of Scythopolis, who repulsed the Zealot attack with the help of their Jewish

fellow-citizens, whom they later treacherously slaughtered in cold blood. Only the people of Gerasa, among all the cities, protected the lives of its Jewish citizens.

Hearing of the outbreak at Jerusalem, the governor of Syria, Cestius Gallus, who was in general charge of the affairs of Judea, decided to intervene (for the local procurator had no legionary troops at his disposal). Taking with him the Twelfth Legion Fulminata ("the Thundering One"), he marched along the coast until he reached Antipatris. Several forays were made by the Romans to intimidate the rebels of Galilee and Joppa. Advancing by way of Lydda, Beth-horon, and Gabaon, Gallus arrived in Jerusalem. He even penetrated into the city, but faltered before the walls of the Temple. As the winter had already begun, he decided to retreat. During the descent the Romans were attacked in the pass of Beth-horon and suffered disastrous losses. The Twelfth Legion lost its eagle, and all its siege equipment, which afterward did good service to Jerusalem. The Romans finally disengaged themselves, but their defeat turned the revolt into a full-scale rebellion. Freed from the imminent menace of Roman intervention, the rebels set up a government in Jerusalem, struck silver coins, and divided the country into seven military districts, each with its own commander. The most exposed post, the command of Galilee, was given to a young priest, Joseph, the son of Mattathias (the future historian, Josephus Flavius), who lacked all military experience.

Galilee was thus now wholly subdued, after affording the Romans a strenuous training for the impending Jerusalem campaign.

(War 4:120)

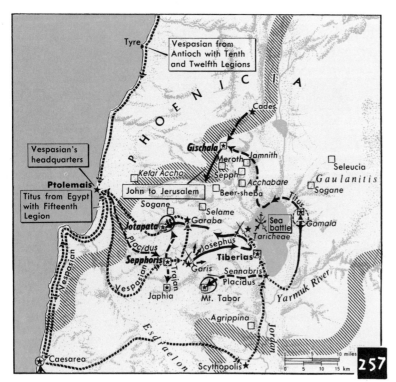

VESPASIAN'S CAMPAIGN IN GALILEE
A.D. 67

Once in his new command, Josephus wasted most of his time in suppressing various opposing factions. He did indeed make some preparations for the coming Roman attack, trying to raise and drill troops in the Roman manner, and fortifying some of the main settlements around Galilee. His efforts were negated, however, by the refusal of the city of Sepphoris to abandon the Romans. In the meantime, the emperor Nero, apprised of the seriousness of the situation, sent his best general, Titus Flavius Vespasianus, with three legions to Judea. Vespasian set up his headquarters at Ptolemais, and from there easily penetrated Josephus' defenses and reached Sepphoris. The Galilean army dispersed almost without fighting and Josephus took refuge in the fortress of Jotapata. There he was besieged and forced to surrender after forty-seven days; he himself saved his life by a trick and was kept prisoner by the Romans. After a short rest, Vespasian again led his army into Galilee in order to complete the conquest. He came from the south by way of the Jordan Valley. Tiberias surrendered, and the remaining rebels were routed by land and sea at Taricheae. Then Vespasian turned against Gamala and took this fortress after a difficult siege, thus cutting the insurgents' life-line to Babylonia. Some minor fortresses, Japhia and Mount Tabor, had also been captured. Before returning to Caesarea, Vespasian sent his son Titus against John of Gischala; the wily Zealot outwitted the Roman and arrived safely at Jerusalem. All Galilee and the Golan, however, were now in the hands of the Romans.

WAR 3:29-34, 59-69, 110-115, 127-134, 289, 409-413, 443-505, 522-542, 4:1-120

Why was the Second Temple destroyed? Because of blind hatred.

(Yoma 9b)

VESPASIAN'S CAMPAIGN IN JUDEA

While the fighting was going on in Galilee, Vespasian sent Cerealis to Samaria to disperse the Samaritans gathered in the region of Mount Gerizim. With the completion of the conquest of Galilee, troops were dispatched to Joppa by land and sea. The city was captured and the Jewish ships there, which had been used to interfere with Roman sea transport, were destroyed in a surprise attack. The Romans also captured Jamnia and Azotus and thereby insured their free movement along the coastal road. Meanwhile the Jews, occupied with their own internecine strife — between the aristocracy and the Zealots, the latter supported by the Idumeans — did nothing to interfere with the Roman advance. The raid of the extremist Zealots from their stronghold at Masada against the village of En-gedi (on Passover eve, of all nights) illustrates the extent of the bitterness of the factional fighting among the Jews. In the years 67-68 other private forces were formed; the most prominent was that of Simon the son of Gioras (Simeon

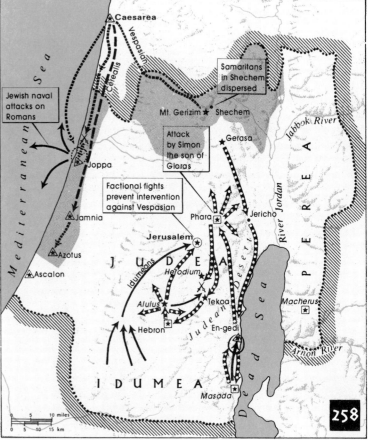

WAR 3:307-315, 414-427, 4:130, 233-305, 399-405

Bar-Giora), who had already taken part in the battle against Cestius Gallus. Simon, who was born in Gerasa, in the district of Acrabeta, was active in the Judean desert. Later he went to Masada and was there accepted after some reluctance. Simon, however, did not remain in the desert, but transferred his headquarters to Phara near Jerusalem, whence he began to extend his influence to Idumea. He captured Herodium, fought his rivals near Tekoa and came to terms with them at Alulus. Having taken Hebron, he went on to Jerusalem where he became one of the Zealot commanders in chief contending all the time with the existing leadership and with John of Gischala his main rival.

Dedicatory inscription on the Arch of Titus, Rome

Vespasian, with a view of investing Jerusalem on all sides, now established camps at Jericho and at Adida.
(War 4:486)

THE CAMPAIGN OF A.D. 68

With the renewal of fighting in the spring of A.D. 68, Vespasian systematically dismembered Judea, subduing district after district. In the spring he embarked on the conquest of Jewish area. Gadora surrendered, and the main part of the Roman army returned to Caesarea. The Zealots among the people of Gadora retreated to the Jordan, pursued by troops of the Roman tribune Placidus. The Romans first captured Bethennabris and slaughtered the refugees on the bank of the Jordan. After this they conquered Abila, Julias, and Besimoth; of all Perea, only Macherus and its environs remained in Jewish hands.

Later in the year Vespasian set out on a second campaign. Marching from Caesarea to Antipatris, he subdued the districts of Thamna and Lydda, and proceeded to Emmaus, where he stationed the Fifth Legion. From Emmaus, Vespasian turned south and captured Betogabris and Caphartobas, where troops were left with orders to harass eastern Idumea. Vespasian himself turned north and passing through Emmaus, left a detachment at Adida. The Romans marched through Samaria to Mabartha, a village between Mount Gerizim and Mount Ebal (which later became the city Neapolis). Vespasian then entered the Jordan Valley by way of Coreae, captured Jericho and advanced to the shores of the Dead Sea. It appears that then Mesad Hasidim (Khirbet Qumran, see Map 226), the center of the Dead Sea sect, was finally destroyed. Trajan (father of the emperor of the same name) joined the main body of the Roman army at Jericho and his legion, the Tenth, was stationed there.

Vespasian then sent a cavalry regiment under the command of Lucius Annaeus to destroy Gerasa (Khirbet Jarish, east to Bethther). Thus the conquest of the toparchy of Natopha and the ascent to Jerusalem from this direction were accomplished.

WAR 4:410-439, 443-450, 486-490, 503-544 ←

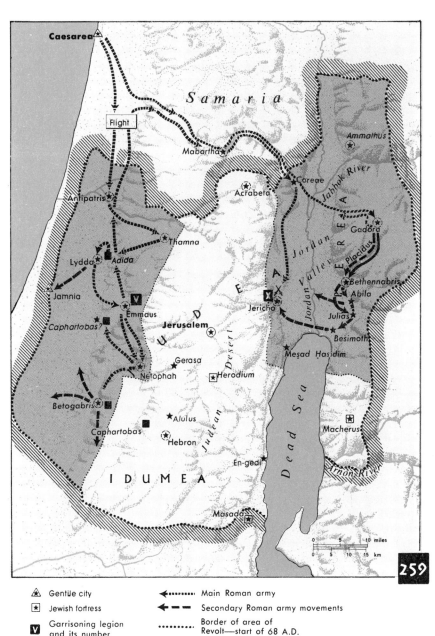

Symbol	Legend
⬟	Gentile city
★	Jewish fortress
V	Garrisoning legion and its number
■	Roman garrison
←	Jewish forces
◄·······	Main Roman army
◄ – –	Secondary Roman army movements
········	Border of area of Revolt—start of 68 A.D.
············	Border of area of Revolt—end of 68 A.D.
	Area lost by Jews during 68 A.D.

He dispatched his son Titus with picked forces to crush Jerusalem.

(War 4:658)

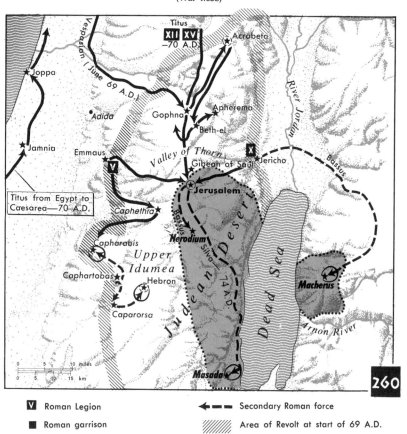

V Roman Legion
◼ Roman garrison
◀━ Major Roman force

◀--- Secondary Roman force
⧹⧹⧹ Area of Revolt at start of 69 A.D.
······ Area of Revolt at end of 69 A.D.

WAR 4:550-555, 566-584, 658-663; 5:39-53, 67-69, 7:17-20, 23-40, 163-177, 190-215

THE CAMPAIGNS OF A.D. 69 TO 70

In A.D. 68, a revolt broke out against Nero in Gaul and Spain, and the emperor committed suicide, seeing his cause was lost. During the ensuing uncertainty as to the imperial succession, Vespasian prudently suspended his operations in Judea. Three emperors — Galba, Otho, and Vitellius — succeeded one another within a year. Even before the suspension of fighting, Vespasian had succeeded in completely isolating Jerusalem, capital of the revolt. In the spring of A.D. 69, he took the districts of Acrabeta and Gophna, and his general, Cerealis, captured Caphethra (Caphar-ther = Beth-ther), Capharabis and Hebron. In the summer of A.D. 69 the Jews held only the triangle of Jerusalem-Herodium-Masada, as well as Macherus on the opposite shore of the Dead Sea. In July, A.D. 69, the troops at Alexandria and Caesarea proclaimed Vespasian emperor; the Pannonian army joined him and defeated his rival, Vitellius. In the spring of A.D. 70, Vespasian ascended the throne in Rome. He sent Titus, his eldest son, from Alexandria to continue the campaign in Judea. Titus assembled two legions at Caesarea and approached Jerusalem from the north; before the gates of the city he was joined by the Tenth Legion, which had arrived from Jericho, and by the Fifth Legion from Emmaus. (For the siege itself, see Map 261). After the fall of Jerusalem, the Zealots retreated to three isolated strongholds, Herodium, Macherus and Masada, all of them in the Judean desert near to the Dead Sea. Masada and Macherus were built by the Maccabeans and Herodium by Herod. He had fortified all three of them, fitted them out as winter palaces and refuge strongholds in the event of siege. Lucilius Bassus, the Roman legate, captured Herodium and Macherus and his successor, Silva, accomplished the difficult feat of conquering Masada (see Map 263) where the last of the rebels met their death in A.D. 73.

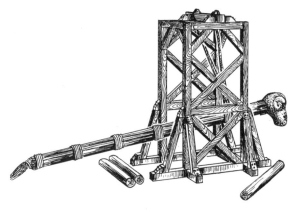

Roman battering ram

Triumphal parade with Temple vessels — Arch of Titus, Rome

THE SIEGE OF JERUSALEM IN THE YEAR A.D. 70

With the approach of the Romans, conflicts among the Zealots finally ceased; their commanders, Simon the son of Gioras and John of Gischala, divided between them responsibility for the defense of the city. Simon was to guard the section running from the northeastern corner of the wall to the Pool of Siloam, while John was assigned the eastern wall. At a later stage, Simon defended the Upper City and John the Temple itself. Their combined armies did not exceed 25,000 men; against them were drawn up four legions (the Fifth, Tenth, Twelfth and Fourteenth), and a great number of auxiliaries,

about 80,000 men in all.

After preliminary skirmishes in the orchards just outside the Gate of Women (no. 1 in the map), the Romans set up their main camp in the west and a secondary one (that of the Tenth Legion) on the Mount of Olives (2). They breached the third wall about May 25th (3) and, about May 30th, the second wall (4); the main camp was then transferred inside the city. About June 16th, the Romans launched an all-out attack on the towers north of Herod's palace and on the fortress of Antonia (5). Great damage was inflicted by the defenders on the siege machinery and dikes, and the assault was fended off.

Titus ordered a siege-wall to be thrown around the city (early in July) to starve out the defenders (6); the results were soon apparent, for much food had gone up in flames during the internecine strife among the Zealot factions. The Romans renewed their onslaught on July 20th-22nd (7). Simon the son of Gioras held fast, but the fortress of Antonia, under the command of John of Gischala, was taken and razed. On August 6th, the perpetual sacrifice ceased in the Temple (8), and the porticoes were burned on August 15th-17th (9). After a ramp had been raised against the inner wall, the Temple itself was entered (10) and burned on the ninth of Ab (about August 28th) (11).

On August 30th, the Romans captured the Lower City (12). Even then, the defenders of the Upper City did not surrender. But after another month of effort the Romans succeeded in capturing the Upper City and Herod's palace (13-14), and only then did resistance cease. By decree of Titus, all the people of Jerusalem were taken captive and its buildings were leveled to the ground. Only the three towers around which the Tenth Legion had camped were left standing, and the ruins of Jerusalem and its region were placed under the surveillance of this legion.

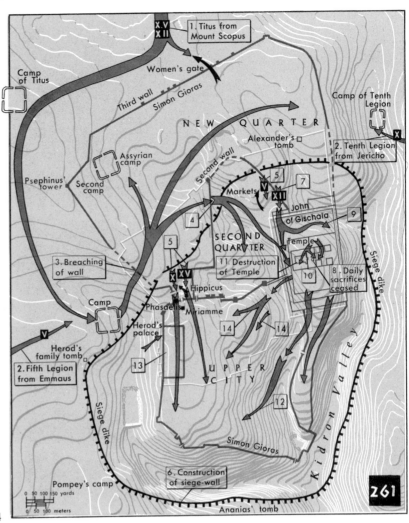

WAR 5:1-38, 52-66, 71-135, 248-361, 420-572; 6:1-95, 112-287, 316-317, 353-434

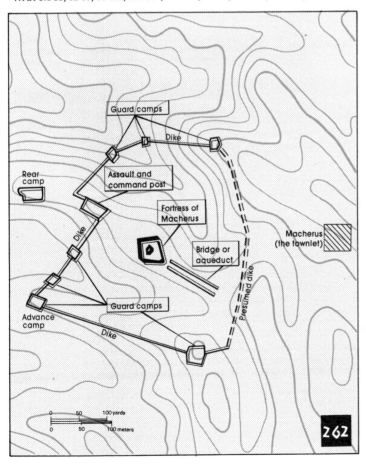

THE SIEGE OF MACHERUS

The stronghold of Macherus consisted of two parts: the upper fortress and the lower city. The Zealots took up positions in the upper fortress and non-members of the Zealot sect did likewise in the city below. The Roman laid a particularly forceful siege to the stronghold and succeeded in capturing one of the Zealot leaders. After negotiations the Romans agreed to give the Zealots safe passage out of Macherus. The non-Zealot defenders, however, were less fortunate as the agreement did not extend to the lower city. Most of them tried to flee but were killed in the ensuing skirmishes.

WAR 4:550-555, 566-584, 658-663; 5:39-53, 67-69; 7:17-20, 23-40, 163-177, 190-215

We determined neither to serve the Romans nor any other save God.

(War 7:323)

THE FALL OF MASADA   A.D. 73

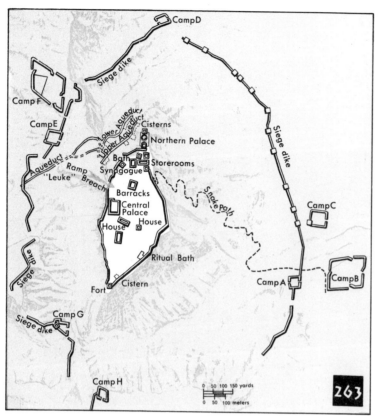

WAR 7:252-259, 275-406

Masada was built atop a rock, its sheer cliffs rising out of the deep ravines surrounding it. The Roman siege-force was divided between the lower camp (B) and the upper camp (F), which also contained the headquarters. The problem facing the Romans was how to get their siege-towers up to the walls of the fortress, at the top of the cliffs. They first built a siege-wall around the whole of the rock, except for the impassable areas. The wall, which was equipped with catapults, completely isolated the defenders, yet there was little prospect of vanquishing them quickly by starving them out, for there were abundant stores of food and water inside.

Silva chose a site to the west of Masada, where there is a low saddle between the two surrounding ravines, and began a ramp from the so-called White Rock (Leuke) up to the defenders' wall, a height of 300 cubits (according to Josephus; in actuality, it is only 260 feet). At 200 cubits the Romans raised a platform of wood and iron, 50 cubits tall; on this they placed a siege-tower reaching a further 60 cubits, its top thus standing about 20 feet above the walls of Masada. The wall was breached with the aid of an iron battering-ram on May 1st, A.D. 73. The defenders hastily put up a barricade of wood which the Romans tried to burn down; at first they had the wind against them, but later in the day it changed and the barricade caught fire and burned.

With victory assured, the Romans put off their final assault until the next day, but the 960 defenders of Masada — men, women and children — the last vestiges of open defiance against Rome in the first Jewish war, committed suicide during the night.

View of Masada, looking south

CHRISTIANS AND JEWS IN PALESTINE AFTER THE FIRST REVOLT   A.D. 73 TO 131

Although the war of A.D. 66-70 was fierce both in Galilee and in Judea — and especially in Jerusalem and a few other places where the fighting was particularly severe — the Jewish population in general remained intact; many lands did, however, pass from Jewish to imperial possession. The evidence of the revolt of Bar-Kokhba (see Maps 265-268) is in itself enough to show that Judea was still settled with Jews at the beginning of the second century. The persistence of Judaism in Galilee in later centuries shows the same trend. After the destruction of the Temple and the uprooting of the leading classes, some Jews did remain in Jerusalem. The reconstituted Sanhedrin at Jamnia (Jabneh) extended its authority over the nation.

The disasters of the Jewish War seem to have caused an estrangement between the Jews and the Judeo-Christians. The Jerusalem community of Christians had left the Holy City on the eve of the siege, taking refuge at Pella beyond the Jordan. Some of its members later returned to continue in Jerusalem; others stayed behind. The communities founded by the Apostles in the coastal plain survived, as did some of the Judeo-Christian groups at Capernaum, Kefar-schania (Sachnin) in Galilee and Cochaba in the Galilee or Syria, and some other places. However, there is little evidence of the thousands of converts mentioned in early sources. The breach with Judaism was not yet formal, though the traditional constancy of most of the Jews, along with other factors, turned the efforts of the Christian missionaries more and more toward the Gentiles in the Holy Land and abroad.

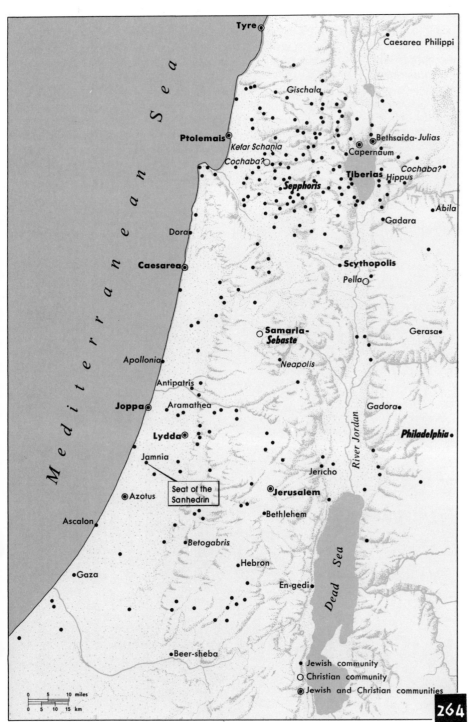

The Tabernacle as represented in the synagogue at Capernaum

Tyre

Caesarea Philippi

Gischala

Ptolemais

Kefar Schania

Cochaba?

Bethsaida-Julias

Capernaum

Cochaba?

Sepphoris

Tiberias

Hippus

Abila

Gadara

Dora

Caesarea

Scythopolis

Pella

Gerasa

Samaria-Sebaste

Neapolis

Apollonia

Antipatris

Joppa

Aramathea

Gadora

Philadelphia

Lydda

Jamnia

River Jordan

Seat of the Sanhedrin

Jericho

Azotus

Jerusalem

Ascalon

Bethlehem

Betogabris

Hebron

Gaza

En-gedi

Dead Sea

Beer-sheba

• Jewish community
○ Christian community
◉ Jewish and Christian communities

0 5 10 miles
0 5 10 15 km

264 ACTS; JOSEPHUS; TALMUDIC SOURCES

THE BEGINNINGS OF THE BAR KOKHBA REVOLT A.D. 131 TO 132

News of Hadrian's plan to found a Roman colony in the city of Jerusalem which would have included the usual pagan temples — thus thwarting all hope of reconstructing the Temple — stirred anew the spirit of the struggle against Rome. The Jews had learned a lesson from the First Revolt, in which proper preparation and unity were lacking. This time they chose the most suitable moment, at a time when the emperor was far from Judea. They prepared fortified positions in the countryside, so as not to be trapped again in fortresses. Preparations also included hundreds of underground hiding systems in the Judean plains and some in the Galilee. These underground systems were quarried into the rock exploiting existing caves and caverns. They made ready quantities of

arms and mobilized all possible inhabitants. A unified command was set up and it remained in control from the beginning of the Revolt to its end.

The Bar Kokhba Revolt lacks a chronicler such as Josephus was for the First Revolt, and we are forced to glean our information from various Talmudic and other sources, and from documents and other archaeological finds from the caves in the Judean desert. The documents reveal that Bar Kokhba (Bar Kosiba) was the same man as "Simeon Prince of Israel" mentioned on Jewish coins from the time of the Revolt, and that his full title was "Simeon son of Kosiba Prince of Israel." It may be assumed that this Simeon, who was regarded as the "Messiah," was descended from the Davidic line.

The Revolt broke out in the fall of A.D. 131, evidently at Caphar-harub, near Modiin. The careful preparations bore fruit: the people of Judea rallied around Jerusalem, where the Tenth Legion was stationed. The Revolt included all of Judea down to the Coastal Plain. There is evidence that some Samaritans joined the Bar Kokhba rebels, and there are also indications that Gentiles, mainly from among the oppressed local inhabitants, also found their way to the rebel camp and joined the "brotherhood" of warriors. The new leader, who was supported by the Sanhedrin, and mainly by Rabbi Akiba, saw his government as the sole legal authority in the land; those who opposed him, such as Christians of Jewish extraction who obviously could not see Bar Kokhba as the "Messiah," were persecuted by the rebel authorities.

The suddenness of the outbreak and the defensive preparations of the rebels were such that the Roman governor, Tinius Rufus, had no alternative but to order the evacuation of Jerusalem. The Tenth Legion and the non-Jewish inhabitants left for Caesarea, and the Jews once again took control of their ancient capital. An orderly administration was set up and a new reckoning of the calendar was instituted. The first year of the Revolt (A.D. 131-132) was declared "The Year One of the Redemption of Israel," and the following years "Year ... of the Redemption" or "of the Freedom of Israel." Documents found in the Judean desert caves reveal the efficiency of the new land registry and the leasing of former imperial lands. District commanders were appointed and the new government issued silver and bronze coinage, struck over imperial Roman and

Rabbi Akiba, when he saw the son of Kosiba, was wont to say: This i the Anointed King.
(Palestinian Talmud, Taanit 84, 68

THE BEGINNING OF THE BAR KOKHBA REVOLT

Coin of Bar Kokhba

Outbreak of revolt

Jerusalem becomes Gentile city named Aelia Capitolina

Seat of Sanhedrin and center of Revolt

--- Roman road
.... Provincial border
••••••• Border
□ Headquarters of the Legion
△ Roman army camp
■ Polis
• Settlement
✪ Rural administrative capital
▽ Hiding complex
X Jewish fortress
▦ Concentration of hiding pla
▨ Scattered hiding places

TALMUDIC SOURCES;
SCROLL OF FASTING;
DIO CASSIUS; EUSEBIUS; CO
JUDEAN DESERT DOCUMEN

265

0 5 10 miles
0 5 10 15 km

provincial city coins.

Upon the success of his uprising in Judea, Bar Kokhba attempted to extend the Revolt to the Galilee. The damage to Sepphoris and to the few hiding tunnels found in the Galilee bears witness to rebellious activity and preparations. Olive groves were uprooted. However, it is clear that most of the Jews of Galilee did not join the rebels. The Romans made every effort to suppress the Revolt, which they regarded as highly dangerous. The proconsul Julius Severus was called from Britain to Palestine. Besides the two legions already stationed in Judea (the Sixth and the Tenth), forces were brought from Syria, Arabia, Mysia on the Danube, and Egypt, in addition to smaller cavalry and infantry units from Panonia, Rhetia and other lands. Pressure was put on Bar Kokhba and his followers from every quarter.

Julius Severus decided to advance slowly, to conquer position after position and village after village, in order to keep up pressure on the rebels. The reason behind this course is evident from the fate of the Twenty-second Legion, which had dared rashly to advance into the interior and was completely wiped out; from this time onward its name disappears from the Roman army list.

Bar Kokhba Letter from the Judean desert

Give me Jabneh and its sages.
(Gittin Tractate 56b)

THE SAGES OF JABNEH

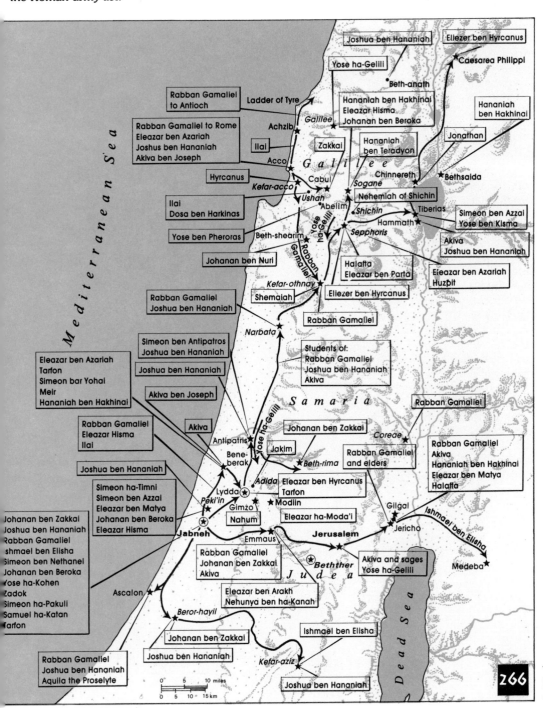

TOSEFTA, MA'ASER RISHON 2:1;
BABYLONIAN TALMUD, SANHEDRIN 32b;
OTHER TALMUDIC SOURCES

266

The wretched Hadrian stationed three guard forces: one at Emmaus; one at Caphar-iaqitiyah; and one at Beth-el.

(Lamentations Rabbah 81)

THE THIRD AND FOURTH YEARS OF THE BAR KOKHBA REVOLT

A.D. 133 TO 134

After the initial successes of the rebels, the military situation changed rapidly. The Romans assembled a large army in Judea and began the conquest of Palestine.

We have little information on the battles proper. Both sides appear to have steered clear of frontal confrontations and were reluctant to engage in decisive battles. Instead, the Romans besieged dozens of smaller villages and persistently reduced the areas held by the rebels. Following each conquest the Romans annihilated the rebellious communities. Sources from this period ascribe the atrocities to Rufus, governor of Judea before the arrival of Severus.

In the third year of the Bar Kokhba Revolt Julius Severus took command of all Roman expeditionary forces. At this time it seems that all of Palestine was in the hands of the Romans except for Judea (as witnessed by coins from the third year of the rebellion found in the Shephelah and Judean mountains). An important battle was apparently fought at Emmaus (maybe the battle in which Horbat Eqed was captured). To commemorate this victory the town was called Nicopolis — city of victory. After this battle, to seal off the rebellious population, the Romans erected barriers at Emmaus, Caphar-laqitiyah and Beth-el or Beth-lehem. In the third year of the rebellion the Romans took the remaining part of Judea including the last stronghold Beththter.

The fighting was very heavy: the historian Dio Cassius tells us that during the Bar Kokhba Revolt the Romans captured fifty fortresses, destroyed 985 villages, and slaughtered more than a million persons. However, the Roman army also suffered great losses, so much so that at the end of the war Hadrian was obliged in his address to the Senate to refrain from using the normal formula "The Emperor and the Army are well."

In spite of heavy losses, Bar Kokhba and his followers kept up their high spirits. From documents dated the "Year Three" of the Revolt, and even of the "Year Four" (the latest document is dated to the month of Marheshwan Year Four), it is apparent that civilian and economic life went on as usual. In Bar Kokhba's letters to his commanders, we can still feel, along with the tension, the care of his staff concerning the fulfilling of religious commandments: along with orders for the confiscation of foodstuffs, for transport of supplies from the small harbor of En-gedi, and for the suppression of opposition elements, we read instructions for the gathering of lulabs and ethrogs for the Feast of Tabernacles.

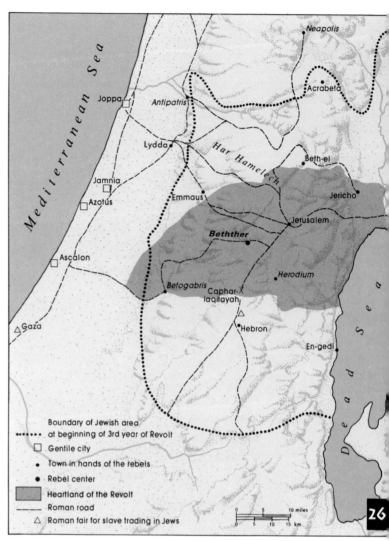

Boundary of Jewish area at beginning of 3rd year of Revolt
□ Gentile city
• Town in hands of the rebels
● Rebel center
Heartland of the Revolt
Roman road
△ Roman fair for slave trading in Jews

DIO CASSIUS; EUSEBIUS; JUDEAN DESERT DOCUMENTS

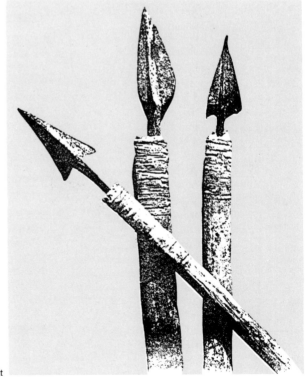

Arrows from the time of the Bar Kokhba Revolt

Once sixty men descended the rampart of Beth-ther,
and not one returned (again).

(Tosefta Yebamoth)

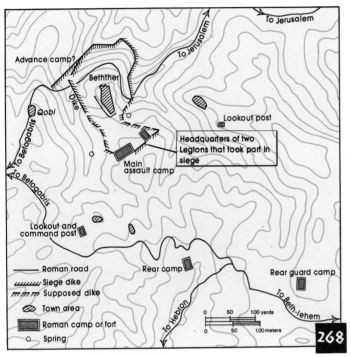

— Roman road
⊥⊥⊥⊥⊥ Siege dike
ʍ ʍ ʍ Supposed dike
⬭ Town area
▬ Roman camp or fort
○ Spring

268

TALMUDIC SOURCES; EUSEBIUS

THE SIEGE OF BETHTHER
A.D. 135

In the fourth year of the Revolt (spring A.D. 135), Bar Kokhba
and his army were driven into the fortress of Bethther (southwest of Jerusalem), to which Severus and his legions promptly
laid siege. (Hadrian had in the meanwhile left Judea, upon the
restoration of Roman control in Jerusalem.) The fortress is situated on a hill overlooking a deep canyon and was protected by
a fosse on the south. The position was quite strong, though it
lacked a sure water supply. The Romans surrounded it with a
siege-wall and, later in the siege, crossed the fosse by means of
a siege dam. At the end of summer A.D. 135, the Romans had
breached the wall and slaughtered the surviving defenders,
including Bar Kokhba himself.

And they were sitting in the cave, and they heard a
noise above the cave.

(Babylonian Talmud, Shabbath 60a)

THE BAR KOKHBA FIGHTERS IN THE JUDEAN DESERT CAVES
A.D. 135

When it became evident to Bar Kokhba's supporters in En-
gedi that the Romans had finally gained the upper hand, they
fled to caves located in the cliffs of the canyons descending
to the Dead Sea. The fates of the several groups were not
the same: in the "Cave of the Pool" east of En-gedi, advance
preparations had been made to provide a water supply and the
refugees there evidently survived. In Nahal Hever, two caves
were used as refuge, on opposite sides of the canyon. As the
Romans could not directly assault the caves, they built camps
above them and waited for hunger and thirst to do their work.
The fate of the refugees in the "Cave of Letters" (including
Babatha of the family of Johanan son of Bayan, one of the
rebel commanders at En-gedi, and possibly also Bayan himself)
is not clear. On the other hand it is known that the refugees
in the "Cave of Horror" (forty men and one woman) declined
to surrender and when it was evident that they had no further
hope they burned all their belongings and perished within the
cave. Remains of rebel hiding places were discovered also in
other caves in the Judean desert and in the Ephraim desert.

JUDEAN DESERT DOCUMENTS

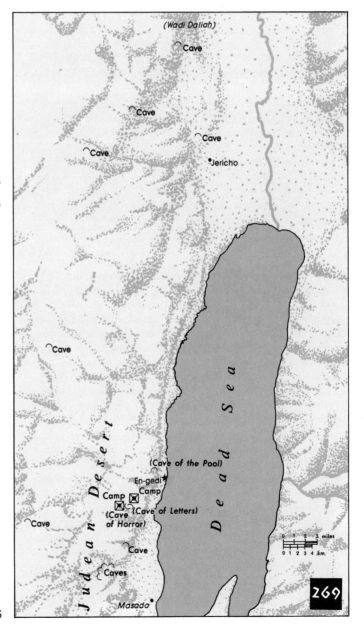

269

I hope to see you passing as I go to Spain.
(Romans 15:24)

THE CHURCH IN THE FIRST CENTURY A.D.

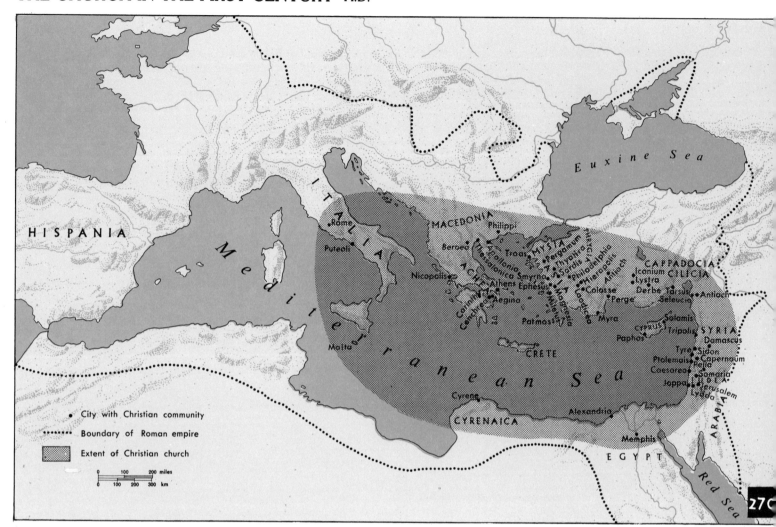

ACTS; EPISTLES; TACITUS: ANNALS 15:44; SUETONIUS: NERO 16

The geographical distribution of Christian communities in the Roman empire in this century reflects the missionary activities of Paul and his fellow Apostles, based on the network of synagogues in the Jewish diaspora. Born as Jews, they were freely admitted to the synagogues, where their teachings often provoked dissension and split the local community; but almost always there remained, after the expulsion or departure of the Apostles themselves, a small group of Christians perpetuating the existence of the church. These scattered communities were assiduously nursed by Paul and his representatives, as is evident from the Apostle's letters. Gradually the missionary teachings attracted a growing number of Gentiles, among whom the Judeo-Christians were gradually absorbed. Apart from Edessa beyond the Euphrates, the Church of the first century A.D. was restricted to the Roman empire. Apparently most of the early Christians were concentrated in Asia Minor, where the Jewish communities had long been established and had created around them a circle of half proselytized "God fearing" Gentiles. It was in these circles that the Christian message based upon a reinterpretation of the venerated Old Testament took root. In the West only Rome and its vicinity, and possibly also Spain, had Christian communities at this early stage. The first persecution (under Nero) was short and did not hinder the growth of the Church.

Nero Caesar

God shows no partiality, but in every nation any one who fears him and does what is right is acceptable to him.

(Acts 10:34-35)

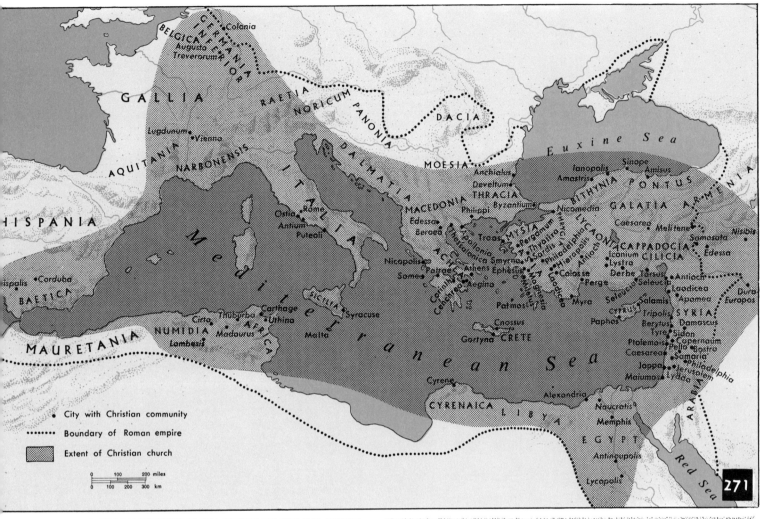

The second century, and in particular the period of the Bar Kokhba Revolt (see Maps 265-268), saw the decisive split of the Church with Judaism. The destruction of Jerusalem and the exile of the Jews from Judea after the war of Bar Kokhba (and the transfer of the Jerusalem bishopric to a Gentile) intensified the breach. Most of the Christians were by then of Gentile origin. The national Jewish catastrophe hindered Jewish missionary work among the Gentiles, the Church profiting greatly from this state of affairs. The Christian communities spread to the west and north, into Gaul and Germany in the second century A.D. Many groups were founded in Africa, laying the basis for the strong African church of the third century A.D. In Egypt, too, Christianity began to extend beyond Alexandria into the countryside. In Mesopotamia, more communities were founded; in Asia Minor the church reached the northern and eastern parts of the peninsula. Under the Antonine emperors, the Christians were left in peace and were no longer molested by the authorities, a state of affairs which greatly helped the growth of Christianity throughout the empire.

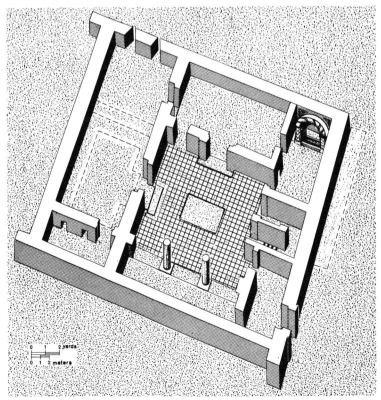

Plan of a church at Dura-Europos

KEY TO MAPS ACCORDING TO BOOKS OF THE BIBLE

CHRONOLOGICAL TABLE – GENERAL

Date	*	East — Mesopotamia	Anatolia-Aram-Tyre	Palestine	Egypt	West
-2800						
-2700	II	FIRST DYNASTRY OF UR / SUMERIAN PERIOD			1st–2nd Dynasties / EARLY KINGDOM	
-2600	EARLY BRONZE AGE					
-2500	III			Beth Yerah Culture	3rd–5th Dynasties (Pyramid Builders)	
-2400		KINGDOM OF ACCAD				
-2300		Sargon I / Naram-Sin		Destruction of city-states	6th Dynasty — Pepi I / Pepi II	MIDDLE MINOAN PERIOD
-2200						
-2150	IV			Pastoralist interlude	First Intermediate Period	
-2100	I	3rd Dynasty of Ur		Renewal of urban centers		
-2000		Gudea of Lagash / Independent Assyria			12TH DYNASTY — Amenemhet I / Senusert I / MIDDLE KINGDOM	
-1950	MIDDLE BRONZE AGE				Amenemhet II / Senusert II	
-1900			EARLY HITTITE KINGDOM		Senusert III	
-1800	IIa				Amenemhet III	
-1750		Mari Period — Hammurabi		Connections with N. Syria	Amenemhet IV / Second Intermediate Period (13th Dynasty)	
-1700						
-1600	IIb	1st (Amorite) Dynasty in Babylon	KINGDOM OF MITANNI	Close ties with Egypt	Hyksos Rule 15th 16th–17th Dynasty	
-1550						
-1500	I	Cassite Dynasty in Babylon	Aramean Invasion	Strengthening of Egyptian Control	18th Dynasty / NEW KINGDOM	
-1400	LATE BRONZE AGE / IIa	MINOR KINGDOMS	KINGDOM OF MITANNI	El-Amarna Period / Strengthening of Egyptian Control		Downfall of Crete / Height of Mycenean Culture
-1300	IIb		NEW HITTITE KINGDOM	Influx of Pastoralists	19th Dynasty	Achean Invasion of Greece
-1200				Philistine Invasion	Syrian Interregnum	Trojan War
-1100	I				20th Dynasty	
-1000	IRON AGE		Aramean Kingdoms / Hiram of Tyre	Institution of Kingship in Israel	21st Dynasty	Dorian Invasion of Greece
-900				Divided Monarchy		
-800	II	Kingdom of Assyria			22nd Dynasty	Etruscan Invasion of Italy / Homer
-700			Assyrian Rule	Destruction of Samaria and Exile of Israel	23rd–25th Dynasties / Assyrian Conquest	First Olympic Games
-600 / 587		Kingdom of Babylonia	Babylonian Rule	Destruction of Jerusalem and Exile of Judea	26th Dynasty	Height of Etruscan Culture
-500	PERSIAN PERIOD	Persian Empire		Return to Zion	Persian Conquest / PERSIAN RULE	Roman Republic Established / Persian Wars / Herodotus
-400			Persian Rule		28th–30th Dynasties	Decline of Athens
-300	HELLENISTIC PERIOD	Conquest of Alexander the Great / Seleucid Rule		Conquest of Alexander the Great		
-200			Seleucid Rule	Ptolemaic Rule	Ptolemaic Rule	Punic Wars / Hannibal
-100		Parthian Empire		Seleucid Rule / Maccabeans		Roman Rule in Greece / Caesar
B.C. 0 A.D.	ROMAN PERIOD			King Herod / Birth of Christ		Roman Empire
-100		Parthian Wars	Roman Rule	Destruction of Second Temple / Bar Kokhba revolt	Roman Rule	

*Archaeological period in Palestine

CHRONOLOGICAL TABLE–DETAILED

Left Panel

*	Meso-potamia	Anatolia and Syria	Palestine	Egypt
1668				Hyksos rule
1640				15th Dynasty at Avaris
1630				16th Dynasty subservient
1620				
1610	MIDDLE BRONZE AGE			17th Dynasty at No-Amon – rivals
1600	1ST AMORITE DYNASTY IN BABYLON			
1590		KINGDOM OF MITANNI		
1580	IIb			
1570				1570
1560		EARLY HITTITE KINGDOM	War in S. Canaan	Ahmose I
1550				1551 / 1545
1540				
1530				Amenhotep I
1524				Thutmose I
1518				Thutmose II
1510			EGYPTIAN RULE	
1504	LATE BRONZE AGE			
1490				(Hatshapsut)
1483	CASSITE DYNASTY IN BABYLON			-----
1470			Renewal of Egyptian Rule	Thutmose III
1453				1450
1430				Amenhotep II
1419				
1410				Thutmose IV
1386				
1370	IIa	Suphiluliuma		Amenhotep III
1350			Weakening of Egyptian Rule (El-Amarna Period)	1349 Amenhotep IV (Akhenaton)
1334		NEW HITTITE KINGDOM		Tutankhamon
1325			Strengthening of Egyptian Rule	Ay 1321
1310		Mursilis II		Horemheb
1300		Muwatall		1293 Rameses I / 1291
1290				Seti I
1280		Battle of Kedesh 1274 Urhi-Teshub		1279
1260	IIb			Ramses II
1250		Hatusilis III	PERIOD OF ISRAELITE SETTLEMENT	
1230		Tudhalia IV		
1220			Pastoralists moving in	
1212				Merneptah
1200				18TH / 19TH DYNASTY

Right Panel

*	Mesopotamia	Aram-Tyre	Judea	Israel	Egypt
1190					
1180	Ia				Syrian Interregnum 1182
1170				1174 Philistine Invasion	
1160					Ramses III
1150	MINOR KINGDOMS				1151
1140	ISRAELITE PERIOD	ARAMEAN CONTROL	PERIOD OF ISRAELITE SETTLEMENT		
1120					Ramses IV to Ramses IX
1116				PERIOD OF THE JUDGES	
1100	Tiglath-pileser I	KINGDOM OF ASSYRIA			
1080	1078				
1070	Ib				1070
1050			Battle of Aphek		21ST DYNASTY
1040			Samuel		
1025	MINOR KINGDOMS	Hadadezer King of Zobah			
1010			Saul		
1000					
990				David	
979		976			
970			970		
960	IIa	Hiram I King of Tyre			Siamun 960
950			Solomon		Psusennes II
943		943			946
930			930 – Division of Monarchy		Shishak I
920			Rehoboam	Jeroboam Son of Nabat	924
913			Abiah 913	910 Nadab / 909	913 Orsokon I 904
900			Asa	Baasha	
890		884	Ethbaal, King of Tyre	886 Elah / 885 Zimri / Tibni 880	890
880	Ashur-nasirpal II	880		Omri 874	
870		Ben-hadad I King of Aram-Damascus	Jehoshaphat 872-848	870	Orsokon II
860	860 / 859	Ben-hadad II King of Aram-Damascus	Jehoram 853	Ahab	860
850	853 Battle at Qarqar	Mattan King of Tyre	Ahaziah 841	853 / 852 Ahaziah / Joram 841	
840	Shalmaneser III 841		Athaliah 835		22ND DYNASTY
830	IIb	Hazael King of Aram-Damascus	Jehoash	Jehu	
824				814	
811	Shamshi-adad			Jehoahaz	
800				798	
796	Adadnirari 796	Ben-hadad III	Amaziah 796-767	Joash	
783				782	
773	Shalmaneser IV		Uzziah 792-740	Jeroboam II 793-753	
760	Asshur-dan III		758	753 Zechariah / Shallum / 752 Shallum	
755	Asshurninari		Jotham 750	Menahem II Pekah	

(Prophets column between Judea and Israel: Elijah, Elisha, Jonah, Amos, Hosea)

* Archaeological period in Palestine

Left Chart

Period markers (far-left margin): ISRAELITE PERIOD · PERSIAN PERIOD · HELLENISTIC PERIOD

Year (B.C.)	Mesopotamia, Persia	Aram	Palestine — Judah	Palestine — Israel	Egypt	West
745	745 Tiglath-pileser III		Jotham 750-732	742 Pekahiah / Pekah (752-732)		753 Rome Founded?
740		740 Rezin / 732	Ahaz 735-716			Height of Etruscan Power
727	727 Shalmaneser V / 722			Hosea		
722	Sargon II			722 Fall of Samaria		Phoenician and Greek Colonization in West
713			Hezekiah 716-687		713 (25TH DYNASTY)	
705	705				Shabako 701	
701	Sennacherib		697		Shibtku	
690					690	
683	681 Esarhaddon				Tirhaqa Assyrian Conquest 671	683 Kingship Abolished in Athens
669	669 Asshur-banipal	(ASSYRIAN PROVINCE)	Manasseh	(ASSYRIAN PROVINCE)	664 Psammtik I (26TH DYNASTY)	
643			643 Amon 640			
633	633 Nabopileser / 625		629			621 Draconic Law
612	612 Fall of Nineveh / 605	609 Egyptian Rule 604	Josiah		610 Necho II	610
609			609 Jehoahaz 609	609 Egyptian Rule 604		
598	Nebuchad-nezzar	(BABYLONIAN PROVINCE)	Jehoiakim 598 / Jehoiachin Zedekiah	(BABYLONIAN PROVINCE)	595 Psammtik II 589	594 Solon's Reforms
586			Destruction 586 of Temple		Hophra	
570	562				570	560
550	550 Nabunaid				Amosis (Ahmose II)	Pesistratos Rules in Athens
539	539 Fall of Babylon / Cyrus	539	538 Return to Zion	538		527
530	530 Cambyses / 522				Psammtik III 526 / 525 Persian Conquest	
516	Darius I		516 Temple built			Roman Republic 509 Established
499		(PERSIAN SATRAPIES)		(PERSIAN SATRAPIES)		499
490	486 Xerxes I					490 Battle of Marathon
484				484-483 Revolt		480 Battles of Thermopylae and Salamis / 479
464	464					461
460	Artaxerxes I		457 / Ezra / Megabyzos' revolt 445	460-454 Revolt		Age of Pericles
440			Nehemiah			
431	423		425			431 / 429 Peloponnesian War
420	Darius II					
404	404				404	404
390	Artaxerxes II					390 Sack of Rome by Gauls
386		386 Evagorus occupies Tyre			Egyptian Revolt against Persia (28TH-30TH DYNASTIES)	
358	358				359	359
350	Artaxerxes III	Tennes' revolt against Artaxerxes III			Philip II	Philip II
341					341	336
335	335 Darius III	332 Conquered by Alexander	332 Conquered by Alexander	331 Conquered by Alexander 323	(WARS OF DIODACHI)	Macedonian Rule in Greece
323	323 Death of Alexander					316 Antigonus Defeats Eumenes
315	312 Seleucus at Babylon	315 Overrun by Antigonus / 312 Overrun by Ptolemy I				
301	301 Battle of Ipsus	301 Conquered by Ptolemy I	Conquered by Ptolemy I		Ptolemy I	

Prophets (column between Aram and Judah): Isaiah, Micah, Hosea, Zephaniah, Habakkuk, Jermiah, Obadiah, Ezekiel, Deutero-Isaiah, Haggai, Zechariah, Malachi

Mesopotamia sub-label: KINGDOM OF BABYLON

Right Chart

Period markers (far-left margin): HELLENISTIC PERIOD · ROMAN PERIOD

Year	East	Palestine	Egypt	West
290 B.C.	Seleucus I	Simon son of Onias High Priest	Ptolemy I	
281	281	Eleazar brother of Simon High Priest	283	
276	276 First Syrian War 272			
270	Antiochus I		Ptolemy II	
264	261 Second Syrian War 259 255	259/8 Zenon's visit		264 First Punic War
250	Antiochus II		246	
246	246 Third Syrian War 240			241
240	Seleucus II	Onias II son of Simon High Priest	Ptolemy III	
226	226 Seleucus III 223		221	
218	Antiochus III	218 Antiochus III in Palestine / 217 Battle of Raphia	Ptolemy IV	218 Second Punic War
200	198 Battle of Panias Conquest of Antiochus III	Simon the Just High Priest	203	201 / 197 Battle of Cynoscephalae
189	189 Battle of Magnesia 187	Onias III High Priest	Ptolemy V	
181	Seleucus IV		181	
175	175 Antiochus IV (Epiphanes)	174 Jason High Priest / 171 Menelaus High Priest / 167 Maccabean Revolt	Ptolemy VI	169 Battle of Pydna Conquest of Macedonia
170			170 Antiochus Campaign to Egypt	
164	164 Antiochus V 162	164 Rededication of Temple / 161 Death of Judas Maccabeus	Ptolemy VII	
152	Demetrius I	152		
150	150 Alexander Balas' 145	Jonathan High Priest	145	146 Destruction of Carthage and Corinth / Conquest of Greece
142	142 Antiochus VI 139 Tryphon 138	143 / Simon High Priest	Ptolemy VIII	
135	Antiochus VII	135	133	Revolt of Gracchi / 121
129	129	John High Priest	Ptolemy IX	
117			117 107	
104		104 Judas High Priest 103	Ptolemy X	
94		94 Civil War 88		
88	88 Mithradates' War against Rome 84	Janneus High Priest and King	Ptolemy XI	90 Revolt of Roman Allies 88 / 87/6 Marius 84 / Sulla Dictator 79
80			80	
76		76 / Alexandra Hyrcanus II High Priest		
66	66 Pompey's Campaign 64	67 War between Aristobulus II and Hyrcanus II 64 / 63 Siege of Pompey	Ptolemy XII	60 58 Julius Caesar Conquers Gaul / First Triumvirate
57	57 Gabinius Proconsul in Syria 55 / 53 Defeat of Crassus at Carrhae	57 Unsuccessful Revolts against Gabinius 55 / 47 Julius Caesar in Judea	51	50 49 Civil War / Battle of Pharsalus / 44 Caesar Murdered
40	36 Antony's Parthian War 33	Parthian Invasion 40 / Mattathias Antigonus / Crowning of Herod at Rome 37	Cleopatra VII	Second Triumvirate 36
31			30 Conquest of Egypt by Rome	31 Battle of Actium
20		Reign of Herod		Augustus Caesar
5		5 Birth of Jesus 4		
0 (B.C./A.D.)		Archelaus		
6 A.D.		6		
14				14
18		18/19 Founding of Tiberias		
29		29 Jesus' Ministry 30		Tiberius
34	34 Parthian Wars 36	34 / 37 Agrippa I Enthroned 39		37 Caligula 41
44		41 44 Agrippa I King of Judea		Claudius 54
54	54 Corbulo's Campaign against Parthia 63	53 / Ministry of Apostles		Nero / 61 Paul to Rome / 64 Persecution of Christians
66		66 First Jewish Revolt / 70 Destruction of Jerusalem / 73 Fall of Masada		68 Revolt against Nero / 69 Galba, Otho, Vitelius
79		Jewish Center at Jamnia		Vespasian / 79 Titus 81
90				Domitian
96				96 Nerva 98
101				101 Conquest of Dacia 106
106	106 Conquest of Nabateans			Trajan
114	114 Trajan's Wars in Mesopotamia 117		115/116 Jewish Revolt in Cyrenaica, Egypt and Cyprus	117
130		130 Hadrian in Palestine / 131 Founding of Alia Capitolina		Hadrian
135		135 Bar Kokhba Revolt / Fall of Beththir / Hadrian's Persecution		138
140		Re-establishment of Sanhedrin		Antoninus Pius

West sub-label: ANTIGONIDS
Egypt sub-labels: PTOLEMAIC RULE · SELEUCID RULE · MACCABEAN RULE · ROMAN RULE
East sub-label: INTER-DYNASTIC WARS · Demetrius II
Between-column labels (Palestine/Egypt): Philip / Antipas · First Procurators in Judea · Later Procurators · Agrippa II

INDEX

The index contains all geographical names appearing in the maps. Only the important occurances of each name are given. Biblical names which have not been identified as to location have not been given in the maps or in the index, except where the sources indicate their general location.

IDENTIFICATIONS: T. Rekhesh = Hebrew name
T. el-Mukharkhash = Arabic name

ABBREVIATIONS: T. = Tel (Hebrew), Tell (Arabic) — "mound"
Ḥ = Ḥorvat (Hebrew) — "ruin"
Kh. = Khirbet (Arabic) — "ruin"

PRONUNCIATION: Ḥ as in Scottish Lo*ch;* Ṣ as in hi*ts*

BEFORE NAME: No sign = Bible (including Apocrypha)
* = Ancient external source
° = Modern source

AFTER NAME: No sign = Identification definite
? = Identification not definite
?? = Identification doubtful
(—) = Not identified

A

ABARIM MTS.: 8
* ABDERA: 172
ABDON: T. 'Avdon, *Kh. 'Abdeh* 108
* ABEL:
— (in Galilee) *'Ain Ibl* 30
— (near Damascus) *Suq Wadi Barada* 30, ABILA 254, 255, 259
— (in Gilead) *T. Abil* 158, ABILA 179, 180, 181, 214, 217, 231, 234, 264, ABILA SELEUCIA 181
— (near Dead Sea) *Kh. el-Kafrein*, ABILA 177, 200, 255, 259
* ABELIM: 266
ABEL-BETH-MAACAH: see Abel-beth-maacha
ABEL-BETH-MAACHA: T. Avel Bet Ma'akha, *Abil el-Qamḥ* 30, 111, 124, 146, ABEL-MAIM 146
ABEL-KERAMIN: *?Na'ur* 78
ABEL-MAIM: see Abel-beth-maacha
ABEL-MEHOLAH: *?Kh. T. el-Ḥilu* 76, 113, 134, 135, 143
ABEL-SHITTIM: *T. el-Ḥammam* 52
ABIEZER: 65, 139
* ABILA: see Abel
ABRONAH: *?Elat, Umm Rashrash* 48
° ABYDOS: 20,182
ACCAD: (country) 4, 20, 43
* ACCAD: (city) 9, 15
ACCARON: see Ekron
ACCHABARE: *'Akhbere, 'Akbara* 257
ACCO:
— (city) T. 'Akko, *T. el-Fukhkhar* 22, 23, 30, 34, 35, 37, 41, 68, 69, 153, 155, 157, 173, 175, 176, 212, 266 PTOLEMAIS: *'Akko,* 177, 178, 179, 180, 184, 191, 202, 206, 217, 218, 219, 220, 243, 244, 252, 254, 255, 256, 257, 264, 265, 270, 271, ANTIOCHENES (in Ptolemais) 181
— (district) 173, PTOLEMAIS 234
ACHEA: 244, 251, 252, 270, 271
ACHMETHA: 9, 11, 157, ECBATANA 166, 167, 174, 183, 243, 244
ACHOR, VALLEY OF: 73, 225
ACHSHAPH: ?T. Regev, *Kh. el-Harbaj* 23, 30, 34, 35, 41, 59, 62, 63, TEL REGEV 17, 18
ACHZIB:
— (in Asher) T. Akhziv, *ez-Zib* 18, 19, 68, 69,

153, 266, ECDIPPA 212, 219
— (in Judah) ?Ḥ. Lavnin, *Kh. T. el-Beida* 140, 154
ACRA: (in Jerusalem) 189, 200, 205
ACRABETA: *'Aqrabba, 'Aqrabba* 190, 200, 211, 259, 260, 267, EKREBEL 212
ADAM: *T. ed-Damiyeh* 54, 76, 120
ADAMAH: *?Qarne Ḥittim, Qarn Ḥattin* 72, 113, SHEMESH-EDOM 30, 32
* ADAMIM: see Adami-nekeb
ADAMI-NEKEB: T. Adami. *Kh. et-Tell* 72, ADAMIM 30, 31
ADASA: *Kh. 'Addasa* 195
ADDAN: (—) 163
° ADER: 17
* ADIABENE: 271
* ADIDA: T. Ḥadid, *el-Ḥaditha* 204, 206, 207, 208, 211, 214, 259, 266
ADITHAIM: (—) 140
ADMAH: (—) 45
* ADORA: see Adoraim
ADORAIM: *Dura* 119, ADORA 177, 210, 214, 217, 265
ADRAMYTTIUM: 243, 254
ADULLAM: Ḥ. 'Adullam, *esh-Sheikh Madhkur* 46, 57, 63, 92, 119, 140, 154, 170, ODOLLAM 192
ADUMMIM, ASCENT OF: *Tal'at ed-Damm* 73
* ADURU: *ed-Dura* 41
* AEGAE: 172
AEGEAN SEA: 172, 251, 252, 253
* AEGINA: 270, 271
AENON: 229
* AFRICA: 271
° AFULA: see Ophrah (in Jezreel)
* AGRIPPINA: see Jarmuth (in Issachar)
AHLAB: *Kh. el-Maḥalib* 68, MAHALAB 153
AI: *Kh. et-Tell* 17, 18, 22, 44, 54, 63
AIATH: *?Kh. Ḥaiyan* 154, 'AYYAH 170
AIJALON: Ḥ. Ayyalon, *Yalo* 34, 36, 56, 64, 68, 107, 108, 113, 119, 120, 145, 201
AIJALON, VALLEY OF: 56, 145
AIN:
— (on border of Canaan) *?Kh. 'Ayyun* 51
— (in Simeon) (—) 108, 140
* AKHETATON: 33, EL-AMARNA 33
* ALALAKH: 24, 26, 43
* ALASHIA: see Cyprus
ALEMA: *'Alma* 190
* ALEPPO: 9, 24, 26, 39, 43, 127, 136, 147, 159,

171, 185, BEROEA 178, 243, 251, 270, 271
ALEXANDRIA: (in Egypt) 174, 178, 182, 183, 184, 218, 243, 244, 253, 270, 271
* ALEXANDRIA: (on Iaxartes) 174
* ALEXANDRIUM: see Sartaba
* ALLAMMELECH: (—) 92
ALMON: *Kh. 'Almit* 108
ALMON-DIBLATHAIM: *?Kh. Deleilat esh-Sherqiyeh* 52, BETH-DIBLATHAIM 128
* ALULUS: see Halhul
AMAAD: (—) 72
AMALEK: 90
AMALEKITES: 45
AMAM: (—) 140
AMANA:
— (mountain) *Jebel Zebedani* 8
— (river) *Nahr Barada* 8
* AMANUS MTS.: 3, 20, 127, 172
* AMASTRIS: 271
* AMIDA: 11
* AMISUS: 271
° AMMAN: see Rabbath-bene-ammon
* AMMATHUS: 214, 217, 230, 259
AMMON: 52, 78, 101, 133, 144, AMMONITIS 181
* AMMONITIS: see Ammon
* AMMONIUM: 174
AMORITES: 45
AMORITES, LAND OF THE: 52
AMORITES, WAY TO THE HILL COUNTRY OF THE: 10, 48
* AMPHIPOLIS: 172, 251
* AMKI: 34, 39
* AMU DARYA: 168
° AMUD CAVE: 225
* AMUQ: 13
* AMURRU: 34, 37, 39, 43, 51, 66, 69, 136, LAND OF THE WEST 20
* AMURRU SEA: see Mediterranean Sea
ANAB: *Kh. 'Anab el-Kebireh* 140
ANAHARATH: ?T. Rekesh, *T. el-Mukharkhash* 30, 32, 72
ANANIAH: *el-'Azariyeh* 170, BETHANY 236, 237, 240
* ANAT: 115, 147
ANATHOTH: *Ras el-Kharrubeh* 94, 108, 143, 154, 170
° ANATOLIAN PLATEAU: 5
* ANCHIALUS: 271
* ANCYRA: 172, 185, 239, 243, 244

K